BEYOND THE PHARAOHS

Beyond the Pharaohs

EGYPT AND THE COPTS IN THE

2ND TO 7TH CENTURIES A.D.

Florence D. Friedman

❖

Museum of Art • Rhode Island School of Design • 1989

EXHIBITION DATES:

Museum of Art, Rhode Island School of Design
February 10 to April 16

The Walters Art Gallery
May 21 to July 16

This exhibition has been prepared by the Museum of Art,
Rhode Island School of Design, in cooperation with The
Walters Art Gallery, Baltimore, Maryland.

The exhibition and catalogue have been organized and
edited by Florence D. Friedman, with the assistance of
Madeleine Cody.

This project has been made possible by generous grants
from the National Endowment for the Humanities, a
Federal agency, and from the Rhode Island Committee
for the Humanities, Textron Inc., the Jesse Metcalf Fund,
Mrs. Gilman Angier, Edward H. Merrin Gallery, Inc.,
Jack A. Josephson, and Joel Cohen and Andrea Toon.

COVER:
Fragment of a Textile with St. Theodore,
6th century, Harvard University Art
Museums (Arthur M. Sackler Museum),
Gift of Mrs. John D. Rockefeller, Jr.
1939.112.1 (cat. no. 128)

FRONTISPIECE:
Isis Nursing Harpokrates,
2nd to 3rd century, Royal Ontario
Museum, Gift of Walter Massey.
910.108.364 (cat. no. 92)

Contents

Contributing Authors, 6

Lenders, 7

Chronology, 8

Foreword, 9

Maps, 10

Color Plates, 12

Introduction, 22

25   HISTORY
Egyptian Historical Background, 26
Everyday Life in Roman-Byzantine Egypt, 28

37   RELIGION
Ancient Egyptian Religion, 38
Christianity, 41
Monasticism in Egypt, 45
Gnosticism, 48

51   ART AND WRITTEN MATERIALS
Pharaonic Themes, 52
An Introduction to the Sculpture of Late Roman
    and Early Byzantine Egypt, 54
Textiles, 65
Pottery and Glass, 73
The Minor Arts of Late Antique Egypt:
    From Relics to Icons, 75
Greek and Coptic Manuscripts, 77
Early Christian Architecture in the Nile Valley, 81

89   CATALOGUE OF THE EXHIBITION
Home, 90
Personal Adornment, 144
Letters, 167
Marketplace, 172
Religion, 182
Christian Church, 206
Monastery, 228
Death, 247
Textiles: Technique and Style, 266

List of Abbreviations, 281

Bibliography, 282

Photography Credits, 296

Contributing Authors

SUSAN AUTH

FLORENCE D. FRIEDMAN

ANNA GONOSOVÁ

PETER GROSSMANN

LUCY-ANNE HUNT

LEONARD LESKO

LESLIE S. B. MacCOULL

BRIAN P. MUHS

BIRGER A. PEARSON

THELMA K. THOMAS

GARY VIKAN

Lenders

Allen Memorial Art Museum, Oberlin College
Anonymous Lender
The Art Museum, Princeton University
Beinecke Rare Book and Manuscript Library,
     Yale University
The British Museum, London
The Brooklyn Museum
Cincinnati Art Museum
Cleveland Museum of Art
Columbus Museum of Art
Corning Museum of Glass
Department of Rare Books and Special Collections,
     The University of Michigan
Detroit Institute of Arts
Dumbarton Oaks, Washington, D.C.
Field Museum of Natural History, Chicago
Harvard University Art Museums
Institute for Antiquity and Christianity, The Claremont
     Graduate School
Jack A. Josephson Collection
Kelsey Museum of Archaeology, The University
     of Michigan
Malcove Collection, University of Toronto
The Menil Collection, Houston
Metropolitan Museum of Art, New York
Minneapolis Institute of Arts
Museum of Anthropology, The University of Michigan
Museum of Art, Rhode Island School of Design
Museum of Fine Arts, Boston
Nelson-Atkins Museum of Art, Kansas City
The Newark Museum
Petrie Museum, University College London
Philadelphia Museum of Art
Pierpont Morgan Library, New York
Royal Ontario Museum, Toronto
The Saint Louis Art Museum
The Tellalian Collection, Newton
The Textile Museum, Washington, D.C.
University Museum, University of Pennsylvania
Victoria and Albert Museum, London
Virginia Museum of Fine Arts
The Walters Art Gallery, Baltimore

Chronology

332 B.C.	Alexander the Great conquers Egypt
305	Beginning of Ptolemaic era
30	Roman conquest of Egypt; Egypt becomes a Roman province
A.D. 40–49	According to tradition, St. Mark introduces Christianity into Egypt
ca. 251–356	Life of St. Anthony, who provides the model for hermetic style of monastic life
303	Beginning of Great Persecution of Christians. Coptic Christians will later date the beginning of their calendar to the "Era of the Martyrs"
286	Roman Empire split into East and West Empires
ca. 288–348	Life of Pachomius, who establishes coenobitic (communal) form of monasticism
313	Emperor Constantine legitimizes Christianity
ca. 318	Arian controversy begins
324	Constantine seizes Eastern Roman Empire, including Egypt: beginning of the Byzantine Period, which ends with Arab Conquest
325	Council of Nicea condemns the heresy of Arianism (which emphasized Christ's humanity over his divinity)
330	Constantine moves the capital of the Empire to Byzantium, renamed Constantinople
328–373	Athanasius (born ca. 293), Bishop of Alexandria
ca. 348–466	Life of Shenoute, Abbot of White Monastery, major figure in history of Coptic church
392	Pagan temples closed in Egypt by order of the Emperor
394	Last official hieroglyphic inscription
451	Council of Chalcedon. Monophysitism is condemned by the Orthodox church.
543	Closing of Temple of Isis at Philae by Emperor Justinian
618–628	Persian occupation
640–642	Arab conquest

Foreword

MANY PEOPLE ARE RESPONSIBLE for the realization of this catalogue. First, my thanks to the National Endowment for the Humanities for generously supporting this exhibition and catalogue. Additional support has been gratefully received from the Rhode Island Committee for the Humanities, Textron Inc., the Jesse Metcalf Fund, Mrs. Gilman Angier, Edward H. Merrin Gallery, Inc., Jack A. Josephson, and Joel Cohen and Andrea Toon.

At the Museum, my thanks to Franklin Robinson, Director of the Museum, and to Kathleen Bayard, Assistant Director, Bianca Gray, Coordinator of Publications, Jean Waterman, Budget Manager, David Stark, Curator of Education, Carla Mathes Woodward, Administrator of Educational Programs, Susan Glasheen, Assistant Curator of Education, Melody Ennis, Coordinator of Slides, Photographs, and Educational Resources, Hannah Myers, Docent Coordinator, and Carole DiSandro, Director of Museum Art Classes. My thanks also to Susan Hay, Curator, and Pamela Parmal, Assistant Curator, of Costumes and Textiles, Joan Hendricks, Registrar, and Louann Skorupa, Assistant Registrar, Terrell Fisher, Chief Preparator, and Gilbert Battista, Frank Sousa, Robert Dohar, Chester Burton, and Mark Moscone; and also, in the Office of Development, Catherine Conover and William O'Neil, and, in the News Bureau, Joan Slafsky and Laura Hart. I wish also to thank all the authors of the catalogue: Susan Auth, Anna Gonosová, Peter Grossmann, Leonard Lesko, Leslie S.B. MacCoull, Birger A. Pearson, Thelma K. Thomas, and Gary Vikan. Thanks also to Lucy-Anne Hunt and Brian P. Muhs for doing additional entries. For all their help and camaraderie while working in Egypt and on the audiovisual presentation, I thank Frank Muhly, script writer, and John Ross, photographer. And for their aid in Egypt, my thanks to Robert Betts and Amirah Khatab of the American Research Center in Egypt, and to May Trad of Cairo and Akhmim for much guidance. Much gratitude especially goes to Gawdat Gabra, Director of the Coptic Museum, Cairo, and to his staff, for their patient help at the Coptic Museum. I thank as well the monks at St. Anthony's and at the Monastery of St. Makarios for their kindness and hospitality.

To many of the authors, and to Arnold Friedman, Diana Wolff-Larkin, Edmund Meltzer, Eugene Cruz-Uribe, and Janice Yellin, my thanks for commenting on portions of my manuscript. And to the many museum interns, Richard Neer, Bruce Jonas, Karen Stern, and especially Toby Kruper and Anne Leinster who worked so diligently, I offer my gratitude. Many thanks as well to Father Timothy Ferguson, Father Steele Martin, and the Reverend F. Anne Ritchings for answering many questions, often at inconvenient times, to Jean-Keith Bennett for all her efforts, and to Pierre du Bourguet for his suggestions. Special gratitude also goes to Leonard Lesko and Gary Vikan, who acted as consultants on the project. I thank them both for their advice, criticisms, and general encouragement.

The curators and staff from all the lending museums, too numerous to mention, were extremely helpful. My thanks especially to Marti Lu Allen, Exhibitions Curator at the Kelsey Museum of Archaeology, Carolyn Kane, Associate Curator of Islamic Art at the Metropolitan Museum of Art, Donald Spanel, Research Associate in the Department of Egyptian and Classical Art at the Brooklyn Museum, and Stephen Emmel at the Beinecke Rare Book and Manuscript Library, Yale University. Everyone at The Walters Art Gallery was exceptionally helpful, especially Gary Vikan, Carla Brenner, John Klink, and Terry Weisser.

For the audiovisual presentation, I thank Frank Muhly for the excellent script and Bogh-AV for the production. For the chapel reconstruction, my thanks to John Marcoux for the expert design and construction, to Patrick Lears for an extraordinary painting, and to Leslie S.B. MacCoull and Pat Jacobson for the superb production of Coptic liturgical music. I would also like to acknowledge my great debt of gratitude to Robert Segal, exhibition designer, for a beautiful exhibition and countless trips to Providence. And to Katrina Avery I extend my heartfelt thanks, for not only typing but often editing the manuscript with great accuracy, speed and dedication. My thanks as well to Bill Rae for typing the Bibliography, and to Gilbert Associates for their catalogue, brochure, invitation, and poster design.

And finally, I am most indebted to Madeleine Cody, Curatorial Assistant. I could not have had a finer assistant. Madeleine's exceptional skill and commitment have been largely responsible for the success of this exhibition and catalogue. My most heartfelt thanks to her.

F.D.F.

Egypt and the Mediterranean World in
Late Roman and Early Byzantine Times

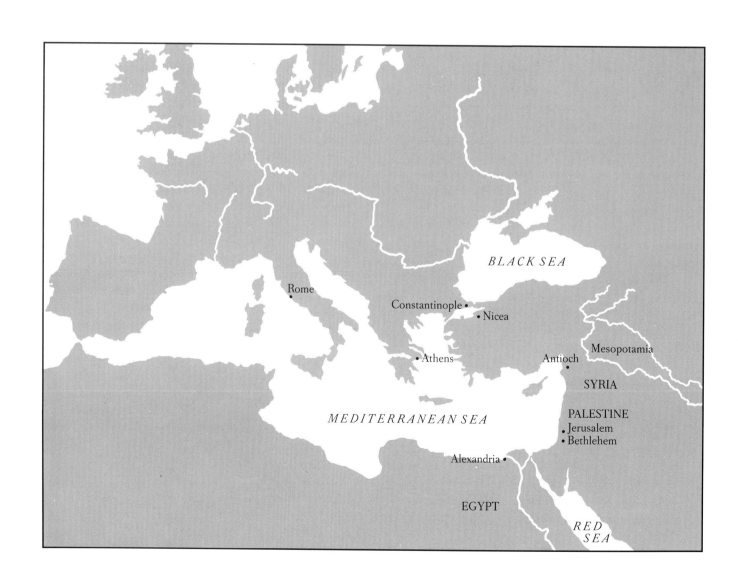

Egypt

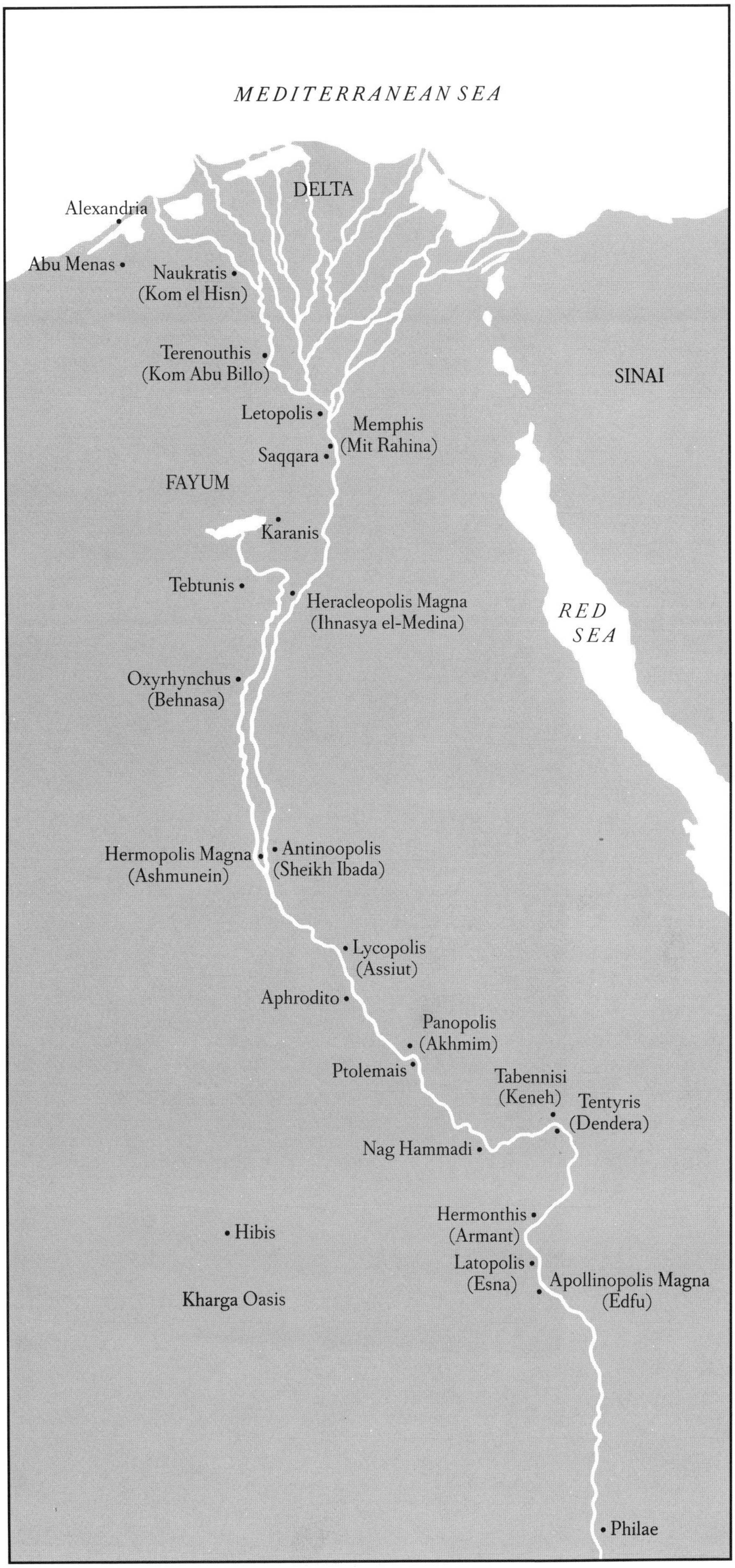

MEDITERRANEAN SEA

DELTA

Alexandria •

Abu Menas •

Naukratis •
(Kom el Hisn)

SINAI

Terenouthis •
(Kom Abu Billo)

Letopolis •

Memphis
• (Mit Rahina)

Saqqara •

FAYUM

Karanis •

Tebtunis •

Heracleopolis Magna
(Ihnasya el-Medina)

RED
SEA

Oxyrhynchus •
(Behnasa)

Hermopolis Magna •
(Ashmunein)

• Antinoopolis
(Sheikh Ibada)

• Lycopolis
(Assiut)

Aphrodito •

Panopolis
• (Akhmim)

Ptolemais •

Tabennisi
(Keneh)

Tentyris
(Dendera)

Nag Hammadi •

Hermonthis •
(Armant)

• Hibis

Latopolis •
(Esna)

Apollinopolis Magna
• (Edfu)

Kharga Oasis

• Philae

Mummy Portrait: Head of a Young Man, first third of the 2nd century, encaustic on wood.
The University Museum, University of Pennsylvania (cat. no. 164)

Group of Objects Found on the Windowsill of a House, 5th century. Kelsey Museum of Archaeology,
The University of Michigan (cat. no. 1)

Funerary Stela: Portrait of the Deceased, C. Julius Valerius, 3rd century, limestone.
The Brooklyn Museum (cat. no. 168)

Nemesis, late 1st–2nd century, limestone. Jack A. Josephson
Collection (cat. no. 169)

Fragment with Quail, late 5th–early 6th century, linen and wool. Museum of Art, Rhode Island School of Design. Gift of Mrs. Henry Sharpe (cat. no. 44)

Lampstand: Aphrodite, 5th–6th century, bronze. The Nelson-Atkins Museum of Art, Kansas City, Missouri (Nelson-Fund) (cat. no. 51)

Pectoral Cross: Christ, 6th–7th century,
gold. Dumbarton Oaks Collection,
Washington, D.C. (cat. no. 52)

Roundel with the Story of Joseph, 7th century, wool and linen. Metropolitan Museum of Art, Gift of Mr. and Mrs. Charles K. Wilkinson (cat. no. 69)

Cabinet Doors, 5th–7th century, wood. The Walters Art Gallery, Baltimore (cat. no. 147)

Fragment of a Sanctuary Curtain, late 5th–6th century, linen and wool.
The Minneapolis Institute of Arts (cat. no. 127)

Introduction

FLORENCE D. FRIEDMAN

THIS IS AN EXHIBITION about life in the Nile Valley in the 2nd to 7th centuries after Christ, when Romans and Byzantines ruled Egypt, before the coming of Islam around 640. Relatively unfamiliar to the public, this period is richly represented through abundant objects of daily life that have survived in Egypt's dry sands. Examples fill this exhibition: decorated tunic fragments, colored glassware, painted pots, pens and cosmetic applicators, wall hangings embellished with pagan gods or saints, simple and fancy jewelry, bed coverlets, tombstones, and written materials ranging from private letters and magical texts to a report of a murder trial and a portion of Psalms. They are objects that illustrate what it was like to live in Egypt in an era of dying paganism and nascent Christianity.

In these early centuries after Christ, Greek and Roman tourists in Egypt climbed the Great Pyramid, marveled at the Colossi of Memnon, and scratched and painted their names on the royal tombs of the Valley of the Kings. Not all of them were strangers to Egypt, however; like those tourists who were native Egyptians, many were residents. As early as the 7th century B.C., Greeks had come to Egypt as mercenaries and traders, though it was only during the Ptolemaic period, after the conquest of Egypt in 332 B.C. by Alexander the Great, that Greeks became a major and enduring presence in Egypt. The Roman Empire altered the picture further. In 30 B.C., Rome conquered Egypt, making it a province of the Roman Empire ruled by prefects who were the personal representatives of the emperor. Thus by the 2nd century A.D., when this exhibition begins, Egypt had a population of Greeks, Romans, and Egyptians, as well as other ethnic groups, living side by side (not always comfortably) in a generally prosperous culture of many languages and religions.[1] People intermarried and produced offspring with Greek-Egyptian and Roman-Egyptian names and cultural heritages.[2] Some still worshiped the ancient gods of Egypt, like Isis, Osiris, and Anubis, though now in Graeco-Roman dress, while others, especially after the early 4th century, devoted themselves to the new religion of Christianity that would leave its mark on every aspect of Egyptian life.

Originally perceived as a Jewish sect, Christianity became a powerful spiritual and political force with increasing numbers of adherents who were often ready to martyr themselves for their faith. After several severe persecutions, the new faith was recognized as the legitimate religion of the Empire under Emperor Constantine in 313 (although he himself was baptized only on his deathbed), and by the end of the 4th century it dominated the religious and secular life of Egypt. But paganism,[3] a thriving, creative faith for millennia, did not simply wither and die, despite the official closing of the pagan temples in 392. Christianity and paganism existed side by side well into the 6th century, often tolerating and sometimes enriching, at other times persecuting one another. Even committed Christians did not totally abandon old ways. Magic, for example, continued to be prevalent, so that we find amulets with images of Jesus and the saints blended with those of the Egyptian gods. Pagans and Christians throughout Egypt – to say nothing of the Jews and Persian Manichaeans concentrated in Alexandria, Egypt's cosmopolitan (but essentially Greek) capital on the Mediterranean coast – created a lively intellectual, economic, and religious life along the Nile in these early centuries after Christ.

1. See Bowman 1986, especially p. 19. The issue of ethnicity is a difficult one, however. See Bagnall 1988b, p. 22.

2. In the Ptolemaic period, however, intermarriage seems to have been relatively rare, and the number of combined Greek and Egyptian names cannot be used as an index of the mixture of peoples. See Mélèze-Modrzejewski 1988, p. 248, and also Bagnall 1988b, pp. 22–3.

3. Paganism is unfortunately a pejorative term in our culture, so it is important to note that no negative meaning should be attached to it in the context of this catalogue.

"Late Roman" and "Late Antique" are the names modern scholars have given to the 2nd to early 4th centuries throughout the Empire, including Egypt. These are the last few centuries during which Egypt was under Roman rule. (Whether one perceives the Romans as benign rulers or oppressive occupiers depends on one's perspective: in Rome's view, Egypt was just one of its many imperial territories; in Egypt's view, Rome was an unwanted foreign occupier.) Though the rulers were Roman, the culture imposed was Hellenic, i.e., Greek. Inspired by Greek civilization, the Romans had in large part adopted it as their own, and a Roman version of Greek culture is found throughout the eastern Roman Empire, including Egypt. The favorite author of the intelligentsia in the Roman Egyptian town of Oxyrhynchus in Middle Egypt, for example, was Homer.

The Greek inheritance in Egypt was further underscored by the Byzantines. The early 4th to mid-7th centuries in Egypt are often termed "Byzantine" by scholars, a designation that may call to mind intricate church mosaics quite foreign to Egypt. But from a historical point of view, Egypt became part of the Byzantine Empire in A.D. 324 when the Emperor Constantine seized the eastern (Greek) portion of the Roman Empire, separated from the (Latin) Western Empire since A.D. 286. In 330 Constantine moved the capital of the Empire to a site along the Bosphorus in Asia Minor then called Byzantium; the remote city was renamed Constantinople. Its official language and that of the Empire was Greek. Originally encompassing territories from Gibraltar to the Indus, the Byzantine Empire was nominally Christian, though even as late as 400, Christians were still in the minority among both the populace and the leaders.[4] As the numbers of Christians in Byzantine Egypt increased during the 4th and 5th centuries, there developed an interpretation and definition of the meaning of Christ's nature that differed from the orthodox view held in Constantinople. The differences resulted in political schism from Constantinople.

Before, during, and even after the advent of Christianity, the objects produced in Egypt often reflect its ancient Egyptian pagan heritage: a Roman-Egyptian gravestone still depicts the deceased in company with the pharaonic deities Anubis and Horus; the pagan tombs at Oxyrhynchus are still sites where meals are shared by the living and the dead; the White Monastery at Sohag still employs the cavetto cornice, a decorative architectural motif 3000 years old; and the Egyptian Christian cross displays its relationship to the hieroglyphic sign for life, the *ankh*. In the area of religion and religious iconography, ancient Egyptian traces in the arts are also apparent: images of the Virgin suckling Jesus probably draw on those of Isis suckling Horus;[5] depictions of St. George and the Dragon are probably modeled on those of Horus overcoming evil in the form of serpents or crocodiles; the iconography of St. Christopher uses that of Osiris.[6] But Egypt after the Greeks and Romans was indeed a different country, and while maintaining some pharaonic features, the arts more often reflect the styles and fashions of the imperial Mediterranean world of which Egypt was a part. What was fashionable in North Africa or Syria was often fashionable in Egypt as well, and thus it is not surprising that the style and iconography of decorated textiles or stone sculpture in this exhibition should often mirror the artistic vocabulary of the Empire.

The major source of uniquely Egyptian cultural contributions in the Christian period, however, was the Copts, who played an important role in the history of Christianity as a whole. Their greatest contribution was the development of monasticism, which spread throughout the world and endures today. Most scholars agree that the word "Copt" is a corruption of the ancient pharaonic name for Egypt (Hwt-k3-Pth; in Coptic, ⲈⲔⲈⲠⲦⲀ), transformed by the Greeks into Aigyptos and over the centuries reduced by the Arabs to Copt.[7] The term refers to native Egyptians, most though not all of whom were Christians at that time. To be a Copt today, however, is synonymous with being an Egyptian Christian. "Coptic" as a noun refers to the last stage of the Egyptian language that developed in the 1st and 2nd centuries A.D. and became standardized as a literary medium about the 3rd century. The language of the native Egyptian population, Coptic was written in a modified form of the Greek alphabet and included many Greek loan-words, but it retained essentially the same grammatical structure as its ancestral pharaonic language written in hieroglyphs. "Coptic" as an adjective refers to the Egyptian form of Christianity practiced by the Coptic Church, and also describes the liturgy and religious literature of the Coptic Church. In addition, some scholars refer to the 2nd/3rd to 7th centuries as the Coptic, i.e., Christian Period, though for others, the Coptic Period is characterized by the fact that Coptic was the primary written and spoken language of the native Egyptian people during these centuries.

The art and architecture of this period is also often called "Coptic." But the question remains among many current scholars as to whether Coptic has any definable meaning

---

4. MacMullen 1986, p. 4.

5. van Moorsel 1979.

6. Millard 1987.

7. For the most current discussion of the etymology of the word Copt, see du Bourguet 1988, pp. 6–12.

in the context of the arts of Late Roman/Early Byzantine Egypt.[8] Is there a specific Coptic style? Did the Copts produce, commission, or use the particular form of lintel decoration, tunic ornamentation, glass goblet, or ceramic plate that has in the past been characterized as Coptic? What we do know is that Greeks and Romans and Egyptians, polytheists and Christians alike, were responsible as a society for the material remains (sculpture, textiles, glass, ceramics, etc.). And we know, for example, that some architectural pieces were produced by pagan Greek-Egyptians and then later reused by Copts in a Christian context. With a mix of intellectuals and farmers, scholars and illiterates, rich and poor, it is difficult to unravel just who manufactured articles of daily or even liturgical use for whom. A ceramic plate with cross decoration might as easily have been used by a Greek Orthodox monk as a Coptic one, unless excavation shows clearly to the contrary. Scholars in this exhibition and catalogue will not necessarily be using the term "Coptic" with complete unanimity, but they will make their opinions on the subject clear.

This is the first major exhibition in twenty-six years of Roman-Byzantine, or "Coptic," material from Egypt.[9] During this time scholarship has made considerable advances, including a Coptic Encyclopedia soon to appear. We present this catalogue and exhibition as a further contribution to the field. The catalogue now begins with a review of the history, religion, and art and architecture of Egypt before and during the 2nd to 7th centuries, followed by a discussion of the objects in the exhibition according to aspects of daily life: the home, personal adornment, letters, the marketplace, religion, and death. This is an exhibition not about kings and emperors or patriarchs of the church, but about the inner and outer life of people, rich and poor, who decorated their homes, worshiped their gods, fled to the monasteries, dressed as they could afford, buried their dead, and equipped themselves with magic just in case. It is about life in Egypt beyond the pharaohs and before Islam.

8. On textiles, see, for example, Trilling 1982, pp. 11–19; and on sculpture, see Torp 1969 and 1973.

9. A brief review of major museum exhibitions and earlier publications on Coptic art includes: *Exposition d'Art Copte*, Société d'Archéologie Copte, 1941; *Pagan and Christian Egypt*, The Brooklyn Museum, 1941; *Late Egyptian and Coptic Art*, The Brooklyn Museum, 1943; *Coptic Egypt*, The Brooklyn Museum, 1944; *Koptische Kunst*, Essen-Bredeny, Villa-Hügel, 1963; *Found in Egypt*, The Textile Museum, 1963; *Myth and Gospel: Art of Coptic Egypt*, The Newark Museum, 1977–8; *The Roman Heritage, Textiles from Egypt and the Eastern Mediterranean 300 to 600 A.D.*, The Textile Museum, 1982. These exhibitions examine Coptic art far beyond the chronological limits of this present exhibition, however.

HISTORY

Egyptian Historical Background

FLORENCE D. FRIEDMAN

THE GREEK HISTORIAN HERODOTUS, in the 5th century B.C, described Egypt as the gift of the Nile, a river that was indeed the source of Egypt's life and prosperity. Each year, swelled from Ethiopian rains, it overflowed its banks and deposited a band of rich, black, cultivable soil the length of the land. This annual replenishment of dark, fertile soil was the basis for Egypt's farming economy. The ancients' gratitude for the Nile's gift is reflected in one of their names for Egypt, Kemet, "The Black Land." A more common name for Egypt, however, was The Two Lands, referring to Upper (southern) and Lower (northern) Egypt. These designations, still used today, follow the course of the Nile from south to north. Upper Egypt refers to the land extending from Aswan to the apex of the Delta, and Lower Egypt refers to the broad Delta region that fans out to the Mediterranean. Many objects and architectural remains survive from the dry sands of southern Upper Egypt; few works survive from the wet, marshy Delta.

The ancient Egyptians did not compose histories in the modern sense, but they did keep king lists and annals[1] that show they marked their cultural beginnings from the unification of The Two Lands, dated by modern scholars to ca. 3150 B.C. Key historical periods that followed (using modern names) were the Archaic Period, when writing and the beginnings of monumental stone architecture were established; the Old Kingdom, which was the Pyramid Age; the Middle Kingdom, when kings reconsolidated their power; and the New Kingdom, the age of Hatshepsut, Thutmose III, Akhenaten, Tutankhamun, and Ramesses II and III. These last two kings were the greatest of the Ramesside pharaohs (13th and 12th centuries B.C.) who repelled foreign incursions, fought enemies abroad, and built splendid temples at home. The Ramesside age was regarded by the Egyptians for centuries after as a golden age of antiquity.[2]

Several of the Ramessides were among Egypt's last great native rulers. In the centuries that followed their demise, Libyans (11th century B.C.), Kushites from Nubia (8th and 7th centuries B.C.), Assyrians (mid-7th century B.C.), and Persians (525–404 B.C. and 342–332 B.C.) occupied (or made incursions into) Egypt. But these foreign powers did not generally impose their own cultures, a situation that changed after the conquest of Egypt in 332 B.C. by the Macedonian Alexander the Great. Alexander, who identified himself as Greek (Macedonia was in northeast Greece), was actually welcomed by the pharaoh as a liberator from the despised Persians. Egyptian pharaohs were long familiar with the Greeks, having used them as mercenaries since the 26th Dynasty (7th century B.C.), and were fully supportive of Alexander's desire to rid the Mediterranean world of the Persians. But what they did not foresee was that Macedonian-Greek domination would change the fabric of Egyptian culture more than any previous occupation.

Alexander the Great stayed less than a year in Egypt, but in that time founded one of the great cities of the ancient world, Alexandria. This new capital of Egypt was known as Alexandria-by-Egypt, a title that reveals the city's intended separation from the rest of Egypt. Situated on the coast of the western Delta, it looked out to the Mediterranean world. Being in essence a Greek city, it attracted other Greeks, especially after the Macedonian Greek general Ptolemy more than twenty years after Alexander's death, took the throne as Ptolemy I in 305 B.C. His name distinguished the Egyptian rulers for the next 300 years.

Greek immigrants now came by the thousands to Egypt looking for a new place to settle and new opportunities to get rich. They came by ship and by land, becoming businessmen, traders, ship owners, tax farmers, land holders, and soldiers. And with them they brought Hellenic culture. They built temples to the Greek gods and exclusive gymnasia where they could exercise and study with others of their class. They had their own law courts. Few learned Egyptian, the language of the land for almost 3000 years, because the administrative language of the country was now Greek. No Ptolemaic monarch, so far as we know, ever bothered to learn Egyptian, with the notable exception of the famous Queen Cleopatra VII.[3]

The Greeks and Egyptians were, on the whole, two separate classes in Ptolemaic Egypt, with two separate

1. Redford 1986.
2. Assmann 1985.

languages, and native Egyptians were often treated as second-class, specially taxed citizens in their own country. There are many Greek references to the 'barbarian' Egyptians. Ten Egyptian revolts between 245 and 50 B.C. are documented.[4] A critical sign of devaluation from the Egyptian point of view was the requirement to learn Greek in order to get a government job. From the point of view of the Ptolemaic or even later Roman Empire, this was not such pointed discrimination, however, since this was the requirement throughout the Greek (and later Roman) territories. The language of the administration everywhere was Greek. If one could learn Greek, adopt the ways of the elite class, in short become Hellenized, one could get along reasonably well.

The lot of the native Egyptians was not entirely bleak. Many Egyptians were bilingual (the Greek administration needed bilinguals) and some landed good jobs in civil and military posts, with opportunities for advancement. A number of Hellenized Egyptians became prosperous, some taking Greek spouses, and adopting Greek names for their children, while in other cases, Egyptian names were preferred. One of the few areas in which the two cultures actually blended is religion, where Egyptian and Greek gods were frequently syncretized, and even the Greek and (later) Roman elite adopted Egyptian funerary customs (cat. nos. 161, 162, 163, 164). Greek may have been the dominant culture, but Egyptian culture still exerted influence.[5] It is the wealthy propertied Egyptians (predominantly the priesthood), who are probably responsible for the transmission of Egyptian religious ideas and practices into the Greek and Roman populations.[6] In the arts, however, where Egyptian iconography was often retained, Egyptian style was almost completely subsumed by Greek Hellenistic traditions.

The Egyptian economy flourished under the Ptolemies. The Greeks introduced technical knowhow, like the Archimedean screw and the ox-driven waterwheel, that significantly improved Egyptian irrigation and farming; and they reclaimed important agricultural land in the natural oasis area of the Fayum, southwest of the Delta, where major settlement took place. Many of the household objects in this exhibition come from the homes of Greek- and Roman-Egyptians who lived in the large village of Karanis and elsewhere in the Fayum (cat. nos. 1–1N).

The Ptolemaic kings maintained the fiction that they were legitimate pharaohs, and embellished old and built new temples to the gods. Some of the finest surviving temples in Egypt were built by the Ptolemies. These kings, like later Roman and Byzantine emperors, functioned in theory as god-kings, though it was not until the development in Christian Egypt of the office of Patriarch of Alexandria that an Egyptian figure would hold the political and religious power once enjoyed by the pharaohs of ancient Egypt. The Ptolemies tried to leave Egyptian customs and beliefs generally undisturbed. They retained, for instance, the ancient division of the land into provinces, which they called nomes, but gave new names to cities, like the Greek Panopolis ("City of Pan") for the Egyptian Akhmim. (Demotic texts continued to use the ancient names, however.)

Politically weakened since the 3rd century B.C., the Ptolemies had maintained friendly relations with Rome. And in the succeeding centuries, when Egypt was threatened by strikes from Syria and by internal dynastic squabbles, Rome settled the problems. But Roman protection ultimately became Roman control and aggression in the 1st century B.C. At the famous Battle of Actium in 31 B.C. off the west coast of Greece, Rome defeated Egypt in the figures of Cleopatra and Mark Antony, and made Egypt a province of the Roman empire.[7] Like the Ptolemies, the Roman emperors continued to build new temples in Egypt. But they also used the old pharaonic temples for their own political purposes: in the 3rd century A.D. they converted an 18th Dynasty columned hall at the Temple of Luxor into a chapel of the Roman legion, replete with Corinthian columns. There is reason to believe that here early Christians, under pain of death, may have been forced (often unsuccessfully) by Roman officials to pledge their allegiance to the state by offering sacrifices to the pagan gods.

After Christianity was made the official religion in 313 A.D., portions of pharaonic temples were sometimes transformed into churches. The ancient Festival hall of Thutmose III (15th century B.C.) at Karnak was converted into a church; the painted figures of the Virgin and saints on the capitals are still visible today. The ruins of the mortuary temple of Hatshepsut at Deir el Bahri (early 15th century B.C.) became the site of a Coptic monastery (cat. no. 160). At the mortuary temple of Ramesses III at Medinet Habu (early 12th century B.C.), Coptic Christians incorporated a church into its third court and built a town along its outer walls. And myriad Egyptian tombs throughout the area were used as retreats by early Christian hermits seeking escape from the world.

3. Lewis 1986, pp. 1–36.
4. For a recent reassessment of this entire period, see Bianchi 1988, pp. 13–20.
5. From the plentiful papyrological evidence, Lewis 1986 believes there was little Egyptian influence (see, e.g., p. 4), while Bowman 1986 maintains the influence was considerable.
6. Johnson 1986; Bagnall 1988, and Peter Grossmann in correspondence.

7. As Bianchi 1988, pp. 19–20 notes, "That battle, the last naval encounter of Antiquity, changed the destiny of the Western world, which, had the war been won by Cleopatra VII and Antony, would have been indebted to the traditions of Ptolemaic Egypt."

Everyday Life in Roman-Byzantine Egypt

BIRGER A. PEARSON and LESLIE S.B. MacCOULL

IN THIS BRIEF SKETCH we attempt to describe what life was like along the Nile during the Roman period, concentrating on the 2nd to 4th centuries, and the Byzantine period, concentrating on the 4th to 7th centuries. In the earlier period Egypt was ruled from Rome; in the later period it was ruled from Constantinople (formerly Byzantium) by Christian emperors. The Roman period is dominated by Greek (Hellenistic) language and culture, whereas the Byzantine period witnesses the flowering of the native Egyptian ("Coptic") language and culture.

Late Roman Egypt

A SPECIAL CASE: OXYRHYNCHUS

The bulk of what is known concerning daily life in Roman Egypt derives from the documentary evidence preserved on papyrus and pottery fragments (ostraka). The most important of the papyrus finds in Egypt come from Behnasa, some 200 km south (upstream) of Cairo, site of the Roman town of Oxyrhynchus (literally "sharp-nose"; the town was named for the "sharp-nosed" Mormyrus fish, the object of a local cult.) Oxyrhynchus was a "metropolis," capital of the nineteenth nome (district) of Upper Egypt.[1]

Since 1897, archaeological excavations at Oxyrhynchus have turned up thousands of papyri that shed much light on daily life in Roman Egypt. Unfortunately, the excavations had as their sole aim the discovery of papyri, and archaeological evidence is now lacking for the topography of the site. No site plan was ever published![2] Even so, the papyri provide evidence of numerous public buildings, temples, street names, and other architectural features.

Located on the left bank of a subsidiary channel of the Nile, Oxyrhynchus was a walled town with five gates. Its theater is estimated to have held over 11,000 spectators. Of the twenty-odd temples in the town, the great temple of Sarapis was the most important. It was not only a religious center but a center of business, where banks and the public notary had their offices. By the end of the 3rd century there were two Christian churches. A 3rd century Jewish synagogue shows evidence of the persistence of Jewish life in Egypt even after the decimation of the Jewish population that resulted from the Jewish revolt under Trajan (115–117 A.D.). On the river were two quays and a Nilometer (a device to measure Nile levels). The gymnasium and at least two public baths were close by. Houses in the town, usually constructed of sun-dried brick, sometimes ran as high as three stories. Each house would normally have a cellar and a small courtyard with a well. Private houses ranged in size of living space from as small as 15 to over 100 square meters.

SOCIAL STRATIFICATION

The governor (prefect) of Egypt was a Roman official based in Alexandria. He was appointed directly by the emperor and served at his pleasure, usually for one to three years and sometimes longer. The governor and his entourage would travel annually to one Egyptian town in the Delta and one in Upper Egypt to hear legal appeals sent from the nomes and to check on the accounts of local administrators. The most visible symbol of Roman rule was the military presence: legionnaires who were Roman citizens and auxiliary troops serving under Roman officers. Veterans of the army were among the few private landowners in Egypt. These and other Roman citizens constituted the top of the social-political ladder.

---

1. "Nomes" as administrative divisions in Egypt originated in the Early Dynastic period. By Hellenistic times 42 had long since been the traditional number of nomes, but the actual number varied over the centuries (see, e.g., Baines and Malek 1980, p. 15). Each nome was governed by a *strategos,* a Roman appointee. Nomes were abolished as administrative units in the early 4th century as part of a major reorganization of Egypt.

2. The meticulous excavations carried out in the village of Karanis by the University of Michigan in the 1920s and 1930s are a conspicuous contrast to those at Oxyrhynchus.

Next in social standing were the citizens of the Greek cities (*poleis*): Naukratis in the Delta, founded in the 6th century B.C., Alexandria in the Delta, Ptolemais in Upper Egypt, and Antinoopolis, founded by the emperor Hadrian in memory of his companion Antinous on the spot where he had drowned. The Greek cities had a modicum of self-government, including a council (*boule*) and an assembly (*demos*).[3] Citizens of the four Greek cities, like the Romans, were exempt from the poll tax (*laographia*) instituted by Augustus Caesar. All other people were lumped together by the Roman administration as "Egyptians," including even descendants of the Macedonians and Greeks who had settled in Egypt under the Ptolemies. To be sure, there were in such nome capitals as Oxyrhynchus local gentry of Greek descent (*metropolites*), who modeled their towns as much as possible on the four Greek cities. They built opulent public buildings, conducted Greek games and festivals, and organized their social lives around the gymnasium.

A metropolite boy was enrolled at the age of fourteen as an "ephebe," identifying him as a member of the gymnasium. Metropolites, though required to pay the poll tax, were nevertheless granted a reduced rate. They were also eligible to serve in various municipal offices, such as gymnasiarch, agoranomos ("market regulator"), "high priest," etc. Such officials served at their own expense. In 200 A.D. the Emperor Septimius Severus ordered the creation of a *boule* in each nome capital. Membership in this council was a mark of status, but also involved considerable personal expense.

The most numerous inhabitants were the native Egyptians, mostly peasants who lived in the rural villages and hamlets. Villages ranged in size from a few houses to towns with populations in the thousands. The larger villages were occupied by mixed populations, including Greeks who tried to emulate the metropolites in aspiring to a high degree of Hellenization. The most important of the larger villages, in terms of what is known from systematic excavation, is Karanis, one of the towns founded in the Arsinoite nome (Fayum) by Ptolemy II Philadelphus in the 3rd century B.C.

Social stratification in Egypt was not simply a matter of chance or custom; it was regulated by law and placed under the jurisdiction of the administrator of the emperor's Privy Purse. For example, Romans could only write their wills in Latin, and severe punishments were visited upon those who styled themselves improperly (e.g., Egyptians as Greeks or Romans, etc.)[4]

3. Alexandria was not granted a *boule* until 200, when Emperor Septimius Severus instituted such councils in all of the nome capitals.
4. Such rules are set down in a papyrus document treated by Lewis 1983, pp. 32–33. It should be noted that much of the information here concerning Roman Egypt has been culled from Lewis's valuable work.

FAMILY AND DOMESTIC LIFE

Metropolite families tended to be rather well-to-do compared with the inhabitants of rural villages. In the villages it was not uncommon that a person owned just a fraction of a house, and living conditions could be very crowded, with domestic animals often sharing living quarters. Organization of space was, therefore, important; much of the day's activities, such as cooking, crafts, etc., were conducted in the courtyards outdoors.

Metropolite families had an average of two or three children, not counting the many who died in infancy. Most metropolite families had a slave or two as well. Rural families tended to be larger. The ancient Greek and Roman custom of exposing unwanted infants (mostly females) also prevailed in Egypt. But native Egyptians, whose religious customs forbade infanticide, often rescued babies from the trash heaps on which they had been thrown. Most such foundlings would be raised as household slaves, since a penalty was attached to adopting them into the family.

Most young men were married by the age of eighteen or so, young women earlier. Endogamous marriages, i.e., marriages within social classes, were the norm, and among the metropolites brother-sister marriage was not unusual. Dowries were provided for daughters and were returned by the husband in case of divorce, which was not uncommon.

The average villager lived mainly on cereals and legumes, supplemented by lotus meal, papyrus stalks, berries and other fruits, milk and cheese, some fish and fowl, and (rarely) other domesticated animals. Barley beer was the usual drink; wine was also available.

But in clothing as in diet, metropolite gentry enjoyed a higher standard. They wore underclothing of linen tunics, and colored outer garments made of linen, wool, or even imported silk. Villagers wore simple versions of the cloaks worn by the townspeople, probably not unlike the gallabiyas worn by Egyptian peasants today. Sandals and shoes made of leather and papyrus rind, often highly decorated, protected the feet of the gentry. Most village peasants went barefoot.

LITERATURE

The level of literacy in Roman Egypt and the literary tastes of the inhabitants are attested by the literary papyri. Works of all the major Greek authors, and many minor ones, were copied and recopied throughout the Roman period. Even some Latin authors were read, especially from the 3rd century on. Homer was by far the most-read author, both in homes and in schools; some 700 manuscripts of Homer are attested. Demosthenes, Euripides, and Hesiod are the next best-attested authors. Of course, most of the literary and biblical finds come from the larger towns of Egypt, but some have even turned up in rural villages such as Karanis and Tebtunis.

Documentary papyri also attest to the copying and circulation of books: we have records of payments to scribes, letters with requests for shipment of books, and orders for specific titles by book dealers. Nor was the devotion to the Greek classics confined only to reading: Greek dramas, such as the tragedies of Euripides and the comedies of Menander, were performed in the theaters. The poetry of Homer was recited by trained performers. We know, too, that actors and performers were very well paid.

Education of metropolite children began at around ten years of age. The pupils were taught to read and write Greek and to appreciate the Greek classics. Higher education would usually require a period of study in Alexandria. Opportunity for elementary education seems to have been available even in the larger villages, at least for those families who could afford it. Most villagers, however, remained illiterate.

AGRICULTURE

Egypt is a vast desert interrupted only by the Nile and a few desert oases. Three main areas of arable land exist: the fertile Delta formed by the seven branches of the river; the Fayum, a natural depression with a lake fed by the river; and the long, narrow Nile valley itself.

Since Egypt was the most important foreign source of grain for the city of Rome, the cereal crops were the foundation of Egyptian agriculture. Wheat and barley were the most important grains. Agriculture in Egypt was also highly diversified, with many cash crops grown. Agriculture was the dominant economic activity of Egypt and occupied the lives of the great majority of people. The agricultural year, dominated by the rise and fall of the Nile, would look something like this:

June	end of the grain harvest; threshing begins
July	threshing ends
August	the vintage begins
September	dates are picked
October–December	sowing of grains; harvest of dates and olives
January	new growing season of vines and olives
February–March	preparation for the grain harvest
April–May	harvesting of grains

Most of the land in Egypt, whether owned by the state, the imperial household, a temple, or privately, was cultivated by tenant farmers, with rent paid in kind or in money. Added to the cost of rent was a substantial amount due the state in taxes, as discussed below. Grain farmers were also responsible for delivering their crops to the state granaries,

whence the grain was shipped to Alexandria for final shipment to Rome.

TRADES AND COMMERCE

While most farmers were "jacks of all trades," a number of trade guilds and associations existed. Apprenticeships of many kinds are recorded in the extant documents, from carpenters and coppersmiths to barbers, scribes, and embalmers. Trade guilds had fixed bylaws, with schedules of dues, meetings, etc. While they served the needs of the membership, providing for assistance to needy members and funerals for the deceased, they were of special advantage to the state. Government officials could place orders for goods and services with the secretaries of the guilds, and hold the groups liable for any problems.

The most important manufactured products, exported in large quantities, were textiles, papyrus, and glass, all abundantly represented in this exhibition. Egypt was very poor in forests, however, and timber was imported from Syria and Asia Minor.

Overland transport was accomplished with donkeys and camels, but the river provided the most convenient means of transport. Boats and barges of all sizes, many with capacities of up to 500 tons, plied the river, powered with sails and oars. There was a state-owned fleet of barges, but most of the shipping was done in privately owned boats.

Banking was an important enterprise in Egypt. The banks' services included not only deposits and withdrawals, but also transfers of funds to third parties. Banking was a lucrative business, and bankers, mostly Greeks, were people of high status.

Other professions that brought wealth and privilege were dramatic acting and athletic competition. A professional career in sports could bring the fortunate competitor enormous sums of money in prizes and lucrative lifetime pensions. Some things never change!

TAXES AND LITURGIES

With the coming of Roman rule the tax burdens on the population increased dramatically, both in actual levies and in efficiency of collection. Conditions could become so intolerable for peasants and villagers that flight became the only way out. Some tax fugitives would move to Alexandria and attempt to melt into the crowds; some would join marauding bands of outlaws; and others would simply disappear into the desert or leave the country altogether.

Egypt's role as the principal supplier of grain to Rome meant that the grain farmer would have to pay a portion of his crop as a tax and deliver it to the state granary. He would also have to take his turn in serving as one of the *sitologoi* (grain collectors) responsible for delivering grain to Alexandria or to a Roman military establishment. Of course, all other agricultural products were taxed as well, but usually in money.

The most general tax was the *laographia* or poll tax, which all male inhabitants of Egypt from ages fourteen to sixty had to pay. Privileged classes, that is, Romans and urban Greeks, were exempt from this tax, however. Numerous other taxes existed: a dike tax, trade taxes, business taxes, plus fees and assessments of all kinds. People were also subject to military requisition of goods and services as needed.

In addition to the taxes there were the "liturgies," compulsory services performed by the people at their own expense. The *leitourgia,* "work for the people," was a feature of civic life in ancient Athens whereby the richest families took turns defraying the expenses of certain public functions. In Roman Egypt this concept was greatly expanded, eventually compelling service from virtually all levels of the population. There were some exceptions: Roman citizens, urban Greeks, prominent athletes, members of learned professions, and some other groups.

From the time of Trajan on, even tax collection became a liturgic function. In that case the abuses of the private tax farmers (*publicani*) were eliminated. But the liturgists had to take responsibility for collecting the full quota of taxes assessed for their nomes, and make up any deficits. Obviously, people would do what they could to avoid liturgical appointments, resorting to bribery if necessary. Sometimes a person would go so far as to surrender all his real property to the nominator and have him perform the liturgy in his place, something the nominator was legally obliged to do.

It is evident from the data that large numbers of people in Roman Egypt were sorely pressed financially, and conditions got worse during the 3rd century, when the entire empire was economically depressed. As noted, a typical last resort was flight. People who fled from the heavy burdens of taxes and other obligations were often called *anachoretai,* from which we get the word "anchorite," a technical term usually applied to the Christian monk who has "withdrawn" to a solitary religious life. We can see that the socioeconomic basis had already been laid in Egypt for the rapid development of monasticism in the 4th century.

RELIGION

Since religion is treated in several of the other essays, we provide here only a bare summary of what can be derived from the papyri regarding religious life in a typical nome capital like Oxyrhynchus in the 2nd and 3rd centuries.

As we have seen, there were many temples in Oxyrhynchus devoted to Greek, Egyptian, and Roman deities. The identities of the deities in question, however, were often easily merged in a Greek-Egyptian-Roman syncretism. Traditional Greek or Roman deities would take on Egyptian functions and attributes, and Egyptian deities would be identified with those of the Greeks and Romans. By far the most popular deity was the goddess Isis, who was worshiped in Greek, Egyptian, and mixed Graeco-Egyptian modes. She was depicted as claiming universal worship and the names of numerous other goddesses. The ruling emperors also had their cults, performed with both Egyptian and Greek and Roman rites. Holidays were observed in the temples in honor of the birthdays and accession days of all the emperors going back to Augustus.

The Greek and Roman temples in Egypt were operated by elected public administrators, as was customary in their homelands. But the temples of the Egyptian deities were run in ancient pharaonic fashion by hereditary priesthoods. Egyptian priests would be clearly identifiable on the streets, with special linen garments and shorn heads. Animal cults were a distinctive feature of Egyptian religion.

The various temple festivals provided the populace with needed diversions from their daily routines: holidays with sacrificial banquets, processions, athletic games, dramatic festivals, music, and dancing. Public religion thus provided the people with the kinds of entertainment that in our day would usually be regarded as purely "secular."

Religion had its more private moments as well. Moreover, the distinction between religion and magic, never very clear, was not at all self-evident in the popular religion of Egypt. Amulets and other charms were everywhere present. Incantations invoking various gods, demons, and spirits were used for all purposes: to cure illness or to visit illness upon someone else, to induce love in a desired woman, to provide victory in a contest, etc. (see cat. nos. 102, 103, 104, 108, 109 and 110).

Oracles were particularly popular, and many of the gods were regularly consulted as oracles. In some cases the priests in charge of the oracles would issue menus with numbered questions from which the consultant could choose. The questions, requiring yes or no answers, covered every conceivable day-to-day concern: "Shall I be sold?" "Shall I be reconciled with my child?" "Is the absent one alive?" "Is my property to be confiscated?" "Shall I become a fugitive?"[5]

Christianity first makes its appearance in the documentary papyri in the 3rd century. From then on people are identifiable as Christians in private letters, financial documents, public records, petitions, wills, etc.[6] Of course, there had been Christians in Egypt for some 200 years by that time, but they were not very conspicuous in public perception and tended to keep to themselves. Their refusal to participate in pagan worship or in the cult of the emperor seems not to have given them much difficulty in Egypt

5. These are some of the questions quoted from selected papyri by Lewis 1983, p. 99.
6. See Judge and Pickering 1977.

until the time of Emperor Decius in the mid-3rd century. In 249 A.D. Decius instituted an imperial edict, presumably directed against Christians, that required everyone to participate in pagan worship and to certify compliance before a government official. (This requirement would have been just as repugnant to Jews as to Christians, but Jews were exempt on the grounds of their traditional legal status in the empire.) Some of the certificates (*libelli*) given to people by the commissioners are extant, certifying that the bearer has poured a libation, sacrificed to the gods of the emperor, and tasted the sacrificial offerings. We know from other sources that numerous Christians were put to death for their refusal to participate in the ritual, while numerous others capitulated and received their certificates. The Decian persecution of Christians lasted only a short time, cut short by Decius's death in battle against the invading Goths. And less than a century later, in 313, under Constantine, Christianity became the official religion of the Empire.

B.A.P.

Bibliography: Baines and Malek 1980; Bowman 1986; Gazda 1983; Judge and Pickering 1977; Lewis 1983; MacLennan 1935; Turner 1952.

Early Byzantine Egypt

Between the early 4th and the mid-7th century of our era, Egypt experienced its greatest cultural flowering since pharaonic times. Under the Theodosian dynasty (379–450), Egypt became a separate administrative unit with its own growing institutions of law and patronage, while Egyptian monasticism began to take on its two characteristic forms, centralized and ermetical. By the reign of Anastasius at the end of the 5th century, the financial and military structure of the province was beginning to coalesce around large landholdings and their powerful administrators, who formed a cultural upper class that provided wide-ranging literary, artistic, and theological patronage. The era of Justinian and his successors in the 6th century saw the separation of the Egyptian church from that of the imperial capital, and a great increase in local prosperity. The Emperor Heraclius (610–641) followed Justinian in making unsuccessful efforts to reunite Egypt (and Syria) ecclesiastically with the rest of the empire; but military over-extendedness offset the economic gains of earlier centuries. Yet even in the 7th century the cultural creativity of Egypt continued under its classically educated, bilingual elite, who led the way in encouraging poetry, philosophy, and the visual arts. In this dynamic period of Late Antiquity, Egypt gave birth to ideas and images whose force is still felt in our time.[7]

This era, often referred to as the "Coptic period," was when the Coptic language, the latest stage of the Egyptian language written in the Greek alphabet, came into its own as a literary tongue and a medium for documents. "Coptic" does not mean exclusively "Christian," since it is well to remember that the Coptic language was spoken and written by pagans as well. "Coptic" also does not necessarily mean exclusively "peasant" or "non-Chalcedonian." The Coptic period of Egypt's history is the period in which the Coptic language was the principal carrier of culture for all classes and ideologies.

This strong and original culture developed out of an economic and institutional base that is documented with a thoroughness unique in Roman times. The dry climate of Egypt south of the Nile Delta has preserved millions of public and private records on papyrus, illustrating every aspect of life from imperial edicts to letters home from college or the army. Using papyri, inscriptions, and narrative sources in Greek, Latin, and Coptic, modern scholars are writing the history of this phase of Egyptian culture. For this history we depend on the accidents of our sources, which are for the most part documents, sermons, and saints' lives: there is no Coptic corpus of historians, no "Book of Kings." But the unfolding of this history can be traced in many media, from written to monumental.

Roman Egypt was a network of cities grown out of the old pharaonic nome (district) capitals and thoroughly interpenetrated with Greek civic institutions, most importantly the city council (*boule*) and the gymnasium. City names were often Hellenized versions of the name of the old tutelary city god, as "Hermopolis" from the equation of Thoth and Hermes; or, in the case of the new foundations, they were named after or by the ruler, like Ptolemais or Antinoopolis. And this superstructure of *metropoleis* rested in turn on a country-wide network of villages, the centers of production: far from being decentralized, the villages collected their produce and their taxes for imperial bookkeeping and transshipment. The towns and villages were adorned with splendid public buildings and the houses of the great families. And this whole apparatus was underpinned by the bilingual education imparted in the town and village schools, where a thorough reading of the standard classical authors was encouraged in order to impart the skills needed for the bureaucracy and the running of the Roman law system.[8] In addition, though the beginnings of Christianity in Egypt are obscure, by the end of the 3rd century much of the Bible had been translated into Coptic, and Scripture too was becoming a "classic" in the minds of the people.

By the early 4th century, the reforms of Diocletian, which supported a more visible Roman military presence

---

7. For the best short survey, see Bagnall 1988.

8. See Bowman 1986.

throughout Egypt, had somewhat bypassed the city councils by introducing fiscal officials responsible directly to the central government. Egypt was not an idiosyncratic "special" province, but was thoroughly integrated into the Mediterranean *koine* sphere. And the country moved from Diocletian's Great Persecution of Christians into the post-Constantinian world of officially recognized Christianity and codified law with a strong champion of its interests in the person of the Patriarch of Alexandria. It was only natural that the economically and culturally strongest city, Alexandria,[9] should seek to further its prestige in the structure of the newly prevailing world view, Christianity.

Egypt was prominent in the 4th century Mediterranean world in the area of speculative thought. While study of the nature of the Trinity was an Alexandrian specialty, Gnostic speculation was translated into Coptic and found its way far south into the Nile Valley.[10] By this time most of Egypt's agricultural land was in the private ownership of city-dwellers, as can be seen from the abundant papyrus tax lists; and while the cities continued to be adorned with physical amenities and the trades and crafts continued to cluster in towns and villages, Egypt's monetary system was thoroughly revamped.[11] In this world, as an attempt to define what it really meant to be a Christian living in the world, arose the enduring phenomenon of monasticism. From the first individual anchorites (from *anachoreuein*, Greek for 'to withdraw out of the *chora* or country') to the establishment of self-sufficient communities whose rules, later transmitted in Coptic, spell out whole universes of trades and crafts, the implantation of monastic settlements and the growth of patterns of monastic landholding are the key to the transition to a fully Christianized Egypt.[12] Monasticism transformed the face of the country, as it would later do in western Europe. In the town and village landscape of Egypt, monasteries, as we can see from the abundant papyrus documentation they produced, were the strongest social force and the foci of loyalty for Egyptian society for many centuries to come. The local monastery was where one went to seek advice, to celebrate, and to touch holiness.

By the 5th century the papyri show us that Biblical, patristic, exegetical, and apocryphal texts in both Greek and Coptic were being read, copied, and circulated all over Egypt, right alongside abundant texts of the standard classical authors of the school curriculum such as Homer and Euripides. The phraseology of papyrus documents and private letters begins to echo the Scriptures and the popular sermons and lives of saints that furnished the stock of people's minds. How Coptic commentators interpreted the Bible demonstrates the specifically Coptic understanding of the Christian messages of incarnation and redemption: their exhortations are practical, attuned to the needs of daily life in a crowded and bureaucratic world. Forms of landholding in this period began to coalesce into large estates dominating the countryside, on which landlords could obtain the right of direct tax-collection (*'autopragy'*) for payment right to the capital, bypassing the local collectors, and being responsible for the global tax quota for their district.[13] At the top of the hierarchy, a patriarch like Cyril, moving at ease among the imperial family, educated in classical rhetoric and rejecting the pharaonic past in the name of an Egyptian Christian identity, embodied the culture of his time.

The movement from a society dominated by the visible symbols and cultural furniture of both kinds of paganism, pharaonic and Graeco-Roman, to a world pervaded by visible saints' images and memorized biblical texts was a profound shift in the very foundations of the whole culture. Unlike what happened in Asia Minor or Syria, there was no battle between 'Athens' and 'Jerusalem,' no effort to move education away from Homer and the myths to concentrate on exclusively Christian texts. It was perfectly natural to decorate the walls of a Christian house with tapestries depicting Dionysus or Prosperity, or to carve Leda and Daphne on Christian tombs, or to adorn the public buildings of a Christian government with sculptures of Zeus's eagle and the god of the Nile, even as our own law courts and banks have statues of Justice and Liberty. And yet the making of this new synthesis entailed a shift in the texture of daily life throughout the province.

The central symbols of an Egyptian city in the 4th and 5th centuries were changing. People found themselves in a world in which Isis Lactans could be seen as the Mother of God, and Leda and the swan could prefigure the Annunciation. By the 6th and 7th centuries, when the majority of Egyptians held a different form of Christian faith from that of the central government, a new set of assumptions underlay the society. The basic postulate of competitiveness and human glory was overtaken by the idea of a world in which the incarnation of the Deity was the transforming reality.

By the time Christianity became politically favored instead of underground, it had been conditioned by the special way of being Christian that had evolved in the

9. Polish archaeologists are working on Late Antique Alexandria; see Rodziewicz 1984.
10. An overview in English is provided by the new edition of Robinson 1988.
11. For a technical study see Bagnall 1985.
12. See Rousseau 1985, and the three volumes of Veilleux 1980–1982.

13. See Gascou 1985.

special landscape of the Nile Valley.[14] Egyptian Christianity was first and foremost strongly Bible-centered. The first texts in Coptic other than horoscopes were Bible texts, and the Scriptures rapidly became the principal fund on which people's speech, writing, and thought drew. We are struck by the early example of St. Anthony, who, upon hearing the Gospel read aloud in church, proceeded to take it literally, selling all that he had and giving it to the poor. When Coptic writers of documents, letters, or wills describe an incident in their lives, they cast it in terms of Bible stories: wicked people are like Cain or Judas, good ones like Susanna or St. John. A good man suffers like Job; a bad one is punished like Ananias. The Coptic style of being Christian is also strongly personal and local, attached to the living examples of holiness embodied in holy people and places like monasteries. A person in any walk of life, farmer or administrator, will journey into the desert to ask a famous anchorite for "a word," an insight into life, and return home treasuring some small object the holy man has touched. Coptic Christianity centers around meditation on the Bible and on sainthood.

The quality of people's experience in a world where Greek and Egyptian elites closely interacted[15] helped new aesthetic and political values to emerge. Particular weight was given to the role played by images in what was becoming Coptic society. The display of public buildings in a city became interwoven with churches and monasteries. And the growth of Coptic as both a literary language and a means of administrative record-keeping further unified the society and provided it with a rich medium of expression.[16] Coptic versions of the Bible, already extant in the 3rd century, took a deep hold on the minds of the people and profoundly conditioned their language, principally through the Christian liturgy. In private letters preserved on papyrus it is easy to see how their phraseology becomes totally permeated with Biblical language and formations, combining a piety accessible to everyone with the Greek erudition imparted by the school curriculum. That same educational combination, of Bible and liturgy with the classical authors, contributed to the growth of a class of Coptic elite – *dynatoi*, "the powerful," literate

landowners who came to hold the highest offices while maintaining their strong local loyalty.[17]

Alongside the civic institutions (like city councils) inherited from Graeco-Roman times, and the government bureaucracy, there grew up under Christianity two influential institutions, monasticism and organized charity. The monastic movement, as discussed above, was born in withdrawal away from the abrasive closeness of Egyptian society, and soon became the focus of intense local loyalty. The patron saint was often a revered local monastic holy man, honored in his lifetime as a wonder-working healer and judge of souls. The local monastery often developed, under the patronage of the curial class, into a large landowning complex, held in affection by its tenants who regarded it as a firmly rooted and tangible source of holiness and stability. The monastery was where you brought a sick child or a perplexing personal question.[18] Hospitals and hospices, along with monasteries, were often founded as works of benefaction by the great families, who kept them up for the honor of their name and out of a new sense of responsibility towards the poor.

Permeating all aspects of daily life was the law,[19] which by the Coptic period consisted of an interweaving of many strands: the native ("*enchoric*") Egyptian customary law of the countryside; Hellenistic law derived from the rulings of Ptolemaic kings; the codified Roman law of jurisconsults and imperial decrees; and the beginnings of a self-consciously Christian law in the form of the canons of councils and local synods. Egypt was very much a part of the Empire, bound to it most visibly by the web of regulations governing taxation and the annual grain shipment that supported Constantinople.[20] Everyone was aware that a large proportion of what they produced went to the capital.

In a flourishing provincial city like Oxyrhynchus or Panopolis, with ties to the great estates of their regions, every imaginable trade and craft could be found, its activities abundantly witnessed in the documentary papyri. Artists and artisans were commissioned by members of the great families and the middle class to decorate their town houses, their country villas, their clothes, their tombs, and the churches and monasteries over which they held patronage. For clerics and laypeople alike these artists created the omnipresent icons, visible reminders of people's friends in heaven, who were there to care for them in adversity and share in their joy in good times. What recent historians have been trying to understand is the role played

14. See Goehring/Pearson 1986.
15. See Fowden 1986.
16. Coptic is a Hamitic language that depends a good deal on word order and on a particular system of verb conjugations (see Shisha-Halevy 1986). It is a good language for locating yourself in a web of spatial relations, up- and downriver, to or from a city or monastery, toward the cardinal points, in and out of your house. It is good for story-telling, for repetitive exhortation, and for puns. You can hammer home a point in Coptic, or plead a case, or tell the story of your life, or come up with a wry and pithy proverb about human existence.

17. See MacCoull 1988b.
18. Illustrated by MacCoull 1979b, which deals with a slightly later period but is relevant to the Byzantine age as well.
19. Steinwenter 1955; MacCoull forthcoming c.
20. Fundamental is Gascou 1985.

by images[21] – icons, building decorations, textiles, the decorated objects of daily life – in the fabric of Coptic society, and especially to try to recreate what the Coptic people of that time saw when they looked at a product of the visual arts and crafts. How they perceived the images with which they surrounded themselves is an index to how they saw their world.

Coptic culture and its characteristic products strike us as being intensely visual. The poetry is full of color and light effects; the sculpture uses polychromy and high contrast to catch the sun; the theology explains itself through visual metaphors and conveys its meaning through the enacting of an impressively decorative liturgy. Coptic craftsmen made things as they did because the forms express deeply held, ingrained beliefs. The long arm of Christ embracing St. Menas in an encaustic painting illustrates the power of divine patronage, not faulty anatomy; the sharply cut acanthus leaves on a capital, ready to be painted, are adapted to the all-pervasive sunshine, and not degenerate copies of a lost idea of Athens. And when a person could top a tunic with bands of Dionysiac dancers and the cloak with praying saints, this was a truly creative synthesis. The objects of Coptic daily life are evocative, "objects to think with." They call up the texture and flavor of a lost Mediterranean way of life that took Homer and the Gospels equally seriously.

Across the middle of the 5th century falls the chasm of the Council of Chalcedon (451), at which churchmen from Old Rome and Constantinople refused any further autonomous growth to the Egyptian/Alexandrian version of Christology. Cyril and Dioscorus I had developed a definition of who Christ was, "one incarnate nature of God the Word," in response to the formulation of Nestorius of Constantinople, felt to be dangerously humanizing of the Savior.[22] The aftermath of this council was to affect all of Egyptian society down to the present day.[23] To understand the nature of Christ was a powerful motivation for people in the 4th and succeeding centuries. If he was just another dying-and-rising god like Osiris, not really human like us, we are not saved. If, on the other hand, he was just

another human moral teacher and healer, he was not really divine, and again we are not saved. How Christ could possibly be simultaneously the God who made and saved the universe, and just like us, our brother, was very important to grasp and make clear to the simplest person. After Cyril formulated a Christology that avoided seeing Christ as too human, the Egyptian church separated from the church of Constantinople, a profound turning point in Egypt's history. The strong adherence of the majority to Monophysite Christianity put its stamp on literature, law, and the entire culture.[24]

After 451 two separate hierarchies evolved gradually, but the culture of Egypt, contrary to many scholars' opinions, did not become radically polarized into upper-class, Greek-speaking Chalcedonians who kept the pagan philosophical tradition on the one hand and on the other Coptic-speaking peasant Monophysites whose mostly illiterate world was bounded by memorized Bible quotations. The phraseology of the papyrus documents shows the deep unity of the culture. Shenoute of Atripe (Panopolis/Akhmim), the 5th century monastic leader, was steeped in classical rhetoric, and brought the Coptic language to a new height of literary expressiveness in his sermons. Nonnus of Panopolis's new metrics had strong roots in Coptic syntax. The inherited mental furniture of classical education – the stories and mythological figures – remained the intelligible foundation of Egyptian culture in both languages, Greek and Coptic.

The 6th and early 7th centuries were the world of the great Coptic *dynatoi*, people of Egyptian birth and education, classically trained, who held high office – sometimes in Constantinople itself – and moved easily about a Mediterranean world linked by its web of cities, monasteries, and dynastic ties.[25] These were the people whose patronage produced opulent visual and literary works of art, who got things done within the bureaucracy, who composed poems in praise of the emperor, local officials, the Deity and saints, who made money from their estates and spent it on learning, ecclesiastical and lay, as well as on beautifying their cities (*euergesia*, "benefaction") and display. People such as these Coptic *kosmikoi* ("people of the world") made the culture work, and they were not just a tiny elite. Literacy in both languages was comparatively widespread, and the 6th and 7th centuries saw the greatest production of both deluxe codices of the authors, pagan and Christian, and elegantly phrased documents turned out by the bilingual, classically educated city notaries. Each Egyptian town boasted several famous writers and thinkers: the map of Egypt's cities is by and large the map

21. See Hunt 1983.
22. It could be said that the decisions of Chalcedon illustrate the mutual unintelligibility of notions in three different language families, Indo-European, Semitic, and Hamitic, which do not conceive of subject and modifier in at all the same way.
23. Until recently, nothing seemed more alien to our minds than the quarrels over the nature of Christ and the Trinity in the early Christian centuries. Egyptian and Syrian Monophysitism was studied only for refutation, from the Chalcedonian point of view; such arguments were at any rate thought utterly silly by post-Enlightment scholars who assumed they were simply coverups for 'real' economic or social needs.

24. See Johnson 1986. There is no up-to-date equivalent for the Coptic world of R. Chesnut's admirable Syriac study.
25. See Gascou 1985, pp. 88–90.

of humane learning of the time. Great magnates like the Apion family and minor scholar-gentry like Dioscoros of Aphrodito[26] combined to make Egypt a deeply rooted heartland of simultaneously classical and Christian humanism and letters: the world of both the "wandering poets," those who produced the hexameter Psalter paraphrase and the drama *Christus Patiens,* and of the fathers and mothers of the desert monasteries, around the hearing of whose pithy sayings a whole pious tourist industry was built.[27] Documentary and literary papyri of the period attest to the opulence of city life, the attachment of the elites to the countryside, the expressive art forms, and the underlying rhetoric that was thoroughly imbued with Biblical language and Hellenic idiom. A governor would be compared both to Solon and to Solomon; a magistrate would be praised for both embodying the spirit of the laws and exalting the faith of the Trinity. And the ubiquity of pastoral and Nilotic imagery shows the high status associated with its use, demonstrating the elite's concern with owning country houses and hunting for pleasure in the old classical way, combined with a Christian delight in creation.

In this high summer of Coptic culture, artists, thinkers and administrators developed an image of the good life that combined the best of the past with a sharp awareness of the eternal aspect of everyday things. The world of Late Antique Egypt had a unique way of apprehending the heritage of antiquity, whose eclipse is an enigma for our own time. For eclipsed it was to be. When Heraclius (610–641) used his power base in North Africa to take over the throne in Constantinople, he appointed one man, Cyrus of Colchis, to have the powers simultaneously of civil and military governor and Chalcedonian patriarch over Egypt. The attempt at religious unity did not work. For ten years, between 618 and 628, Egypt was occupied by Sassanian Persian troops; by 642 it was fully occupied by the Moslem Arab army. The papyrus documentation of Heraclius's reign attests to the vitality of the economy, the world of learning, the monasteries, the estates and the law-courts. But the golden age of Late Antique Egyptian culture was to pass into oblivion as the indigenous population of Egypt, now defined by religion as a subject people, abandoned its classical languages and lost the meaning of its inheritance. There were to be no more wandering poets. Coptic culture adopted a fortress mentality that emptied learning of the value it had enjoyed in earlier centuries, to become merely a liturgical memory for the financial officials of the Caliphs' courts.[28] Only after the Moslem conquest did the surviving Copts begin to date their works and their tombstones by the "Era of the Martyrs."[29]

L.S.B.M.

Bibliography: Bagnall 1985; Bagnall 1988a; Bell 1944; Bowman 1986; Fowden 1986; Gascou 1985; Goehring 1986; Goehring/Pearson 1986; Hardy 1932; Johnson 1986; Keenan 1984; MacCoull 1979b; MacCoull 1981; MacCoull 1988a; MacCoull/Worp 1989; Martin 1985; Robinson 1988; Rodziewicz 1984; Rouillard 1928; Rousseau 1985; Sorabji 1987; Steinwenter 1955; Timbie 1986; Veilleux 1980–1982; Ward 1980; Wildberg 1987.

---

26. MacCoull 1988a.
27. Study of the *Apophthegmata* (*Sayings of the Desert*) has become quite an academic industry. See Ward 1980.
28. See Martin 1985.
29. See MacCoull/Worp 1989.

RELIGION

Ancient Egyptian Religion

FLORENCE D. FRIEDMAN

THIS ESSAY WILL CONCENTRATE on a few of the most important aspects of ancient Egyptian religion and will also touch on some features that may have influenced Coptic Christianity. Religion permeated every aspect of Egyptian life. The rising sun, the flooding Nile, the corn harvest, even the named and ritually enlivened doorjambs of a temple gate were infused with the divine. The life of the gods was generally open to everyone, though the official state religion of the king, who was both god and man, differed from the popular religion of the masses. We may never fully know what the average farmer in the Pyramid Age believed, since so little documentation remains. Most of what we know comes from material produced for the king or high-ranking members of society. Their religious texts are especially instructive. Hymns, prayers, magical spells, guides to the underworld, and compilations like the so-called Book of the Dead (called by the Egyptians the Book of Going Forth by Day[1]) provide glimpses into many levels of religious life.

Egyptian religious texts are sometimes difficult to understand and often seem confusing and contradictory to modern eyes. For example, the god Amun, the "Hidden One," originally a god of air, could appear as a man in one text and a goose in the next. In one theology, Ptah, patron of craftsmen, created the world through "what the heart thought and the tongue commanded," while in another, Atum performed the same feat through masturbation. Sophisticated and primitive notions existed side by side, local folk traditions being sustained alongside formal theologizing. The Egyptians did not discard old ideas, they added to them. Thus, in the next world one could at the same time dwell in the sky as an immortal star, or in the funerary statue as the ka-spirit; in the underworld with Osiris, King of the Dead, or in the sky, towing the sun boat of Re. The Egyptians perceived no contradictions in this fluid form of thinking,[2] since each experience was complete and valid in itself. Perhaps because of this tolerance and flexibility, Egyptian religion never acquired an exclusive form of holy writ. It had no Bible, no revealed word at the center of its multifaceted faith. And it offered no one god who embodied the essence of all belief, as Christ would in Christianity.

There was one concept, however, called Maat, that was operative throughout religious, social, and political life in Egypt. (Social, political, and even economic life were in large part inseparable from religious life in Egypt.) Although frequently translated as justice and truth, Maat especially meant harmony and balance, particularly the harmony that pervaded creation "in the beginning." This was a mythical moment, reenacted again and again in temple ritual, when a creator god (there were many in the many different creation myths) brought the world into being out of chaos. Each creator god was a self-creator who preexisted what he created. He created the natural world, including light, and then a myriad of gods and mankind. Man did not, however, dominate the animal and natural world; he coexisted with them.[3] Preserving the harmonious balance of Maat within one's life, country, and cosmos, by commitment to the truth and performance of just deeds, was the ethical as well as pragmatic duty of every person, and most especially of the king.[4]

The king was the intermediary between the gods and man. Called Pharaoh (literally, "Great House") since the New Kingdom (ca. 1500 B.C.), the king was the most important figure in Egyptian society. He was both god and man. Divinity was implicit in his office: to be a king was to be a god. The living king on earth was identified with the falcon god Horus, but at death he became Horus's father, the god Osiris, lord of the underworld. The king thus played the role of son in this world and father in the next, son and father being two eternal aspects of kingship. This idea was so embedded in Egyptian thinking that it perhaps facilitated the later Egyptian understanding of the

---

1. For an interesting example of a guide to the underworld available to those who could afford it, see Lesko 1977. And most recently on the Book of the Dead, see Lesko 1987, pp. 270–1.
2. Frankfort 1948, p. 22.

3. Te Velde 1980.
4. See, for example Morenz 1960, pp. 110 ff on ethics and its relationship to Maat; and Hornung 1982, pp. 213–6.

unity of Christ and the Father as two aspects of godhead. It has also been suggested that pharaoh's central position in Egyptian society may have provided the religious structure within which Christ could be later understood. For as pharaoh was king of Egypt and thus of mankind, Christ was king of the world.[5] And (though the interpretations of this concept were vastly different) both were sons of gods.[6]

Since Dynasty 4 (ca. 2500 B.C.), the king was called the son of the sun god Re. This relationship was given special emphasis in the mid-14th century B.C. by the so-called monotheist king, Akhenaten, who prohibited the worship of virtually all gods except his father, the solar disk, called the Aten. Representations and inscriptions make it clear that the king and the Aten, an aspect of Re, were seen as equivalents. Inscriptions state that the king was the solar manifestation of his father, that he was daily created through the Aten's sunbeams. One possible translation of "Akhenaten" suggests that he was the very light of his father.[7] Though this union of son with father is more intimate than any previous, the merger of creator and creation, as well as father and son, appears repeatedly in Egyptian religious thinking.[8] One might suggest that the ideas of Akhenaten influenced later notions of the unity of Christ and the Father, though this seems doubtful, since the ideas of this heretic king were rejected after his death and probably had little effect on Egyptian religion as a whole.

Though the monotheistic tendencies of Akhenaten were condemned, Egyptian theologians routinely sought unity within the diversity of numerous deities. Triads of gods were sometimes created to express aspects of a single godhead in three different forms. One famous New Kingdom hymn to the state god proclaims that "All gods are three,"[9] while another declares that "One is Amon...."[10] Many religious passages of the New Kingdom to the Ptolemaic period stress the unity of Re, the sun god, and Osiris, the King of the Dead, thus trying to reconcile the apparent opposites they represented. Many gods were also seen as aspects of Re alone "in all his forms." Thus there was an attempt to understand the force of the divine in a variety of guises and names.

Another notion reflecting a unifying concept beneath multiple forms is the soul, covered by the ancient Egyptian terms *ba, ka,* and *akh,* among others. While the meaning of these terms is complex, each reflects a concept of the whole person. As a *ba* one might assume any form one wished in the afterlife; the *ba* is typically depicted as a human-headed bird ascending from the tomb to enjoy the haunts of the living. The *ka* is a person's second self produced at birth, which could inhabit the funerary (or *ka*) statue; food offerings, essential for the deceased's afterlife, were consumed by the *ka*. The *akh* is the spirit of the deceased that could assume forms of light, especially sunlight. These three sorts of soul were not parts of the person that added up to a whole, nor did they separate the spiritual and material person: each represented the individual in his totality. This monistic view of man[11] may have encouraged the later Monophysite interpretation of Christ (as being of only one nature, human and divine combined) among Coptic Christians.

These notions of the soul, though originally the prerogative of the king, had long been absorbed by the general populace. But the ideas of most of the theologians had scant effect outside the royal circle. The popular religion of the masses differed from the official state religion of the divine king. The ordinary person concentrated more on deities who directly affected his daily life: for example, the household gods who protected women in pregnancy and childbirth, or the gods of his craft, or of a particular locality (just as there were later saints of particular localities) where he lived or worked. The interiors of the temples were barred to the ordinary person. Unlike later churches, which were large assembly halls for worshipers, the temples were not places of communal worship. They were houses where the gods lived, and the function of the temple priests (the king was theoretically the high priest of every temple) was to tend to the daily care of the gods in their statue form. Except for major festivals, which involved the whole community, the average individual had little association with the temples, and then only from the exterior. Contact with their major resident deities was still possible, however, by inscribing supplications on the outer walls of the temple. From the New Kingdom on, appeals to personal savior deities like Amun are common.

Personal appeals of non-royal individuals are well known from a New Kingdom Ramesside workmen's village. Their hymns and prayers recorded on stelae recall later Christian prayers of supplication, penitence, and thanksgiving: "You are Amun... when I call to you in my distress, you come to rescue me."[12] And: "... the lord is disposed to forgive,... may you forgive; it shall not happen again."[13] Or, from a late Ptolemaic text known from a 1st century A.D. copy, comes the plea: "The sin which I

5. Horn 1985, pp. 59–60, 66.
6. Brunner-Traut 1981.
7. Friedman 1986, p. 101; but see also Redford 1976, p. 54.
8. Morenz 1960, p. 175. On the human mind originating in and partaking of the divine mind, see Federn 1949, pp. 317–8.
9. Pritchard 1969, p. 369.
10. See Gardiner 1905, p. 34.

11. Žabkar 1968, p. 97.
12. Berlin Museum 20377 in Lichtheim 1976, p. 106.
13. Lichtheim 1976, p. 107.
14. Papyrus Insinger, Twenty-fifth Instruction, 35, lines 4–5 in Lichtheim 1980, p. 213.

have committed unwittingly, . . . I call to the god to have mercy on me. . . ."[14] Emphasis on living a moral life is evident in a tomb inscription of a man living at the time of Alexander the Great. Echoing themes from Old Kingdom Wisdom texts, the speaker says that the realm of the dead "is the abode of him who is faultless, . . . No man will attain it, unless his heart is exact in doing right."[15]

Every person could also make contact with the gods through their statues. At the temple festivals, which continued even into Roman times, the gods' statues were removed from the temple sanctuaries and paraded before the people. Contact with the statue, the living image of the god, was not simply idol-worship (though it appeared as such to later Christians), any more than adoration of an icon is today. The statue was the vehicle within which the godhead resided and provided a focus for prayer and petition. Statues also acted as oracles: questions and legal disputes, for example, could be settled by a movement of the statue's head for "yes" or "no." Statuettes of deities could also be kept in the home or worn as amulets for protection. Use of oracles, amulets, and other forms of (what we call) magic continued right into Byzantine times.

A more intimate form of a relationship with a deity ultimately was also possible through identification with Osiris, god of the dead. If one could afford the proper mummification, spells and tomb offerings, one could at death become "an Osiris." Through this identification, which was at the heart of Egyptian funerary beliefs, each person could be resurrected as Osiris had been. According to fragments of the myth (the Egyptians did not record full narratives of their myths), Osiris was a man unjustly slain, but resurrected with the aid of his dutiful sister-wife Isis, who then conceived by him and bore their son Horus. The family triad of Osiris (in the form of Sarapis), Isis, and Horus (as Harpokrates) became especially popular in Graeco-Roman religion in Egypt (see Pharaonic Themes, below).

The Greeks left Egyptian religious practice relatively untouched during the almost 300 years of Ptolemaic rule. Unused to the fluid world of Egyptian thinking, they were puzzled by Egyptian religion, but also in awe of its legendary mystery and antiquity. Some Greeks adopted the Egyptian deities, though many Romans were repelled by Egyptian animal cults. Under both Greek and Roman domination, however, conflations of Egyptian and Graeco-Roman deities occurred. The most enduring example was Isis, who absorbed the features of virtually all divine aspects of nature, life, fertility, and death. Her cult spread throughout the Mediterranean world, even into Roman Britain, and in Late Antiquity when her cult merged with that of the Virgin, belief in Isis was clung to tenaciously even in the face of spreading Christianity.

Clear lines of transmission from ancient Egyptian religion to Coptic Christianity are not easily discerned.[16] Yet notions fundamental to Egyptian religion often provided a framework within which Coptic Christianity was understood. For example, the tendency to discern godhead in multiple forms may be found in the concept of the Trinity; the eternal continuum of father and son in the figure of the king parallels that of Christ and the Father; the role of pharaoh as king of Egypt is assumed by Christ as king of the world; and the single god-man nature is found in both the pharaoh and Christ. The monistic view of man may also be evident in the Coptic Christian belief that Christ was of one nature only (i.e., human and divine combined into one), and not two as the orthodox church maintained.

Early Christians unfortunately viewed the ancient representations of gods and their monuments as reminders of an "unholy paganism." Having no understanding of or respect for the profundity or richness of Egyptian religion and faith,[17] they desecrated the Egyptian temples, mutilating figures of the gods and damaging inscriptions. Sadly, their Christian monuments suffered similar desecration at the hands of Muslims after the Arab conquest.

15. *The Long Biographical Inscription of Petosiris* in Lichtheim 1980, p. 46.

16. Säve-Söderberg 1981, p. 71 rightly cautions against "motif hunting" in order to establish lines of continuity from pharaonic to Coptic Christian religion. See also Zandee 1960, ch. 4 and p. 342; I thank Edmund Meltzer for this reference. For other recent contributions on lines of continuity see Bresciani 1981; Junge 1982; Horn 1985; and Schenkel 1977. See also Viaud 1978 for a discussion of pharaonic practices that have influenced the life of the Coptic Church. My thanks to Leslie MacCoull for obtaining for me a copy of Horn 1985.

17. For a moving description of Egyptian religion and faith, see Goyon 1988, pp. 29–39.

Christianity

LEONARD LESKO

FOLLOWING THE CRUCIFIXION of Jesus of Nazareth in the principate of Emperor Tiberius, his disciples, who acknowledged Jesus as Christ, the messiah whose coming had been prophesied by the Jews, recorded his teachings and the miracles he performed and began a religion that was to spread around the world and dominate much of Western civilization. According to tradition, these disciples dispersed throughout the ancient world, teaching and often working wonders of their own.

Although there is virtually no documentation for earliest Christianity in Egypt, it has certainly been correctly surmised that its origins were in the Jewish community at Alexandria in the 1st century.[1] The disciples of Christ who went to Egypt would have assimilated most easily into the large and diverse Jewish community that constituted perhaps a quarter of the population of cosmopolitan Alexandria. With more Jews there than any place other than Jerusalem, there was a receptive audience. Most of the Alexandrian Jews would have been interested in the news from Jerusalem and many would have been won over by the convincing testimony of these enthusiastic witnesses to Christ. Clearly, freedom of movement in the early Empire made it easier for missionaries to spread the gospel, and a letter of Emperor Claudius to the Alexandrians refers to Jews still coming there from Syria, while in Acts 2:10 Jews from Egypt were said to have listened to Peter's sermon.

Coptic tradition, but no historical evidence, traces the origin of the Egyptian church to Saint Mark the Evangelist. Clement of Alexandria (ca. 215) is the first to mention that Mark came to Egypt,[2] and Eusebius, "Father of Church History" (ca. 260–340), provides the earliest account of Mark's activity there, including preaching, founding churches, and converting large numbers of men and women. From the 4th century Egyptian *Acts of Mark*[3] we also learn that Mark had appointed a bishop, three priests, and seven deacons in the thriving Christian community that he founded at Alexandria, but he also greatly angered the pagan community who in about year 66 dragged him through the city, eventually killing him. Whether this particular martyrdom story is properly attributed to Mark has been questioned, but it is still possible that this late legend holds some truth. Interestingly, there was no mention of Mark's work in Egypt earlier by other prolific writers, and the martyrdom story could have been that of the later archbishop Peter (died ca. 311).[4]

Just as Jewish beliefs and practices in the Hellenized setting of Alexandria had considerable diversity, so the Christian traditions would have had variations, and it is now thought that what was later judged by the "Fathers of the Church" as heterodox (nonconforming), Gnostic (distorted), or otherwise heretical grew up right alongside the orthodox (approved) tradition.[5] Several forms of Gnosticism (belief in a power come down from heaven to redeem man through *gnosis* – knowledge, (see essay on *Gnosticism*), as well as several variants of orthodox Christianity, are represented in the literature of the 2nd century. Portions of the standard "canonized" Gospels of Matthew and John are known from 2nd century Egypt, together with the non-canonical "Gnostic" *Gospel of Thomas*, the *Gospel of the Hebrews*, and the *Gospel of the Egyptians*, none of which gained acceptance in any surviving form of Christianity.

The earliest known Christian sites in Egypt were located in the Jewish quarters of Alexandria, and these probably grew in importance after Trajan suppressed the Jewish rebellion (115–117).[6] Portions of the ancient city have sunk below water level now and much would have been

---

1. Cf. Roberts 1979, pp. 49–93, and Pearson/Goehring1986, pp. 132–7.
2. Cf. Smith 1973.
3. In addition to the Coptic version of this text there are also Greek, Latin, Arabic, and Ethiopic versions. For a discussion of the manuscripts and contents of this work see Pearson/Goehring 1986, pp. 140–5.

4. As suggested by Pearson/Goehring 1986, pp. 143–4.
5. Cf. Pearson/Goehring 1986, pp. 245–6, Säve-Söderbergh 1961, pp. 287–293, and Bowman 1986, pp. 199–201.
6. Cf. Pearson/Goehring 1986, pp. 147–55.

rebuilt in modern times, so it is uncertain how much will ever be recovered through archaeology. Again, though documentation is almost entirely lacking, it seems likely that there was a connection between Trajan's punishment – the almost total extermination of the Jews – and the end of Jewish influence on Christianity.

Shortly after this, in the mid-2nd century, the famous Christian Catechetical School at Alexandria was founded, and this contributed greatly to the further dissemination and development of Christianity in general. Egypt had a long tradition as a melting pot as well as an intellectual and cultural center, and the Egyptians' tolerance of new religious ideas would have been a contributing factor in this independent development. The school was founded to instruct catechumens (those being taught the principles of Christianity), and the sophisticated environment demanded strong intellectual leadership. The first three heads of the Catechetical School, Pantaenus (died ca. 200), Clement (died ca. 215), and Origen (died ca. 253) had their background in Greek philosophy and adopted the ethics of the Stoics, the logic of Aristotle, and the metaphysics of Plato. Origen alone taught so many of the early Church Fathers that without him the teaching mission of the early Church would not have been as successful as it was. The philosophical and theological writings and teaching of these scholars provide a clear antecedent to the earliest faculties of the later medieval and modern universities.

In 2nd century Alexandria there was also a Gnostic school with teachers such as Basilides and Valentinus. Patrons sponsored young scholars in one or the other or both schools. Both the Christian Origen and the pagan Plotinus (Neoplatonist *par excellence*) were students of the same teacher, Ammonius, and both of these Neoplatonists, schooled in the rational tradition of Greek philosophy, became influential scholars in their own separate traditions. Their teaching methods were similar, as were the philosophical texts that they read, and they shared a disdain for Gnosticism, which they perceived as revelatory and illogical. While the Catechetical School may actually have been formed to counteract Gnosticism, in succeeding centuries the school was actually condemned as not being orthodox enough. Origen, as a good Christian, abandoned traditional Greek theological views and assumed the difficult task of trying to express new Christian interpretations, combining philosophy and theology. He also taught himself Hebrew and wrote commentaries on the Old Testament. It is for his voluminous writings and for having taught many Church Fathers that Origen is best known, but some of his teachings were later (553) condemned as heretical.[7]

His role in sustaining orthodox Christianity over pagan Platonism and Christian Gnosticism should not be underestimated, however, and his influence on later theological education certainly was unparalleled. Both Clement and Origen, it is important to note, fostered the role of women in spreading Christianity. While Clement said that women were no different from men in their spiritual abilities, Origen, according to Eusebius, went so far as to castrate himself to avoid possible scandal in admitting women to his school.

In the 3rd century, under Emperor Decius, persecution of the Christians began; though sporadic and not really a threat to Christianity, the persecution of those who refused to acknowledge the pagan gods of Rome became particularly severe in the reign of Diocletian in 303, and reputedly tens of thousands were sent to their deaths. Clearly Christianity would not have survived if all had rushed to martyrdom as some are said to have done,[8] but it is also understandable that the documentation about Christians in this particular period is limited. The situation changed rapidly further into the 4th century, however, first with Rome's Edict of Toleration in 311 and then when Christianity was granted official status by the Edict of Milan under Emperor Constantine in 313. By the end of the 4th century, Christians turned the tables and began to persecute pagans, a process that was to continue for another century.

Among the early heretics condemned by orthodox Christianity were the Manichaeans, Christian followers of the Persian prophet Mani, who were outlawed at Alexandria by Diocletian at the beginning of the 4th century. Their books were to have been destroyed, but documents pointing to their existence even into the 6th century survive.[9] Apa Shenoute, the abbot of the great White Monastery in Upper Egypt, attacked not only pagans but also Manichaeans, whom he accused of rejecting fundamental Christian doctrines.

Whereas earlier Christians would have met in private homes or house-chapels, after 313 they could worship publicly in large churches, first in converted temples that were often taken by force from the pagans and later in edifices of their own construction. Many monasteries were established in earlier pharaonic temples and tombs, but some very large new establishments also grew up in this period.

The most important centers for early Christianity were Jerusalem, Antioch in Syria, Alexandria, Constantinople, and Rome. These became the patriarchal sees that provided leadership, resolved differences, gained suzerainty over smaller sees, and eventually competed with one another.

7. This was at the Fifth Ecumenical Council, the second council of Constantinople. During his lifetime Origen had also been banished and deposed from the priesthood, and at the end of the 4th century was condemned by Anastasius I.

8. Cf. Bowman 1986, pp. 191–2 (Eusebius, *History of the Church* 8.9.5).

9. Cf. Bowman 1986, p. 199, and Stroumsa in Pearson 1986, pp. 307–19.

Antioch had early displaced Jerusalem in importance. Alexandria as a patriarchal see may have been third after Antioch chronologically, but clearly rivaled Constantinople and to some extent paralleled Rome in development into the 5th century. In addition to many liturgical features in common, Alexandria and Rome each had "popes" with more centralized jurisdiction than the other patriarchates. A hierarchy, with the bishop at the top over priests and deacons (this latter group including women), would have developed early, but the subordination of local bishops to the Patriarch of Alexandria was a gradual process completed in the 6th century. Synods or councils of bishops were held to discuss and resolve differences, and this was frequently accomplished in an unruly way. Condemnation of heretics resulted in both strained relations among clerics and their supporters and often strong feelings of nationalism that involved the masses.[10]

It was the doctrinal conflicts at Ecumenical Councils that shaped Christianity now that the persecutions were over and paganism was dying. The most serious doctrinal conflict involving Egypt developed in the early 4th century when a cleric at Alexandria named Arius taught that the "Son of God" was divine but not as divine as the Father. This teaching, quite logical from the point of view of the traditional Egyptian concept of divinity, had been presented earlier by a student of Origen, but had been condemned by the Bishop of Rome, Dionysius. Now Arius was also condemned by a synod of Egyptian bishops in 318, but Christians elsewhere in the eastern Empire defended him. Emperor Constantine first tried to defuse the situation, then in 325 personally convened the first Ecumenical (or general) Council of more than three hundred bishops at Nicea in Asia Minor, where the Nicean Creed with its doctrine of consubstantiality (Christ and God the Father being of one substance) was formulated. At the same time Arius was condemned and sent into exile. There was an appeal, the Council was reconvened in 327, and Arius together with the other dissenters accepted the Nicean Creed, with of course their own interpretation of "homoousios" (same essence). Athanasius, the new Bishop of Alexandria, refused to reinstate the heretic Arius, however, and the latter appealed in vain to the Emperor for permission to establish his own church at Alexandria. Constantine ordered Arius's writings to be burned, but Arius appealed and convinced the Emperor of his orthodoxy. Bishop Athanasius was deposed by the Council at Tyre and exiled to Gaul, but Arius, who was given permission to return to Alexandria, did not live long enough to do so. In 337, Constantine, on his deathbed, was baptized by an Arian bishop. Following Emperor Julian's proclamation of complete religious toleration, Athanasius was restored to the See of Alexandria, but because of the resulting disturbances in the East, Athanasius was again deposed, but restored yet again in 364 by the emperor Jovian. Emperor Valens, who was an Arian himself, attacked eastern Catholics but let Athanasius stay on in Alexandria, where he died in 373. Subsequently, the intolerance of the Catholic Emperor, Theodosius, led to the destruction of the Serapeum at Alexandria, attacks on pagan temples by Shenoute's monks, and the stoning to death of the famous pagan woman philosopher, Hypatia, in Alexandria in 415.

Clearly, in the long fifty-year tenure of the Patriarch Athanasius, who had been exiled five times, there had been a great deal of dissension within the Egyptian church, and this continuing dissension certainly contributed to the transfer of authority from Alexandria to Constantinople in the middle of the 5th century. Egypt, under attack from Blemmyes to the east (savage inhabitants of the area between Meroe and the Red Sea) and Nubians to the south, was inadequately defended by its Roman overlords, so that the Egyptian monasteries, which had already attracted thousands to religious life, now had to provide for tens of thousands of refugees within their walls. This new rural and ascetic, rather than doctrinaire, Coptic Christianity would grow ever stronger and more self-assured, and also more unwilling to bow to distant Byzantium.

Monks were involved in the teaching and spread of many doctrines and eventually influenced the very tenets of the patriarch of Alexandria. Even though the monks were not educated in the Catechetical School (i.e., scholastic tradition), they were involved in the discussion of these conflicts and their ideas often prevailed, particularly when politically advantageous to the Patriarchs. They were definitely involved in the next doctrinal issue to be resolved, concerning the nature of Mary as "Mother of God." This doctrine, being taught by monks in the Eastern Church, had been condemned as heretical by Nestorius, a priest of Antioch who became Patriarch of Constantinople. At the Council of Ephesus in 431, Cyril, Patriarch of Alexandria defended the monks' doctrine that accepted the Virgin Mary as Theotokos, the Mother of God.

In 449 (again at Ephesus) under the succeeding Alexandrian Patriarch, the doctrine of Monophysitism that had been formed by an influential monk at Constantinople gained acceptance. This doctrine stated that Christ was of one nature, his human nature after his birth being absorbed into his divine nature. This issue was critical to the development of the early church and led to the first great schism in Christianity. The Egyptian church wholeheartedly endorsed the doctrine, considering it very logical and concrete. They perceived that if Mary was "mother of God," as had been declared, then Christ was God. Two years later in 451, at the Fourth Ecumenical Council at Chalcedon, the monophysite doctrine was condemned, and the Egyptian church, which considered the diophysite doctrine of Christ's two natures (both human and divine)

10. See Jones 1959 and Griffiths 1984, pp. 1027–9.

as equivalent to Nestorianism, refused to acquiesce. It was also decreed at Chalcedon that monks should be subject to the authority of bishops and should not interfere in ecclesiastical or secular business. This served to galvanize the Eastern monks in their Monophysitism. Thirty years later, Emperor Zeno tried but failed to reconcile the Monophysites by suggesting a slightly modified interpretation of Christ's nature. This was followed by attempts to make converts to one or the other churches – an interesting example being Justinian's sending of a Chalcedonian mission to convert the Nubians, while his wife, Empress Theodora, sent a Monophysite group whose mission was successful. Shortly after Justinian's reign there were two separate patriarchs in Egypt, a non-Egyptian Chalcedonian patriarch brought in from outside to serve at Alexandria and a Coptic patriarch to serve the bulk of the Egyptian Christians.

By 618, Persians conquered Alexandria, and while they terrified some Egyptians familiar with the tales of what the Persians had inflicted on Egypt when Cambyses invaded more than a thousand years earlier,[11] this intervention certainly delighted others who clearly despised the Byzantines. When the Arab general Amr Ibn al As conquered Egypt in 642 A.D., he was probably welcomed by many of the Copts who had endured several years of persecution by the Chalcedonian Patriarch Cyrus.[12] Although the new invaders made it advantageous for many to convert to Islam, this shift in religious identity was also precipitated by the disunity and persecutions the Copts had witnessed. Still to this day, the Coptic church has managed to survive and maintain its independence with a substantial number of adherents worldwide.

11. For this text see Jansen 1950, no. 2, and MacCoull 1982a, pp. 185–8.
12. Cf. Bowman 1986, pp. 52–3, and Moorhead 1981.

Monasticism in Egypt

LEONARD LESKO

A REMARKABLE PHENOMENON of early Christianity was the desire of many to escape the attractions and pitfalls of the world and devote themselves to the spiritual life. As counterparts to the missionaries who preached the gospel and used intellectual arguments to win converts, these contemplatives, by their example and dedication to the biblical injunctions concerning perfection, showed how the gospels could best be lived and thereby attracted many more converts to the comparatively new religion.

Christian monasticism developed in Egypt in the 4th century A.D. beginning with ascetics (those who practiced some strict form of self-discipline or renunciation) who embraced the eremitic (solitary) life, often in caves or ancient tombs in the mountain deserts on either side of the Nile. Various attempts have been made to trace models of the monastic life back to the Jewish community in Egypt and even to earlier pagan customs. A link to the therapeutai, a 1st century Jewish contemplative sect located near Alexandria, had already been suggested in antiquity by Eusebius of Caesarea (260–341), the "Father of Church History."[1] At any rate, Christian monasticism was not a direct result of the Roman persecutions, a way of escaping martyrdom, as Sozomen (died ca. 450) suggested;[2] but this way of life rather developed after the persecutions as a substitute for martyrdom, a self-surrender or self-immolation. The "Era of the Martyrs" in Egypt during the reign of Diocletian was followed by the flowering of monasticism, after the Edicts of Constantine that first tolerated and then officially established Christianity in the Roman Empire.

The traditional founder of monasticism, St. Anthony, was born in about 251 A.D. in Middle Egypt. He inherited a farm which he sold, and he gave all to the poor, having taken literally the Gospel injunction for one seeking perfection.[3] His *Life* recounts the temptations he fought for thirty-five years, his miracles, and his simple, idyllic life, presented as an attractive alternative, a solution to life's problems. Anthony's fame was greatly enhanced by publication of his life, and it is indeed significant that the author of Anthony's *Life* is said to have been Athanasius of Alexandria. The fact that this long-lived, strong-willed, internationally known patriarch championed the cause of monasticism would have promoted the ascetic Christian life worldwide, while it also helped to cement the bonds between the Hellenized patriarchal see and the bulk of the Egyptian Christians who would more easily have identified with the monks. This *Life* was translated into Latin, and by the end of the 4th century it had already been read far and wide. Many of the early church fathers make reference to it.

Anthony is often identified as the first hermit, but this is hardly accurate, since Paul of Thebes was clearly his forerunner as an anchorite, and there may well have been others. Anthony does, however, represent the ideal of the Christian ascetic, and he clearly had a role of the formulation of coenobitic or community life, as well as in the eremitic life of the anchorite.

Generally, however, monasticism was of the coenobitic type, consisting of communities of men or women that congregated near a master or great teacher. Because of increasing numbers and social requirements, coenobites had to be governed by rules. Pachomius (ca. 321 A.D.) is credited with establishing the first rule for monks living in a community, and thousands of early Christians flocked to his carefully planned and well-governed establishments to live a perfect Christian life. The monasteries were essentially self-sufficient, and provided security as well as life's necessities.

Two important distinctions between the anchorites and the coenobites were in their choice of a place to live and their attitudes toward book learning. Anthony loved the desert and chose to retreat there, even from the community that came to be close to him. Pachomius founded his community, Tabennisi, near the river and allowed nine separate communities (including two for women) in close proximity to one another. Pachomius insisted that his monks learn to read and also memorize portions of the scriptures, while Anthony appreciated nature more than book learning and had to dictate his own sermons and letters to scribes.

1. Eusebius, *History of the Church* 2.17.17, which was based on Philo, *On Contemplative Life* 4.1–20; cf. Workman 1927, pp. 90–1 and Meinardus 1961, p. 8.
2. Sozomen, *History of the Church* 10, 12.
3. "If thou wouldst be perfect, go sell all that thou hast and give to the poor," Matthew 19:21.

The plan of the Pachomian monasteries was based on a military establishment, probably reflecting Pachomius's early background as a soldier. Pachomius led his disciples gradually to the ascetic life. He freed them from day-to-day concerns by assuming responsibility for their clothing, food, and shelter, and gave them a monk's habit. The buildings of his monastery were of sun-dried brick within an enclosing wall. There were a gatehouse, assembly or oratory for prayer, refectory with kitchen, bakery, storerooms, infirmary, and buildings containing the individual cells for the monks. Separate houses would weekly rotate the daily chores. Agriculture was a principal occupation and various other trades and crafts were practiced. Certain monks were entrusted with the monastery's outside business and they maintained river transport in boats that could travel from the Thebaid in the south as far as Alexandria in the north.

The written rule of Pachomius survives in several copies in Greek, Latin, Coptic, and Ethiopic.[4] It does not appear to have been a carefully organized or complete guide, but rather a collection of precepts that were added to as necessary to deal with problems. While some discipline would have been required in such large communities, Pachomius certainly seems to have been inclined toward leniency. His monks' daily meal at noon was followed by an instruction, scriptural reading, and prayer. There was some time for meditation and discussion dealing with the instruction before retiring. Morning prayers began very early and tardiness was rebuked. Sweetmeats, often gifts from relatives, could be enjoyed but had to be shared. Just how orthodox the Pachomian monastery was has come under discussion recently, because the Nag Hammadi codices with their Gnostic texts could have come from a Pachomian source.[5]

Antonian monasteries were also established at several sites, including one at Scetis in the Wadi Natrun by Apa (i.e., Father) Makarius, whose disciples were very austere and rigorous. Another established at Nitria by Apa Ammoun was also inspired by Anthony. At Nitria some monks were allowed to become priests, wine was used and sold, while linen- and rope-making were important occupations. Though the life at Nitria might seem easier, there was a certain competitiveness to outdo the rigors of the Pachomian coenobites.

Regarding important women ascetics, Mary of Egypt was a semi-legendary hermit who sought God in the desert where she roamed like an animal. Another Mary, the sister of Pachomius, guided one of the monasteries of women near the Pachomian settlement which provided for all the sisters' subsistence and apparently kept them cloistered from all men. It is clear, therefore, that there were Egyptian antecedents for convents or monasteries for women with women directing them, such as are later found in the West.

In addition to the writings about the Egyptian monks that reached the West in translation, there is also the case of John Cassian who visited Egypt near the end of the 4th century and spent seven years at Scetis before ultimately returning to Marseilles to found a monastery of the Egyptian type. With this bridge between East and West, it would appear that St. Benedict, who through his "Holy Rule" became "Father of Western monasticism," had been foreshadowed in the East by Pachomius and his "Rule," while Benedict's sister, St. Scholastica, "patroness of Benedictine nuns," had also been prefigured by Pachomius's sister Mary.

The *Apophthegmata Patrum*, a collection of stories and sayings of the early monks, was assembled in the 5th century. This pious work, intended to edify, tells us much about the most famous Egyptian monks and their way of life, but contains much that is fanciful and unhistorical as well. From the *Apophthegmata* we learn something about the monks' barest essentials, their renunciation of other worldly goods, and their social obligations:

It was said [about Apa Dioscorus] that he said, "God has given me three blessings: a good eye, an abode in a cell, and a bodily illness."

Concerning his clothing – a linen garment with a linen hood and another linen garment are his according to the rule. If one asks it of him, he should give one and keep the other. Again concerning his nourishment – he should taste nothing at all except bread, salt, and water. Concerning his resting – he should not place a reed-mat or a skin-garment or anything of this kind (under him), but he should rest on the ground according as we have heard, and it is absolutely impossible for him to put oil in the cell.

An old man said, "I have never loved anything that would give profit to me and cause loss to my brother, for I had this hope that the profit of my brother was a thing of fruitfulness for me."

Apa Hyperechios said, "The treasure of the monk is not taking anything material for himself. Load up for yourself within, and you will gather for yourself in heaven, because for you eternal rest is ceaseless."

We also learn from these sayings about the monks' concern for safety, and about their trust in God, and self-discipline:

Apa Moses from Scetis said, "If we keep the commands of our fathers, I will guarantee to you before God that no barbarians will come to this place, but if we do not keep them, the place will be destroyed.

It was said about Apa Daniel from Scetis that when the barbarians came, the brothers fled, and the old man said, "If God does not take care of me, why do I live?" He came through the barbarians and they did not see him. The old man said, "Behold,

4. Cf. Goehring in Pearson 1986, pp. 236–57.
5. Cf. Barns 1981, Pearson 1986, pp. 248–9, and Veilleux in Pearson 1986, pp. 271–306.

God has taken care of me, and I did not die, you yourself should act like the human ones and run like the other fathers."

The priest of Scetis went once to the archbishop of Alexandria and when he returned to Scetis the brothers asked him how the city was. He said to them, "Truly, my brothers, I did not look at the face of anyone except the archbishop alone." When they heard, they became strong because of the saying that they should guard themselves from raising the eyes.

Among the most famous of the Egyptian monks was an abbot whose lengthy sermons, letters and *Life* written in Coptic have made him the principal literary figure in the Egyptian church. Apa Shenoute, who in ca. 370 became a monk at the White Monastery of Apa Pjol at Sohag in Upper Egypt, later became abbot of this monastery and regarded it as a proving ground for the strenuous life of the solitary. He ranted against infractions of his rules and punished offenders with blows. He dictated the exact number of blows to be inflicted on sisters for individual faults, and he himself inflicted punishment on his brothers, in one case accidentally beating a monk to death.

But Shenoute also performed good works that included providing large quantities of his monastery's stores for the needs of the thousands of refugees from the Nubian invasions. Rigorous discipline and something approaching vows were his principal contributions to Egyptian monasticism. Trained with such violence, it was perhaps easier for these particular monks to be driven to excess in their attacks on heretics and pagans.

Following Constantine's conversion in the early 4th century there were tax exemptions that favored the monasteries and their inhabitants. Monks were drawn from the fellahin (peasants) primarily and were interested in mystical and ascetic rather than intellectual, doctrinal matters. The monks exemplified the Christian life in different ways, choosing one or another scriptural passage as the basis for their ideal life.[6] While familiarity with the scriptures would have been urged on some monks, the study of philosophy or theology was not. The differences between the urban Alexandrian bishops, priests, and scholars and the rusticated monks of the rest of Egypt were very great. Yet Egyptian Christianity made a transition eventually from the former to the latter, certainly helped by Athanasius's praise of Anthony and the growing differences between Alexandria and Constantinople.

The Alexandrian clergy tried to win converts by persuasion, while the monks used example and on occasion force. Some scholars are convinced that the two types of Christian communities worked together very well, at least for some period of time. As evidence for this cooperation the story from Shenoute's *Life* of his accompanying Cyril, the Patri-

arch of Alexandria, to the Council of Ephesus is cited.[7] Others challenge the historicity of this episode and point rather to the monks' use of the Coptic language and translations from Greek to Coptic to show how different they were. By the time of the Chalcedonian Council in 451, the unity of the Egyptian church, achieved through the common support by hierarchy and monks of the Monophysite doctrine, was assured. Whether this was achieved through decisions at local synods, a sense of nationalism that opposed any foreign leadership, or self-confidence based on two recent victories at Ecumenical Councils, the fact that actions were taken at Chalcedon prior to the arrival of the Egyptians finally contributed directly to cutting off the Egyptians totally from Catholicism and later Orthodox Christianity.

The decline of monasticism in Egypt after the coming of Islam was probably related to the imposition of a head-tax on monks in the 8th century.[8] Since many Christians had already converted to Islam to avoid such a tax, it is not surprising that many monks, including some who may have chosen monastic life in order to be free of taxes, left when this immunity was taken away. Other factors may have been the relative lack of religious sophistication or theological knowledge on the part of the monks that would have made their leaving seem less a denial or failure than a transformation.

While some of the old monasteries have disappeared completely, several have survived and still attract disciples, who continue to pursue perfection and preserve a way of life by selling what they have and giving to the poor.[9]

---

6. For the Beatitudes of the Sermon on the Mount, see Matthew 5:1–13, and for Christ's retreat in to the desert to overcome temptation see Mark 1:12–13.

7. Besa, *Life of Shenoute*, 128 (CSCO 42:34, 95, 219). Cf. Timbie in Pearson 1986, pp. 258–70, and Säve-Söderbergh 1961, pp. 296–7.
8. Cf. Attiya 1968, pp. 85–6.
9. Most notably, the Monastery of St. Makarius at Wadi Natrun and the Monastery of St. Anthony on the Red Sea.

Gnosticism

BIRGER A. PEARSON

I. GNOSIS AND GNOSTICISM

SOMEWHERE IN ASIA MINOR early in the 2nd century a concerned Christian teacher, writing in the name of the Apostle Paul, warned his readers, "Avoid the godless chatter and contradictions of what is falsely called 'knowledge' (gnosis), for by professing it some have missed the mark as regards the faith" (1 Timothy 6:20–21). The author of this warning was referring to a heretical form of Christianity whose elaborations of gnosis were considered mortally dangerous to adherents of the Christian faith, particularly as that faith was coming to be defined by ecclesiastical leaders of the catholic Church.

About a half-century later, St. Irenaeus, Bishop of Lyons (Lugdunum) in Gaul, wrote a five-volume work entitled "Refutation and Overthrow of Knowledge Falsely So-Called" (referred to in scholarly literature as *Adversus Haereses*). In that work the bishop gives an extensive account of the various heretical teachers and groups known to him, and traces the heresy we call "Gnosticism" back to a Samaritan "magician" called Simon, about whom there is a garbled account in the New Testament (Acts 8:9–24).

What kind of "knowledge" is at issue here? How does Gnostic knowledge differ from the kinds of spiritual knowledge that would have been valued by the anti-heretical Christian writers? A famous Gnostic formula in use among the Valentinian Gnostics describes the requisites of salvation in this way: "(What saves is) the knowledge (*gnosis*) of who we were, and what we have become; where we were or where we have been thrown; whither we hasten, from what we are redeemed; what birth is and what rebirth."[1]

In the Gnostic view, it is not faith or works that saves but a special kind of knowledge having to do with the origin and destiny of the human soul. The Gnostics (*gnostikoi*, "knowers") developed the answers to these questions in an elaborate mythology, based on radical reinterpretations of older religious traditions rooted in the Jewish scriptures, especially the Book of Genesis. According to the Gnostics, the soul of the Gnostic originated in God, but, in a tragic

cosmic fall, it has come to be encapsulated in a material body in which it languishes in a state of oblivion. The soul needs to be awakened by *gnosis* and thus provided with a means of returning to its divine origin. The world itself is regarded as the product of this cosmic fall, for it was created not by the transcendent God but by a lesser being who, in his ignorance and arrogance, claims that he is the only God. This lower creator, with his cohorts, attempts to hold human beings in thrall.

Many scholars look upon Gnosticism as a religion or world view in its own right, rather than simply a deviant form of Christianity. The origins of Gnosticism are obscure, but it seems to have developed in the eastern Mediterranean around the same time as Christianity, and existed in close symbiosis with Christianity for many centuries. In Christian forms of Gnosticism it is Jesus Christ who is considered to be the heavenly revealer of *gnosis*; that is his role as "savior." But there are other forms of the Gnostic world view that are not Christian at all. A specifically Egyptian form of Gnosticism looked upon "Thrice-Greatest Hermes" (Egyptian Thoth) as the revealer of gnosis. The Mandaeans ("Gnostics") of Iraq and Iran, a still existing religious group whose origins can be traced to 1st century Palestine, reject Christ and Christianity altogether. Their chief savior is a mythological being called *Manda de Haiyi* ("Knowledge of Life"); they also regard John the Baptist as one of their precursors.

It was in the form of Manichaeism that Gnosticism became a world religion, one that persisted in China into the 17th century. Smaller Christian heresies of recognizable Gnostic stamp (Bogomils, Cathars, etc.) existed throughout the Middle Ages in the West. Even today there are some Christian groups that claim to preserve the ancient *gnosis*.

II. GNOSTICISM IN EGYPT

The earliest Christian teachers active in Egypt of whom we have any substantial historical evidence were the Gnostic heresiarchs Valentinus and Basilides. (I omit from consideration here the legend of the founding of the Alexandrian church by St. Mark the Evangelist.) Both of these teachers were active in Alexandria in the time of Emperor Hadrian (117–138). Alexandria was then the cultural and educational center of the Roman world. Basilides had come to

---

1. Clem Alex. *Exc. Theod.* 78.2.

Alexandria from another place, probably Syrian Antioch. His teachings were elaborated by his son, Isidore, and other followers, and gained considerable currency in Alexandrian Christian circles. Basilidian Gnosticism persisted in Alexandria for at least two centuries.

Valentinus was born in a village in the Egyptian Delta, and was educated in Greek rhetoric and philosophy in Alexandria. It was there, too, that he became a Christian. Something of the relationship between Christianity and Gnosticism in Valentinus's thought can be ascertained from the following remark made by Bishop Irenaeus in his great work *Against Heresies*: "Valentinus adapted the fundamental principles of the so-called 'Gnostic' school of thought to his own kind of system."[2]

From this statement we can deduce that a well-developed Gnostic system already existed in Alexandria before the time of Valentinus. Whether or not this system already had some Christian features in it, it is clear from the evidence that Valentinus "Christianized" it with liberal use of such non-Gnostic Christian writings as the gospels of Matthew and John and the Epistles of Paul. Fortunately we now have, as a result of the Nag Hammadi discovery (see below), a beautiful writing of the great heresiarch himself, a meditative discourse on Christian Gnostic themes called *The Gospel of Truth* (NHC I,3; XII,2). A complete copy exists in the Lycopolitan dialect of Coptic (I,3); fragments of a Sahidic Coptic version are also extant (XII,2). (Valentinus originally wrote in Greek.)

Valentinus moved from Alexandria to Rome during the episcopate of Hyginus, Bishop of Rome (138–41). His teachings, as modified by a number of brilliant pupils, spread over the entire Roman world and eastward into Syria and Mesopotamia, and in some places persisted into the 7th century.

It should also be pointed out that "the so-called 'Gnostic' school of thought" referred to by Irenaeus in the statement already quoted, is partially summarized by him in chapter 29 of the first volume of his lengthy treatise. The basic myth is also extant in four different Coptic manuscripts, three of them in the Nag Hammadi collection (NHC II,1; III,1; IV,1) and one in the closely related Berlin Gnostic Codex (BG, 2). The tractate in which this system is incorporated is called *The Apocryphon of John*, a "secret book" in which are purportedly revealed the post-resurrection teachings of Jesus to his disciple John. According to some scholars, the basic system originally featured a female revealer figure. In the version we now have Jesus Christ has taken over that role.

As has already been implied in our references to Coptic versions of Gnostic writings (all of which were originally written in Greek), Gnosticism spread rather rapidly from the Greek-speaking metropolis of Alexandria into the native Egyptian ("Coptic") areas of Upper Egypt. First, of course, the Gnostic writings were transmitted in their original Greek versions to the main towns of Egypt, where Greek was the language of commerce and education. Papyrus fragments of Greek versions of several Gnostic writings have turned up in the massive papyrus finds at Oxyrhynchus. Some of the writings in question are now extant in complete Coptic versions (*The Sophia of Jesus Christ* and *The Gospel of Mary*). Fragments of three different copies of *The Gospel of Thomas* (which not all writers agree is "Gnostic") are also included among the Oxyrhynchus papyri. They were identified as such as a result of the publication of a complete Coptic version of *The Gospel of Thomas*, part of the Nag Hammadi find.

Up the river from Oxyrhynchus, at Lycopolis (Assiut), various forms of the Gnostic religion were well established by the 4th century. Late in the 3rd century a learned Platonist philosopher, Alexander of Lycopolis, wrote a polemic treatise *Against the Doctrine of Mani*. (Lycopolis was the birthplace of the founder of Neoplatonism, Plotinus.) As it happens, a large number of Gnostic texts are extant that are written in the Lycopolitan dialect of Coptic (also known as "Subakhmimic"). These include some of the Nag Hammadi tractates, as well as the large collection of Manichaean texts discovered at Medinet Madi in the Fayum in 1930. Indeed, many of the Nag Hammadi tractates written in Sahidic represent impure forms of that (classical) dialect of Coptic, "contaminated" by influences from Lycopolitan. All of this shows that Lycopolis was an important center for the spread of Gnosticism.

III. THE NAG HAMMADI LIBRARY

In December of 1945 a group of peasants from the Upper Egyptian village of al-Qasr (ancient Chenoboskeia) were digging for sebakh (a nitrate used for fertilizer) at the base of the Jabal al-Tarif, nine km west of the ruins of the Basilica of St. Pachomius. (Pachomius was the founder of the "coenobitic" communal form monasticism.) Suddenly they uncovered a large earthenware jar. One of the men, Muhammad Ali al-Samman, broke the jar, and out fell 13 leatherbound books (codices). Since Nag Hammadi is the most important town in the vicinity, this collection of manuscripts is now often identified by the name of that town. The discovery of the Nag Hammadi Codices is of inestimable importance for the scholarly study of Gnosticism and the general history of the religions of the ancient world.

After a number of vicissitudes, including the loss of some of the material, the manuscripts were gradually studied and published by scholars. One of them had been smuggled out of Egypt and was eventually purchased for the Jung Institute in Zurich, Switzerland. This manuscript (NHC I, often referred to as "The Jung Codex"; see cat. no. 154 for the binding of this codex) contains a number of

2. *Adv. Haer.* I.II.I, as translated by B. Layton.

Valentinian Gnostic treatises, including the aforementioned *Gospel of Truth*. When all of the material in it had been published, it was returned to Egypt. It is now housed, together with the other extant Nag Hammadi Codices, in the Coptic Museum in Old Cairo.

The manuscripts, all inscribed in Coptic, date from the latter half of the 4th century. They contain 52 tractates in all, 46 different ones (some are represented by more than one copy). Most, but not all, of the texts are Gnostic. One of the non-Gnostic tractates consists of a very bad Coptic translation of a passage from Plato's *Republic*. The liberties taken by the Coptic translator in that case may reflect (in addition to his poor knowledge of classical Greek) a tendency to interpret the material in a "Gnosticizing" fashion. In any case, all of the texts in the Nag Hammadi collection, including the non-Gnostic ones, are such as could be read with profit by readers religiously oriented to Gnosticism. Such readers would be inclined toward renunciation of the material world, and a disciplined asceticism.

Now it is of considerable interest, in this connection, to mention here three major factors pointing to a monastic provenance for the Nag Hammadi Codices: (1) The jar containing the manuscripts was found in an area that had been used both for monastic retreats and for burials. Indications of monastic use include Coptic psalm inscriptions in one of the caves of the Jabal al-Tarif. (2) The cartonnage (scraps of discarded papyrus glued into the leather covers to stiffen them) contains evidence of a monastic provenance, such as private letters and documents, even part of a biblical manuscript. The manuscripts were therefore manufactured in one or more of the monasteries in the Nag Hammadi area. (3) The manuscripts contain colophons and scribal notes consisting of prayers and other indications of monastic piety. These features show, too, that the persons who copied the various texts into the codices treated them as edifying religious literature.

Can it be that some of the monks living in monasteries founded by the great Saint Pachomius were given to reading and copying "heretical" literature? It would seem so, from the nature of the evidence relating to the manufacture, copying, and burial of the Nag Hammadi manuscripts.

We know that a purge of heretical books was carried out in the Pachomian monasteries by the saint's successor, Theodore, who caused to be read in the monasteries a Coptic version of the paschal letter sent out by Archbishop Athanasius of Alexandria in 367 A.D. That letter contained a lengthy condemnation of the reading of heretical literature. Theodore's purge could have resulted in the burial of heretical books on the part of recalcitrant monks who wished to preserve them from destruction. (Banned books were either burned or thrown into the Nile.) Such a scenario can plausibly be argued in the case of the "Nag Hammadi Codices." They lay buried beneath the cliff of the Jabal al-Tarif undisturbed for almost sixteen centuries, only to be brought to light again by the random digging of Muhammad Ali and his companions on a December day in 1945.

Bibliography: Layton 1987; Robinson 1988; Rudolph 1983.

ART AND WRITTEN MATERIALS

Pharaonic Themes

FLORENCE D. FRIEDMAN

PHARAONIC THEMES NOT ONLY SURVIVE under Greek and Roman domination, in some respects they flourish. The terracotta industry of the Fayum especially reflects the continued use of pharaonic religious subjects that were used for home worship and as votive temple offerings. In the Fayum and elsewhere the most important figure represented was Isis. An extraordinary blend of Egyptian and Graeco-Roman ideas surface in a new understanding of her in this period, but she was rendered in a predominantly Hellenistic style. While the subjects and iconography of Egypt were used, the style of the dominant class was imposed.

During the Ptolemaic and Roman periods, Greek and Roman deities were absorbed into the Egyptian pantheon, and similarities between the Egyptian and Greek gods provided easy correspondences. As Herodotus noted in the 5th century B.C., Apollo could be equated with Horus, Demeter with Isis, etc. But such equivalences were rather superficial. On the other hand, when a deity absorbed the characters and attributes of another god, a more profound conflation occurred that often resulted in a richer and broader concept of each god. This process of absorption of identities and the sharing of similar attributes is called syncretism (see cat. no. 116). Though gods could be syncretized for political purposes, the conflation of one deity with another was successful religiously and politically only if it was experienced by the believer. One of the best examples of a syncretistic deity in Late Roman and Early Byzantine Egypt is Isis, who absorbed the essence of virtually every god of birth and death and nature itself. She was Isis "of the many names," all things to all men, and a personal savior to mankind.

In Egyptian mythology, Isis was the sister and wife of Osiris, the god-man who was murdered by his evil brother. According to variants of the myth, Isis found Osiris's corpse, enlivened it, became pregnant by her brother-husband, and bore their son Horus. The jackal-headed god Anubis embalmed Osiris, ensuring his eternal life, and Osiris's mummification and resurrection provided the model for all Egyptians. Isis nurtured their son Horus to maturity, protecting him from his father's enemies, and when grown, Horus avenged his father's death and took

his rightful place on the throne. This Osirian story of wifely, maternal, and filial love held a prominent place in Egyptian religious thinking and influenced artistic themes into Roman times.

As mother and protector of children, Isis is typically shown nursing Horus, who in this role is called Harpokrates (literally, "Horus the child") (see cat. nos. 92 and 93). Though an extension of an ancient theme, the cubic design and rigid pose of pharaonic bronze prototypes were abandoned for a more naturalistic treatment of the subject in the Roman period. Conceptually, Isis's fertility as mother was extended to the fertility of the fields, as well as to the realm of the dead that inevitably yields new life. Thus in Roman Egypt when she is syncretized with a host of other deities related to creation and death, she appears as a serpent goddess of the grain, who is also a funerary deity (cat. no. 94); as the Greek goddess of love and fertility, Aphrodite; as Nemesis, a winged griffin goddess of fate (cat. no. 169); and as the Roman goddess of good fortune, Isis-Fortuna. Egyptian iconography is usually maintained in these small terracottas or bronzes, though it is frequently misunderstood. The cow's horns and sun disk of the Egyptian Isis, for example, are often ill-conceived and poorly executed. Artists were sometimes copying forms that they did not understand, much as they might transcribe garbled copies of hieroglyphic texts on Roman mummy shrouds. Craftsmen were obviously being trained in the Graeco-Roman tradition: the execution of the figure, often standing with the weight shifted onto one leg (cat. no. 160), and sometimes with added Graeco-Roman iconography (like a cornucopia for an Isis-Fortuna) are all Hellenistic. And while a voluptuous Isis may harken back to earlier Egyptian forms (e.g., in Amarna art) that were revived under the Ptolemies,[1] it is doubtful that the Late Roman artists in Egypt had any knowledge of or familiarity with such earlier pharaonic prototypes.

---

1. That the voluptuous female figure in Egyptian art was revived under the Ptolemies was noted in conversation by Bernard V. Bothmer.

Harpokrates also assumes a dominant role in Egyptian artistic products, especially at Karanis in the Fayum, where his agrarian and fertility aspects were emphasized.[2] He appears with a sidelock of youth and holding a finger to his mouth, the ancient Egyptian designations for "child" that identify him as Harpokrates (cat. no. 114). But as with Isis, there the similarity with things Egyptian ends. He is depicted as a chubby little boy, often engaging in some childish behavior that characterized him in Roman-Egyptian eyes as a patron of children. But whether riding the back of a hen, on horseback like a Thracian god (cat. no. 95), suckling from Isis's breast (cat. no. 92), or dressed as a Roman emperor (cat. no. 115), he generally is depicted according to Greek artistic conventions.

The most important new deity to emerge in Hellenistic and Roman times was Sarapis. The concept of this god was closely linked to that of the funerary and fertility god Osiris, so that Sarapis could therefore assume Osiris's position in the new family triad of Sarapis, Isis, and Harpokrates (cat. no. 96). But much more often in Egypt, Sarapis was appealed to alone; like Isis, he became a savior deity. In a fascinating process of syncretism, he absorbed the identities of a multitude of Egyptian and Graeco-Roman gods. Both he and Isis appealed to individuals of all social strata (though he may have had more appeal to Greeks than native Egyptians), and spoke to the innermost needs of the everyday man and woman. His appearance, dictated probably by the early Ptolemies in the early 3rd century B.C., was clearly Greek (cat. no. 116), however, and his iconography, though sometimes alluding to that of Osiris and/or Amun, was depicted in Greek style.

What is remarkable in the statuettes of Sarapis, Isis, and Harpokrates, among others, is that the Greek and Roman dominant ruling class was willing to adopt Egyptian religious subjects and iconography, but unwilling to use Egyptian style. The images of these gods may represent a blend of ideas and iconography, but the artistic vocabulary used to depict them was Greek.

Greeks and Romans in Egypt continued the tradition of Egyptian cult worship, the use of funerary stelae, and the practice of mummification, probably influenced, at first, by wealthy propertied Egyptians. But they often altered original Egyptian intent. The Romans, for example, honored the personification of the Nile, a deity non-existent in ancient Egypt but now represented as a reclining Classical river god (cat. no. 118). Stelae integrate Egyptian gods like Horus and Anubis with a decidedly non-Egyptian frontal depiction of a deceased Roman youth (cat. no. 168). And Egyptian products associated with mummification, like shrouds (cat. no. 163) and mummy masks (cat. nos. 161 and 162), now include lifelike Roman likenesses. The use of mummy portraits, in place of the three-dimensional Egyptian mask, is the most telling example of a Graeco-Roman interpretation of a pharaonic subject. These panels' dramatic use of light and shade and slight turn of the sitters' heads were significant deviations from standard Egyptian representations.

Bibliography: Dunand 1973a, 1973b, 1979; Gazda et al. 1978; Heyob 1975; Hornbostel 1973; Junge 1979; Kaufmann 1913; Müller 1969; Perdrizet 1921; Plutarch in Griffiths 1970; Shier 1978; Solmsen 1979; Stambaugh 1972; Tran Tam Tinh 1973, 1983; Vanderlip 1972; Vidman 1969; Weber 1914.

2. See Gazda et al. 1978, p. 60.

An Introduction to the Sculpture of Late Roman and Early Byzantine Egypt

THELMA K. THOMAS

MOST OF THE EXTANT SCULPTURES of Late Roman and Early Byzantine Egypt were polychromed (painted and/or inlaid) architectural reliefs in stone and wood from tombs, houses, monasteries, churches, and other public buildings. With their polychrome these reliefs created colorfully lavish interiors with overall decorative programs that often illustrated the purposes of the buildings they decorated. Much rarer was free-standing statuary such as statuettes that were deposited in domestic shrines and tombs; statues, chiefly imperial portraits, were erected in public spaces.

Only a fraction of this vast body of work survives today and, unfortunately, those that remain have been prematurely assessed without regard for their original architectural surroundings, the materials from which they were made, the techniques employed in their production, or their present conditions.[1] In fact, the sculptures have never been closely examined. Only recently has it been recognized that the polychromy of these sculptures is integral to their style. That the sculptures are usually fragmentary and in poor physical condition is scarcely noted in evaluations of their artistic achievements.[2] Compounding these oversights is a longstanding lack of critical research into the cultural contexts of the sculptures.

Early scholarship often reduced the diversity and richness of the cultural background of Early Byzantine Egypt to a limited concept most clearly characterized by the inaccurate use of the term "Coptic." "Coptic" identified the Egyptian Christians of poor peasant stock who were thought to be united in their hostility to all things Greek, Roman, and Byzantine, due to a long history of oppressive foreign rule. In mistakenly assuming that the arts had been produced exclusively by and for Copts, art historical studies promoted the notion that particularly "Coptic" issues formed the mainstream of artistic expression in Early Byzantine Egypt.[3]

Thus, the artistic remains came to be described within the framework of an Egyptian Christian art which, in its quest for sprirituality, had deliberately broken away from the naturalistic illusions of Graeco-Roman artistic traditions. In sculpture, this "anti-hellenistic" style was seen to be based on shapes created by the simple play of light versus shadow.[4] "Coptic" imagery was found to be similarly naive and culturally limited. The pagan images on many of the surviving sculptures were generally interpreted as out-dated copies of earlier models, their authentic meanings either lost or subverted to fit the new Christian age. Clearly Christian images, on the other hand, were inter-

---

1. The sculpture of Late Roman and Early Byzantine Egypt has been studied in some depth since the turn of the century. The most important scholarly works are: Beckwith 1963; Kitzinger 1937, pp. 181–215; Gayet 1902; de Gruneisen 1922; Duthuit 1931; duBourguet 1967, English translation Paris 1971; Riegl 1893, pp. 113ff.; Strzygowski 1904, nos. 7001–7394, 8742–9200; Wessel 1963; Effenberger 1976.

2. Some early publications record traces of polychromy remaining on these sculptures (Strzygowski 1904) and publish photographs illustrating the polychromatic remains (Duthuit 1931) but do not discuss or reconstruct how the paint and inlays would have looked when in pristine condition. See, an example of such a discussion in Vikan and Boyd 1981.

3. Cf. Riegl 1893, Gayet 1902, Strzygowski 1904. Writings of a more popular nature continue to repeat this reading of the cultural background of "Coptic" art. See also Ross 1941, pp. 47–50. More recently, duBourguet 1967 (1971 English translation) and Wessel 1963 (1965 English translation) have promoted similar interpretations.

4. DuBourguet 1971 elaborated on this notion when he wrote of "the coloristic" versus "the plastic arts" (see, for example, p. 21). Typically, duBourguet considered painting to be an entirely separate field from that of sculptural form.

"Anti-Hellenism" in "Coptic" art was introduced as part of the larger question of how Christian art developed as distinct from its Graeco-Roman forerunners. The essence of the alleged "anti-Hellenistic" style was seen to be its emphasis on spirituality rather than the representation of physical beauty. "Coptic style, in particular" was interpreted as a particularly concentrated version of this spiritualized Christian style. Cf. Gayet 1902, p. iii, and more recently duBourguet 1967 (1971 English translation) and Wessel 1963 (1965 English translation).

preted within the narrowly defined "Coptic" scenario.[5]

It is now clear that these early theories of "Coptic" art (and culture) are, largely, unfounded. In the first place, Egyptian Christians of the early Byzantine period cannot be described so narrowly. In this period that witnessed the origins of Coptic orthodox Christianity, the new adherents also included sophisticated and wealthy city-dwellers and rural landholders, members of the middle classes, and monks drawn from among all socio-economic ranks. While the majority of Egyptian Christians may have come to follow Coptic orthodoxy as it was established in the middle of this period, some remained Greek orthodox.[6] A sizeable portion of the population of early Byzantine Egypt did not convert to any form of Christianity; pagans, pagan communities, and their arts survived even after the Arab conquest of Egypt.[7] Nor were all inhabitants of Egypt purely Egyptian in blood or cultural heritage. The previous six hundred years of Greek and Roman rule had introduced new civic, religious and artistic traditions into the cultural life of Egypt.[8]

Secondly, no evidence has been submitted to support the theories of particularly "Coptic" trends in artistic patronage and production.[9] Failing to consider how much a work would have cost, earlier scholarship also missed the fundamental question of who among the population could have afforded to pay for the statuary or architectural reliefs. The issue of expense as it relates directly to sculptural production or as it might explain the socio-economic background of the artisans has also been overlooked.

Finally, while it is evident that this period witnessed the formation of a Coptic identity in language and Christian theology, it is difficult to discern the subtleties of these distinctions in the sculptural remains. Yet, broader changes in the direction of artistic impulses which correspond to the increasing conversions from paganism to Christianity can be charted. It is also possible to describe how the physical and formal characteristics of the surviving sculptures of Early Byzantine Egypt developed. The polychromy of these sculptures, in particular, offers abundant evidence to counter previous stylistic assessments and interpretations. The well-preserved sculptures testify to an aesthetic that was both naturalistic in the Graeco-Roman tradition and ornate in the taste of contemporary early Byzantine arts.

The imagery of the surviving sculptures reflects their wide variety of interpretive settings – public and private, funerary and domestic, monastic and ecclesiastic – and the wishes of their patrons, whether they were pagans, Egyptian Christians of the Coptic Church, or Greek orthodox. Accordingly, the chief aim of this essay and the related entries is to introduce some of the hitherto unexplored artistic and documentary evidence for this wider reading of the art historical and historical backgrounds of the sculptures from Early Byzantine Egypt.

To begin, an assessment of the physical characteristics of the materials from which the sculptures were made and the techniques employed by the artisans contribute to an evaluation of their artistic achievements. Damage is especially telling. Deteriorated surfaces and loss of original paint on many of these works (not always evident even to trained observers) give an incomplete and strikingly less powerful impression.

The poor preservation of the Early Byzantine Egyptian sculptures is at least partially due to the materials from which they were made. Typically, the few works in hard stones – including imported Greek marbles (cat. no. 118), porphyry from the Sinai (cat. no. 91), and granite from the Sinai and Upper Egypt (cat. no. 120) – are best preserved. These are densely compacted metamorphic and igneous rocks, which are very difficult to work but are more resistant to erosion, deterioration due to changes in the environment, and breakage. The more common sculptural materials were sandstone and limestone, sedimentary stones which are relatively soft and easy to carve, but quick to deteriorate when not protected from the hazards of the environment (cat. nos. 165, 174, 175, 176). Sandstone, most readily available in Upper Egypt, was the material used for the majority of sculptures from that area. The limestones quarried along the full length of the valley, however, were the most popular sculptural materials. Very few sculptures in terracotta and wood survive as these materials are extremely fragile[10] (see fig. 1 and cat. nos. 100, 138 and 147).

The choice of materials, in part, determined the sculptural techniques employed. Hard stones, such as porphyry and marble, were usually polished by abrasion to smooth their surfaces. But most of the surviving reliefs are in local soft stones which, due to their grainy texture, do not take a high polish and were not finished with the same gloss or precision. Carving in wood and modeling in terracotta could be exceptionally meticulous due to the fine texture of those materials, but the works in terracotta are usually on such a small scale that minute details were not molded (fig. 1).

5. See, for example, Gayet 1902, Strzygowski 1904 and, more recently, Torp 1969, pp. 104 ff.
6. For an overview of the situation, refer to Pearson/Goehring 1986.
7. See, for example, Remondon 1952, pp. 63–78.
8. Excellent general histories covering these periods in Egypt's history are Lewis 1986 and 1983, and Bowman 1986.
9. Trilling challenged the notion of "anti-Hellenism" in Trilling 1987, pp. 469–476.

10. Few sculptures in these materials are represented in this exhibition, due to their fragility. The availability of sculptural materials is discussed briefly in Severin 1977b.

Fig. 1
Figurine, terracotta
Metropolitan Museum of Art (12.185.4)
Photograph courtesy of the author

Sculptures in the local soft stones, or in terracotta or wood were not complete until they had been polychromed.[11] Works now lacking their polychromy may yield valuable information on sculptural technique. When the final layer of paint is lost, the carver's tool marks are often clearly visible. The two most important types of tools used in early Byzantine Egyptian stone carving were chisels and drills. Large straight-edged chisels roughly blocked out general shapes, which were refined by smaller implements. In a 5th century limestone relief from The Brooklyn Museum (fig. 2), small pointed chisels were employed to create overall patterns such as rows of triangular gouges to indicate a furry pelt, and narrow flat-edged blades carved parallel wavy lines to indicate a shaggy coat or circles to indicate the curly nap of a fleece. A variety of decorative effects were also fashioned by the widespread use of drills, elaborating on a trend begun in the Roman period. The shadows thrown by a drill hole carved with a triangular bit are irregular; when such drills are used to indicate the iris of an eye, as in this relief, the irregularities of the borders make the eyes lifelike in their variability.

After a sculpture was carved or molded, a thin layer of plaster was applied as a sizing ground to prepare the surface to receive and retain the paint. The sizing ground also smoothed the sculpted shapes, obscuring the toolmarks and the texture of the stone, wood, or clay. In addition, the sizing ground de-emphasized the rigid geometrical form underlying this relief's carving style (fig. 2). Thus, the shallowly incised schematic markings of the animals' hides would have been covered by the layer of ground so that, hardly visible, they would have served more as guidelines for the painter than as textural effects in their own right.

The colors and the matte finish of the paint completed the artisans' work. As seen on a 6th century capital from the monastery of Apa Jeremias at Sakkara (fig. 3), painted colors both traced the carved shapes, and created patterns where none had existed in the sculpted forms. Note, for example, the painted rinceau on the abacus of this capital. Color also created details impossible to sculpt. On the body of the capital, such details make up the variegation of the lotus leaves. In a 5th century statuette now in the Metropolitan Museum of Art (fig. 1), the warmth of flushed cheeks is created by a ruddy red fading to a lighter pink, and the opulence of golden jewelry is rendered in a metallic paint as opposed to the flat finish of the yellow used for the pedestal.

The underlying sculpture, therefore, was transformed by the addition of color. Consequently, assessments of

11. Some hard stones, such as purple porphyry, were not necessarily or completely polychromed, since their natural colors already carried symbolic meaning (cat. no. 91). Other hard stones, such as marbles, were painted.

Fig. 2
Stela, limestone
The Brooklyn Museum (41.1266)
Photograph courtesy of the author

sculptural quality by forms alone neglects one of the most important aspects of the sculpture of Early Byzantine Egypt: the precision and detail provided only by the paint. If, by way of an extreme example, one were to imagine this statuette stripped of its paint, it would present only the simplest of forms. In the statuette, the priority of painting over the modeling of forms is most obvious in the treatment of the figure's clothing. Vaguely modeled drapery folds are articulated by the paint to indicate the positions of the underlying anatomical forms. More crucial to the intricacy of the statuette's visual effect is that the painted folds depict two garments: a diaphanous robe over a heavier dress with embroidered stripes. The thicker folds of the heavier garment are modeled and articulated by thick grey lines. The shallower set of folds is not modeled at all; instead, the folds of the lighter garment are painted by thinner grey strokes. A broad black outline is all that depicts the deep and shadowy space between the edge of the garment and the yellow pedestal (see also cat. nos. 167 and 172).

Comparisons of such extraordinarily well-preserved works demonstrate that neither the carving nor the painting of sculpture was based solely on the observation of nature. Instead, the carvers and painters relied on formulas. In carving, we have seen such short-hand methods used to indicate the different textures of the animals' hides. One example of the most basic kinds of formula used in Early Byzantine Egyptian polychromy was a base of a light solid color which was then overlaid with brushstrokes of darker colors. The use of this formula can be detected in the faint traces of paint remaining on the claw of one of the animals in the 5th century relief (fig. 2: detail) and in the drapery folds of the statuette (fig. 1, see also cat. no. 172).

Throughout the period, sculptural styles developed from pre-existing techniques and mannerisms. In general,

Fig. 2 (detail)
Stela, limestone
The Brooklyn Museum (41.1266)
Photograph courtesy of the author

this stylistic development combined progressively schematized carving with increasingly naturalistic painting effects. Polychromatic formulas developed gradually from the Egyptian and Greek practices of using solid blocks of colors over meticulously sculpted forms. In the earliest stages of these developments, as seen in 2nd and 3rd century funerary stelae (gravestones) from the cemetery of the Greek town at Terenouthis, carving and painting follow the earlier conventions. Strands of hair were carved individually and painted over with solid black. The painters were not unaware of the freer, sketchier Graeco-Roman manner of painting on flat surfaces: when in its original setting at the head of the tomb, the stela was surrounded by other decorations painted in the more impressionistic Graeco-Roman manner (fig. 4).

Fig. 3
Capital, limestone
Coptic Museum, Cairo
Photograph Courtesy of the author

Fig. 4
Terenouthis, view of the tomb of Isidora
Kelsey Museum of Archaeology, The University of Michigan

Fig. 5
Frieze, limestone
Metropolitan Museum of Art (09.217 a,b)
Photograph courtesy of the author

It is clear in this 2nd century example that the stela and the wall paintings are both integral parts of the tomb's overall thematic program. The deceased stands in the gateway to the afterlife, modeled on a temple entrance, around which garlands are festooned. All elements worked "to convey the impression that a perpetual festival was in progress in front of and presumably beyond the tomb structure's symbolic entrance."[12]

By the middle of the Early Byzantine period, we find increasingly impressionistic polychromatic effects made by casual strokes of the brush and fewer sculpted details. In the 5th century statuette, for example, strands of hair were no longer sculpted individually and painted over all in the same color (fig. 1). Rather, sculpted masses of hair that fit the head like a cap were painted with finer strands: a coppery orange overlaid by black strokes of varying thicknesses.

The natural optical effects of color were, of course, intentionally heightened and intensified by the use of the formulas outlined above, as well as by the texture of the chosen materials. Other means of providing color were inlays of glass and stone. Hard stones, polished to a glistening smoothness and pieces of glass, faceted to glint in the light, made striking contrasts to the matte texture of the paint. In this 6th century frieze from the Coptic monastery of Apa Apollo at Bawit (fig. 5), inlays of red and green glass indicated the focal points of this abstract meandering design. Inlays of hard stones were sometimes used to create the glittering irises of eyes. Since few of the surviving sculptures preserve their paint or inlays, however, only the carving remains.

Two photographs dramatically illustrate the importance of polychromy to the intended visual effect of an architectural relief (figs. 6 and 7).[13] In the black and white photograph from around 1930, taken soon after this 5th century relief was excavated at Oxyrhynchus, it is clear that the paint covered all available surfaces – background, figures, and decorative motifs – sometimes adding details not indicated in the carving, such as the woven strips of basketry (fig. 6).

Even in this black and white photograph, it is evident that the new layer of sizing ground concealed the graininess of the limestone and the roughness of the carving, and that color enlivened the entire composition. Colors also worked to define the pictorial space inhabited by the carved shapes. Dark outlines, for example, represented deep shadows which worked to anchor the figure in the illusion of three-dimensional space. The simulation of spatial recession,

12. McCleary 1987, p. 5.
13. The two photographs are reproduced from Duthuit 1931 and Villa Hügel 1963.

then, was not so much indicated in the shallow carving as it was depicted in the paint. Dark shadows and colored backgrounds effectively opened up the otherwise visually impenetrable barrier of the flatly finished stone. The setting of the scene, too, would have been clarified by the blue of the water in the background. The slight projection of the carved forms, in contrast, served a different purpose. The elements carved in relief linked the background with the figure, and figure with the real space of the viewer: her head barely tilted, the figure looked down at the viewer.

Seen again in the later photograph, taken around 1960 in honor of the relief's inclusion in a major exhibition on "Coptic" art, the ground and paint have been removed and their effects have been obliterated by overzealous cleaning (fig. 7). The shapes have lost the clarity imparted by the layer of ground and the precision of the painted features. The new work, however, fits more neatly into the generally accepted art historical theories of a "Coptic" folk style based on simple abstract forms. Little remains but the juxtaposition of shadows next to expanses of bare stone.

The later photograph also shows that the relief has even been recarved. The removal of paint and the recarving have transformed the figure into the misunderstood motif that scholars expected. The first photograph shows a pagan image – halo notwithstanding – of a nymph surrounded by fish and a dolphin. Originally the physically immature and virginal figure of Greek myth, the reworked figure has full breasts and exaggeratedly emphasized genitalia. Now, the figure is more easily interpreted within the conventional framework.[14]

14. For a typical interpretation, see Morey 1942, p. 36, who emphasizes the primitive and sexual aspects of the mythological motifs; and Wessel 1965, p. 36. For a representation of an authentically physically mature female water divinity also drawn from Greek myth, see cat. no. 171.

Fig. 6
Niche decoration, limestone
Graeco-Roman Museum, Alexandria (23552)
From Duthuit, *La Sculpture Copte*, 1931, pl. XXXXb

Fig. 7
Niche decoration, limestone
Graeco-Roman Museum, Alexandria (23552)
From *Koptische Kunst: Christentum am Nil*, Vienna, 1964, cat. no. 81

Sadly, this relief does not present an unusual case of forcing the sculptures to fit the art historical theories.[15] The history of this particular relief should, however, underscore the caution with which we must approach both the physical evidence of the sculptural remains of Early Byzantine Egypt and the art historical assumptions. Its most significant implications are the need to recognize the continued coexistence of pagans and Christians and the general availability of Graeco-Roman artistic traditions. In the necropolis of the city of Oxyrhynchus where this relief was discovered, monumental tombs with interior niches were commissioned for both pagans and Christians. The niches were inserted high up in the walls and decorated with such polychromed reliefs as that of the nymph. Appropriately distanced from the viewer by their location within the wall, the polychromed niche decorations presented exceptionally animate scenes of the afterlife. The relief of the nymph reflects the belief of the patron that the deceased, most probably a young girl, has metamorphosed into a nymph upon her death. As a nymph, she would live on in the never-ending cycles of nature.[16] (See also cat. no. 171)

Other archaeological finds from tombs in the cemeteries at Oxyrhynchus, Heracleopolis Magna, and other Greek cities of Byzantine Egypt demonstrate that the niche decorations formed only one part of an overall decorative program including friezes, frescoes and, sometimes, inscriptions. Thus, as is evident in the smaller middle-class tombs of Terenouthis where the stela formed only one part of the thematic program, the niche decorations of the monumental tombs did not necessarily constitute the whole artistic statement. At times, for example, the tombs were reused to house additional members of the family. New decorations were then inserted which referred to those others recently interred in the tomb. In such circumstances, the program was enlarged to accommodate other scenes from the afterlife which had personal significance, and was altered to tell the larger story of the family. Since most of these cemeteries were destroyed during the course of their excavations, the entire programs and their individual histories are now lost.[17]

In Christian settings, overall decorative programs also combined polychromed reliefs, wall-paintings, and inscriptions. The Coptic monastery at Bawit, a major pilgrimage center, was a large architectural complex including numerous churches, chapels, and satellite buildings such as the cells where the monks lived and refectories where they gathered to eat. At the monastery, pilgrims had devotional inscriptions carved or painted. Such inscriptions are found in the churches and chapels, on walls and columns, and, most frequently, on niches and doorways. Often, they were painted over polychromed relief decorations. Some areas carried layers of paint from the original decorative scheme, pilgrims' inscriptions, and subsequent repainting (fig. 8).

These elements of monastic buildings, then, could serve more than strictly architectonic and decorative purposes. They also functioned as a kind of living skin, displaying both the original didactic and artistic intent of the overall thematic program and the individual prayers of the pious visitors who daily poured into the monastery.

The architectural setting is also extremely important for understanding how Christian reliefs came to have the appearances they have now. Both polychromed reliefs and wall-paintings were integral parts of the overall schemes and intended to be seen as such. It is crucial to note the impossibility of determining where the polychromy of architectural relief ends and wall-painting begins (fig. 9).

The early Byzantine development of the intertwined effects of polychromy and wall-painting, as exemplified at Bawit, tended to cover the flat wall and its relief decoration with color. Reliefs from Bawit were sometimes deeply undercut in the manner that is usually described as the typically "Coptic" style based on the interplay between the superficial effects of light and shadow. But the reliefs were also polychromed. Instead of light reflecting off of bare stone and contrasting with inky shadows, there were bright reds, greens, blues and yellows on the surfaces and in the depths. This aesthetic is also found in the major monuments of the capital of the Empire, at Constantinople, and in architecture throughout the Byzantine territories.[18]

If we compare the sculptural styles at Bawit to those evident at other sites, it becomes clear that Byzantine Egyptian sculptural styles can be chronologically and geographically defined. Stylistic groups can be distinguished within relatively extensive geographical areas.

15. There is evidence of a widespread recarving and faking of "Coptic" sculpture. For a brief discussion of this problem, see Vikan and Boyd 1981.

16. An inscription from the 2nd century tomb of Isidora in the Roman period cemetery of the Greek city of Hermopolis Magna eloquently expresses a father's belief that his young daughter has, upon her death, become a nymph. Later references to this belief are found in the Greek verses of the 5th century Graeco-Egyptian poet, Nonnos of Panopolis.

17. This is most regrettable for historians of Late Antique and Early Christian artistic trends in those cases where there is some evidence of earlier pagan decorations being supplanted by Christian imagery when a tomb has been reused or rebuilt.

18. Although various scholars have traced how this early Byzantine aesthetic evolved over the centuries from the Graeco-Roman traditions, none has investigated how the Egyptian monuments fit into this development. For a clear, general outline of this international development discussed both in terms of the architectural surroundings and religious settings, see Krautheimer 1965. Kitzinger 1977 offers more speculative discussions of stylistic developments (especially pp. 20 and 42–3).

Fig. 8
Capital, limestone
Musée du Louvre (E16901)
Photograph courtesy of the author

Fig. 9
Bawit, entrance to the South church, view from the West
From *MIFAO*, vol. 13 (1911), pl. lxii

Locally defined styles can also be distinguished further within relatively small geographical areas (fig. 10 and cat. no. 143). In reliefs found at the monastery of Apa Jeremias at Sakkara, which was contemporary to that at Bawit, artisans working in the same techniques and decorative motifs created slightly different styles. At Sakkara, for example, more details are crowded into smaller areas creating busier designs. The similarity between motifs and techniques also suggests that these artisans received the same kind of instruction or, in other words, that these reliefs were the work of skilled craftsmen.[19]

Written sources from the period describe who the artisans were, as well as how they were trained and organized. A well-known reference in the Theodosian Code, a compilation of Early Byzantine legislation, indicates that artisans were skilled and respected middle-class professionals, whose chosen areas of expertise were likely to have been family traditions.

We command that the practitioners of the arts enumerated in the appended list, whatever city they shall live in, shall be exempt from all public services, on condition that they devote their time to learning their crafts. By this means they may desire to become more proficient themselves and to train their sons: Architects, makers of panelled ceilings, plasterers, carpenters, physicians, stonecutters, silversmiths, builders, veterinarians, stone-masons, goldweavers, makers of pavements, painters, sculptors, makers of perforated work, joiners, statuaries, mosaicists, coppersmiths, blacksmiths, marble masons, gilders, founders, dyers in purple, makers of tessellated pavements, goldsmiths, ivory workers, fullers, potters, plumbers, furriers.[20]

The larger context of the Early Byzantine artistic training is fundamental for an understanding of the practical aspects of how the sculptures were made. Surviving papyri from Early Byzantine Egypt indicate that the artisans and their activities were closely monitored to determine whether their actions were in accord with the law. Written in Greek rather than Coptic, these documents tell us that the artisans belong to guilds, registered their whereabouts with local officials, and conformed to internationally fixed prices

19. It is extremely important to note, however, that many of the sculptures used in the monasteries at Bawit and Sakkara appear to have been re-used, that is, taken from other locations and inserted within new monastic structures. For a thorough review of the excavations and the arrangement of sculptures at the sites, see Severin 1977a, pp. 113 ff; Severin 1981a, pp. 299 ff; Severin 1981b, pp. 315 ff; and Severin and Grossmann 1982, pp. 155 ff.

20. *Cod. Theod.* XIII, 4, 2: Edict of Constantine to the Praetorian Prefect Maximus in A.D. 337.

Fig. 10
Saqqara
From J. E. Quibell, *Excavations at Saqqara*, vol. 3, *ASAE* (1907–9), pl. XIV, 2

set by law.[21] There are also contracts among the surviving papyri indicating that artisans were trained in apprenticeships during which they learned their specialized trades.[22]

Fig. 11
Karanis. Decorative Niche in House CI19 for private devotion
Kelsey Museum of Archaeology, The University of Michigan

21. That the documents were written in Greek does not necessarily mean that the artisans were Greek speakers or were literate in Greek. In fact, in the documents, the artisans are often described as illiterate (meaning illiterate in Greek). However, the use of Greek does indicate that the artisans were working in a Greek milieu. One documentary example of this situation also confirms that artisans were restricted to work in given regions. " . . . To Aurelius Sarapodorous, *logistes* of the Oxyrhynchite nome, from Aurelius Gunthus, son of Amois, from the village of . . . , stonemason. In conformity with the commands issued by the might of my lord the most glorious *praeses*, Flavius Eumathius Parthenios, I agree, swearing by the august divine oath of our masters Valentinian and Valens and Gratian, the eternal Augusti, that I shall go . . . to . . . and there practise . . . my trade and shall not withdraw until I am released or (may be) liable (to the penalties of the divine oath)" Then, in a second hand, we read "I, Aurelius Gunthus, have sworn the divine oath and shall go and practise my trade as is aforesaid. I, Aurelius Dorotheus, son of Neilos, wrote on his behalf." P. Oxyrhynchus 3308 (A.D. 373). See also *Theod. Code* 14,7,1 (A.D. 397) for an example of legislation meant to bring guildmembers back to their own municipalities.

22. Westermann 1917.

These documents also indicate that the carving, plastering and painting which together created the finished appearance of architectural relief work were specialized processes. Architectural relief decoration, such as was found in the monasteries of Bawit and Sakkara and in the monumental tombs of Oxyrhynchus and the cemeteries of other Greek cities, constituted only a part of the larger architectural ensembles which required the skills of additional specialized artisans. One grade of mason cut the stones so that they were the appropriate sizes and shapes. Another grade of mason carved the ornamentation. After the building was constructed (with the help of additional masons and laborers who laid the stones) and the ornamentation had been carved, then the plasterer prepared the walls and reliefs with the layer of sizing ground. Finally, the painter completed the decoration of the building.

The materials and skilled artisans needed to produce architectural ensembles were expensive and not affordable by the peasantry or lower-middle class as was previously thought by some scholars.[23] Imperial patronage often paid for the foundation, maintenance, and decoration of arenas, theatres, and other public works, as well as Christian centers, such as the monasteries of St. Menas in the Maryut and St. Catherine in the Sinai. It is likely, however, that much monastic architectural decoration was sometimes commissioned by wealthier members of the monastery, and perhaps even executed by trained monks.[24] Private citizens could decorate their homes or tombs in any way they wished, spending any amount they could afford. Architectural relief in stone is rarely found in domestic settings probably due to its expense (fig. 11).

Patrons could request purely ornamental decorations in general negotiations with the craftsmen and, in more detailed requests, they could commission sculptures which were to have meanings relevant to the project at hand.[25] Because no written documents can be tied to individual monuments, art historians can avoid inappropriate interpretations of the meanings of those sculptures only by establishing their intended settings, that is to say, whether they were meant for secular or religious monuments, pagan or Christian audiences.

Generally, the historical background for pagan religious works moved from the public to the private spheres. As the Empire was converted to Christianity, pagan temples lost their imperial funding and open acts of paganism came to be forbidden.[26] But it is clear that various forms of paganism did continue. Among other evidence, there was the continual reintroduction of laws forbidding it. Not all pagan worship required temples and priests. There were, as mentioned previously, niches for private devotions in tombs and in houses (fig. 11). The extensive sculptural remains with overt pagan imagery from the early Byzantine period were, primarily, architectural relief decorations from funerary monuments.[27]

Religious attitudes toward free-standing statuary underwent significant changes during the Early Byzantine period. When pagan temples lost their official status, temple statuary lost their patrons, their caretakers, and their audience. Statues housed in temples had been cared for by special ranks of the priesthood and, as if living beings, the statues

23. See, for example, Gayet 1902 and duBourguet 1967 (1971 English translation). Diocletian's *Edict on Maximum Prices*, meant to be enforced throughout the Empire, gives us an idea of what the costs were likely to have been. A camel driver, such as those who would have hauled the stones from the local quarries to the building sites, could earn 25 denarii daily. A carpenter could earn 50 denarii daily. A wall painter could earn 75 denarii daily. A picture painter, on the other hand, could earn 150 denarii. For another example of the range of earned incomes (as opposed to inheritances or income property) and an illustration of the fact that the artisans themselves were members of the middle classes, it is useful to note that the *Edict* permits an advocate to earn up to 1,000 denarii daily.

24. In the Theodosian Code (Novels of Valentinian 20.I) there is the recall of guildmembers (in Rome) to complete the terms of their service "Even if he should be found in the number of the clerics" (A.D. 445). At Bawit, the day to day carving and/or painting of pilgrims' inscriptions can be accounted for only by craftsmen living at the site.

25. Comparisons of contracts from earlier periods of Egyptian history to those from the Early Byzantine period make clear that the processes of commission also followed Graeco-Roman traditions. Compare, for example, the Ptolemaic period P. Cairo Zenon (ca. 255 B.C.) and the early Byzantine P. Oxyrhynchus 896 (A.D. 316). These two Greek documents from Egypt are especially telling as concerns the continuity of Graeco-Roman processes of commissioning the works of craftsmen. These estimates for repainting architectural elements – the first refers to a large house and the second to a public bath – discuss the same concerns in the same order. The wall-painters describe what work is to be undertaken on which elements and then they list the estimate of the cost.

26. See, for example, Pharr 1952, p. 452 in Sirmondian Constitutions, and p. 488, A.D. 438. Note also that temple of Isis at Philae was not shut down until the 6th century A.D.

27. This may be due to the fact that the majority of excavations were carried out in cemeteries, where the archaeologists were searching for pharaonic period remains and papyri. There were few archaeological investigations of Byzantine Egyptian cities and towns such as those carried out by the University of Michigan at Karanis and Terenouthis. It is important to note that the surviving sculptures are either from the cemeteries of Greek cities or from monasteries and that there is no signficant stylistic difference distinguishing the Christian from the pagan works.

participated in religious ceremonies.[28] In short, pagan religious statues had functioned as idols.

With the rise in the Christian population, Christianity developed sculptural traditions of its own. Significant for the future virtual disappearance of sculpture in the round was the pervasive belief that the spirits of the gods that the statues represented resided in them.[29] This belief fueled a major theological controversy which gained importance throughout the Early Byzantine period, in Egypt and all parts of the Empire. Epiphanius of Thebes (A.D. 315–413) wrote as an *iconoclast* ('breaker of images') against the Christian use of representations of holy beings. For Epiphanius, such images were inherently idolatrous: "Remembering this . . . bring no images into churches nor into the resting place of saints, but always remember God in your hearts. Neither bring them into your common dwelling; for it becomes not a Christian to be unsettled by the eye or the fancies of the mind."[30]

Apologists for the necessity of images, called *iconodules* ('adorers of images'), ultimately triumphed. All along, they had emphasized the meditative and didactic qualities of images: the viewer learned to recognize holy persons by their depictions; the illiterate viewer, in particular,

learned to follow scriptural narratives; exegesis, interpretation of the scriptures, was available for all to see. So wrote John of Damascus (A.D. 675–749):

When we set up an image of Christ in any place, we appeal to the senses, and indeed we sanctify the sense of sight, which is the highest among the perceptive senses, just as by sacred speech we sanctify the sense of hearing. An image is, after all, a reminder; it is to the illiterate what a book is to the literate, and what the word is to hearing, the image is to sight.[31]

Whereas the styles of the sculptures of Late Roman and Early Byzantine Egypt present ever more mannered facsimiles of purely visual effects – mass, color, texture, and space – their meanings remain inextricably bound up in their settings and uses. There were, indeed, changes in sculptural trends corresponding to the religious shift from paganism to Christianity, but it is difficult, if not impossible, to discern particularly "Coptic" characteristics. Previous scholars, inspired by turn of the century notions of the otherworldly inclinations of the Oriental mind and the legendary asceticism of Coptic monasticism, considered spirituality to be the goal of artistic expression in Egypt during this period. The present generation of scholars, however, in reviewing the physical and archaeological evidence, finds the sculpture to be more firmly rooted in the rich traditions of the early Byzantine empire. Thus, examples of imperial sculpture, votive statuary, funerary stelae, architectural reliefs from monumental tombs, and reliefs from ecclesiastic and monastic settings are included in this exhibition. Entries describing these works attempt to take into account their functions and settings, who commissioned them and who made them, as well as the material and technical components of their styles.

28. The following document from the monthly accounts of the temple of Jupiter Capitolinus at Arsinoe (see Berlin, *Griechische Urkunden* 1895–1970, 362 (A.D. 215)) describes these activities in passing: ". . . for polishing all the statues in the temple with oil 20 drachmae, wage of a coppersmith for polishing the statues 4 drachmae, to porters who carried the image of the god in procession to meet the praefect 32 drachmae, for crowns for the said image 4 drachmae . . .". A similar text from Early Byzantine Egypt, from an affidavit of priestly rank (P.Oxyrhynchus 1265 (A.D. 336)), refers to priests charged with caring for temple statuary: "To Flavius Paranius also called Macrobius, *logistes* of the Oxyrhynchite nome, from Aurelius, Thonius son of Demetrios, of the same city, priest of the temple of Zeus, Hera, and the associated most great gods, celebrant of the divine images and their advancing victory. Your grace enjoined me to state in writing whence I obtained the aforesaid rank. Accordingly, I acknowledge, swearing the holy, divine oath by our masters the Emperor and the Caesars, that I received the said rank in succession to my aforesaid father Demetrius, who was himself one of the priests and celebrants of the divine images, and that I have made no false statement, under penalty of the consequences of the divine oath."

29. Mango 1963, and Kitzinger 1954. Trilling 1987, p. 471, n. 16 notes that "the decrease in the importance of freestanding sculpture in the late antique world parallels the process of dematerialization in two-dimensional imagery."

30. Byer and Herrin eds. 1977, p. 180; excerpt from Epiphanius's *Treatise against those who are engaged in the making, after the fashion of idols, images in the likeness of Jesus Christ, The Mother of God, martyrs, angels, and prophets.*

31. *Oratio* I, PG 94 col. 1258 c–d as translated in Byer and Herrin eds. 1977, p. 183. Some three hundred years earlier, Athanasius of Alexandria (328–373) had offered a similar defense based on secular imagery:

This will be easier to understand from the example of the Emperor's image which displays his form and likeness. . . . The likeness of the Emperor, and anyone looking at the Emperor recognises that the image is his likeness. . . . He who worships the image worships the Emperor in it. (In *Oratio contra Arianos*, iii, 5: P.G. 26, col. 332) in Byer and Herrin eds. 1977, p. 181.

Textiles

ANNA GONOSOVÁ

INTRODUCTION

THE BODY OF TEXTILE MATERIAL from Roman and Byzantine Egypt is vast. It has been estimated that there are as many as 100,000 pieces, now mainly small fragments, scattered in public and private collections. These textiles survived in the dry Egyptian soil as clothing of the dead and as the padding and wrapping of their mummies. Most were found in the last decades of the 19th and the first decades of the 20th century in both official and clandestine explorations of the vast burial grounds of Saqqara, Akhmim, Antinoopolis and Hawara.[1] Unfortunately, even official excavations were conducted in haste. The better preserved clothing and coverings were stripped from the bodies and preserved only as countless fragments. Bared of their archaeological context their study has proven to be exceedingly difficult. Even the occasional bits of archaeological evidence mentioned by early excavators must be treated cautiously. Some limited help has been provided by textile scraps from trash heaps of Karanis accumulated before the city was abandoned around A.D. 460 and which were more soundly archaeologically explored and documented.[2] In spite of these difficulties, through the effort of generations of scholars great strides have been made in organizing and interpreting these textiles.[3]

In general, the textiles date to the period between the 3rd century and the Middle Ages. The custom begun in the 3rd century of burying the dead fully clothed and wrapped in multiple layers of fabrics establishes the lower chronological limit for their dating; but it is impossible to set the upper limit. While many textiles undoubtedly date to the Middle Ages, the majority belong to the Late Roman, Byzantine, and early Islamic periods of Egyptian history. Although found in graves, only a small number were actually made as funerary clothing and shrouds.

Much of the clothing of the corpses was not new, and all the padding and wrapping was done with discarded and otherwise available textiles. These include various kinds of clothing, household pieces (such as towels, blankets, table cloths, curtains, and hangings) as well as textiles, mainly curtains and hangings, that may have been used in public and religious contexts. Once they are better understood, these textiles will become an important source for the study of Late Roman and Early Byzantine economy, and for the techniques of weaving, artistic styles and, through the content of their decoration, the cultural and religious climate of their times in Egypt, as well as in the rest of the Late Roman and Byzantine world.

From contracts and business agreements, price lists and inventories, personal correspondence and wills much is known about the textile industry in Egypt.[4] Like the textiles themselves, these documents, written on papyri, survived because of the dry Egyptian soil, and they furnish valuable information on all stages of textile production, from yarn preparation and weaving to distribution and pricing. The use of extensive technical terminology suggests a considerable degree of specialization at every level of textile production. Yet much is unknown and not all information that papyri provide is well understood. For example, many terms pertaining to textiles have not yet been satisfactorily translated, and as is the case with all archaeological material, the papyri finds are spotty. Although they have been found throughout Egypt, they are almost completely lacking for Alexandria, the largest and commercially and artistically most important center in Egypt. It is assumed that in Alexandria most of the weaving was done in large workshops, while the papyri indicate that in the rest of Egypt the work was done in smaller workshops by individual weavers who either worked on their looms or hired them-

---

1. For a good survey of early excavations see Kendrick 1920, pp. 5–24.
2. Wilson 1933.
3. Reil 1913, pp. 93–122; Calderini 1946, pp. 13–83; Johnson and West 1949, pp. 119–125; Jones 1960, pp. 183–192; Wipszycka 1965.

4. Especially Kendrick 1920–22; Dimand 1924a; Wulff and Volbach 1926; from Pfister's writings esp. 1932a, pp. 433–459; 1934; and 1936, pp. 1–16, 73–85; Beckwith 1959; du Bourguet 1964; Nauerth 1978 and Nauerth 1986; Renner 1982; Thompson 1985, pp. 145–156. Also Baerlocher 1983 and de Jonghe 1985, pp. 5–23.

selves out to loom owners.[5] Not only was owning a loom an investment,[6] but such commercial use of looms is suggested by actual textiles many of which had to be made on very large looms. Tunics, woven in one piece lengthwise from hem to hem, for example, required a loom at least seven to eight feet wide. Although some weaving for private consumption must have been done on large estates, textiles of all quality, including decorative weavings, were produced primarily by commercial weavers who acquired their skills through apprenticeship.[7] Within the textile industry, weavers like other professions of the times were organized into guilds according to their specialization.[8]

Following the textile practices established under the Ptolemies, weavers of the Roman and Byzantine periods worked primarily in linen (*linon*) and wool (*erion* and *pokas*). Based on the documents and terminology in use, both productions were separate and highly specialized.[9] Since a great portion of surviving textiles are of linen, the importance of wool in the Roman and Byzantine centuries remains largely undervalued by textile scholars. Ignoring the evidence of the papyri, which indicate that wool clothing was very much in use, it is generally believed that wool was needed mainly for decorative weaving and that all-woolen cloth was commonly made in Egypt only after the arrival of the Arabs. Thus the presence of all-wool textiles among the extant pieces from the pre-Muslim period has often been explained by their identification as imports from the Eastern provinces of the Empire, in particular Syria.[10] However, all-wool textiles have been found at many Egyptian sites, and those from Karanis[11] can be dated archaeologically to the 4th and 5th centuries, well before Arab influences occurred. The majority of all-wool textiles from Egypt was surely locally produced.

Silk (*serikos* and *metaxis*), the threads from cocoons of several species of silk worms, must also have been a well-established fabric in Byzantine Egypt.[12] The majority of extant samples of early silk – imported and domestic alike – were found in Egypt, especially in the cities of Akhmim and Antinoopolis,[13] and the use of silks in Alexandria is indicated by a variety of ancient sources.[14] Surprisingly, however, the papyri themselves are silent about this choicest fabric of the Late Roman and Byzantine empire.[15]

Well known for some time in the Mediterranean world, by the middle of the 5th century, silk textiles had become the ultimate status symbol and the use of certain types was even restricted by decrees to the imperial household and to certain privileged persons. At first production of Roman and Byzantine silk was quite limited since it was almost wholly dependent on yarns imported from China, where the industry first developed and the finest yarns were produced, from Central Asia, and possibly from India. However, it continued to be highly prized even after it was produced domestically following the introduction and cultivation of the silk worm during the reign of Emperor Justinian in 552.[16] Two explanations may elucidate the puzzling silence of the Egyptian papyri concerning silk weaving. One is that silk weaving was a new industry which had not yet fully established itself throughout Egypt before the Arab conquest of 640; the other is the possibility that the manufacture of silk stuffs was concentrated in the largest commercial and artistic centers of the Empire, those with access to expensive raw materials and a wealthy clientele for the costly final product. Since Alexandria was one such major producer and consumer of luxury goods, the lack of the papyri and other specific documents from this city is particularly regrettable.

Another luxury product of the Alexandrian workshops might have been textiles woven with gold threads, actually thin strips of gold foil wound around a silk or linen core (cat. no. 60). Also among the materials known to Egyptian weavers in the Roman and Byzantine periods is cotton, or tree-wool as they called it, but its use was very limited.[17] All of these yarns, except for gold thread, were employed in their natural state or colorfully dyed. Wool and silk were dyed most frequently since these yarns hold dyes particularly well. Dyed linen is mentioned, but in the Late Roman and Byzantine periods linen was typically used undyed or occasionally bleached.

In addition to indicating yarns, the papyri contain references to different weaves, and possibly to decorative designs, such as Laconian cloth (*lakonia*)[18] and Tarsian linen (*lina tarsika*), probably named after the city of Tarsus where such textiles were initially made.[19] The latter was

5. Wipszycka 1965, pp. 53–56.
6. P. Oxyrhynchus 1705 (A.D. 298); see also Hunt and Edgar 1932, I, no. 36, pp. 106–109
7. Wipszycka 1965, pp. 57–63.
8. Fikhman 1965, pp. 25–7, 121–127.
9. Wipszycka 1965, pp. 15–37.
10. See Bellinger 1951. On the use of wool in the Dynastic period, see Hall 1986, p. 10.
11. Wilson 1933.
12. Forbes 1964, pp. 50–58.
13. Forrer 1891, Guimet 1912; also Martiniani-Reber 1986, pp. 36–97.

14. Lucan *Pharsalia* X. 141–143, indirectly also Schoff 1912; Wipszycka 1965, pp. 37–39.
15. Wipszycka 1965, pp. 37–39.
16. Procopius, *History of the Wars* VIII. 17. Also Forbes 1964, pp.54–8.
17. *Erioxylon* and *erion apo xylou* (Wipszycka 1965, pp. 39–42).
18. Reil 1913, p. 118; often referring to striped decoration (*lakonosemon*: P. Tebt. 406, for A.D. 266, see also Hunt and Edgar 1932, I, no. 189, pp. 428–9).
19. P. Oxyrhynchus 109 (3d–4th c.).

even woven on a special type of loom by weavers known as *tarsikarioi*.[20] Unfortunately, it has not yet been possible to identify these weaves among the extant textiles. Importantly, cloths and clothing were also differentiated into several grades and priced accordingly. Actual textiles amply bear out this variety of weaves and grades of quality.[21]

Linen textiles were woven mainly in a weave we now call a plain cloth or tabby. Linen, and for that matter woolen, tabbies vary in texture from thin and fine to thick and quite coarse. Tapestry weave, frequently used for decorative weaving, produced denser and heavier cloths. Even thicker and warmer cloths were made with a loop-pile of supplementary weft yarns. Weft-loop-pile cloths, especially of linen, were used for clothing and household textiles already in Dynastic Egypt.[22] In the Byzantine papyri they are called *malotta*,[23] referring to their shaggy, fleece-like appearance (cat. nos. 38, 44, 45). Woolen loop-pile cloths, referred to as *kaunakes*, were made as well.[24] In the Late Roman and Byzantine periods, the loop-pile technique was successfully employed for decorative weaving in which linen was replaced by dyed woolen yarns (cat. nos. 36, 40). Twill weaves, quite frequent among ancient textiles from Northern Europe,[25] are rarer in Egypt, although fragments of woolen twills were found in Karanis.[26]

Technically, most complex fabrics found in Egypt are compound weaves made on a more mechanized type of loom than any of the three basic weaves already mentioned. These weaves are characterized by the repeat patterning produced by mechanized weaving. It is still not known what these looms looked like, but they must have operated on a drawloom principle with numerous extra leashes or heddles to make possible an orderly warp control. The appearance of such a loom sometime in the 4th century may be connected with a demand for patterned weaving, possibly as a labor-saving device.[27] It is also possible that the weaving of silks and the suitability of silk thread for such mechanized techniques may have affected the development of the drawloom.

Both linen and wool tabby and twill weaves exist in compound versions (cat. no. 194). Patterned silks were made primarily as compound twills (cat. nos. 131, 192, 193). The difficulty of reconciling the reading of some terms with actual textiles is illustrated by the word *polymita*, a term that has traditionally been translated as woolen or silk "compound weaves." This reading has recently and convincingly been changed to "multicolored" woolen tapestries, since the occurrence of *polymita* in ancient sources predates by many centuries the appearance of compound weaves.[28]

An important component of any textile is its decoration, which is an integral part of much ancient costume and other textiles. Depending on the technique and the complexity of the design, the weaver could execute the decoration from memory, from detailed cartoons and samplers (isolated examples of which, drawn and painted on papyrus, actually survive),[29] or in a mechanized process, as in patterned compound weaves.

Decorative weaving in tapestry technique is most common, followed by loop-pile weft designs and tabby brocading. Other techniques include mechanized patterned weaving, needle embroidery, and resist-dyed painting. Needle embroidery and tapestry weaving are the simplest. Decorative tapestry weaving, as the most manual of all weaving techniques, involves covering the warp with weft yarns, color by color, motif by motif, as required by the design. Wool and more rarely silk are used for dyed yarns; linen, wool, and silk for undyed ones. This technique could be used to imitate the effect of illusionistic painting (cat. nos. 35, 180) as well as to create two-dimensional designs through strong outlines and extensive colored surfaces (cat. nos. 68, 70). The majority of hangings and the woven-in and applied decorations of costume and other textiles are executed in tapestry technique.

Much of the decorative weaving was done in monochrome silhouette style in which the main decorative field – in the form of panels, bands, or figures – was executed in one solid color, mostly purple, with internal details indicated partly in linen weft and partly with a supplementary yarn placed over the woven surface, probably with a needle. The finished designs resemble embroideries, except that this detailing was done simultaneously with the tapestry weaving of the rest of the textile. Much of the ornamental and figural detailing in the monochrome details was done in this way, which is now referred to as the flying shuttle technique (cat. nos. 61, 62, 181).

Related to the flying shuttle technique is the so-called soumac wrapping used to execute strong outlines of the main design elements. Here weft yarns, both linen and

20. P. Oxyrhynchus 1705 (A.D. 298) and P. Oxyrhynchus 3626; see also Wipszycka 1965, pp. 110–112; Fikhman 1965, p. 126.
21. E.g., in a declaration of prices from Oxyrhynchus, A.D. 343 (P. Oxy. 3776).
22. Most recently Hall 1986, pp. 16, 38–9.
23. Roberts 1950, no. 44, pp. 101–102.
24. Wipszycka 1965, p. 114.
25. Strong and Brown 1976, pp. 174–5.
26. Wilson 1933, nos. 11–15, pp. 16–17, pl. 2
27. The exact evolution of mechanized patterning has not yet been convincingly reconstructed, but for a review of the problem see Geijer 1979, pp. 96–106, 117–123.

28. Wild 1967, pp. 151–155.
29. Berlin, Staatliche Museen, Papyrussammlung, P. 13.275, 9922–26 (Scheller 1963, cat. no. 2, pp. 46–48, fig. 2–3); another fragment is in Victoria and Albert Museum, inv. T15.1946.

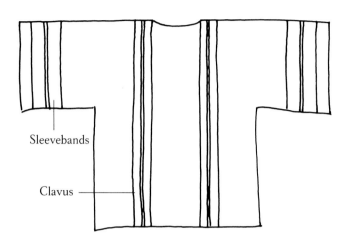

Sleevebands

Clavus

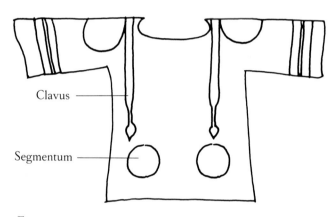

Clavus

Segmentum

Fig. 1
Tunic Ornamentation

wool, are wrapped directly around warps. A group of color tapestry weavings executed on plied warps and used as sets of applied decorations are excellent examples of soumac wrapping (cat. nos. 68, 69, 70). Both of these techniques required great skill, as well as the good eye and hand of a draftsman.

In spite of their frequent use, however, we do not know whether these techniques were carried out by ordinary weavers or by specialists. The flying shuttle technique may even be referred to in papyri as "embroidery" (*ploumarisma*). Mentions of embroiderers (*ploumarioi*)[30] are frequent, including their guilds, while actual needle embroideries are not very common among the extant textiles. In some instances, the content of a document may warrant translating *ploumarios* and *ploumarisma* as pertaining to the flying shuttle technique rather than the traditional needle embroidery.[31]

Large pieces such as wall hangings and covers often carry decoration in loop-pile of supplementary weft in polychrome wool. Similar to tapestry technique, this technique can also imitate the illusionistic effects and fine coloristic nuances of painting, or be used for defined geometric patterning or for the more linear figural style of the 6th and 7th centuries (cat. nos. 36, 40).

FUNCTIONS OF TEXTILES

As is to be expected, a great number of the extant textiles belonged to clothing. The costume found in Egyptian graves is that represented in paintings, mosaics, and other arts of the Late Roman and Early Byzantine periods, as can be judged from the late 3rd and 4th century wall paintings from Luxor, Silistra, or the floor mosaics in Piazza Armerina, as well as from the 6th century wall mosaics in S. Vitale in Ravenna and contemporary wall paintings from Antinoopolis.

The principal garment worn by everyone in the Late Roman and Early Byzantine period was a shirt-like tunic. One tunic, usually very simple, was worn as an undergarment; another, decorated with ornaments and usually wider, was worn over it. Tunics could be short or long, sleeveless or with narrow or wide sleeves. They were mostly woven in one piece lengthwise from hem to hem, with the work starting at the cuff of a sleeve. They were made of linen and woolen plain cloth, loop-pile cloth, in tapestry-weave, and presumably in silks. The decoration of the upper tunics could be quite elaborate, often consisting of a set of ornaments (fig. 1). Ornaments, many examples of which are in this exhibition, consisted of *clavi* (vertical stripes running from the shoulders toward the hemline, either part way or for the entire length of the tunic) (cat. nos. 62, 71); *segmenta* (pairs of round or square panels

30. Also called *poikiltes*; Wipszycka 1965, pp. 125–6.
31. P. Ant. (above, n. 22).

Fig. 2
Icon of the Virgin, Egyptian tapestry,
Byzantine period, 6th century
Wool. 70 3/8 × 43 1/4
The Cleveland Museum of Art,
Leonard C. Hanna, Jr., Fund, 67.144

worn over the shoulders and on the front and back of the skirt of the tunic) (cat. nos. 60, 67); U-shaped hem bands (cat. no. 63); bands edging the neck openings (cat. no. 61); breast and back panels; and wide or narrow cuff-bands over the sleeves (cat. nos. 72 and 73). Some tunics would have only some, others all of these ornaments. Executed normally in tapestry weave, these ornaments were either woven directly into the ground fabric of the tunic or woven separately and only sewn on as appliqués. From the 6th century onwards, applied ornaments would also be made of patterned silks (cat. nos. 131, 193). These ornaments contain the widest range of ornamental and figural motifs and themes.

Various types of cloaks and mantles were worn over tunics. Some could be hooded, others may have had fringed hemlines. Like tunics, these too were made of various linen and wool cloths. They could be brightly dyed in addition to having woven-in or applied tapestry ornaments. Women also wore veils, and both sexes used scarves as well as many other accessories.[32]

Household textiles were even more varied than costumes. They included towels, bed sheets, mattress covers and blankets, cushions, bolsters, wall hangings and curtains, and, of course, carpets. Many were made by specialized weavers.[33] Decoration would have been even more important for household textiles than for costume. The houses of the well-to-do, in particular, offered opportunities for the use and the display of fine weavings, whether they were the coverings and cushions of diningroom couches or the door curtains and wall hangings that would complement the designs of carved furniture and decorated walls and floors. The chairs and couches seen in painting and other arts of the period are customarily covered with decorative textiles and cushions (cat. no. 50).

The use of curtains in contemporary architecture is recorded in the wall mosaic of the Palace of Theodoric in S. Apollinare Nuovo in Ravenna (cat. no. 39). Curtains and other textiles were used in official and religious architecture, and this use was continued in Christian churches. Curtains were needed in doorways and as altarcloths, the uppermost ones decorated, on the altars. The practice of separating the altar area from the rest of the church with curtains developed very early in Egypt. The textile with the cross from Minneapolis (cat. no. 127) may have been used as such a sanctuary curtain. The St. Theodore fragment (cat. no. 128) and the Icon of the Virgin in the Cleveland Museum of Art (fig. 2) are examples of monumental weaving executed in the style of wall and panel painting and used as religious devotional images, much like icons.

32. Houston 1966.
33. E.g., *tapetarioi* made carpets (*tapetes*), while *tylophantai* and *tyloplokoi* made pillows and cushions (Wipszycka 1965, pp. 118–120; Fikhman 1965, pp. 26–7).

MOTIFS AND ICONOGRAPHY

The decorative repertory of these textiles is characterized by its richness and endless variation of motifs. Geometric, vegetal, and figural designs, in monochrome and in color, fine and coarse, small and large, appear in every type of textile in all decorative techniques. Geometric patterns can be very simple or very complex. The most frequent geometric motif in this family of designs is the braid and its most advanced form, the interlace, whose looped and knotted strands are arranged in the most elaborate compositions, and seem ever-present (cat. nos. 129, 181). As an ornamental motif the interlace became more widely used only from the late 2nd century onwards, at first mainly in floor mosaics. Its textile versions from Egypt represent the finest realization of the ornamental potential of this pattern. In the area of vegetal ornament, probably the most ubiquitous is the grape vine in all possible variations and styles, followed by acanthus and ivy-leaf scrolls, and foliate and floral garlands. The scrolls can be plain or populated with hunters, erotes, animals, and birds, or enriched with fruits and flowers. The repertory of decorative motifs used by Egyptian weavers was never fixed. New motifs were constantly being added to existing ones, often from other arts and from imported objects. A distinctive group of such motifs, consisting of composite palmettes, rosettes, masks, and exotic animals combined in unusual arrangements, was taken over from imported Sassanian silks (cat. nos. 48, 191). Creation of other patterns was the direct result of the methods used in weaving, as may be the case with the repeat patterns of compound weaves (cat. nos. 192, 193, 194).

The wealth of figural motifs in the textiles matches that of the geometric and vegetal ornament. Figures come from a variety of sources, mainly classical mythology and literature; Christian subjects derive from the Old and New Testaments and include images of saints and worshipers as well. The figures appear as individual motifs, in groups, or in compositions that are often based on other works of art. By far the most numerous are images of Dionysus and his followers (cat. no. 42). In addition to various myths and portrayals of divinities, important classical subjects (cat. no. 37) include representations of the hunt and hunting motifs, pastoral themes, the Seasons with their symbols and related subjects, and marine scenes with nereids and sea monsters, often combined with boating and fishing (cat. no. 68). Child-like erotes are often shown hunting and engaged in other activities (cat. no. 36). When the figural motifs and subjects fill *clavi*, *segmenta*, and other ornaments of clothing or household textiles, they seem at first glance to play a purely decorative role. But when they are the subjects in wall hangings or curtains, they have the same role as wall paintings and mosaics, and their iconographic content and meaning is more focused.

Despite the fact that most extant textiles date from the period after the official recognition of Christianity, Christian themes form only a small group in the figural repertory. Moreover, the majority of them cannot be placed earlier than the 6th century. Large-scale weavings (cat. nos. 127, 128), like the monumental wall and panel paintings that they imitate in style, format, and to some extent use, show holy images, crosses, and other symbols. Narrative cycles from the Old and New Testaments have survived in the fragments of resist-dyed curtains,[34] probably used in churches, and in small-scale costume ornaments. David, the Sacrifice of Isaac, and the story of Joseph (cat. no. 69) are the most popular Old Testament subjects. The story of Joseph seems to have been especially popular, since it has survived in several sets of tunic ornaments. Scenes from the life of Christ appear on similar tunic ornaments (cat. no. 130).

Another important group of decorative themes includes motifs taken from or related to imperial art, such as the images of victorious emperors and charioteers. These subjects, which first appeared in 6th century weavings, may have been designed initially for silk textiles, and only later adapted by tapestry weavers to their technically different linen and wool versions (cat. no. 70).

This review of the iconographic repertory shows that classical subjects and motifs are prominent in textile art in Egypt at a time when one would expect a much stronger Christian presence. In Egypt, as elsewhere, Christian art developed rapidly in the religious and funerary spheres, but in other areas as well, after the official recognition of Christianity in the early 4th century. How then is one to understand this preponderance of classical subjects in such a large body of material as these textiles?

Traditionally, the classical content of Egyptian art of the Late Roman and Byzantine periods has been seen in two ways: on the one hand, as an example of the Hellenistic culture patronized by the Greeks, the Romans, and a Hellenized Egyptian elite; on the other hand, as evidence in part for the popularity and continuation of pagan religious cults, especially the worship of Dionysus that was introduced to Egypt by the early Ptolemies. Grafted onto the traditional Egyptian belief in the afterlife, the cult of Dionysus – the god of regeneration and rebirth, among other things – is believed to have been particularly strong and still flourishing even after the introduction of Christianity and its establishment as the official and eventually the only allowed religion. Studied primarily as examples of religious and funerary art, the textiles, with their frequent display of Dionysiac themes, have been cited as important evidence for the continuation of such pagan practices in Egypt.[35] But at the same time, many of these

---

34. Kendrick 1922, pp. 60–68 and Illgen 1968.
35. E.g., Friedländer 1945, pp. 27–41; also Metropolitan Museum of Art 1979, nos. 120, 121, 125, pp. 141–3, 146–7.

same textiles have been cited as examples of a native Egyptian Coptic artistic tradition that emerged during the centuries of Byzantine rule in Egypt. Given this interpretation, they reflect a cultural climate in which the various Hellenistic, Roman, and Byzantine traditions were rejected under the impetus of an emergent native Egyptian-Coptic Christian orthodoxy.[36]

These contradictions and dichotomies in the explanations offered for the thematic content and stylistic character of these textiles lead – because of their vast numbers – to the Gordian knot in the study of Egyptian art of the Late Roman and Byzantine periods. Touched upon above this can be characterized in one question: Whom does this art represent; i.e., for whom was it produced? The Greek-Roman minority and the Hellenized Egyptians? All inhabitants of Roman-Byzantine Egypt, irrespective of their ethnic and religious background? Or at some point only the native Egyptians-Copts? Were they practicing pagans or the militant Christians of the contemporary Christian sources? Another question that needs to be asked is whether there is sufficient iconographic, or for that matter stylistic, justification for interpreting these textiles (and thus much of the art of the period) from a strictly Egyptian perspective. These questions are obviously complex, and there are many ways of addressing them. One way, which is pursued here, is to understand the textiles neither as provincial versions of Late Roman and Byzantine art, nor as indigenous Egyptian-Coptic art, but rather as part of the mainstream of Late Antique art.

There is no doubt that, even in Egypt, the progress of Christianity was much slower than contemporary Christian writers wanted posterity to believe, and pagan religions – native and foreign – continued to be practiced there for some time. Moreover, the evidence of the textiles can shed light on a broader and less studied aspect of Late Roman and Early Byzantine society than the specific religious situation in Egypt during the 4th, 5th, and 6th centuries. As has been mentioned, these works represent the largest surviving body of textiles from the Roman and Byzantine world, and although found in graves, they happen to be at the same time the largest surviving body of objects used in secular as well as private domestic contexts. Thus a comparison with other examples of secular and domestic arts from Egypt and elsewhere in the Late Roman and Byzantine world should yield a more satisfactory explanation for the thematic content of these textiles than traditional funerary and strictly religious interpretations have done.

Decorations for private houses from all areas of the Late Roman and Early Byzantine world, whether on walls or floors (the quantity of floor mosaics is considerable), depends on the same and similarly distributed classical repertory of themes and motifs as seen in the Egyptian textiles: the Dionysiac cycles and motifs, the seasons and their symbols, hunting and pastoral scenes, marine and Nilotic subjects, as well as grape vines, vegetal scrolls, and garlands. This same repertory also decorated furniture fittings, silver plate, and other table utensils, and numerous personal objects, including jewelry.

This repertory has been thoroughly studied in the context of religious and funerary art,[37] but its use in the domestic and private sphere in particular is only now attracting the attention of scholars. Nevertheless, it is becoming increasingly apparent that the presence of this repertory in the domestic sphere was not accidental or motivated only by fashion or decorative appeal. The most frequently used classical subjects were seen not simply as visual illustrations of mythology and classical literature, but came to be understood as broad allegories of life's blessings and its renewal, and as allusions to prosperity and continued good fortune.[38]

It is clear that the thematic content of Egyptian textile decoration was not unique to Egyptian art of the Late Roman and Byzantine periods, but was used throughout the Late Antique world. Even such a characteristically Egyptian subject as a Nilotic landscape (usually showing marshes and water with specifically Nilotic flora and fauna, and known since Early Dynastic times) may have entered the textile repertory, along with other related figural subjects, such as marine scenes, in the Roman period, since from the 1st century B.C. onwards Nilotic landscapes became widespread in the art of the Mediterranean.[39] The extant textile renditions of this subject do not differ from those found in the rest of Late Roman and Early Byzantine art.

Placing Egyptian textiles in the context of Late Roman and Early Byzantine domestic art helps to explain the seemingly anomalous lack of weavings with Christian subjects from the 4th and 5th centuries. On the one hand, the classical themes had become so entrenched in the decorative repertory of this art that they continued to be used even though their meaning may have become less understood, and as time passed their appeal became largely decorative. On the other hand, even with the greater Christianization of the Empire, the use of Christian subjects in many areas of domestic art appears to have been restricted.

36. Such a break is particularly strongly advocated by du Bourguet 1971 and Zaloscer 1974.

37. This bias is evident in the discussion of the majority of Late Antique and Early Byzantine objects, see e.g., Metropolitan Museum of Art 1979.

38. In the context of the floor mosaics, discussed by Dunbabin 1978.

39. Foucher 1965, pp. 137–143.

Although the existence of clothing with Christian decorations is already known from the sources from the end of the 4th century,[40] neither the textiles themselves nor any portrayals of them in art has survived. One of the earliest artistic representations is the border of Empress Theodora's *chlamys* with an embroidered Adoration of the Magi in the sanctuary mosaic in S. Vitale in Ravenna (ca. 547). Extant examples of costume ornament with Christian subjects, like their representations in art, appear only as an addition to the already existing figural repertory. One such group of Old and New Testament subjects appeared in the course of the 6th century, first in silk weavings together with images inspired by imperial iconography, and later also in wool and linen tapestries, many examples of which are extant. Some of these tapestries are completely dependent both compositionally and stylistically on the silk models. The appearance of the Old and New Testament themes on costume ornament in the 6th and 7th centuries reflects the overall increase in the use of Christian imagery at that time. Jewelry of the same period, for example, was also increasingly decorated not only with Christian symbols but with scenes from the life of Christ.

SUMMARY

To summarize, the textiles were made for and used by the widest possible segment of the population of Late Roman and Byzantine Egypt. They were made commercially in small workshops and by individual weavers. Unlike the more expensive artistic media of wall painting and floor mosaics, for example, textiles were more affordable and varied in price, depending on the quality of the weaving as well as the quality of the yarns. While most textile decorations were mass-produced, many – both for costumes and the household – must have been individually ordered. Weavings with mythological and other classical subjects were certainly commissioned for pleasure and displayed by the well-to-do, educated class, which even in the Early Byzantine period cultivated classical culture. The vast majority of the textiles found in Egypt were made there; although it is known that some of the extant pieces had to be imported from other parts of the Empire,[41] because of their clearly shared style and iconography they cannot be securely identified. (An exception to this, of course, is the group of Sassanian silks found at Antinoopolis.)[42] Qualitative assessment of Egyptian textiles should not, as has been

the tradition, be confused with their stylistic character. As the discussions in the individual catalogue entries show, in Late Roman and Early Byzantine art two stylistic modes are used side by side – one more naturalistic and the other more abstract and stylized. The use of either must have been a matter of choice. For example, the change seen in the proportions of human figures to an emphasis on large heads and large, wide-open eyes, taken as evidence of a gradual transformation of weaving in Egypt into a folk art, is in fact a common stylistic trend in representing small figures, also found in the finest examples of Byzantine manuscript painting, jewelry, and such an expensive medium as ivory carving. Examination of the extant weavings confirms that Egyptian weavers of the Late Roman and Early Byzantine periods did not work in artistic isolation or only for a selected purpose. Interpreting their work only as Egyptian-Coptic art or, because of the manner of its survival, as funerary art, is misleading, and ignores the contributions these textiles make to our knowledge of the art and society of the time.

*I wish to express my most sincere thanks to my friends and colleagues Ann Bermingham, Linda and George Bauer, Christine Kondoleon, and Laura Allen for their support, encouragement and their patient and most helpful reading of this essay and my catalogue entries.

40. E.g., by Asterius, bishop of Amaseia (Mango 1972, p. 51; see also cat. no. 130).
41. E.g., a hanging with erotes in the Textile Museum in Washington, although believed to be found in Egypt, has been attributed to a workshop in Herakleia Perinthos near Constantinople (inv. 71.10; Trilling 1982, no. 1, p. 31).
42. Geijer 1963.

Pottery and Glass

SUSAN AUTH

POTTERY

IN ANCIENT CULTURES clay was the most common material for household utensils from cooking pots to water jugs. People lit their way to bed with clay lamps and honored the gods with dedications of terracotta statuettes. Later, Christian pilgrims brought back holy water in clay souvenir flasks. In Coptic Egypt the clays of the Nile river and the desert were skillfully fashioned into many forms, often decorated with painted geometric and animal motifs similar to those of contemporary textiles and sculpture.

An overwhelming mass of pottery has been found on Egyptian sites of this period. However, with some exceptions such as Kellia, noted below, careful retrieval, study and publication of pottery have been lacking. Thus we are missing the many types of information that can be derived from the humble but useful potsherd. We know of the pottery used at some monasteries and at the town of Karanis, but very little of that in use at Alexandria, the capital.

At Kellia, a monastic complex in the desert southeast of Alexandria, four centuries of occupation from ca. 390 to 750 A.D. produced four tons of pottery and 12,000 sherds for modern excavators.[1] At other monastic sites as well pottery was widely used, often serving as a more austere and cheaper substitute for metal and glass.[2]

A 3rd century A.D. papyrus document details the lease of a pottery works in order to make 15,000 wine jars a year, certain evidence of ancient mass-production.[3] Earlier excavators solved the problem of quantity by saving only complete examples of pottery[4] or by giving their workmen bounties for saving decorated or choice sherds.[5]

Many examples of pottery in this exhibition have been borrowed from the Kelsey Museum of Archaeology at the University of Michigan and come from Michigan's 1924–1935 excavation of the rural town of Karanis in the Fayum Oasis.[6] This fertile area supported an extensive agriculture carried on by the inhabitants of the small towns and villages. They grew wheat both for their own use and as taxes to Rome, along with legumes, vegetables, olives, fruit and wine grapes. Artisans, for example in the cloth-making trades, produced goods for local consumption and export. Some of the surplus above each family's needs went to pay the numerous taxes in money and in kind that included grains, draft and food animals and even woven cloaks for the Roman army.[7] Although some luxury goods were shipped in, especially from the capital, Alexandria, these were not wealthy people and their pottery and other household items reflect the modest lifestyle of the average person in Egypt.

Since Karanis was inhabited over a long period of time, its pottery gives a good idea of the range of shapes, clays and decoration used in a single place from about the 1st century B.C. to the mid-5th century A.D. or possibly later.[8] Items chosen for this exhibit generally fall within the 3rd–5th century chronological range. Examples include a jug of porous clay for cooling and storing water (cat. no. 4), a

1. Egloff 1977, p. 18.
2. From the monastic site at Kellia, for example, four centuries of occupation produced only 34 examples of glass (Egloff 1977, p. 170). Compare the more than 1000 examples catalogued from the first five seasons of work at the town site of Karanis (Harden 1936, pp. 1, 306). See also Jacquet-Gordon 1972, p. 3.
3. P. Oxyrhynchus 3595 (243). Cited in Bowman 1986, ch. 4, p. 109, no. 35, p. 244.

4. As at Karanis, Johnson 1981, pl. 1. According to information kindly provided by Dr. Marti Lu Allen, representative sherds were saved at Karanis and pottery counts were made of pots that were not kept. However, this material has not been studied or published.
5. Myers in Mond and Myers 1940, p. 75.
6. Summary of the goals and results of the excavations of Karanis in Gazda et al. 1983, pp. 4–5.
7. Gazda et al. 1983, pp. 9–15.
8. Johnson 1981, p. XIII. On the basis of comparison of Karanis pottery with other datable Mediterranean ceramics, there is some controversy on the date of the abandonment of the town, whether mid-5th century A.D. or later. See Hayes 1972, p. 2; Hayes 1980, pp. 516–7, and Bailey 1984b, pp. 186–7.

massive wine jar with humorous faces and garlands (cat. no. 2), good tableware, lanterns, lamps and statuettes (cat. nos. 2–34). Some fine red-slipped and stamp-decorated pottery was imported from North Africa and later copied by local potters (cat. no. 1A).[9] The discovery of potters' kilns at Karanis suggests that much of their clay ware was locally manufactured.[10] Kilns found in other regions of Egypt probably made wares primarily for local use,[11] although some especially fine or specialty wares were traded widely.[12]

Some of the pottery shown here cannot be identified precisely by region or date of manufacture, since it was not found and recorded in carefully conducted archaeological excavations. We still lack fundamental information concerning manufacturing sites, regional variations, and trade patterns for later Egyptian pottery. However, the great range of shapes, surface finishes and decoration indicates that in the later period of Egyptian culture pottery was not merely a ubiquitous utilitarian product but could share in the fine craftsmanship and the artistic and religious expression of other media of Coptic art.

GLASS

Like pottery, the glass of Coptic Egypt was the heir to a long and distinguished history of fine craftsmanship.[13] The raw materials of glass, sand, soda, and lime were readily available in the Egyptian deserts. From as early as 1500 B.C. glass had been a relatively rare and luxurious material in Egypt, made to imitate precious gems such as turquoise and lapis lazuli. However, the discovery in about 50 B.C. that molten glass could be blown through a hollow tube revolutionized glass manufacture by making it quick to produce, and thus a common commodity rather than a luxury item.[14] Moreover, the thinness and translucency of blown glass made it suitable not only for tableware but for lamps and even window panes.

Along with plain glassware, Egypt excelled in the production of luxury wares such as finely engraved glass, painted glass, sandwich gold-glass, and millefiori glass made much like modern paperweights (cat. nos. 25–28; 121). Much of the earlier Hellenistic and Roman luxury glass of Egypt is thought to have been produced at Alexandria. Later fine glass, such as the intarsia St. Thomas panel

(cat. no. 121), must have been made in one or two specialized workshops, but there is no evidence either literary or archaeological to indicate their location. It is quite remarkable that the Egyptian glassmakers maintained their highly skilled and painstaking technical secrets for four or five hundred years and adapted them to the new requirements of large-scale architectural decoration.

The quantity and simplicity of most later Egyptian glass suggests the existence of a number of small-scale factories producing glass for local consumption.[15] Shapes such as oval bowls (e.g., cat. no. 16) and some decorative techniques distinguish Egyptian glassware from that produced elsewhere around the Mediterranean. In general, Egyptian everyday glass of this period was comparable to contemporary products from adjacent regions.

The dry Egyptian climate has contributed to the remarkable preservation of much of this glass, which gives the deceptive impression, after more than 1500 years of burial, that it could have been made yesterday. As with pottery, the town of Karanis provides evidence for the glass used by ordinary people. One group of objects exhibited here was found on the windowsill of an ancient Karanis house of the 5th century A.D. Along with other household items, it contains a few individual glass vessels – bowls, a plate, a jar, a decanter – rather than the complete table service that might have been found in the larger cities and wealthier households.

Egyptian monasteries such as that of St. Jeremias at Saqqara show some later uses of glass, such as lamps in hanging chandeliers, small clear or brightly colored window panes, and wall and apse mosaics of multicolored and gold glass cubes.[16] Especially striking is the "painting" of St. Thomas fashioned of millefiori canes and large sheets of flat glass (cat. no. 121). This was undoubtedly part of an elaborate church wall decoration. In contrast, glass vessels were so cheap in later Egypt that the deacon of a poor village church in A.D. 300 explains that their church liturgical vessels were only of glass[17] rather than of bronze or silver.[18]

9. Johnson 1981, pp. 1–3, n. 9; 9–10, n. 60.
10. Gazda et al. 1983, p. 16, fig. 25, n. 37.
11. Egloff 1977, p. 191, n. 2 gives a list of Egyptian kiln sites of the 5th–10th centuries. Adams 1986, pp. 31–2 gives information on the design of two kilns, taken from the better preserved and more numerous Nubian examples.
12. Jacquet-Gordon 1972, p. 9; Adams 1986, p. 26.
13. For a recent summary of earlier Egyptian glassmaking, see Goldstein in Museum of Fine Arts, Boston 1982, pp. 1061–2, nos. 1–15.
14. Auth 1976, p. 17.
15. Harden in Mond and Myers 1940, p. 199, details the slight traces of glass manufacture found at Armant in the region of Thebes. On Roman glass furnaces, see Clairmont 1975, pp. 59–63, n. 37 and Charleston 1978, p. 10. Furnace remains are often so slight that they may have been overlooked in earlier excavations of Egyptian sites.
16. Quibell 1909, p. 6, *idem* 1912, pp. 2 and 43. Glass windows are attested for secular buildings as well. A 4th century papyrus details repairs to the windows of the public baths at Oxyrhynchus by the glassworkers' guild (Hanson 1976, vol. II, no. 81, p. 541).
17. Corning Museum of Glass 1987, no. 11, p. 34 and Auth forthcoming.
18. Balestri and Hyvernat 1908, p. 82; Codex Vaticanus Copt. 66, F. 96 V.

The Minor Arts of
Late Antique Egypt:
From Relics to Icons

GARY VIKAN

Fig. 1
Monza, Treasury of the Cathedral of
St. John the Baptist, ampulla 2: later 6th
century; Annunciation, Visitation,
Nativity, Baptism, Crucifixion, Women
at the Tomb, Ascension.
    From A. Grabar, *Ampoules de terre
sainte* (Paris, 1958), pl. V (and *passim*).

WITHIN THE RICH AND VARIED WORLD of Late
Antique art, the minor arts of Egypt have their
own special character and importance. This is
due in part to an accident of nature, for the arid climate
and abundant sands of that region have together preserved
whole categories of the artifacts of daily life which otherwise would have been lost forever. Consider, for example,
the everyday act of writing, certainly one of the most basic
and essential ingredients in any developed culture. Where
but in Egypt can one find the full paraphernalia of a private study of the 6th century? Indeed, united in *Beyond the
Pharaohs* are a wooden writing stand, reed pens and a pen
case, a terracotta inkwell, and the papyri they produced
(shopping lists, wills, and curses on your neighbor!); elegant bone styluses once used on wax tablets to take notes,
a bronze peacock lamp to illuminate the study, a wooden
storage cabinet for valuables, and on the floor, a pair of
abandoned leather slippers. In this respect, Egypt is to the
Byzantine Empire what Pompeii is to the Roman Empire.

But even more than that, the minor arts of this region
and period provide important clues to a momentous yet
somewhat puzzling development in the history of Early
Byzantine piety, namely, the emergence in the 6th and 7th
centuries of the cult of icons out of the cult of relics.[1] Consider, for example, the tiny pewter flasks of sacred oil carried home by pilgrims from the Holy Land (fig. 1).[2]

Typically, they bear religious scenes evocative of the
various holy sites the pilgrim had visited and words indicating that the liquid inside had once been touched to the
wood of the True Cross – thus its miraculous power to
preserve the traveler on his journey homeward, or to cure
his ailments or drive off his demons once he got there.
This "True Cross oil" was a common sort of contact relic
which, in early Byzantium, was valued by Christians

1. Grabar 1943/1946; Vikan 1988, pp. 6 ff.
2. Monza, Treasury of the Cathedral of St. John the Baptist,
   ampulla 2: later 6th century: Annunciation, Visitation, Nativity,
   Baptism, Crucifixion, Women at the Tomb, Ascension. See
   Grabar 1958, pl. V and *passim*.

Fig. 2
Silver Amuletic Armband
Cairo, Fouquet Collection: late 6th to
7th century; (left to right) Ascension,
Annunciation, Nativity, Chnoubis,
Baptism, Cruxifixion, Women at the
Tomb, Holy Rider.

From J. Maspero, "Bracelets-amulettes
d'époque byzantine," ASAE 9 (1908),
246 ff., fig. 1.

throughout the Mediterranean basin and beyond.[3] But it seems to have been specifically in Egypt, and among the minor arts, that the notion emerged of dispensing with the relic and relying instead on the miraculous efficacy of the Holy Land images. This phenomenon, which in essence marks the subtle but momentous shift from relic power to icon power, may be documented among several types of objects, but nowhere more clearly than in a group of amuletic silver armbands (fig. 2).[4] On them one encounters the cycle of Holy Land pictures that had been developed for the Jerusalem oil flasks, but now, in Egypt, there is no relic oil, and so the pictures alone are the primary source of the object's miracle-working powers. And indeed, that these armbands were intended to be amuletic and not simply decorative is clear from their customary inscriptions, most notably *Heis Theos ho nikon ta kaka* ("One God conquering evil") (as on cat. no. 107) and Psalm 90 ("He that dwells in the help of the Highest...").

But the more basic question remains: why, specifically, should the Christians of Early Byzantine Egypt have initiated (or at least significantly facilitated) this revolutionary change? An important part of the answer lies with these armbands, for in the central medallion of the example illustrated here, toward the bottom, is the Chnoubis, the lion-headed snake which for centuries pagan Egyptians had believed to be miraculously efficacious in combating afflictions of the abdomen (fig. 3; see also cat. no. 107).[5] The Chnoubis has been added here, to a Christian's armband, doubtless for the same reason, to combat abdominal diseases. But more important, its very presence attests to the strength and continuity of an ancient Egyptian belief,

namely, that an image in and of itself can convey magical power. For certainly, in a society in which this is accepted as true, and in which there is a long, deeply ingrained tradition of giving that belief artistic expression – as was true in Egypt, among Roman period gem amulets[6] – there remains but a very short step to impute comparable powers to comparable Christian images. The Chnoubis/Holy Land silver amulet (fig. 2) is Christianity's functional descendant of the pagan Chnoubis gem amulet (fig. 3). This is one of the most crucial stories to emerge from a study of the minor arts of Late Antique Egypt, for it is a story that bears heavily on the emergence of the icon, the very embodiment of the Byzantine Middle Ages.

Fig. 3
Paris, Cabinet des Médailles, no. 2189;
Graeco-Egyptian gem amulet of the
Roman period; inscribed on the reverse:
"Guard in Health the Stomach of
Proclus."

From A. Delattre and P. Derchain,
Les intailles magiques gréco-égyptiennes
(Paris, 1964), no. 80.

3. On such contact relics in general, their role in the life of the pilgrim, and their relationship to art, see Vikan 1982.
4. Cairo, Fouquet Collection, late 6th to 7th century (left to right): Ascension, Annunciation, Nativity, Chnoubis, Baptism, Crucifixion, Women at the Tomb, Holy Rider. See Maspero 1908, pp. 248 ff, fig. 1. For the group in general, see also Vikan 1984, pp. 74 ff.
5. Paris, Cabinet des Médailles, no. 2189: Graeco-Egyptian gem amulet of the Roman period, inscribed on the reverse: "Guard in Health the Stomach of Proclus." See Delattre and Derchain 1964, no. 80, and Vikan 1984, pp. 75 ff.
6. For the Chnoubis in general, its Egyptian origins, and its popularity on Egyptian gem amulets, see Bonner 1950, pp. 54 ff.

Greek and Coptic Manuscripts

BIRGER A. PEARSON and LESLIE S.B. MacCOULL

A "MANUSCRIPT," as its Latin etymology indicates, is something "written by hand." Nowadays, the word often has a broader meaning, but before the invention of the printing press all writing was done "by hand," with various implements ranging from stone chisels to quill pens. Many materials were used for receiving writing in ancient times, such as stone, bone, wood, palm leaves, tree bark, various metals, clay tablets, broken pottery and limestone flakes (ostraka), animal skins (including parchment and vellum), and papyrus. In Roman-Byzantine Egypt, documentary manuscripts (legal documents, receipts, private letters, etc.) were written in Greek and Coptic, usually on papyrus, parchment, or ostraka. For Greek, Latin, and Coptic literary manuscripts, papyrus and parchment were commonly used.

Literary Manuscripts

I. PAPYRUS AND PARCHMENT

The elder Pliny, writing in the first century A.D. and citing a famous writer of the previous century, says the following about the development of the use of papyrus and parchment for the production of literary works:

"According to Marcus Varro we owe even the discovery of paper to the victory of Alexander the Great, when he founded Alexandria in Egypt, before which time paper was not used.... Subsequently, also according to Varro, when owing to the rivalry between King Ptolemy and King Eumenes about their libraries Ptolemy suppressed the export of paper, parchment was invented at Pergamum; and afterwards the employment of the material on which the immortality of human beings depends spread indiscriminately."[1]

In this discussion of the two basic writing materials of the ancient world, papyrus (from which we get our word "paper") and parchment (derived from the adjective *Pergamena*), it is interesting to note that their use is connected respectively with the two greatest repositories of literature in antiquity, the libraries of Alexandria and Pergamum. The details are wrong, however. The earliest papyrus rolls known, from Egypt, date from a time some two and one-half millennia before Alexander's conquest. The oldest piece of papyrus found outside Egypt is written in Hebrew and dates to around 750 B.C. The oldest extant Greek papyrus dates from the 5th century B.C.

As for parchment, derived from the skins of sheep or goats, Pliny's account may be correct in that a particular mode of preparation of the skins, by tawing with alum and sifted chalk, was apparently developed at Pergamum. ("Vellum" is a finer version of the same thing, for which skins of younger animals were used.) But writing on animal skins was known long before the time indicated in Pliny's account; the oldest extant text on skin (leather) is from Egypt and dates to the 12th dynasty (early second millennium B.C.).

The preparation of "paper" from the papyrus plant involved a complicated and ingenious process. The rind of the reed was removed, and strips of the underlying pith were laid out side by side, barely overlapping each other. A second set of strips was placed at right angles over the first layer, and the two-layer mass was beaten together with a wooden mallet. The juices of the plant are sufficient to hold such a sheet together. When dried and polished with pumice, it is an ideal material for receiving writing.

Papyrus sheets were pasted together to form rolls. Theoretically rolls could be as long as desired, but they were normally marketed in standard sizes. From a roll of blank papyrus, pieces could be cut off for small items such as letters or bills of sale. Whole rolls would be used for literature, and for longer works two or more papyrus rolls could be glued together.

It is rather striking that the best-quality papyrus is also the oldest. The quality of papyrus deteriorated in the Roman period, and by the 7th century most papyrus was thicker and rougher, and not as supple as the earlier product. By that time parchment had replaced papyrus as the

---

1. *Nat. Hist* XIII.21.69–70, trans. H. Rackham. The word translated here as "paper" is *charta*, the material of which is papyrus. Pliny goes on to describe the making of *charta* from the Egyptian papyrus plant. The word translated here as "parchment" is *membranae* ("skins"), invented "at Pergamum" (*Pergami*).

standard writing material for literary purposes.

Modern knowledge of ancient papyrus manuscripts is largely based on archaeological discovery. One of the earliest papyrus finds took place in excavations at Herculaneum, Italy, in 1752. Discovered there were 800 papyrus rolls buried in ash during the eruption of Mt. Vesuvius in 79 A.D. (The elder Pliny, quoted above, was a victim of that eruption.) Unfortunately these rolls were "carbonized," turned into hard masses by the combination of a damp environment and the hardening of the tufa deposit. Only a small fragment of this material has been susceptible of study, enough to determine that the papyri were Greek books belonging to a library of the Epicurean school of philosophy. Perhaps some day a method will be developed for unrolling these manuscripts so that they can be read.

The vast majority of ancient papyri have been found in Egypt, thanks to a dry climate which is best for the preservation of papyrus. Thousands of papyri have been found at Behnasa alone (ancient Oxyrhynchus), and the papyri recovered there from 1897 are still being edited and published. The very first sheet of papyrus found there (P. Oxyrhynchus 1, published in 1898), inscribed in Greek on both sides, contains sayings of Jesus. It is from a codex dated to the end of the 2nd century. With the discovery of the Nag Hammadi Codices in 1945, including a *Gospel of Thomas* completely extant in a Coptic translation, the Oxyrhynchus fragment could be identified as part of a Greek version of the *Gospel of Thomas* (Sayings 26–33).

II. FROM ROLL TO CODEX

The earliest books were rolls (scrolls). Indeed, our English word "volume" is based on the Latin word for a book roll, *volumen*. A book in roll form is really a very inconvenient thing, requiring two hands to open and unwind it so that the columns of writing can be seen. Early in the Roman period a revolutionary development took place in the history of book manufacture: the development of the codex, the precursor of the book as we know it.

The Latin word *codex* originally referred to a set of hinged wooden tablets, coated with wax and inscribed with a stylus. The form of the early wooden codex was, in fact, the model for the development of the codex book, the simplest and oldest form of which consists of a stack of sheets of papyrus or parchment folded once, stitched together, and protected by bindings made of wood or leather. An intermediate stage in this development was the use of parchment notebooks in "codex" form for notes and rough drafts. (Ink could be washed off, so the notebook could be used more than once.) The New Testament provides interesting evidence for this intermediate stage. In 2 Timothy 4:13 (a pseudonymous work of the early 2nd century) "Paul" makes the following request of "Timothy": "When you come, bring the cloak that I left with Carpus at Troas, also the books, and above all the parchments." Here "books" (*biblia*) refers to scrolls of either papyrus or parchment; "parchments" (*membranas*) refers to parchment notebooks.

It is quite likely that the use of the codex for the composition and copying of literature was first developed in the Christian church. The oldest Christian manuscripts in existence, dating from the 2nd century and discovered in Egypt, are all in codex form. Most of these are biblical manuscripts (containing portions of the Old Testament or New Testament); but four non-canonical Christian texts are included in the list: the aforementioned *Gospel of Thomas*, another non-canonical gospel (Pap. Egerton 2), *The Shepherd of Hermas*, and St. Irenaeus's treatise *Against Heresies*. In contrast, the available evidence shows that the scroll was the predominant book form used for pagan literature well into the 4th century.

Why did Christians adopt the codex for the production and preservation of their literature? Several practical reasons have been advanced: economy, compactness, convenience, ease of reference, and comprehensiveness. The last two are especially important: the ease with which biblical passages could be found and cited in a scripture-oriented community, and the possibility of including several authoritative texts within a single book, a consideration that has possible consequences for the development of the Christian canon of scripture.

If Christian scribes were responsible for the invention of the codex books, where and when did this development take place? The Christian community in Rome has been suggested in this connection, but the same scholar who put forward this hypothesis, Colin H. Roberts, now favors Antioch or Jerusalem as more likely possibilities. If Jerusalem is the place where the Christian codex originated, this momentous event must have taken place in the 1st century, and before the Jewish War of 66–70.

III. FROM GREEK TO COPTIC

During the past century more new manuscripts of Greek literature have been found than in any period since the Renaissance, and most of these new manuscripts are papyri from Egypt. Previously, Western knowledge of Greek literature was based on medieval parchment, vellum, and paper manuscripts brought during the Renaissance period from the Byzantine world, where a rich tradition of classical scholarship persisted until the sack of Constantinople in 1453. The works of Greek authors previously known are well represented among the papyri (almost 700 papyrus texts of Homer alone), but the papyrus discoveries have provided classical scholarship with numerous ancient works previously lost or unknown, such as the poems of Bacchylides, the comedies of Menander, Aristotle's *Constitution of Athens*, and many others.

The dissemination of Greek literature throughout Egypt, where the papyri have been found, is itself an important fact. This dissemination took place largely during the Hellenistic period, i.e., during the centuries following the death of Alexander the Great (323 B.C.), though it probably began even earlier. With the founding of the great Library in Alexandria by Ptolemy II Philadelphus, Alexandria became the cultural and scholarly center of the entire Mediterranean world, and provided the impetus for the dissemination of Greek learning and literature throughout Egypt. Unfortunately, the damp Delta climate of Alexandria is such that no papyri could have survived there.

The scribes of the oldest Greek manuscripts wrote in capital ("majuscule" or "uncial") letters, with no separation of words. (It was not until the 9th century A.D. that minuscule letters were first used, when a distinction between "capital" and "small" letters became possible.) Of course, different writing styles are observable in the manuscripts, and stages of development in hands over the centuries; but there is always a clear distinction observable in manuscripts between literary or "book" hands on the one hand and "documentary" hands on the other. Documentary hands are usually cursive and much more difficult to read (cat. nos. 150 and 155).

Greek scribal practices provided the model for the development of scribal practices among early Copts. Indeed, a page from a Coptic manuscript of, say, the 4th century resembles very much one from a Greek manuscript of the same period: the same "uncial" letters, for example. A closer look at the page will, however, reveal the presence of letters that do not occur in Greek manuscripts.

The Coptic language, of which there are several dialects, is linguistically unrelated to Greek.[2] It is, in fact, the latest stage in the evolution of the language of the pharaohs, both in terms of linguistic development and in terms of writing. From the earliest form of Egyptian writing in hieroglyphics, there eventually developed "hieratic" and "Demotic" writing forms, which are very cursive forms of hieroglyphs. Coptic, on the other hand, instead of using hieroglyphs, for the most part used the Greek alphabet.

The oldest Egyptian texts written with Greek letters date from the first century A.D. They are magical in character. In some of these texts Demotic letters are used along with the Greek letters, betraying an intention to accurately represent sounds not occurring in Greek. It is in this way that the Coptic alphabet developed, i.e., by the addition of new letters based on Demotic characters. For the Sahidic Coptic alphabet these added letters are as follows: ⲱ (š), ϥ (f), ϩ (h), ϫ (ǧ), ϭ (č), and ϯ (ti). Literary Coptic developed among Egyptian Christians. The earliest examples of Coptic literature consist of translations of Greek

Biblical texts. A standard Coptic language (Classical Sahidic) was developed by the 4th century. Its basic expression is the Sahidic New Testament. In the Coptic language, the influence of Greek was evident not only in the alphabet used but in the language itself. Numerous Greek loan words were incorporated into the Coptic language as a regular part of the vocabulary. The oldest surviving texts composed in Coptic, i.e., not translated from Greek originals, date from the 4th century (St. Pachomius), but it is possible that efforts to write in Coptic began somewhat earlier (Hierakas of Leontopolis, according to St. Epiphanius).

Coptic literary history, for the most part preserved in manuscripts yet to be edited, is unique in that it is not only the product of a Christian culture but consists entirely of works of a religious character. The eclipse of Coptic culture that resulted from the Arab Conquest of the 7th century also prevented its further development in more "secular" literary forms. For secular literature, even among the Copts, Greek, and eventually Arabic, was felt to be the more appropriate medium.

Bibliography: Kahle 1954, vol I; MacCoull 1986b; Orlandi 1986, pp. 51–81; Pearson and Goehring 1986; Roberts and Skeat 1983; Turner 1968; Turner 1971.

Documentary Manuscripts

Manuscripts are cultural objects that say something about the underlying assumptions, the mental and physical world, of the culture that produced them. They attest to every variety of activity in the public and private realms. In the world of Coptic Egypt, documentary manuscripts come in several materials: papyrus, parchment, and ostraka (potsherds or limestone flakes used for writing).[1] It is thanks to the documents fortunately preserved by the dry climate of Egypt that we know this province of the late Roman empire better and in greater detail than any other.

At first excavators looked for literary manuscripts, being primarily interested in possible lost works of classical authors and early patristic and biblical texts. But the discovery of large numbers of documents at Oxyrhynchus made historians aware of the great value of this material for reconstructing the details of the province's history. Today documents are valued alongside literary texts as primary sources for the period.

Public documents, such as copies of imperial rescripts, tend to be in Greek (or occasionally Latin); private documents are found in both Greek and Coptic, with Coptic increasing in number in the 6th and 7th centuries. As documentary phraseology becomes more elaborate with

---

2. The word "Coptic" means "Egyptian." It is a corruption of the Greek word *Aigyptos*. Beside Sahidic, the other main dialects of Coptic are Bohairic (the language of much of the Coptic liturgy still in use among the Copts), Fayumic, Akhmimic, Lycopolitan ("Subakhmimic"), and Middle Egyptian ("Oxyrhynchite").

1. There is as yet no collection of Coptic documents comparable to the Greek *Sammelbuch*. See MacCoull 1986b, and the Coptic bibliographies issued in the journal *Enchoria* (Würzburg).

the passage of time, we can discern local provincial variations in scribal practice and even in the notaries' handwriting, as well as dialectal variations in Coptic. And the sheer number of documents produced also increases with time: Egypt's Byzantine bureaucracy generated a great deal of paperwork, such as tax rolls and receipts, official correspondence, and the account-keeping of great lay and monastic estates. With the adoption of the Greek alphabet for writing Egyptian, the ability to read and write ceased to be the property of a small priestly and scribal class, and the level of literacy rose considerably for those who spoke and used Coptic. Both Coptic and Greek were the vehicles of an extensive polite private correspondence,[2] written according to the best rhetorical norms of late antique education. The volume of every class of documents reaches its greatest height in the 6th century and the first half of the 7th.

In fact, all kinds of documents become more rhetorical, more ornamentally composed according to the rules taught in the higher schools, than had been the case in Hellenistic times.[3] Petitions and especially wills tell the life stories of their writers with elaboration and feeling; in sales, leases and accounts of each party to the transaction are marked out by an appropriate epithet, such as 'the illustrious' magnate, 'the most humble' priest, 'the most learned' lawyer, or 'the most pious' abbot; even inventories and tax receipts are drawn up in the careful phrasing of the schools. Explicit Christian phraseology, such as prayers and echoes of the Bible, makes its way into the composition of documents early on. A favorite, though risky, pastime of historians has been to try to infer whether the writer of a private letter was a Christian from particular formulas, such as 'I pray to God for you' (instead of 'the gods'). In 591 the emperor Maurice decreed that all documents must be headed by an invocation, either of Christ or of the Trinity;[4] and this invocation remains a feature of Coptic documents as long as the Coptic language continued to be used for record-keeping, openly proclaiming Christianity even under Moslem rule.

Each category of documentary manuscript is rich in information about the society of its times. We can perceive the linguistic and manual fluency, or lack of it, of the writer (some people are skilled scribes with a large repertoire of classical and biblical phrases at their command, while "slow writers" have trouble signing their own names). We can compare regional writing styles, for example, different dialects and modes of address. From sales, leases, and wills we can estimate in detail the material prosperity of Egypt and the richness of its infrastructure in the Coptic period, and examine the economic workings of the skilled trades (textiles, building, wine, and cheese), the upward mobility of self-aggrandizing land entrepreneurs, the growing role of the Church as a property-owner and -manager, and the year-to-year functioning of agriculture as the mainstay of the economy. The wills of the prosperous also attest to their founding of monasteries, churches and hospitals; and the archives of these latter institutions show how patronage could continue over several generations. The abundant cadasters, tax lists, and tax receipts are a window into the most basic functioning of the whole province.[5] Private letters, especially between Coptic monks, are full of everyday concerns: requests for prayers, for foodstuffs, for writing materials, for the transmission of messages (cat. nos. 15, 157, 158 and 159). Inventories of house or church property enable us to reconstruct what a building of the period must have looked like and contained.

The documentary papyri from Late Antique Egypt furnish our best way to understand the history, the structures, and the mentality of its culture. There is no area of society they do not illuminate. They show us in the most basic way how ideas moved out from the small worlds of their originators into the common currency of the culture at large and the actions and experiences of individual people. Documents are our open window into the world of Coptic Egypt.

The last Greek documents from Egypt come from the late 7th century. Coptic continued to be used for letters, wills, and other documents into the 9th century, and in some areas (near Hermopolis/Ashmunein) even the 11th. But Coptic ceased to be understood except for some memorized parts of church services, and was replaced in Egyptian record-keeping by Arabic, to the great impoverishment of the Christian community.

L.S.B.M.

Bibliography: Bagnall/Worp 1981, pp. 112–33, 362–5; Biedenkopf 1983; Gascou/MacCoull 1987, pp. 103–58; MacCoull 1986b, pp. 42–50; Zilliacus 1967.

---

2. See Biedenkopf-Ziehner 1983.
3. An early study is Zilliacus 1967; but it needs to be superseded by a modern work, since it still subscribes to old ideas of "Byzantine servility."
4. See Bagnall/Worp 1981.

5. For a 6th century village see Gascou/MacCoull 1987.

Early Christian Architecture in the Nile Valley

PETER GROSSMANN

THE FOLLOWING IS A DISCUSSION of Christian architecture in Egypt during Late Roman and Early Christian times, that is, the period between the Edict of Constantine and Galerius in 313 A.D. and the Arab conquest in 640/42 A.D. The Edict of Constantine brought to an end the Diocletian persecution of Christians, so that from this date on Christianity enjoyed increasing governmental protection throughout the Roman Empire. In Alexandria, Egypt's capital, Christianity was already well established by the end of the 2nd century A.D., as it is attested in the historically well-known personality of Bishop Demetrius (189–231), Patriarch of Alexandria.[1] No remains of Christian architecture in Egypt from this early period have yet appeared, however, that can be dated before the end of the 4th century. Besides some unpublished new discoveries, probably of the 4th century, in Antinoopolis, Shams al-Din (al-Kharga Oasis) in Upper Egypt, and Marina (at the ancient site of Leucapsis, west of Alexandria), the oldest known churches are two very modest early 5th century buildings of the large monastic settlement of Kellia in the northwest Delta. A 4th century basilica (an early Christian church type, used throughout the Roman Empire, in which the main hall for the congregation is divided into a central nave and two lateral aisles) may well also exist in the area of Faw Qibli, the site of the Pachomian monastery of Pbow. The other early foundations in Alexandria (Theonas church and Athanasius church[2]), as well as in other towns (Antinoopolis, Lykopolis, Oxyrhynchus, Thmuis and others) are known only through the written sources.

There are a number of reasons for this absence of early churches in Egypt. Certainly only a few were ever built.

And presumably at the start they were modest in scale and design and were therefore as a rule quickly replaced by larger foundations. Consequently, the early churches that survive are in sites abandoned soon after their erection. But here another difficulty arises. At the end of the 18th century, Egyptian farmers discovered that the earth of ancient townsites was rich in organic elements that made excellent fertilizer (sebakh), and the widespread search for the fertilizer destroyed many ancient remains.[3] Its use ended only in this century, and by then, many ancient towns had almost completely disappeared, leaving only vast dead fields covered with little hills of stones and broken pottery.

In Alexandria, where the majority of the Late Roman remains are to be expected, the destruction still continues. And what is not already lost will soon be destroyed by modern building activities. The interest in antiquities today primarily concerns works suitable for museum exhibit, and as a result the architectural context of the surviving paintings, sculptures, capitals, and other forms of architectural decoration has been largely ignored.

5TH AND 6TH CENTURY CHURCHES

Churches were where the early community of the faithful gathered for thanksgiving and prayer. But since few remain from this period, it is difficult to trace their architectural origins. Their development can really be traced only from the beginning of the 5th century onward in a few Upper Egyptian churches, including the large transept-basilica of

1. Eusebius of Caesarea VI, 3.8.14.19.26; Hist. Patr. (ed. Evetts, P.O. I, 1948).
2. The material mentioned in the sources has been recently restudied by Martin 1984.
3. Descriptions of these activities can be vivid indeed; see Schweinfurth 1886 on the destruction of Arsinoe-Krokodilopolis in the Fayum. This same article also describes the so-called "brickfinders" whose business it was to salvage fired bricks from ancient buildings. That such people existed is well attested by the fact that in many Roman buildings only the floors survive, surrounded with trenches where the walls once stood.

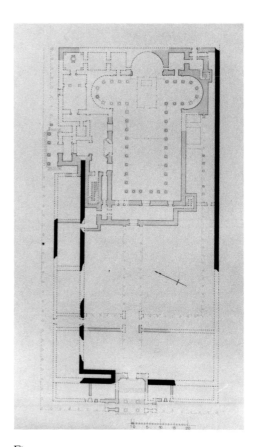

Fig. 1
Hermopolis Magna (Ashmunein),
Transept Church

Fig. 2
General view from southeast of Deir
Anba Shenouda (so-called "White
Monastery)

Hermopolis Magna (today called Ashmunein) (fig. 1) of the first quarter of the 5th century, and two famous 5th century monastery-churches. The first is the famous "White Monastery," the surviving church of Deir (monastery) Anba Shenouda near Sohag (fig. 2), founded around 440 by the Abbot Shenoute; most of its main body is still standing today (fig. 3). The second monastery-church is the large five-aisled basilica of the main Pachomian monastery at Pbow (modern Faw Qibli) (fig. 4) founded in 459 A.D. (Remains of a smaller church with a similar ground plan were recently discovered below this latter basilica.[4])

Both of these monastery-churches were monumental representations of their time and both clearly drew on earlier architectural sources. From pharaonic temple architecture they borrowed their generally cubic structure[5] and the design of some of their moldings, e.g., the cavetto cornice along the door lintels and the outer exterior walls.[6] In addition, the grouping of the different rooms of the sanctuary behind a straight outer eastern wall, especially striking in the church of Deir Anba Shenouda, is adopted from pharaonic temple architecture. Further pharaonic elements are the stairs, often embedded in the walls,[7] and the small recesses behind many doors into which the door wings swing when opened. In their basilican shape, however, both churches follow the general Hellenistic-Roman trend of the Empire. The columns, too, are of truly Roman form; Roman columns were even reused in the nave.

On the other hand, the large transept basilica of Hermopolis Magna, probably the episcopal church of that town, shows the strong influence of Hellenistic-Roman town architecture. In contrast to the modest doors and passages of the monastic basilicas discussed above, the main entrances here are designed as rich propylaea. Where western churches have an atrium (rare in Egyptian churches, though a few exceptions are found at the pilgrimage site of Abu Mina,[8] and pharaonic temple architecture offers many examples), the church of Hermopolis Magna has a large court with the crossing colonnaded streets familiar in Imperial architecture (Palmyra, Spalato). The builders here used only elements of classical Roman architecture – columns with Attic bases and Corinthian capitals, and architraves, door jambs and lintels carved

4. Grossmann forthcoming.
5. Deichmann 1938.
6. Remarkably, however, the half-round torus below the cavetto cornice in pharaonic temples is always lacking in the Christian adaptation.
7. Deichmann 1938, pp. 35 ff.
8. See the example of the North Basilica, as discussed in Jaritz 1980 (see fig. 6) and the East Church, as discussed in Grossmann 1980 (fig. 7).

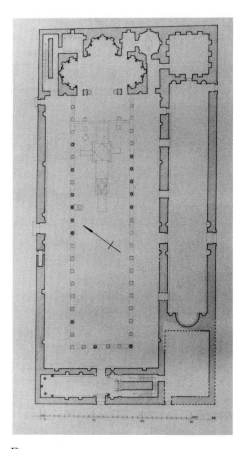

Fig. 3
Church of Deir Anba Shenouda
(so-called White Monastery)

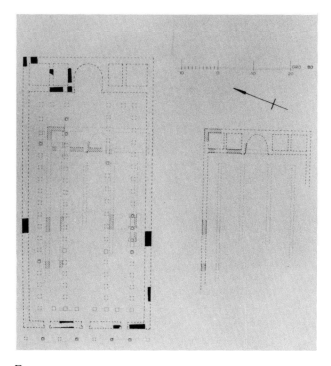

Fig. 4
Faw Qibli, site of the Pachomian
Monastery
A. large church (459 A.D.)
B. earlier church (early 5th century)

in Late Roman style.[9] In the nave, as in the monastery-churches mentioned above, all columns were spoils, that is, building elements, such as columns, door lintels, etc. reused from earlier buildings.

The Imperial style of this transept basilica, which characterized Egypt's later architectural development, is noteworthy since public and private architecture in Egypt followed pharaonic tradition almost exclusively until the 3rd century. The few exceptions are found only in Alexandria and such other places as Antinoopolis, Naukratis, Ptolemais and Paraetonium, areas that enjoyed the special attention of the Imperial government.[10] Graeco-Roman features are rare elsewhere before the 4th century. From the very start, however, Christian church architecture, in its spatial arrangements and architectural design, followed the models of Late Roman architecture developed in Europe and along the coast of Asia Minor. With the spread of Christianity, these classical architectural features were carried to the farthest Egyptian villages and became a new basis for the design of architectural monuments throughout Egypt. In larger cities, building complexes had colonnades, peristyles, arches, and other classical elements rare in earlier times, and only a few pharaonic elements were retained.

The main reason for the adoption of classical models in church architecture was liturgical requirements. Christian liturgy required a large assembly hall illuminated by many windows, and pharaonic temples, being houses of a resident deity and not places of communal worship, offered no model for adaptation. The rapidity of the change from pharaonic to classical forms was probably also enhanced by the political climate. Under Diocletian (284–305), Egypt ceased to be governed directly by the Emperor or his representative and became a normal province, part of the diocese Oriens, whose capital was Antioch in Syria. Egypt thus became more open to cultural exchange with the other imperial centers, and its church architecture moved almost in parallel to developments abroad. Perhaps as important, however, was the effect on the viewer of the pharaonic versus classical styles. Pharaonic features had been used for thousands of years for temples and tombs, many still visible, and were thus strongly associated with the ancient Egyptian pagan religion. Classical features, on the other hand, had long since entered the standard (although often highly provincialized) decorative repertoire of rich private houses and secular public buildings. Classical elements thus had a neutral religious character,

9. Many of these pieces are reused spoils, although of unknown origin (the huge neighboring Komasterion of the Antonine period of similar fabric was still standing when the church was built); cf. Bailey 1984a.
10. Jones 1983, pp. 309 ff.

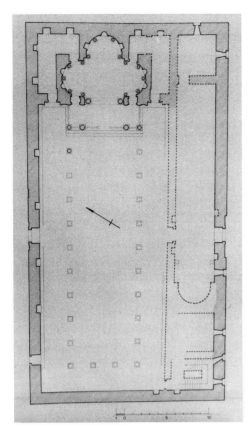

Fig. 5
Church of Deir Anba Bishuy
(so-called Red Monastery)

and were much more acceptable than pharaonic ones for use in Christian churches.

It is worth noting, however, that even though enough Egyptian workshops existed in the 5th and 6th centuries to produce architectural elements in the classical Late Roman design, the Egyptian churches still made extensive use of spoils (reused materials).[11] In the church of Deir Anba Shenouda, only the smaller columns and frames of niches are newly produced for this church; the tall Roman 3rd century granite columns, as well as many other pieces, come from earlier, pagan buildings of the neighborhood. The 6th century churches at Abu Mina are furnished nearly exclusively with elements of 4th and 5th century buildings of Alexandria,[12] and the late 7th century main church of the monastery of Apa Jeremias at Saqqara uses material from a number of 5th and 6th century mausolea of the Memphite necropolis whose owners left the country during the Arab invasion in 640/42.[13] (One of the few exceptions is the so-called Red Monastery, the 5th century church of

Deir Anba Bishuy near Sohag (fig. 5).[14]) The general use of spoils gives an idea of the speedy exchange of all these materials. Apparently the practice was carried over from the pharaonic past, when kings not infrequently dismantled the structures of their predecessors. In no other region of the Roman Empire were spoils reused on such an extensive scale.

GENERAL CHARACTERISTICS OF EGYPTIAN CHURCH ARCHITECTURE

In Egypt, as in other provinces of the Empire, the three-aisled basilica became the most important type of church and remained so until the Fatimide period. This basilica design provided the largest spatial area that can be covered by a single roof. Its basic design is similar to that used in other parts of the Empire. The central nave is usually larger and higher than the aisles, and a series of windows (clerestory) is often opened in the upper wall that rises above the colonnade on both sides of the nave. Examples exist with and without galleries, that is, a second floor over the lateral aisles of the basilica, usually used by women and children. The sanctuary is usually designed as an apse. As elsewhere in the Empire, five-aisled basilicas were built in Egypt.[15] Examples of transept basilicas are known from several sites;[16] at Hermopolis Magna and Marea-Hauwariya, the transepts had half-rounded endings on both sides, elements heretofore unknown in the Empire.

All churches are aligned approximately with the east, the direction of sunrise, where the day begins and whence the return of Christ is expected.[17] In Upper Egypt this orientation generally follows the direction of the Nile. With a few exceptions due to topographical reasons, the main entrance typically lies on the western side. Frequently there is a narthex (narrow entrance hall) on the west side, where people could wait until the church was opened.[18]

11. Deichmann 1975, pp. 53 ff.
12. Severin 1984.
13. Grossmann and Severin 1982. The same is apparently true of the monastery of Bawit; see Severin 1977a.

14. The same is apparently the case, at least for the major sculpture, of the late 6th century church in front of the pylon of the temple of Luxor, but unfortunately all the capitals were not finally worked out; see Grossmann forthcoming.
15. At Faw Qibli, Medinet Habu, Armant, Qasr Ibrim, Old Dongola and even in smaller places such as Makhura and Medinet Madi.
16. Hermopolis Magna, Abu Mina, Merea-Hauwariya, Dakhayla (the site of the famous monastery of Ennaton, unpublished) and again in Old Dongola.
17. Peterson 1959, pp. 15 ff.
18. This is also where penitents stood who were not allowed to enter the church proper. In some cases these narthices were richly outfitted with lateral conches (half-round extensions of a room) usually covered with a half dome (at Deir Anba Shenouda, Dendera, and in the Great Basilica at Abu Mina). Such lateral conches also occur elsewhere, mainly in the western part of the Empire.

The inner supports separating the nave from the aisles in Egyptian churches are generally columns bound together with architraves or arches. There seems to be no regularity in the number of columns or the length of the churches, although later churches are generally shorter. The naves were presumably nearly always covered by gable roofs over a wooden framework, a construction that allows a wide span. Only some very narrow churches had barrel-vault roofs, and in these cases heavier pillars were used to carry the upper part of the walls instead of columns. The aisle roofs were probably always flat, and the outer walls of the aisles – evident in a few surviving examples – contained continuous rows of small, usually rectangular windows (as in Sohag, Luxor, and Qasr Ibrim). In some churches, remains of seats have been found, usually lined up along the inner sides of the walls. They might have been just for the elderly, since there are too few to accommodate the whole congregation.[19]

A feature typical of Egyptian church architecture is the large number of wall niches appearing at roughly regular intervals in the side walls of the churches. This feature itself is of Roman origin, but was abandoned in the rest of the Empire.[20] The niches in Egyptian churches, which are the primary reason for their thick outer walls,[21] are usually arranged in accordance with the distribution of the colonnades. Their purpose is, however, only decorative. In several churches these niches are framed with pilasters or engaged columns and form a considerable part of the interior ornamentation (as at Deir Abu Hinnis, Dendera, and Deir al-Naqlun). In the richly outfitted church of Deir Anba Shenouda at Sohag, half-round niches alternate with rectangular ones. In some sections doors replace rectangular niches, and in the triconch sanctuary, indeed, where the wall decoration is composed in two stories, this alternation is also observable in the vertical view: half-round niches on the lower floor correspond with rectangular ones on the upper floor, and vice versa. What we have here is a typical Roman niche alternation.[22] Less regularly, this alternation is also found in the slightly later church of Deir Anba Bishuy, north of Sohag. In earlier and more provincial churches, as in Sketis, the actual Wadi Natrun (Deir al-Syrian, Deir al-Baramus), and in Philae (east church), the niches take the form of simple rectangular cupboards.

Except for a few examples near the Mediterranean coast, the sanctuary at the eastern end of the church is divided into at least three room units.[23] Usually all rooms are of equal depth, a feature making it possible to build the eastern wall of the church in a straight line. The center is occupied by the apse, open to the nave. In episcopal churches, the throne of the bishop is located at the apex of the apse, flanked on both sides by the seats of the other priests. In front of the apse – in a few mainly monastic churches inside the apse as well (which points to the fact that this arrangement probably derives from an earlier rule) – slightly extending into the nave, is the presbytery, surrounded with screens. In the center of the presbytery stands the altar for the celebration of the Eucharist. The two lateral rooms serve secondary liturgical functions, such as storage

19. Beyond these general characteristics, there are several features typical of early Egyptian architecture that are not found elsewhere. First, the Egyptian basilica contains a western return aisle (that is, aisles at the western end of the basilica; see Grossmann 1982b). In a gallery church it offers the opportunity to form a transverse passageway at the western end of the church which makes it possible to have one common staircase for both lateral galleries. During the second half of the 5th century, at least in Upper Egypt, the western return aisle became a standard church element, and after that time appears also in churches that lacked galleries.

However, galleries are not as widespread as return aisles; they rarely appear in churches of smaller communities or in monastery churches. That the two monastic churches at Sohag have galleries is quite an exception. One should also not be surprised by the many stairs often found beside the churches, which give access principally to the roof, not to the galleries. The same circumstances might be responsible for the fact that Egyptian church architecture developed no standard position for the stairs. For example, in Abu Mina, where no churches have galleries, the position of the stairs is always different.

20. See Hornbostel-Hüttner 1979, pp. 73 ff.

21. Deichmann 1937, p. 34.

22. Hornbostel-Hüttner 1979, pp. 70 ff, 82 ff.

23. Exceptions were discovered in the church extra muros of Taposiris Magna (see Grossmann 1982a, pp. 152–54, fig. 11), in the church of al-Akhbariyya (unpublished) in the 6th century tetraconch, the Gruftkirch of Abu Mina (in press) and in both periods of the East Church of Abu Mina (Grossmann 1980, pp. 222–4, figs. 7 and 8).

of liturgical vestments and books.[24]

SPECIAL FEATURES OF EGYPTIAN CHURCH ARCHITECTURE

In the first half of the 5th century, a new triumphal arch based on two columns begins to appear, just in front of the main opening to the sanctuary, in Upper Egyptian churches with a three-foil sanctuary (the first example is Deir Anba Shenouda). The two columns were connected to the lateral colonnades of the nave and originally served to embellish the central opening of the sanctuary, which for technical reasons was relatively small. In earlier examples these columns were usually larger than the other

columns of the nave. Later on the same installation was also used in churches with simple half-circular apsides (in three examples at Luxor, Medinet Habu and Esna). In architectural terms, the area behind this new triumphal arch still belongs to the nave of the church, since the aisles of the basilica do not show a similar interruption at the same position. From the late 7th century onward, however, the *khurus* of Egypt's medieval churches developed out of it[25] (the first known example is the main church of the monastery of Apa Jeremias at the Saqqara necropolis). The *khurus* was a transverse room unit just in front of the sanctuary whose middle section opened to the naos of the church through a short row of columns. Later yet, in the early Middle Ages, it was reduced to a single tall but not very large door, of which several examples survive in Wadi Natrun. This development may have arisen from a desire to separate the priests and their holy operations at the altar more definitively from the congregation of the laity. A corresponding feature is the iconostasis in the Greek Orthodox church, which developed much later.

Churches with a centralized groundplan are very rare in Egypt, perhaps because such churches belong to an urban kind of architecture, which is less developed in Egypt. However, a few examples are known from two tetraconch churches at Abu Mina (Tomb church II and Eastern church, both of the Justinian period, 527–565 A.D.). To a certain degree, the little church of al-Hayz Oasis may also be understood as a central-plan church, although the transverse axis does not have the same architectural value as the long axis. Other examples are to be expected in Alexandria. A full circular church was recently discovered in Tall al-Farama (Pelusium) (unpublished). The tetraconch churches have a square or rectangular central aisle surrounded by rows of columns interrupted on all four sides by half-circular conches also formed of colonnades. The planning of the outer walls varies somewhat. In Tomb church II of Abu Mina (fig. 6) they are arranged on a rectangular groundplan; only in the apex of the lateral conches were small niches placed projecting slightly outward. In the Eastern church of Abu Mina the shape of the outer wall simply echoed the inner arrangement on a larger scale. These tetraconch churches are not native Egyptian inventions but may rather have come to Egypt from Asia Minor and Syria, where they are most prevalent.[26]

Apart from these very rich churches, the only significant Egyptian buildings with a centralized groundplan are the four-pillar type, consisting of a square room with pillars at each corner, usually covered with a hanging dome. (The ancient name for this building type is "tetrapylon," which

24. Since the purpose of these rooms is not totally clear, one should avoid calling them such names as "prothesis" and "diaconicon," especially since the rite of the prothesis was not developed before the beginning of the 8th century (see Descoeudres 1983, pp. 91 ff.; note, however, that the term "diaconicon" for part of a church appears in the 5th century *Apoph. Patr* 178 (= Gelesaios 3).

Early Christian churches in Syria have a similar arrangement of the sanctuary, again with a straight eastern wall (see Butler 1929). It seems, however, that the Egyptian examples are an independent development. In larger and richer churches such as Hermopolis Magna and Deir Anba Shenouda, even more than three rooms are grouped behind the same straight eastern wall.

The apses in the east are occasionally replaced by rectangular altar chambers, most frequently in provinical buildings as well as in some of the simpler monastic churches (in the large *laura* of Kellia, all the churches found so far have rectangular altar chambers; the recently excavated church CH E at Medinet Madi, Fayum; cf. Grossmann 1987, pp. 77 ff, and fig. 1). On the other hand, Egyptian architects often liked to ornament their apsides with rich architectural decoration. In eleven instances (Medinet Madi church G, Deir Anba Shenouda and Deir Anba Bishuy, Deir Abu Fana, Dendera, Luxor, Armant-Hermonthis, Esna, al-Bagawat, Elephantine, and Faras), an additional inner circuit of columns was erected against the walls of the apse. Some smaller churches (Deir al-Naqlun, Deir Abu Hinnis) have instead, in the same location, a series of niches each framed with engaged columns; such niches are also present in some of the churches mentioned above. In the two monastery churches near Sohag of Deir Anba Shenouda and Deir Anba Bishuy, these niches, with their columns, are grouped in two stories with a regular alternation of half-round and square niches. In other examples the opening of the apse (triumphal arch) is flanked with columns (Abu Mina: North Basilica, Medinet Madi, Bawit, Armant, and Bigai). The highest quality is represented, however, in those churches in which the central part of the sanctuary has the form of a triconch. Seven examples of this type are now known in Egypt, all in Upper Egypt and dating from the 5th to late 6th century: both churches at Sohag, Dendera, Deir al-Bakhum, Antinoopolis South, Deir Abu Fana and Deir Abu Matta in Dakhla Oasis.

25. Grossmann 1982b, pp. 112 ff.
26. Grossmann 1983, pp. 167 ff.

contrary to our modern thinking draws attention to the openings between the pillars rather than the pillars themselves.) The architectural design resembles that of the Iranian fire-temples, but there is no reason to suggest any historical relation between the two building types. In the variants of this type found in the early Christian necropolis of Hibis (al-Bagawat), the spaces between the corner pillars are filled with thinner walls and interrupted only on one side by a small door. Opposite the door a small niche is often present in the wall. To transform this building type into a functioning church, only a normal tripartite sanctuary need be added on the eastern side, and this adaptive step was taken in several instances in al-Bagawat and Oxyrhynchus. In principle what resulted was a single-aisled chapel with a domed naos.

This building type is often made richer by surrounding the central space with another wall curtain so as to form a kind of corridor (*ambulacrum*) encircling the inner part of the building. This type is generally constructed with four inner columns, as at Saqqara, Oxyrhynchus, and Luxor. In Elephantine there is an example with corner pillars dating to the second half of the 6th century. Churches of this form also appear from this time on in Nubia, where church architecture always lagged somewhat behind that in Egypt.

SUMMARY
Although the remains of early Christian church architecture in Egypt are all of rather late date, and no examples survive from Alexandria, there are nonetheless some

outstanding examples that demonstrate their own unique architectural character while at the same time being fully in accord with general Imperial trends. The Christian buildings in Egypt are strongly dependent on the art and architecture of Constantinople, the capital of the Eastern Empire, where nearly all new developments originated.[27] The windblown and so-called basket capitals with stylized acanthus found in the monastery of Apa Jeremias at Saqqara are characteristic of this dependence, being local limestone imitations of 6th century Constantinopolitan originals in marble.[28] The character of this art is thus rather un-Egyptian. It is merely the art which the foreign invaders, i.e., the Ptolemies and Romans, brought into the country; the art cannot in this period be called "Coptic." In the late Roman period members of the upper classes, who influenced cultural development the most strongly, were with a few exceptions of Greek or Roman origin. Only with the conquest of the country by the Arabs under Amr Ibn al-As in 640/42, during which most of the Greeks left Egypt and relations with the center of the Empire were interrupted, did Christian Egyptian art and architecture become more independent.

FUNERARY ARCHITECTURE
We know very little about early Christian funerary architecture in Egypt, and generalizations are thus dangerous. We can say, however, that the burial customs and tomb architecture retained more of the pagan – Hellenistic-Roman – tradition than might be expected. Thus, most tombs were simple rectangular holes dug deep into the earth or hewn into the rock and covered with slabs of stones or a small barrel-vaultlike structure of bricks.

Wealthy families continued, like their pagan predecessors, to be buried in underground burial chambers (*hypogea*), accessible usually through a vertical shaft but sometimes also by stairs. Small mausolea were usually erected above the ground; these take a variety of forms, especially in the Ptolemaic and Roman periods. Most fashionable were mausolea in the shape of a small temple with pronaos, cella, and some additional lateral rooms.[29] The majority, however, are a simple house-form with a barrel-vaulted or domed ceiling and a little niche in the eastern wall. In some cases they consist of a domed chamber open

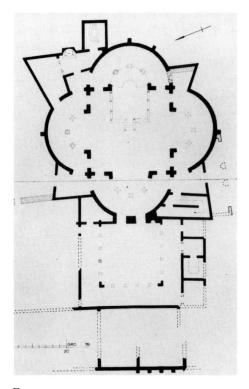

Fig. 6
East Church II of Abu Mina

27. A contrary opinion has recently been expressed by Vermeule 1987; however, he cites no examples of architectural elements to support his view and seems to have forgotten that almost all the marble used in Egypt for architectural carving in late antiquity came from the islands of the Proconnesos at Constantinople.
28. Severin 1977b, pp. 243 ff.
29. Many examples are known from Tuna el-Gebel, the necropolis of Hermopolis Magna; cf. Gabra 1941.

on four sides with arches on four corner pillars and bearing a symbolic tomb (*cenotaph*) above ground in its center. In this form it was used in the Christian and even the Islamic period. From the late 4th century on a variant of this type also appears, a closed building with thinner walls between the corner pillars.[30] Just as in former times, during the Hellenistic and high Imperial period, wealthy pagans often made their mausolea in the shape of small temples. After Christianity became the dominant religion, some Christians likewise built little chapels over their tombs or added one to the normal house-like mausoleum. Several examples are known from al-Bagawat, the necropolis of Hibis in Kharga-Oasis.[31] In the marginal areas of Abu Mina some underground burial chambers were recently discovered, the upper structure of which is a normal chapel suitable for regular services.

The ordinary mausolea served as sites where the family of the deceased could gather and share a meal (*silicernium*; Christian *refrigerium*) in memory of the deceased. Half-round clines have been found in the near neighborhood of some pagan as well as Christian mausolea at al-Bagawat that attest such meals.[32] During the later periods this habit went out of use, presumably because its relation with the pagan tradition was too close.

MONASTIC ARCHITECTURE

Monastic architecture developed to meet the needs of two sorts of monks, anchorites and coenobites. Anchorites, the earlier of the two, lived alone or, when in a larger congregation (*laura*), dwelt far from each other and took care of their personal needs individually. They prayed, ate, and worked alone, meeting with other brothers only during the church liturgy. Anchorites were accommodated in little houses (*kellia*) of two rooms, one for living, working, and reception, and the other (generally the smaller) for sleeping and prayer.[33] The rock-cut caves in the area of Deir al-Naqlun in the Fayum and in the neighborhood of the East Church at Abu Mina[34] are typical examples. In Kellia during the 6th and 7th centuries a very well-organized house type (*kellion*) was developed with separate sleeping rooms for two monks, storerooms, an oratory, kitchen, and reception room, all placed in the northeast corner of a small court.[35] Many of these were later enlarged by adding similar units, probably reserved for guests and additional pupils.

The *laura* in the area of Esna (Adayma) and west of Samalut (Kum Namrud, unpublished) had different types of houses. Of particular interest are the accommodations at Esna, which were built rather irregularly and below ground, each with a large central court open to the sky.[36] The reason for this unusual design was probably the threat of invading nomads. The method, however, was not successful, and after occupation for about 40 years the site was abandoned. The house units at Kum Namrud are more regular, with rooms distributed all along the eastern side of a small rectangular court.

Coenobites lived communally. According to the organization described by Pachomius (ca. 346),[37] the monasteries were surrounded by walls inside of which were large dwelling houses in which each monk had a room. Food was served once a day in special refectories (in several sittings, due to the large number of monks). There was also an infirmary as well as a guesthouse, the latter outside the wall to avoid communication with the secular world.

Unfortunately, no Pachomian monastery has yet been excavated. But remains of a similar monastery can be recognized in the Deir al-Balayza south of Asyut, also called "Monastery of Apa Apollo" after the texts found in its ruins.[38] Although this monastery does not follow Pachomius's rules precisely, it has sufficient similarities to be taken as an example. It is situated on a hillside, surrounded by a wall that encloses a roughly trapezoidal area.[39] The buildings in the area stand close together, leaving space only for some narrow streets or stairs. Most of the houses are long and narrow, accessible directly from the street through a door in the short side wall. They are clearly dormitories for a number of monks, with sleeping places lined up along the long side walls. In two- or three-storied houses of the same kind, three narrow rooms were placed parallel with a common corridor and stairs along the entrance side. In the lower area of the slope there are two large refectories, each probably composed of six aisles divided by five rows of vertical wooden supports. The monks probably sat on small circular benches such as survive in other earlier monasteries.[40]

The churches of this monastery are of lesser importance. An earlier and larger one is constructed inside the huge cave of a Roman quarry in the upper zone of the hill, and there is a small mud-brick chapel in the northeastern region. The building with several rooms outside the wall but near the main gate may well be the guesthouse.

30. A group of such tombs was excavated by an Italian mission at the south border of Antinoopolis; cf. Donadoni 1974, pp. 141 ff.
31. See Fakhry 1951.
32. Grossmann 1982b, pp. 78 ff.
33. Contemporary descriptions are given by Palladius, hist. Laus 8 (Hermitage of Amun), 19 (Hermitage of Macarius the Alexandrian), 35 (Hermitage of John of Lycopolis), and in the hist. Mon. 20.9 (Hermitage of Ammonius).
34. Grossmann 1967, pp. 463 ff.
35. See Weidmann 1986.

36. Sauneron and Jacquet 1972.
37. The texts have recently been republished in a very careful study: Bacht 1983.
38. Cf. Kahle 1954.
39. Grossmann 1986.
40. See Severin and Grossmann 1982 for the Saqqara monastery of Apa Jeremias, Monneret de Villard 1927, pp. 105 ff., fig. 114 for Deir Anba Hadra, and Scanlon 1972 for Qasr al-Wizz in Nubia.

CATALOGUE OF THE EXHIBITION

In the entries, dimensions are in centimeters; height precedes width and, where relevant, depth and outer dimensions.

Home

1

GROUP OF OBJECTS FOUND ON THE WINDOWSILL
OF A HOUSE

5th century
From Karanis, house BC61
Kelsey Museum of Archaeology, The University of
Michigan
Provenance: Excavated in 1926

*The people of Karanis often stored their household possessions
in wall niches with open fronts. In this house a window was bricked
up to make such a storage niche. The objects placed there provide
a fascinating glimpse of everyday life, since they appear as they
were left by the ancient householders. Fine tableware was placed
there – a large imported red-ware plate from North Africa (modern Tunisia), and a few nice but not fancy locally made glass
dishes, not enough for a matched set. When found during excavation, some of the glassware was carefully covered with baskets.
Much of this glass looks almost as it did when in use more than a
thousand years ago.*

*The two weavers' combs show the importance of cloth-making
in Egypt. The long spindle and spindle-whorl of wood were used
for the spinning of thread for cloth. Although skilled weavers turned
out fancy work and quotas of garments for the Roman army, it
is likely that some cloth was also made at home (see essay on
Textiles).[1] Note that one of the weaver's combs was broken and
mended in antiquity. The hair-combs with wide teeth at one end,
narrow at the other, are of the usual Egyptian type. The broken
comb was not thrown out but was thriftily saved. These items are
all quite plain, suggesting a household of moderate means.[2]*
S.A.

Bibliography: Boak and Peterson 1931; Peterson 1933, p. 53;
Gazda et al. 1983, fig. 43, p. 26.

1. Gazda et al. 1983, pp. 15–6, n. 35, with reference to a papyrus receipt
   from Karanis for compulsory tax weaving.
2. The contents of house BC61 windowsill are shown here as much as
   possible as they were found. The following items have had to be
   substituted, however, primarily because the originals were too fragile
   to travel: 5123 substitute for 5553; 7415 substitute for 51415 in Cairo
   Museum; 5898 substitute for 5511; 3461 substitute for 3903A–B;
   5163 addition inside basket; 3441 basket omitted. The group is discussed in Gazda et al. 1983, p. 26, fig. 43. The 2nd century date given
   there for the house is in my opinion too early, given the objects
   found on the windowsill, which are all of Late Roman type.

Color plate, page 13

1A

North African Red-Ware Bowl,
first half of the 5th century

Red-slipped pottery. 8.7 × 28.7

Kelsey Museum of Archaeology,
The University of Michigan. 3658

This type of good-quality pottery,
which was probably more durable than
the local wares, was imported from
North African workshops and later
imitated in Egypt. The fine pottery of
North Africa was shipped throughout
the Mediterranean region.[1] This deep
bowl is of dense orange clay with a
red-orange slip applied to the interior
and a third of the way down the exterior.
It is decorated on the interior with a
circle of feather rouletting. A brownish
stain marks the bottom of the interior.
S.A.

Bibligraphy: Johnson 1981, p. 48;
cf. no. 231, pl. 36;

1. Hayes 1972, form 91, type B/C 12, p. 141.
   Hayes 1980 modified his original chronology for this shape, putting it earlier, in the
   first half of the 5th century. This new
   dating affects the dates at which the town
   of Karanis is thought to have been abandoned. Hayes notes that the proposed
   sequence may need modification as new
   finds are made. For the dating, see also
   Bailey 1984b, p. 186.

1B

Lamp, late 3rd–6th century

Molded pottery. 3.9 × 11.5 × 7.3

Kelsey Museum of Archaeology,
The University of Michigan. 3634

This everyday lamp is blackened at
the nozzle from use. Like most Roman
pottery lamps, this one is formed in a
two-part mold that makes a raised
design on the top. It is of light brown
clay with a dull red slip. The design
consists of raised circles, dotted circles,
rays, and ribbed rectangles. There is a
splayed ring handle.[1] Such ancient lamps
give about as much light as one candle.
S.A.

Bibliography: Shier 1978, p. 145,
no. 430, pl. 45.

1. Shier 1978 dates this lamp to "the late
   3rd century A.D." However, see Bailey
   1984b, p. 186, who feels that these
   types "probably extend well into the 6th
   century."

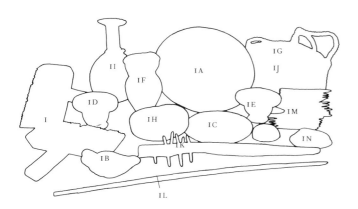

1 C

Oval Dish, 4th–5th century

Pale yellow glass with purple streaks.
5.2 × 21.5 × 14.6 (max.)

Kelsey Museum of Archaeology,
The University of Michigan. 5898

These oval dishes are especially characteristic of Egypt, and are not seen in
contemporary glassware elsewhere in
the Roman Empire.[1] Their rims are
folded out and down, and they have
high pad bases with pointed kicks and
pontil marks. A kick is an indentation on
the bottom of a glass formed during
manufacture. A pontil mark is made
when a piece of blown glass is knocked
off the solid metal rod that was used to
hold it at the base while the rim and
upper portions were being finished.
Harden notes that this type of oval dish
was among the most popular shapes of
glass at Karanis in the later occupation
period of the town.
S.A.

Bibliography: Harden 1936, no. 25,
p. 55.

1. Harden 1936, p. 54, describes the manufacturing technique used for this shape;
dating is discussed on p. 47.

1 D

Deep Bowl with Vertical Rim,
4th–5th century

Yellow-green glass. Rim D. 11.5
Base D. 5.7; Base H. 10.5

Kelsey Museum of Archaeology,
The University of Michigan. 5532

The bell-shaped body splays out horizontally at the top with a deep vertical
rim folded out and down; the high pad
base has a pointed kick and pontil mark.
S.A.

Bibliography: Harden 1936, no. 228,
pp. 106–7.

1 E

Deep Bowl with Vertical Rim,
4th–5th century

Pale forest-green glass. H. 6–6.5;
Rim D. 12.4; Base D. 5.5; Base H. 1.3

Kelsey Museum of Archaeology,
The University of Michigan. 5533

This bowl is of the same shape as the
preceding one (cat. no. 1D), but is more
lopsided and made of a more bubbly
fabric.
S.A.

Bibliography: Harden 1936, no. 229,
p. 107.

1 F

*Jar with à-Jour (Openwork) Thread
Decoration,* 4th–5th century

Pale yellow-green glass with green neck
threads. H. 16; Rim D. 9–10; Base D. 6.7

Kelsey Museum of Archaeology,
The University of Michigan. 5123

Note the indents in the body formed
during the blowing process. The splayed
base is marked with slanting tool marks,
a characteristic of Karanis glass. There is
a small kick with pontil mark.[1]
S.A.

Bibliography: Harden 1936, p. 321,
class VIII.

1. Cf. Harden 1936, p. 321; cf. nos. 497–8,
and see p. 174 for dating.

1 G

Flask with Thread-Decorated Rim,
4th–5th century

Pale yellow-green glass with self-colored
threads. 14.6

Kelsey Museum of Archaeology,
The University of Michigan. 5163

The base has kick and pontil mark.[1] The
flask has been placed in the palm leaf
basket (1J).
S.A.

Bibliography: Harden 1936, p. 327,
class XIIB.

1. Cf. Harden 1936, no. 783, p. 262, pls. 10,
20; the dating is discussed on p. 254. The
glass found on the windowsill all compares
with Karanis examples found in later
4th–5th century levels.

1 H

Straight-Sided Footed Bowl,
4th–5th century

Light yellow-green glass with slight
purple streaks, many bubbles and
impurities. 4.5 × 14.9; Base D. 7

Kelsey Museum of Archaeology,
The University of Michigan. 5524

This bowl, a common shape at Karanis,
is characterized by a rim which is folded
outwards, a short base with diagonal
tool marks and a pontil mark with pronounced triangular kick.[1]
S.A.

Bibliography: Harden 1936, no. 100,
pp. 73–4.

1. See Harden 1936, pp. 63–5 for the type.

1 I

Decanter, 4th–5th century

Colorless glass with yellow-green tinge.
Slight mauve streak in body. Medium
green glass neck thread. H. 23; Rim
D. 8.3; Base D. 7.5; Neck H. 9

Kelsey Museum of Archaeology,
The University of Michigan. 5563

This decanter of thin, almost transparent
glass is typical of the fine-quality wares
produced in Coptic Egypt. The green
frill around the neck was formed from
a thick glass thread quickly pulled out
into points while still hot. Note the
decorative indents on the body.[1]
S.A.

Bibliography: Harden 1936, no. 535,
p. 198.

1. For a discussion of the dating, see Harden
1936, p. 191.

IJ
Palm Leaf Basket, 4th–5th century

Palm fiber. 12–15.5 × L. 28.5 × W. at top 10.7

Kelsey Museum of Archaeology, The University of Michigan. 3461

This basket closely resembles the one found on the windowsill of Karanis House BC61, which is badly disintegrated. It is closely woven of flat plaited palm fibers reinforced by single and double strands of palm-fiber rope fastened to the rim, in an "x" pattern on the base, and in a vertical and diagonal pattern below each of the two handles. The pale orange-beige color has darkened to brown, and there are some holes in the bottom. A glass flask (1G) has been placed in the basket to indicate a common use of baskets at Karanis as containers for glassware. Many glasses were found protected by baskets.
S.A.

IK
Stirring Stick, 4th–5th century

Wood. 42.3, length of pegs 10

Kelsey Museum of Archaeology, The University of Michigan. 7415

This is a long tapering piece of wood in which holes were drilled for the insertion of pegs, originally eight in all. Without additional evidence its use cannot be determined. It would have been large enough for stirring wool in a dye vat, but in that case the wood ought to show signs of staining. There are long cracks in the stick, and some pegs are broken, with one missing.
S.A.

IL
Spindle and Spindle Whorl, 4th–5th century

Dark wood. Spindle 60.2; whorl 2.7 × D. 6.6

Kelsey Museum of Archaeology, The University of Michigan. 3669, 3860

The fiber woven on this spindle was probably linen, the material used in many garments, covers, and hangings. Some spindles found at Antinoe with whorls of comparable size have twists of ancient linen attached.[1] The carved wood whorl has a flat base and a rounded grooved top with a small center hole. It fits onto the spindle, which is merely a slightly curved stick. This spindle seems unusually long; however, a number of others found at Karanis are about the same length.[2]
S.A.

1. Closest is Rutschowscaya 1986, p. 44, no. 65. Rutschowscaya notes that many spindles are made of the wood of the olive tree that was cultivated in the Fayum region.
2. Cf. Kelsey Museum 3353A–B of which the spindle is 61 cm. long.

IM
Two Hair Combs, 5th century

Wood. 1: 13.5 × 7; 2: 13 × 4

Kelsey Museum of Archaeology, The University of Michigan. 3567, 1017

Like many Coptic combs, these are made of a light-weight dark brown wood, almost certainly imported boxwood.[1] The portion between the rows of fine and coarse teeth is incised with simple line-and-circle motifs.[2] The second comb is broken in half lengthways.
S.A.

1. Rutschowscaya 1986, p. 15; pp. 26–35. Of 38 Louvre wooden combs catalogued, all but two were made of boxwood. The wood came from Asia Minor, North Africa, or Europe.
2. Rutschowscaya 1986, no. 27, p. 32 is similar in size and shape, without decoration.

IN
Shell Found in Basket on Windowsill, 5th century

From Karanis, House BC61

Pale yellow. 10.5 × 6.3

Museum of Anthropology, The University of Michigan (formerly Kelsey Museum 3708)

This shell was probably picked up casually by a Karanis resident and kept as a souvenir. Although fossilized prehistoric shells have been found near Karanis, this one is not of that type. The species has recently been identified as a fresh water shell from the Nile, called *Aspotharia rubens*. It was probably used as a container for small items. Other shells of this species from Karanis were ground down on one end for use as scrapers for working leather or decorating pottery.[1]
S.A.

1. Information from David S. Reese, Field Museum of Natural History, Chicago.

2

Wine Jar with Faces and Grape Vines in Relief, 4th–mid-5th century

From Karanis

Clay. H. 50.5, rim D. 14.2, foot D. 11.6

Kelsey Museum of Archaeology,
The University of Michigan. 3425

The unexpected decoration of this wine jar lends a sense of fun to an otherwise utilitarian pottery vessel and reflects both the skill and playfulness of the Karanis potter. This hefty thick-walled wine jar is made of pinkish-brown clay with a dark brown surface coating. It was thrown in at least two parts, with one horizontal join clearly visible part-way up the body, the other concealed at the junction of the neck and shoulder. The shape combines the cylindrical neck and vertical handles of a wine amphora with the flat base and body shape of a water jug.[1] On each side of the neck a face is worked in relief.[2] Small circles of raised clay called barbotine decoration ring the vessel at neck and rim, giving the impression of a necklace and hair. Barbotine decoration on the shoulder forms a raised design of grape clusters springing from the vine. A group of punched circles at the top of each handle also indicates grape clusters.
S.A.

Bibliography: Johnson 1981, no. 148, pl. 21, pp. 5–6, 38.

1. Cf. Quibell 1912, pl. 48, 5 for a large two-handled jar with a face on the neck.
2. Two examples are illustrated in Murray 1935, pl. II, 2, p. 2 and pl. VII, 2, p. 2.

3
Cylindrical Vase with Three Ring
Feet, late 3rd–4th century

From Karanis

Painted pottery. H.11

Kelsey Museum of Archaeology,
The University of Michigan. 7740

This cylindrical vase has a most unusual
feature – its three looped feet are formed
like handles from flat clay strips. The
exterior is blackened but not the exterior,
suggesting that something, possibly
incense, was burnt inside. Five additional complete examples of this type
are recorded from Karanis; additional
fragments may have been found as well.
The surface is carefully finished with a
smoothly burnished red slip on which
bands of matte purple with white dots
have been applied.
s.a.

Bibliography: Johnson 1981, no. 45,
pl. 5, pp. 2–3, 25.

4
Water Jug with Shiny Black Design,
4th–mid-5th century

From Karanis

Clay with bitumen decoration.
H. 19.6–20.2; Rim D. 6.8, Base D. 5.4

Kelsey Museum of Archaeology,
The University of Michigan. 8094

This is one of a group of similarly decorated water jugs found at Karanis. It has the practical feature of a three-hole strainer inside the rim to keep out insects and a drinking spout on the side. The porous cream-yellow clay allows gradual evaporation from the surface to cool the contents, while the black bitumen makes a waterproof coating for the base, rim, and spout. The bitumen also forms a design on the body in the shape of a stylized bird within a wavy-line frame. This type of decoration with bitumen may have been peculiar to the Fayum area.[1] Water jugs from other areas have a different type of ornamentation.[2]
s.a.

Bibliography: Johnson 1981, no. 160, pl. 25, pp. 6–7, 40.

1. Same type, probably from Hawara in the Fayum: Bourriau 1981, no. 180, p. 92. Several examples of this type shown in pl. 7 of Murray 1935 may also be from Petrie's excavation at Hawara.
2. Water jugs from Kellia have a white slip with red and black painted decoration (Egloff 1977, II, pl. 23 and color pls. 1, 2, 3; he notes that the capacity of these jugs is slightly less than half a liter, about one U.S. pint). The hermitages at Esna in Upper Egypt have yet another decoration: Jacquet-Gordon 1972, p. 50, pl. 216, 21.

5
Tall-Necked Jar with White Painted Motifs, probably 3rd century

From Karanis

Slipped clay. H. 24, Base D. 8.6

Kelsey Museum of Archaeology,
The University of Michigan. 20678

The decoration of this jar is intriguing in its depiction of birds pecking at grapes, a motif from Graeco-Roman art that was popular in Coptic Egypt. The whimsical addition of fish and a donkey is a characteristic local adaptation. The design is quite unlike contemporary pottery elsewhere in the Mediterranean world.

The jar originally had a tall cylindrical neck with slightly out-turned rim. The reddish-brown slip covers the upper half of the pot, with streaks dripping lower down. Finely drawn cream-colored designs ornament the neck and upper body. Three vertical branches running from the rim to the middle of the body separate the design into three panels. The first shows two birds pecking at a grape cluster that hangs from a stylized branch. A fish swims to the right above each bird. The second panel has the same design as the first, with the addition of a Greek inscription. Fish above birds swim towards each other. The third panel is the same as the previous one, but lacks the inscription, and depicts a donkey in place of the left-hand bird. The lower portion is intact, but there has been mending and some restoration to the shoulder and neck. The upper neck and rim are missing.

S.A.

Bibliography: Johnson 1981, no. 184, pl. 29, pp. 7–8, 42; n. 47, p. 92.

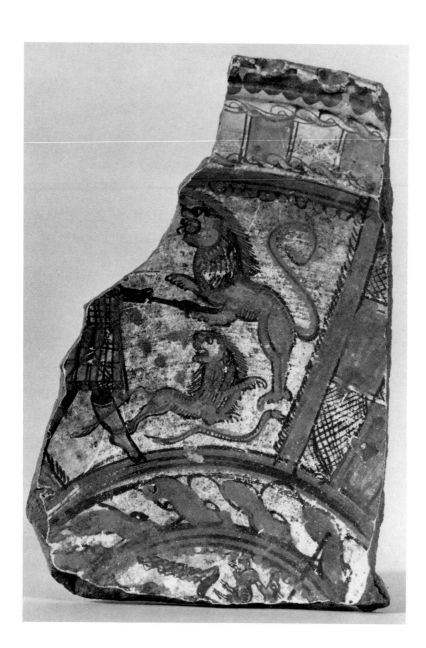

6

Fragment of a Deep Bowl with a Design of a Wild Beast Fight, 6th century (?)

Friable pale brown clay, white-slipped, with black and orange painted decoration. H. 15; Rim D. 32, Base ring D. 18, thickness 1.5

Museum of Fine Arts, Boston, Gift of Herbert Hoffman. 64.130

This tantalizing fragment comes from an impressively large and elaborately decorated bowl. What remains shows a scene from a *venatio* or wild beast fight in the arena.[1] A figure clad in boots and a short tunic, perhaps covered with a leather cuirass (indicated by the black cross-hatching), spears a lion. Below, a second, smaller lion and a snake move off to the right. The scene is enclosed in a rectangular frame with what looks like a paneled door to the right. Above the figure scene is a band of alternating white and orange rectangles, and below, a band of guilloche that frames a central tondo.

Only a small gazelle and an unidentifiable decorative motif remain from the tondo design. Perhaps the tondo showed the wild animals being captured, while a series of rectangular pictures above showed fights with various animals in the amphitheater.

Chariot races and gladiatorial contests of various kinds were very popular in the Roman and Byzantine periods throughout the Mediterranean region. Each major town and city had its arena, and mob excitement and violence were features of the contest. The Alexandrians were notable for their volatility at these events.[2]

S.A.

Bibliography: Museum of Fine Arts, Boston 1976, no. 251, p. 209.

1. Metropolitan Museum of Art 1979 illustrates some early Byzantine representations of various types of beast fights.
2. Bowman 1986, pp. 215–6.

7
Fish-Shaped Vase with Scales,
date unknown

Painted clay. 14 × 26.7

Collection of the Newark Museum.
29.1064

Provenance: Purchased in Egypt in 1929

This wine jug in the form of a broad-
backed fish has a strainer opening for
filling on the top between the loop
handles, and pours out liquid through
its gaping mouth. The coarse orange-red
clay has been roughened to suggest
scales and covered with white slip highlighted with black outlines. The humor
of this appealing wine jug was certainly
intentional!
S.A.

8

Large Wide-Mouthed Vase with Animals Under Arches,
5th–6th century

Painted clay. H. 26.5, Rim D. 16.5, W. at shoulder 21.5, Base D. 10

Collection of the Newark Museum. 84.299

Provenance: Fouquet Collection; Dikran Khan Kelekian Collection; R. Sturgis Ingersoll

This vase, intact but with some whitish incrustation, belongs to a group of painted pottery with similar designs and stylistic peculiarities. The elaborate design and fine painting of these vases stands out from more ordinary Coptic ceramics. One example has been found at Karanis[1] and two at Saqqara,[2] while a number of others are in American and European museum collections.[3] One workshop and in some cases even one artist must have produced these distinctive wares. We are not sure where the factory was located, but it is clear from some surviving examples that production continued past the Islamic conquest.[4]

This large vase is covered on the exterior with an orange-brown slip on which a very detailed, precisely drawn design has been outlined in black. A wide frieze band on the body is divided by overlapping arches that frame floral and animal motifs; a deer, a winged griffin-crocodile, a three-stalked flower and a complex interlace pattern. Interlace, leaf, and vine scroll bands ornament the neck and shoulder; plain black horizontal lines, the space from the bottom of the frieze to the foot. Fleurs de lys fill the spaces between the arches, while groups of dots on stems fringe their interior. Groups of dots accent the outlines of the animals. Animal and geometric motifs overhang their groundlines; the feet of the animals hang down limply. The dense, flat, space-filling design echoes the patterns on many contemporary textiles.

S.A.

1. Kelsey Museum of Archaeology 7967; Johnson 1981, p. 33 under 108; H. 22.5 cm.
2. Quibell 1912, p. 140, pl. 51, H. 80 cm. (paired doves, gazelle pair, lion and gazelle, flower). Severin and Grossmann 1982, p. 159, pl. 24A, B, C ("various animals" including gazelle, horse, lion, bird).
3. Berlin, Staatliche Museen 3500, Bröker 1970, fig. 66; Wulff 1909, no. 1509 (horse, lion, bird and gazelles). Allard Pierson Museum, Amsterdam, 3840. A similar design is transferred to a large plate in the Louvre (du Bourguet 1971, color pl. p. 116 (birds and gazelles)).
4. A very large example is in the Metropolitan Museum of Art, 23.2.74; Dimand 1924b, pp. 123–4; Dimand 1924c, pp. 269–73, as "8th century."

9
Jar with Design of Cocks,
5th century

From Egypt

Painted, slipped clay. H 17. Rim D. 11.4,
Base D. 7.2, Max. D. 18.2

Royal Ontario Museum. 910.176.42

Like many large painted Coptic storage
jars, this one is made of a surprisingly
coarse red-brown Nile river clay. The
rim is thickened with horizontal groov-
ing on the exterior, and there is a rope-
like band just above the shoulder. The
surface is coated with a cream-yellowish
slip on which the design is applied in
brownish-black outlines with orange
filling and black detailing. The white
slip continues up to the interior of the
rim and is enlivened by a design of
orange on black stripes alternating with
plain black bands. The wide central
pattern band is bordered above by a
cable pattern and below by a series of
plain horizontal ground lines. Four
sketchily drawn animals fill the frieze
space: three cocks facing to the right
separated by rosettes and a long-eared
animal (a hare?) with its face turned up
and back. Diagonal and horizontal bands
of black arrow shapes fill in the spaces
between the animals. The hooves and
claws of the animals dangle below the
groundline, a stylistic feature seen in
other Coptic painted pots (for example,
cat. no. 8) and also on textiles. It shows
the lack of interest in the weight and
solidity of objects and their existence in
space that is typical of other art of this
period.[1]

This jar is broken and mended, with a
hole in its shoulder, and the surface is
worn away in small patches.
S.A.

Bibliography: Hayes 1976, no. 261, p. 50.

1. Lowrie 1965, pp. 4–5.

10

Storage Jar with Spiral Decoration,
probably 5th century

From Egypt

Painted, slipped clay. 29.7–30.3 (Rim
D. 24.7–25, Base D.15.5, Max D. 31.8)

Royal Ontario Museum, Walter Massey
Collection. 916.1.76

This hefty storage jar is made of the
same red-brown clay as the previous jar
with animal design (cat. no. 9) and
shares with it a thickened rim with
orange and black design bands. There
are two pattern bands: a top one of black
and orange wave pattern with spirals
above and below each crest, and a bottom one of broadly painted alternating
black and orange horizontal lines.
Despite their differences in scale and
fineness of slip and decoration, these
pots look so similar that they could well
have been made in the same workshop.
S.A.

Bibliography: Hayes 1976, no. 262,
pp. 50–1.

11

Red-Ware Plate with Bird Design,
ca. 1000–1200

From Nubia

Dense pinkish-buff clay with orange-red slip and black painted decoration. H. 8.2, Rim D. 27.3, Base ring D. 8

Museum of Fine Arts, Boston. Harvard University – MFA Expedition. 47.1672

Provenance: Excavated at Sarras, Nubia in 1931

This very well-made large plate (with whitish incrustation and pitting) is set on a small ring base and looks very like the pottery bowl imported from North Africa and used at Karanis (cat. no. 1A). It was in fact made in Nubia to the south of Egypt, at a much later date.[1] Unlike the North African pottery which had stamped decoration, this example is ornamented with black painted designs: a square-tailed bird in the center and a line-and-wave pattern around the rim. Potters in Egypt, particularly at a factory in Aswan, adapted the North African wares and exported them to Nubia. It must have been from these imports that the Nubian potters derived tableware of this type. It is striking how long this basic type of pottery continued beyond its original Roman prototypes.

S.A.

Bibliograpy: Reisner and Wheeler 1967, vol. 2, pp. 131, 137, fig. 6, pl. 67; Museum of Fine Arts, Boston 1976, no. 252, p. 209.

1. W. Y. Adams kindly informs me that this plate is a well-defined type of Nubian ware (Adams 1986, Group N.V., Ware 21, Form D23, Decoration style N. VA). See Adams 1986, Pt. I, p. 53 for the general type, pp. 330–1, figs 182–3 for the decoration, Pt. II, pp. 496–8, fig. 282, D23 for the shape and chronological range.

12

Very Flat Round Plate,
2nd–3rd century

From the Fayum

Colorless glass with pale green tint. Rim folded down and out. Tubular base ring.
2 × 17.5

Kelsey Museum of Archaeology,
The University of Michigan. 5001

Provenance: Askren Collection

This remarkably well-preserved flat plate[1] is earlier and rarer than some of the other specimens shown. It is an excellent example of the translucent qualities of blown glass. More popular than very flat plates such as this were ones of pottery, glass or precious metals with small lips or rims to prevent the contents from tipping out.
S.A.

Bibliography: Harden 1936, p. 318.

1. See Harden 1936, pp. 49–51 for a discussion of the shape. See also Root 1982, p. 39, Vitrine XIV, 10.

13
Tall One-Handled Jug,
4th century

From the Fayum

Blown glass, rim folded in, glass bubbly, with blowing spirals. H. 20.5, Rim D. 7.5, Base D. 6

Kelsey Museum of Archaeology, The University of Michigan. 5157.

Provenance: Askren Collection

This pale yellow-green jug has a tall oval body, cylindrical neck with circular mouth, and a small pad base with diagonal tool marks. The sturdy vertical strap handle is of bubbly pale-green glass. Variations on this useful vessel shape were made in workshops throughout the Roman Empire.[1]

S.A.

Bibliography: Harden 1936, pp. 232, 326.

1. For an example, see Auth 1976, no. 121, p. 106 from Syria.

14
Flask with Patterned Body,
4th–5th century

From Karanis

Blown and pattern-molded glass; rim
folded in. H. 21.5; D. at shoulder 14

Kelsey Museum of Archaeology,
The University of Michigan. 5944

This simple but well-proportioned
flask was undoubtedly used as a wine
decanter. It was given its fluted body
design by blowing into a mold followed
by twisting and free-blowing. The
shape, with its tall funnel-shaped neck,
is similar to Late Roman glass made
on the eastern Mediterranean coast.
S.A.

Bibliography: Harden 1936, no. 612,
p. 211, pls. 8, 18; Root 1982, p. 41, no. 9,
pl. 6, p. 12.

15
Flask with Contrasting Handles,
4th–5th century

From Karanis

Blown glass bubbly. Funnel rim, folded
up and in. Pointed kick. H. 14

Kelsey Museum of Archaeology,
The University of Michigan. 5945

Even an ordinary flask like this one is
carefully decorated. It has multiple twists
of green glass under the rim and ring
handles of the same color. The green
contrasts with the yellowish-brown
color of the body.
S.A.

Bibliography: Harden 1936, no. 784,
p. 262; Root 1982, p. 39, case 15, no. 2.

16

Stemmed Cup, 4th century

From Karanis

Blown pale olive-green glass; H. 9;
Rim D. 7; Base D. 3.5

Kelsey Museum of Archaeology,
The University of Michigan. 5964

This delicate stemmed goblet was the
most common type of drinking glass
in the Late Antique and Byzantine
world. In many excavations only the
sturdier feet of the goblets are found,[1]
but at Karanis the ancient inhabitants'
habit of carefully storing their glass in
boxes, baskets, and pottery containers
preserved fragile pieces such as this
complete.[2]

S.A.

1. Von Saldern 1980, pp. 53–8, pl. 24; Auth
   in Clairmont et al. 1975, pp. 164–5,
   table 7, pl. 31.
2. Harden 1936, pp. 34–7 lists groups of
   glass found in containers at Karanis. See
   also Root 1982, p. 10, pl. 1.

17

Censer, 5th century

Said to have come from northern Iraq

Bronze. 24.5 × 7.5

The Art Museum, Princeton
University, Museum purchase. 33–5

This anthropomorphic incense burner,
probably used in the home, has two
parts: a tall conical hat with suspension
ring and two rows of air holes; and,
connected by a hinge, a stylized female
head atop a thick flaring neck. The
figure's face is distinguished by small
puckered lips, broad puffy cheeks, and
continuous nose and eyebrows atop
elongated, bulbous eyes with drilled
pupils. The neck, which rises from three
simple feet, bears four incised rings; in
addition, the figure wears a necklace,
earrings, and a simple fillet.

   This form of censer derives from
more elegant Roman-period antecedents.[1] Although it is said to have been
found in Iraq, this striking piece of
bronze figurative sculpture bears close
comparison with a pair of anthropomorphic bronzes (a censer and a water jug)
in Berlin, known to have come from
Egypt.[2] Moreover, its protruding eyes
and pursed lips are like those of several
familiar pieces of Early Byzantine limestone sculpture in the Coptic Museum,
Cairo.[3] Indeed, such expressive stylization is characteristic of the best art of
that region and period.
G.V.

Bibliography: The Art Museum, Princeton University 1986, no. 53. Baltimore
Museum of Art 1947, no. 275.

1. For example, Baltimore Museum of Art
   1947, no. 276.
2. Wulff 1909, nos. 978, 1035.
3. Duthuit 1931 (e.g., pl. XXXIIA).

18

Spoon, 4th–7th century

Bronze. L. 16.4

The Brooklyn Museum, Charles Edwin
Wilbour Fund. 70.90.1

Significant numbers of spoons survive
from Late Antiquity in wood, bone,
bronze, and silver. This example is
unusually elaborate. It is distinguished
by a large round bowl with serrated
forward edge, and a richly profiled flat
handle terminating in a pair of juxtaposed birds; both bowl and handle are
covered by circles with punched centers.
The round bowl identifies it as a *cochlear*
(vs. the larger *ligula,* with its pearshaped
bowl), which is believed to have been
used for eating shellfish and eggs.[1] The
circles with punched centers are common
on the decorative arts in all media during
this period in Egypt.
G.V.

1. Walters Art Gallery 1986, nos. 18, 22.

19

Key, 5th–7th century

Said to have come from Egypt

Bronze. 9.1 × 5.1

The Walters Art Gallery, Baltimore.
54.1023

Among the most essential implements for security in any culture are keys. This particular type, shared by many cultures, is called a "turning key," because after being inserted into the lock it is turned in order to advance or retract the bolt.[1] Security is provided by the fact that only a bit of the proper size can successfully engage the bolt as it is positioned over or to the side of the keyhole. Yet its technology – which was invented by the Romans and survives to this day in "skeleton keys" – is obviously very simple and, predictably, such locks were easily picked.

A complementary dimension of security was often provided by a personal seal, most often applied with a ring intaglio. In this key, as in most others of its type, the function of the seal was incorporated into the design of the key by the inclusion of a swivel ring handle, as shown here. Although lacking a personalized intaglio, the ring handle bears a sealing bezel. As one walked around the house the ring would be slipped over the finger and the key neatly folded into the palm of the hand. G.V.

Bibliography: unpublished

1. For the typology and functioning of keys see Vikan and Nesbitt 1980, pp. 2 ff.

20

Furniture Decoration: Apollo,
3rd–4th century

Bone. 14.9 × 5.3

The Walters Art Gallery, Baltimore.
71.43

Provenance: Purchased from Polovtsoff,
Paris, 1928

Bone and ivory inlays were used to
decorate household furniture objects
such as couches and chests. Mythological subjects, like this example of a nude
Apollo, are common and testify to the
continued use of classical imagery in
Early Christian Egypt. Most pagan
subjects, however, held no religious
meaning and were simply decorative
elements used throughout the Empire
by the well-to-do who identified themselves with the educated elite.

The inlay reflects a naturalistic style
characteristic of Hellenistic art that was
still maintained in much Late Roman
Egyptian work. The languid pose of the
god as he leans against the tree, grasping
a branch in one hand and resting the
other arm on his lyre, recalls a 4th century B.C. prototype, the Apollo Lykeios
of Praxiteles.[1] The lyre is set on a tripod,
with a snake coiled around one leg.
F.D.F.

Bibliography: *The Art News*, March 4,
1939, p. 10, ill; Wessel in Villa Hügel
1963, no. 213; Randall 1985, no. 121.

1. Randall 1985, no. 121.

21

Furniture Decoration:
Panel with Dionysus, Ariadne,
and a Cupid, 4th–5th century

Bone. 5.4 × 9.2

The Walters Art Gallery, Baltimore.
71.1127

Provenance: Purchased from the Estate
of Dikran Khan Kelekian, New York,
1951

Figures of the god Dionysus figure
prominently on Early Byzantine objects,
ranging from textiles and mosaics to
smaller works like this lunette-shaped
panel from a chest. Aside from its decorative function, the image of Dionysus
also had considerable religious significance in Egypt where he became a god
of immortality (see Textile essay). On
this small plaque a half-nude, draped
Ariadne reclines to the right, with
Dionysus standing above to the left.
The Cupid alludes to the romantic subject matter. Dionysus and Ariadne
became lovers after her abandonment by
Theseus on the Mediterranean island of

Naxos. A number of sculptural renditions
of this mythological subject, found even
on sarcophagi, show a sleeping Ariadne
just before Dionysus finds her.[1] The
associations with rebirth and immortality connected to Ariadne may possibly
be alluded to here.

According to Randall, such plaques
"filled lunettes above paired columns of
a figure or other subjects."[2]
F.D.F.

Bibliography: Randall 1985, no. 143.

1. Ridgway 1972, p. 129.
2. Randall 1985, no. 143.

22

Furniture Decoration:
Figure of a Woman, 4th–5th century

Bone. 9.1 × 4

The Walters Art Gallery, Baltimore. 71.6

Provenance: Purchased before 1931

The deep linear carving of this furniture inlay was originally filled with colored wax that would have emphasized the volume of the figure and the folds of drapery. Like much sculpture that has lost its original polychromy (see Sculpture essay), the smaller decorative arts could also bear bright colors.
F.D.F.

Bibliography: Baltimore Museum of Art 1947, no. 191; Randall 1985, no. 152.

23
Furniture Decoration:
Female Figure, 4th–5th century

Bone. 5 × 9.5

The Walters Art Gallery, Baltimore.
71.56

Provenance: Purchased from Dikran
Khan Kelekian, Paris, before 1931

A nereid (sea-nymph) is probably the
subject of this inlay, originally one of
many inlays that composed a decorative
border on a piece of furniture.[1] With her
drapery billowing behind, she appears
to be swiftly moving across the seas, not
unlike the limestone relief of a nereid
from the Columbus Museum of Art (cat.
no. 171). Her long, boneless limbs and
attenuated torso typify the breakdown
of naturalism in the art of the Early
Byzantine period.
F.D.F.

Bibliography: Baltimore Museum of Art
1947, no. 175; Randall 1985, no. 142.

1. Randall 1985, no. 142.

24
Appliqué From a Chest: Eagle With Monogram,
later 6th to 7th century

Gilt bronze. 10 × 9

The Malcove Collection, University of Toronto. M82.396

This energetic eagle, with its stylized wings, splayed tail, sharply curving beak, and bulla, has close parallels from Coptic Egypt in a variety of media.[1] Its size, material, and the attachment holes in its wings, tail, and feet suggest that it was once applied to a wooden object, and indeed a similar eagle (without monogram) appears with four other animals as part of an openwork appliqué handle on a Coptic chest lid now in Berlin.[2]

In Late Antiquity the eagle often appeared as an emblem of power and victory, for example, on grave stelae (see cat. no. 176). Yet at the same time it was clearly used for its purely decorative value and was often, as here, made to display a monogram. The form of this (apparently Latin) monogram – comprised of N-K-I-N – is a cross, indicating a date no earlier than the mid-6th century.[3] It no doubt identified the owner of the chest or other object to which it was attached.

G.V.

Bibliography: Campbell 1985, no. 94.

1. See, for example, entry 23 in Vikan forth-coming catalogue of the sculpture in the Dumbarton Oaks collection.
2. Wulff 1909, no. 831.
3. See Weigand 1931, pp. 412 ff.

Most of the glass vessels found at Karanis represent the commoner everyday types used in ordinary households. However, fragments and complete vessels of finer glass, some treasured in antiquity as heirlooms, have been found in Egypt as well. This luxury glassware was a specialty manufacture of the city of Alexandria in Egypt.[1] This manufacture is more clearly documented in ancient literature than in archaeological finds from Alexandria itself, for that ancient city is now partially submerged by the rising water levels of the Mediterranean.

Egyptian luxury glass was shipped in antiquity as far away as Roman Germany and Britain to the west, and the Kushan kingdom in Afghanistan to the east.[2] The figure-engraved and painted glasses on view here have subject matter from Graeco-Roman culture that relates to later Coptic art.

1. For the relationship between the Alexandrian and Western Roman glass industries, see Harden 1969, pp. 54–5, and Grose 1983, p. 45.
2. Auth 1983, p. 42, with refs. For western finds, see Harden 1969, p. 54, n. 49.

25
Fragment of Bowl Engraved with a Bird, 2nd–3rd century

From Egypt

Blown glass decorated with engraving.
5 × 5.7

The Corning Museum of Glass, Corning, New York. 55.1.89

This fragment of reddish-purple glass probably came from a small deep bowl with an outcurved rim.[1] Horizontal cut bands frame a design of a bird in hollow cutting with the feathers indicated by fine narrow incisions. The closely observed bird is typical of the Egyptians' interest at all periods in the natural world around them. A branch and flower are indicated also. The cutting was probably done with copper wheels using emery powder and water as abrasives. Some details were scratched in by hand.
s.a.

Bibliography: Smith 1957, no. 369, pp. 182–3.

1. The shape may have resembled that of the Artemis and Actaeon bowl in Corning Museum of Glass 1987, no. 107, p. 197.

26
Fragment of Painted Glass Bowl,
2nd–early 3rd century

From Egypt

Blown glass with enameled decoration.
3.5 × 3.3

The Corning Museum of Glass,
Corning, New York. 59.1.84

This greenish-colorless fragment of
glass (the surface is crackled from weathering) is curved as if from a bowl. The
design is applied on the exterior in matte
opaque pigments fired in the kiln to fix
them to the surface. The preserved
design shows the legs of a male figure in
a short tunic and boots with part of a
semicircular object to the left of the
figure, perhaps a shield. The painting is
outlined in a sketchy brown contour and
filled in with pink for the skin, yellow
for the boots and tunic, and pink and
brown for folds and interior details. A
very small section of a groundline is
preserved below the feet.

This figure may be a lightly armed
gladiator from a scene of pairs of fight-
ing gladiators.[1] Curiously, the largest
number of complete enamel-painted
glasses has been found in the hoard of a
Kushan prince at Begram in Afghanistan.[2] Imports from Alexandria combined
with ones from India at this site. The
painted glasses show a great range of
finely painted themes done in a very
competent painterly style that must
reflect both book illustrations[3] and
larger-scale wall paintings that have
now disappeared. A later development
in Egypt of painting on glass is seen in
luster painting (a low-fired metallic
stain), which begins with Coptic and
Christian motifs and continues in the
Islamic glass of Egypt.[4]
S.A.

Bibliography: Smith 1957, no. 345,
p. 169.

1. See Hamelin 1954, pl. 19 for more
complete examples
2. See Hamelin 1953, pp. 121–3 on the
Kushan hoard with references to original
publications.
3. A possible example of this is the Cohn
Collection beaker now in Los Angeles
County Museum, Weitzmann and Turner
1981, pp. 39, 43–8.
4. For a complete beaker with Tree of Life in
urn in luster paintings, see Honey 1946,
pl. 16 D; compare this same theme on a
number of Coptic textiles. For two fragments with Christian subjects from the
Monastery of St. Jeremias, Saqqara, see
Lamm 1941, pl. VI, 1 and VII, 1. Claimont
1977, pp. 36–8 gives a good summary of
the early history of luster painting on
glass in Egypt.

27

Fragment of Bowl Engraved with Mythological Figure, late 2nd century

From Egypt

Blown glass with engraved decoration. 7.5

The Corning Museum of Glass, Corning, New York. L. 59.1.138

This greenish-colorless glass fragment (the interior surface is crackled with weathering) is from the curving surface of a bowl. It is engraved on the exterior with deep cutting filled in with more shallowly scratched details. The head of a male figure looks to the left towards an inscription scratched from right to left in Greek. This inscription is intelligible, however, only when read from left to right as seen from the inside by someone drinking from the bowl. The name (ΙΠΠΟ) then possibly reads as Hippolytos. Hippolytos, son of Theseus and the Amazon Antiope in Greek myth, met a tragic end when his horses bolted before a sea monster sent by the god Poseidon. Complete examples show that these small bowls were generally engraved with a single mythological scene in which the human figures' names could be read correctly from the interior as the bowl was used.

It may seem strange that glasses with Greek myths and Greek inscriptions were made in Egypt. Yet the city of Alexandria where these were made had served since its foundation as a bridgehead of Greek culture in Egypt. Such products would have appealed to the large population of Greeks living in Egypt, and show the strong underpinning of Greek artistic ideas that underlies much of later Coptic art.
S.A.

Bibliography: Smith 1957, no. 361, p. 179.

28

Fragment of Bowl Engraved with Mythological Figure, late 2nd century

From Egypt

Blown glass with engraved decoration. 6

The Corning Museum of Glass, Corning, New York. 61.1.10

Like the previous fragment, this scrap of an elaborately ornamented glass bowl depicts a mythological scene with the figures identified by Greek inscriptions. The male figure here, of which just the torso, left arm, and upper legs survive, is identified as Orestes. In Greek myth and drama Orestes was destined to avenge the murder of his father, committed by Orestes's mother and her lover, Aegisthos. As described in one of the classic tragedies of ancient Greece, he was compelled to kill them both. Specific mythological scenes such as this fade away in later Coptic art in favor of more general themes that required less accurate knowledge of the ancient Greek myths.
S.A.

Bibliography: Smith 1957, no. 365, pp. 180–1; Harden 1969, p. 54.

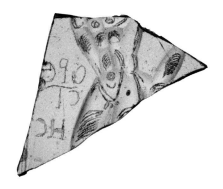

29

Frog Lamp, early 3rd century or later

From Karanis

Molded clay. 5.3 × 10.7 × 8.2

Kelsey Museum of Archaeology,
The University of Michigan. 4767

This egg-shaped lamp of fine cream-colored clay is decorated on the top with a frog in raised and incised relief.[1]
S.A.

Bibliography: Shier 1978, no. 251,
pp. 30, 103, pl. 30.

1. For the frog motif on these lamps see
   Shier 1972, pp. 349–58.

30

Lamp with Christian Designs,
6th–7th century

From Egypt

Light red clay with a pale red slip.
4.8 × 8.5 × 7.5

The Malcove Collection, University of
Toronto. M 82.488

This round-bodied lamp was held by a strap handle, now missing. Christian motifs in high relief decorate the top disk and sides. Four equal-armed crosses surround the filling hole with rosettes, leaves, and grape clusters in a larger circle around the central motif. A Greek inscription around the sides reads, "Glory and light," a reference to the proclamation that Christ is the light of the world.

   This type of lamp, of which a number of variants exist, was probably made in the Aswan region far to the south in Upper Egypt.[1]
S.A.

Bibliography: Campbell 1985, no. 53,
p. 56.

1. Hayes 1980, no. 509, p. 127, pl. 58 shows
   an example close in shape and decoration.
   For a discussion of the type with references, see pp. 124–5.

31
Conical Lamp, 4th–5th century

From Karanis

Blown glass, green with slight yellow tinge. Knocked-off rim. Hollow flattened Base. H. 20.5; Rim D. 12.2, Base D. 2.5

Kelsey Museum of Archaeology, The University of Michigan. 5932

This well-made lamp was decorated with four bands of shallow wheel-cutting and a band of applied blue blobs, two large ones alternating with two sets of ten small ones in a triangle pattern.[1] Harden, who published the Karanis glass, noted that most of the vessels of this shape felt oily on the interior.[2] They were apparently filled with water on which floated a layer of oil with a wick. When lit they were set onto individual holders or in groups onto bronze hanging candelabra. One example was found at Karanis with four dice inside.[3] Clearly it is hard for archaeologists to second-guess the people of antiquity!
S.A.

Bibliography: Harden 1936, no. 457, p. 162, pls. 6 and 16.

1. A general discussion appears in Harden 1936, pp. 155–8. See also Root 1982, p. 42, no. 2, pp. 10 and 20; and Auth 1976, no. 201, p. 153 with references.
2. Harden 1936, p. 155.
3. Ibid.

32
Shrine Lantern or Votive Head,
3rd century or earlier

From Medinet el-Fayum in the Fayum

Pinkish brown molded clay, originally covered with red slip. H. 16.7, W. at base 8.0, D. at base 4.5, H. of hole in back 3.5, W. 4.0

Kelsey Museum of Archaeology, The University of Michigan. 22462

Provenance: Purchased from E.E. Peterson, 1935, who bought it in Medinet el-Fayum

Small portable clay lamps were used extensively by the Greek-Egyptian and Roman-Egyptian residents of the Fayum, and many were found in the streets, homes, granaries and temples of Karanis.[1] Lanterns, which were larger, were probably kept on a shelf or table.[2] The relief decoration on the front of this lantern depicts grapes and leaves wound around the face of either a woman or more likely Dionysus, the Greek god associated with wine. At the lower rear portion of the lantern is a square hole inside of which a small lamp, with castor or sesame oil and wick, was inserted; the light emanated through the open latticework at the base of the front.

Images of Dionysus on objects ranging from mosaics to tapestries are common throughout the empire, and thus have no necessary religious or mythological significance. In this case, however, the lantern shows no signs of wear, and has such a small lamp space that it was probably a devotional object dedicated to Dionysus. The ecstatic cult of this Greek god held out the promise of immortality to its followers, and in Egypt Dionysus was identified with Osiris and later Sarapis.[3]

F.D.F. and S.A.

Bibliography: Shier 1978, pl. 55, p. 171, n. 73.

1. Shier 1978, p. 1. For a similar head, though not from the same hold, see Perdrizet 1921, pl. 64, bottom, no. 195; pl. 73 top is a head of Telesphoros with the same type of pierced base. A different type of Dionysus head with shoulder drapery is shown in Bailey 1975, p. 282, p. 116.
2. Shier 1978, p. 8.
3. For Dionysus worship in Egypt, see Bell 1951, pp. 8, 18–9, 20–1.

33
Lantern with Suspension Hole,
late 3rd–early 4th century

From Karanis

Wheel-made painted clay. 24 × 17;
H. of opening 9.5

Kelsey Museum of Archaeology,
The University of Michigan. 7716

Unlike the Dionysus head lantern
(cat. no. 32), this piece is solidly made
for actual use, and in fact is blackened
on the interior and on the handle from
the lamp it once held. The modern rope
indicates how this lantern might have
been suspended.[1] The thick, coarse red
clay is coated with a pinkish cream slip
and ornamented with sketchy bands and
circles in orange-brown and deep purple.
The front opening is strengthened on
the sides by a thickened band with pie-
crust crimping.
S.A.

1. Cf. Johnson 1981, no. 131, pp. 36, 111,
   pl. 76. Several similar complete clay
   lanterns were found at Karanis: Gazda et
   al. 1983, p. 25, fig. 41. For an illustration
   of a lamp inside a lantern, see Shier
   1978, pl. 55.

34
Fish in Basket Lamp,
date unknown

Said to be from Alexandria

Bronze. L. 10

The Malcove Collection, University of
Toronto. M82.392

Egyptian artists through the centuries
closely observed the details of the life
around them. This bronze lamp, a product
of that keen observation, reproduces in
metal an oval palm-leaf basket just like
the one from the Karanis windowsill
(cat. no. 1J). The handles are pulled in
tight to contain the nice plump Nile fish
whose head bulges out of the end of the
basket. A wick hole for the lamp is at the
other end.

This piece is in the tradition of fine
bronze-working known at Alexandria.
Since it is unique, it is very hard to date,
and without further context, it is not
possible to say whether or not in this
instance the fish is a Christian symbol.
S.A.

Bibliography: Campbell 1985, no. 41,
p. 48.

35
Tapestry Bands from a Curtain,
late 3rd–early 4th century

Tapestry weave in wool and linen.
15 × 91 and 12.2 × 90.1

Museum of Fine Arts, Boston, Charles Potter Kling Fund. 66.377 and 66.378

These two tapestry bands, one slightly higher than the other, were originally woven into a linen curtain or hanging.[1] The main design component of both is a colorful laurel leaf garland with birds, fruit, and blossoms placed on a dark red ground; continuous in the narrow band, it incorporates a central motif of two flying nude putti carrying a yellow *clipeus* with a male head in the higher band. The head, shown in a three-quarter view to the right, has long, dark hair covered with a green reed wreath. The birds of the garland are arranged in pairs, one on each side of the putti and three pairs in the narrow band. Some birds are surrounded by blossoms, others feed on grapes, while two pairs of waterfowl nest among lotus buds and seed pods.

The blending and interweaving of fine-textured, dyed woolen yarns of the bands represents the illusionistic style of tapestry weaving at its best. The plasticity of the figures is so painterly that it can be described as impressionistic; also the play of light and shadow over the figures of the putti and the head of the *clipeus* is consistent with their foreshortening. The understanding of the three-dimensionality of the figures is so profound that the bands must have been executed at the time when illusionism and naturalism were still the commonly practiced styles, in this case not later than the late 3rd or early 4th century.

Thematically, the bands fit into the decorative aspect of textile art. Both the garland and the putti with the *clipeus* are standard in the decorative repertory of ancient art. The putti carrying a *clipeus* often serve as the focus of a composition and often carry specific iconographic meaning. As here, the head may be more than just an ornamental filler. With its reed wreath, it may be either a personification of Winter[2] or a river god; both types use the reed as their most characteristic attribute.[3] This identity is strengthened by the presence of the floral garland with birds, which in other arts often complements representations of the Seasons.[4] These two bands could have come from one out of a set of curtains decorated with the four Seasons, as was often the case in textile and domestic decoration in general (see also cat. no. 37). Employment of a river god in this context would be more unusual but not entirely without precedent. Just as personifications often appeared in floor mosaics,[5] so they could also decorate domestic textiles.

A.G.

Bibliography: Zaloscer 1974, fig. 87; MacMillan Arensberg 1977, fig. 17, p. 17.

1. Technical information: warp: undyed linen (S-spun); weft: red, blue, green, pink, yellow, beige, gray, purple, orange wool (all S-spun). Tapestry over 2–3 warps; ca. 7 group warps per 1 cm, ca. 18 more wefts per 1 cm.
2. Parrish 1984, with bibliography.
3. A similar problem of identification is posed by a polychrome loop-pile panel with a youth wearing a reed wreath and holding a reed in his hand. Pushkin Museum, Moscow, inv. 5195 (Šurinova 1969, pl. 1, no. 1).
4. E.g., a fruit garland from the Annus and the Seasons mosaic from the House of the Dionysiac Procession in El Jem in Tunisia (Parrish 1984, cat. 25, pl. 37, pp. 147–9); also the Mosaic of Ananeosis, Antioch (Levi 1947, I, pp. 320–321, II, pl. 73).
5. E.g., busts with the Tigris and Pyramos from the House of Cilicia and the House of Porticoes, Antioch (Levi 1947 I, pp. 58 and 109–110, II. pls. 9b, c and 18a, c).

36

Loop-pile Hanging with Boating Putti, early 4th century

Linen and wool. 102 x 128.5

The British Museum. 20717

Polychrome weft-loop pile weavings[1] are among the most effective wall decorations of the Late Antique and Early Byzantine periods (see also cat. no. 40). This dramatic hanging, which might have decorated the wall of a dining room, is decorated with putti boating, and although not intact, it is one of the finest surviving examples of this type of textile. One pair of putti and their miniature boat on the left are almost intact; at least one more pair is indicated by a set of wings and a prow of another boat visible in the now separate fragment on the right. Playfully tending their boat, the fair-haired putto in a red *tunica exomis,* a short tunic that bares one shoulder, handles the rudder, probably being helped by his companion in a blue tunic, who is now armless. The background is filled with flower petals above the figures and with fish and waterfowl below the boat. The boating scene is framed by a colorful laurel-leaf and flower petal garland with corner disks displaying masks, a satyr's on the left and a maenad's on the right. The piece is executed in an illusionistic style particular to a group of 4th century paintings and mosaics. Similarly proportioned and modeled putti populate the floors of the villa at Piazza Armerina (ca. 350) and the ceiling panels at the palace in Trier (ca. 310).[2]

Late Antique art abounds in putti enacting genre and other subjects, among which marine and Nilotic scenes of boating and fishing are common.[3] The meaning of putti in art, however, is many-sided. Depending on the context, they could have religious, funerary, or even propagandistic significance, although most of the time, they appear as convenient and endearing figural motifs.[4] But even when boating and fishing putti are included in marine subjects teeming with life, which were understood as allegories of regeneration, they still had a decorative function. It is in this way that they are employed in this hanging and other related textiles.[5] Themes similar to this playful subject were also used to enliven the floor and table utensils of the dining room.

A.G.

Bibliography: Beckwith 1959, pp. 5 and 6; Wessel 1965, p. 192, pl. 105; Zaloscer 1974, fig. 78; MacMillan Arensberg 1977, pp. 20–21, fig. 22.

1. In the loop-pile technique of decoration, the designs are woven into the plain cloth with extra polychrome woolen yarns. These designs can be geometric and very two-dimensional, or figural and illusionistically modeled through the blending of colors. Such mixing of dyed yarns approximates the impressionistic effect of polychrome mosaics. Because of the texture of the pile, the designs project in relief from the plain cloth backing, further enhancing the painterly effect of the decoration.

2. E.g., rooms 4, 29 and 40 (Carandini 1982, II. pls. XXIII, XXXVII, LVIII; Simon 1986.)

3. Dunbabin 1978, pp. 125–30 and *passim.*

4. Stuveras 1969.

5. E.g., playing putti decorate several other loop-pile textiles: Victoria and Albert Museum, inv. nos. 286.1891 and 307.1891 (Kendrick, 1920, nos. 24–6, pp. 48–9, pl. 10); The Brooklyn Museum, inv. no. 38.683 (Thompson 1971, no. 3, pp. 16–17); Haifa, Haifa Museum, inv. no. 6039 (Baginski and Tidhar 1980, no. 23, p. 48); another hanging in a private collection in Haifa(?) must have been made in the same workshop as the British Museum piece (Baginski and Tidhar 1980, no. 24, p. 48).

37
Panel with a Personification of Spring, ca. 400–450

Possibly from Akhmim

Wool. 25 × 22.5

Metropolitan Museum of Art. Gift of George F. Baker, Jr. 90.05.848

Provenance: Emil Brugsch (Bey), Cairo

This small intact wool tapestry panel[1] with blue background presents a bust of a woman haloed and turned in a moderate three-quarter view. The folds of her mantle are held high and filled with pink and red blossoms. Her face, dominated by large outlined eyes and eyebrows, is small and round, its shape stressed by the simple modeling along the chin, cheekbones, and nose. Her short hair is tied above the forehead with a pearl-studded headband. The weaving of the panel proceeded in the direction of the design.

This panel was originally used as an appliqué for a larger textile, probably as one of a set of such panels.[2] Its prominently displayed blossoms help in identifying the figure as a personification of Spring.[3] Although in the past it has been referred to as Ceres and Goddess Earth,[4] these goddesses are usually portrayed with a richer selection of Nature's bounty, while roses and blossoms are one of the principal symbols of Spring.[5]

This tapestry panel can be dated to the late 4th and early 5th century. Its three-dimensional, but simple and clearly defined forms appear almost as pure geometric shapes, only minimally disturbed by the demands of such surface detail as facial articulation characteristic of the Theodosian period (i.e., from the end of the 4th through the middle of the 5th century). Seasons are typically shown holding their attributes in a cloth[6] or even, as here, in the folds of their mantles, as on a 4th century floor mosaic from Carthage.[7] As a motif associated with prosperity and continuous good fortune, Seasons and their symbols are frequently used in Late Antique domestic art, including textiles (e.g., cat. nos. 187 and 35).[8]

The panel is said to have come from Akhmim, and though this provenance cannot be confirmed, it is likely, since the textile belonged to the Emil Brugsch (Bey) collection of Cairo, formed at the time of major textile finds at Akhmim.[9]

A.G.

Bibliography: The Brooklyn Museum 1941, no. 184, pp. 61–2; Ostoia 1969, pp. 36–7, no. 12.

1. Technical information: warp: undyed wool (S-spun); weft: undyed, beige, pink, tan, red, blue, green, yellow and purple wool (all S-spun); tapestry over 1 warp.
2. A similar panel with a personification of Summer was once in the Figdor collection in Vienna (von Falke et al. 1930, I, no. 2, pl. 1).
3. Parrish 1984, pp. 34–7.
4. The Brooklyn Museum 1941, no. 184, pp. 61–2; Ostoia 1969, no. 12, p. 37.
5. Cf. the Mosaic of Ge and the Seasons, Antioch (Levi 1947, I, pp. 346–7; II, pl. 81).
6. Antioch-Daphne, now at the Louvre (Levi 1947, I, pp. 230–1; II, pl. 54; also Baratte 1978, no. 45, pp. 99–118, figs. 96–125).
7. Parrish 1984, no. 12, pp. 120–2, pl. 21.
8. Parrish 1984, pp. 12–13; Dunbabin 1978, pp. 158–61.
9. Ostoia 1969, no. 12, p. 37.

38
Looped Cover with Tapestry Inserts,
ca. middle of the 4th century

Possibly from Akhmim

Linen and wool. 89.5 × 90.2

Metropolitan Museum of Art, Gift of
George F. Baker. 90.05.899

Provenance: Emil Brugsch (Bey)
Collection, Cairo

This piece is one of a large group of
common domestic textiles [1] used since
pharaonic times as blankets and covers
made in loop-pile cloth for added
warmth.[2] From the Late Roman period
onwards, they were decorated with
woven-in inserts, first in monochrome
and later also in polychrome tapestry, as
seen in this example and several other
textiles in this exhibition. They are
known from a very large number of
fragments. These textiles were certainly
manufactured throughout Egypt,
although several that are particularly
close to this weaving are, like this example, circumstantially associated with
Upper Egypt and Akhmim.[3] Some are
so close that they might be considered
the products not only of the same area
but even of the same workshop.[4]

The fragment bears three ornamental
inserts, consisting of a roundel and a
pair of narrow horizontal stripes. The
roundel (D. 41 cm.) has a stylized garland band framing an eight-point star
filled with an interlace whose complex
pattern is formed by flat bands looped
into tight coils arranged into four
medallion-like motifs. A fringed edge
and its adjoining selvage indicate that
the fragment was the end corner of a
much larger piece that would have been
decorated with two or three additional
roundels in the main field and a set of
stripes on the other end.[5] This specific
type of interlace design, together with
other ornamental motifs, suggest a mid-
4th century date for its manufacture.[6]
A.G.

Bibliography: Dimand 1930, p. 126,
fig. 3.

1. This sizable fragment is made of a linen
   cloth with a thick weft-loop pile constituting most of its surface except for the areas
   reserved for ornamental inserts, here a
   roundel and a pair of narrow horizontal
   stripes woven-in in tapestry technique in
   dark purple wool and linen. All three
   ornaments are filled with delicate interlace
   designs executed by a flying shuttle during weaving. The interlace of the stripes
   consists of two flat bands looped into
   pointed ovals separated by pairs of tight
   coils. The ovals are lined on the outside
   by dotting, and filled on the inside with
   several types of vegetal motifs as well as
   abstract-looking dolphins and birds. Technical information: looped linen cloth: warp,
   weft, and loops: undyed linen (S-spun);
   tapestry: warp: undyed linen (S-spun);
   weft: undyed linen (S-spun), purple wool
   (S-spun).
2. Hall 1986, pp. 16, 38–39, figs. 28–29.

3. Such early collections as those of Emil
   Brugsch (Bey), Franz Bock, Wladimir
   Bock, Robert Forrer, and Theodor Graf
   were formed in the 1880s at a time when
   textiles originating in Akhmim were
   most available.
4. Especially the Metropolitan Museum
   of Art inv. no. 89.18.151 (cat. no. 181)
   and Victoria and Albert Museum, inv.
   nos. 665.1886, 365.1887 and 40.1936
   (Kendrick 1920, nos. 251, 191, pp 115,
   101); also Louvre, inv. x4567 and x4325
   (du Bourguet 1964, B34 and C60, pp. 80
   and 109); Trier, Simeonstift, no. VII. 29
   (Nauerth 1978, no. 32, p. 46, fig. 21).
5. Brussels, Musées Royaux d'Art et
   d'Histoire (Errera 1916, no. 85, pp. 36–
   37). Such textiles are also represented
   on painted mummy wrappings from
   Antinoopolis (Guimet 1912, no. 74,
   pl. 45, p. 39).
6. Cf. cat. no. 181

39
Fragment of a Curtain,
late 4th to early 5th century

Linen and wool. 42.5 × 17.7

Virginia Museum of Fine Arts,
Richmond, The Glasgow Fund 64.56.1

Provenance: Paul Mellon Collection,
Paris

Wearing a red, green-spotted *nebris*
(fawn skin) and an orange loin cloth,
this youth holds a garland or branch in
his left hand. The figure is executed in
dark purple, almost black wool.[1] It is
well drawn, with the body and the facial
features clearly articulated, although
much of the fine surface detailing in the
face is now gone. This isolated figure,
probably a shepherd, is a fragment from
a larger curtain, very similar to one now
in the British Museum.[2] The number of
extant fragments suggests that these
curtains were common. Although their
origins, as in the case of this shepherd
and the British Museum piece, are
mostly unknown, they must have been
manufactured throughout Egypt.[3]

The Virginia shepherd, and other
hunters, dancers, and similar figures that
decorate the linen curtains belong to the
standard repertory of Roman and Early
Byzantine domestic art. In addition to
their purely decorative role, their iconographic association with Dionysiac
themes and seasonal and pastoral activities made them broad allegories of
life's blessing and renewal that continued
to be popular well after Christianity
replaced its pagan rivals as the reigning
faith. As themes and as individual motifs,
this type of decoration was very common in the art of the 3rd to 5th centuries,
although those of the curtains compare
most closely with the late 4th and 5th
century art. The fine articulation of this
figure and the high quality of its execution suggest that this textile was made
relatively early, in the late 4th or early
5th century.
A.G.

Bibliography: Gonosová and
Kondoleon forthcoming.

1. Technical information: warp: undyed linen
   (S-spun); weft: undyed linen (S-spun),
   dark purple, yellow, orange, blue and
   green wool (all S-spun). Tapestry over
   2–3 warps; 6–7 group warps per 1 cm;
   ca. 17–25 wefts per 1 cm.
2. British Museum, inv. 43049 (Wessel 1965,
   p. 199, fig. 118). These curtains were made
   of plain linen cloth with woven-in decoration in tapestry weave, usually in the
   form of wide bands alternating with large
   figures, which like the Virginia shepherd
   were taken from a Late Antique pastoral
   and hunting repertory. The bands, filled
   with ornamental elements, divided the
   curtains into independent fields occupied
   by the figures. The designs, both figural
   and ornamental, were executed mainly in
   dark wool; other colors played only a
   secondary role.
3. E.g., Textile Museum, no. 71.79 (Trilling
   1982, no. 42, p. 57); Coptic Museum,
   inv. 7948, said to be from Antinoopolis
   (Cairo 1984).

40

Hanging with Victories,
early 5th century

Linen and wool. 96 × 223

The Brooklyn Museum, Gift of
Howard M. and Dorothy C. Pack. 74.155

All that remain of this still impressive
hanging are two flying victories carrying a fragmentary wreath, and portions
of bordermotifs.[1] The motif of wreath-bearing victories developed in the sphere
of triumphal imperial imagery[2] and was
then adopted by funerary and later
Christian art. In the Late Antique and
Early Byzantine periods such victories
were frequently used in an honorific
context. The meaning of this hanging is
unknown, however, since we lack the
content of the wreath, but being an early
5th century work it was most likely
intended for formal use either in a public
or religious setting.[3] A strikingly similar
composition of victories, carrying a
wreath with a Tyche of Constantinople
on an imperial consular diptych of ca.
500, illustrates such traditional imperial
meaning.[4] On the other hand, a slightly
later tapestry in London with the wreath
containing a cross is obviously Christian
in content.[5] The intentions of several
other textiles employing this motif are
less clear. The presence of a betrothal
scene inside a wreath on the pair of
curtains in the Hermitage suggests a

more ceremonial use,[6] while the victory
motif on a late 6th century curtain in
New York is strictly decorative.[7]

This type of loop-pile textile (see also
cat. no. 36) is characterized by a blending
of colors combined with the texture of
the pile, a technique that gives the victories a distinct relief quality. Graded
flesh tones model their bare arms, feet
and the one remaining face; varied reds,
blues and yellows do the same for the
bodies beneath the clinging clothes. The
definition of the figures is reinforced by
outlines. On the whole, the victories,
now wingless and moving freely through
the air with their cloaks billowing
around them, are conceived and executed
in the simplified naturalism of the art of
the Theodosian period (end of 4th
through mid-5th century).
A.G.

Bibliography: Metropolitan Museum of
Art 1979, no. 70, p. 82.

1. The hanging has a linen backing with the
   design in a weft-loop pile of dyed woolen
   yarns. Each victory is dressed in a chiton,
   a peplos, and a cloak draped over the
   shoulders. Each is also adorned with
   bracelets, armlets, anklebands, and elaborate belts. The wreath, the center of which
   is lost, is made of pink and yellow petals
   accented with jewels. The top of the hanging is bordered by a colorful cable and the
   sides by bands of red and yellow petals.
2. Daremberg and Saglio 1919, v, esp.
   cols. 850–854.
3. Cf. the Column of Arcadius in Constantinople (Metropolitan Museum of Art
   1979, no. 68, pp. 79–81).
4. Volbach 1976, no. 49, pp. 48–49, pl. 26.
5. Victoria and Albert Museum, inv.
   no. 349.1887 (Kendrick 1921, no. 317,
   pl. 7, p. 15; also Metropolitan Museum of
   Art 1979, no. 480, pp. 535–6).
6. Hermitage, Leningrad, inv. no. 11643
   (Mat'e and Ljapunova 1951, no. 4, pp. 76,
   90–91, fig. 17, pl. 4).
7. Metropolitan Museum of Art (Grabar
   1967, fig. 385, p. 328).

41
Roundel with Two Figures:
Orpheus and Eurydice (?),
late 5th–early 6th century

Wool and linen tapestry. 48 × 51

Walters Art Gallery, Baltimore. 83.466

This textile may have been just one roundel in a set of tapestry ornaments from a household textile. The principal motif is two standing figures inside the central square: a female dressed in a long tunic with yellow bands and a red mantle is shown to the right, a nude male leaning on a lyre is to the left. The surface is strewn with leaves. The figures can be identified in several ways. The attribute of the lyre establishes the male figure as either Apollo or Orpheus. If the figure is Orpheus, the female must

be his wife Eurydice, although the lack of Opheus's traditional Phrygian cap weakens the identification (see also cat. no. 39).[1] If he is Apollo, his companion may be one of the nine muses[2] or the nymph Daphne, although Daphne is usually shown escaping the deity's amorous advances by transforming herself into a laurel tree.[3] The male figure is poorly preserved, making a more precise identification difficult. All these interpretations are plausible since gods, heroes, and other figures of classical mythology and literature constituted even at this late date (the late 4th and 6th centuries) the largest category of figural subjects decorating objects of daily use. Quite popular were portrayals of pairs of famous lovers of the classical past, often used in sets, as this example probably was.[4]

Recurring motifs and similar weaving details characterize much monochrome tapestry weaving, so that many examples appear, if not alike, at least related. It is possible, however, to isolate distinct groups. One is represented by the present roundel, whose decoration is distinguished by an extensive use of a mixed purple-and-white middle tone, along with the usual contrast of light and dark. The effect is achieved by a technique of hatching, by which white and purple yarns are used simultaneously.[5] The group is stylistically and technically homogeneous, suggesting that these textiles were produced in one geographical area, possibly Upper Egypt. Their motifs are traditional and consist of hunting scenes, isolated warriors, mythological and marine figures, and animals, baskets and other such motifs. All design elements are rendered in a simple, stylized manner. Human figures and animals display disproportionately large heads with wedge-shaped eyes with the white strongly pronounced. While the outlines are essential, the internal detail of the motifs is minimal. The motifs are executed with a certain disinterest in naturalistic representation shared by much of the late 5th and 6th centuries, which helps in assigning the group to this period. The majority of the fragments, mainly square panels and roundels, are quite large and some are still preserved with their surrounding clothes, often in loop-pile technique; they were used to embellish household textiles.[6]

This roundel, woven in wool and linen on linen warps, displays all the important features of this group. The roundel and its interior square panel are framed by narrow fillets. The surface around the square is executed in hatching, inside the square in undyed linen; the ornamental motifs are primarily in dark purple wool with details in linen and red, green and yellow wool. The hatched surface contains several sets of ornamental discs.

A.G.

Bibliography: The Brooklyn Museum 1941, pp. 64–65, no. 195; Brommer 1976, III. p. 342.

1. This is the traditional identification of the subject of the Walters Art Gallery roundel (Brommer 1976, III. p. 342).
2. As, e.g., on the floor mosaic from a private house at Sousse in Tunisia (Foucher 1960, no. 57.042, p. 19, pls. VIIIb and c).
3. This myth is well illustrated by a tapestry panel from the so-called shawl of Sabina from Antinoopolis; Louvre, GU 1230 (Metropolitan Museum of Art 1979, no. 112, pp. 134–5).
4. See a tapestry panel with Aphrodite and Adonis (Elsa Bloch Diener collection, Bern; Metropolitan Museum of Art 1979, no. 119, p. 141); also an ivory diptych in the Museo Cristiano in Brescia (Volbach 1976, no. 66, p. 38, pl. 38).
5. Although hatching appears in many tapestries, it plays a particularly important role in this group, where it is used for major surface areas. The basic purple-and-white scheme can also be enlivened with touches of red, green, and yellow, especially when figures are included in the designs. An emphatic containment of the main compositional parts in simple, narrow fillets is another distinct stylistic feature.
6. E.g., Detroit Institute of Arts, inv. 22.253.1; Louvre, inv. x4196 and x4344 (du Bourguet 1964, c42 D92, pp. 101, 153); Pushkin Museum, inv. 5385 (Šurinova 1967, no. 94, pl. 44). See also a roundel from Akhmim in Gayet 1900, no. 436, p. 216.

42

Wall Hanging with Dionysiac Busts, late 5th–early 6th century

Said to be from Antinoopolis

Tapestry in wool. 91 × 134.6

Metropolitan Museum of Art, Gift of Edward S. Harkness. 31.9.3

The worship of Dionysus was particularly strong in Egypt , but the use of Dionysiac motifs during the Late Antique and Early Byzantine periods is not unique to Egypt: images of the god appear on objects throughout the Empire. Floor mosaics, silver plate, furniture ornaments, and so forth are more often than not decorated with Dionysiac or other mythological imagery.[1] Considering the use of textiles as hangings, covers, and curtains, it is therefore not surprising that they should be decorated with the same or related motifs. In Egypt as elsewhere in the Early Byzantine world, objects like these were made not so much for diehard traditionalist pagans as for the members of a well-to-do, educated class. For these patrons, visual representation of pagan myths, like the reading of classical literature or contemporary poetry on classical themes, such as the *Dionysiaca* of Nonnos of Panopolis (Akhmim), were acknowledgments of the culture of the past rather than expressions of religious sentiment.

The decorativeness of Late Antique textiles is vividly demonstrated by this hanging, a precious relic of Early Byzantine weaving as well as a beautiful wall hanging. Twelve busts (there were originally fifteen), each placed inside a yellow roundel, fill the loops of a delicate leafy interlace covering a red-rose background.[2] The busts portray participants of *thiasoi*, revelric festivals of the god Dionysus, among which wreathed maenads and horned satyrs are most prominent. The bold male at the bottom center right is Silenus, the diadem-wearing youthful female in the top central roundel is a Victory, and her bearded neigh-

bor to the left is Heracles. The last two are often included in depictions of Dionysus's triumphal return from the conquest of India.[3] The busts could have been included to give the hanging a specific meaning or, more likely, as stock members of the Dionysiac entourage. The identities of the three missing busts are conjectural. It is quite possible that Dionysus himself was portrayed in the central roundel. The continuous tendril of the interlace, and its clearly displayed interstitial vine leaves and grape clusters, as one of Dionysus's principal attributes, further emphasize the Dionysiac content of this textile. Although the figures are presented in bust form, they retain the impression of movement associated with Dionysiac figures; the cast glances and disheveled hair of the maenads in particular convey the revelric mood of more extensive Dionysiac scenes.

In spite of its overtly pagan subject, the hanging dates from the Early Byzantine period, specifically the late 5th and early 6th century. Its stylistic features – prominent outlines and reduced modeling of the busts combined with a more schematic arrangement of their costumes – are present in other late 5th and early 6th century monuments.[4]

The hanging is also an excellent example of Late Antique and Early Byzantine decorative composition in general. The busts are part of an overall patterned design in an ornamental frame. The same combination of surface patterning, enriched with figural fillers and framed, is used in floor mosaics. The latter also provide further compositional and iconographic analogies for the Dionysiac hanging. For example, a field of a garland interlace, filled with Dionysiac figures (busts and full figures) and the Seasons, decorates a 2nd century floor in a house in El Jem (in Tunisia).[5] A mid-4th century floor from a villa from Antioch-Daphne with a bust of Dionysus and full figures of his companions, including Heracles, is also related.[6] Dionysiac figures, in fact – full figures, busts, and head masks – are the largest single category of main and auxiliary motifs in Late Antique and Early Byzantine art. The interlace pattern, used in floor mosaics from the 2nd century onwards, became especially common in the 5th and 6th centuries. The compactness of this interlace pattern agrees with the 5th and early 6th century development of this motif.[7]

A.G.

Bibliography: Winlock 1932, pp. 157–8, fig. 1: The Brooklyn Museum 1941, no. 238, p. 76; Ostoia 1969, no. 14, pp. 40–1; Metropolitan Museum of Art 1979, no. 129, pp. 150–1; Brown University 1987, no. 4, pp. 34–5.

1. For an overview of this material see Metropolitan Museum of Art 1979, pp. 141–54.

2. The interstices of the interlace contain naturalistically rendered vine leaves and grape clusters. The hanging is framed by a garland of stylized pink flower petals on a yellow ground edged by a dark blue outer rim. The hanging is an example of a large-scale textile woven in tapestry technique mainly in wool, including the warps. Much of the vegetal ornamentation, except for the interstitial leaves and border petals, is executed in solid colors, while the busts, although distinctly outlined, are rendered in a more illusionistic style of hatching and interweaving of colors. The weaving proceeded perpendicularly to the design, which may account for a certain amount of distortion in the drawing of the images. Technical information: warp: off-white natural wool (S-spun); weft: yellow, red, blue-green, pink, gray, purple, etc. wool (S-spun); some undyed linen also used. Tapestry over 1 warp.

3. Dunbabin 1978.

4. Cf. the figures of the original mosaic program in S. Apollinare Nuovo and in the Archepiscopal chapel, both in Ravenna. Deichmann 1969, pls. 112–3, 136–51, 219–44.

5. The House of the Peacock, see Foucher 1961, pp. 8–9, pl. VI.

6. Levi 1947, I pp. 244–246; II pls. 53b and 58.

7. Levi 1947, I pp. 457–67; also Trilling 1985, pp. 29–42, and Gonosová 1981, pp. 49–52.

43
Tapestry with a Shepherd Milking a Goat, late 5th–early 6th century

Said to be from Akhmim

Wool and linen. 33.7 × 34.3

The St. Louis Art Museum, Museum Purchase. 48.1939

The decoration of textiles consists of the widest selection of themes and motifs. In this square panel, a more stylized border of grapevines with vases and doves is combined with an almost anecdotal milking scene in the central square. A continous stem of the vine arbor outlines the four trapezoidal sections of the border. Each section is filled with a pair of doves juxtaposed across a vase motif supporting the vine. A freer form of the vine grows above the shepherd, portrayed in the central field wearing a *tunica exomis*. Crouching on his left knee, he milks the goat standing in the middle. The pastoral scene is completed with a kid in the lower right corner of the field.[1]

Pastoral scenes in Roman and Late Antique art were inspired by bucolic poetry, as represented, for example, by an illustration in Vergil's *Eclogues* (*Vergilius Romanus*, fol. 44r), and by representations of rural activities; the latter often appeared in connection with representations of Seasons, as for example in the floor mosaics from Oudna and Carthage.[2] Sometimes the scenes were more general without specific associations.[3] In textiles, the pastoral scene is used frequently in tunic ornaments. Some may have been inspired by a more specific source;[4] others, like this piece, follow the more general iconographic type.[5] Because of the direction of the weaving, this panel also may have come from a tunic, although other uses are possible as well (cf. cat. nos. 61 and 62).

It is difficult to date the St. Louis panel. Although it is executed in the monochrome style, the actual rendition of the figures differs from other weavings. Even though the figures are distorted and stylized, they appear very lifelike, as if the artist had invented this pastoral scene instead of relying on the use of stock figural types and conventional compositions. The doves with vases are more helpful in this respect: they were a particularly favored motif in late 5th and early 6th century religious

and funerary art, and it was probably during this period that they were adopted for other decorative uses, as here.

A.G.

Bibliography: Whittemore 1932, p. 387, pl. 60; The Brooklyn Museum 1941, no. 182, p. 61; Metropolitan Museum of Art 1979, no. 234, p. 253.

1. The panel is woven in tapestry technique in undyed linen and purple and red wool. The design is carried out in purple except for the legs and the beaks of the doves, which are red. Inner details are minimal; some are executed in an extra yarn with the flying shuttle. The weaving proceeded perpendicularly to the direction of the design, which would agree with the position of the panel as one of the hem *segmenta* of a tunic (cf. cat. no. 63).

2. Oudna, Villa of the Laberii and Carthage, the Mosaic of Dominus Julius (Dunbabin 1978, Oudna 1, f. 1 and Carthage 32, pls. 101 and 109).

3. E.g., on a silver plate from the Carthage treasure in the British Museum (British Museum 1977, no. 99, pp. 50–1) and in the Hermitage, inv. w277 (Effenberger 1976, cat. 7, pp. 97–101, fig. 14); or on an ivory pyxis in the British Museum (Volbach 1976, no. 106, pl. 56, pp. 75–6).

4. The Brooklyn Museum, inv. nos. 44.143A–F (Thompson, 1971, no. 4, pp. 18–9; Metropolitan Museum of Art 1979, no. 227–230, pp. 249–51).

5. E.g., Louvre, inv. nos. x4193, x4351, x4252, x4126 (du Bourguet 1964, B23, p. 74; c38 and c39, p. 99; D47, p. 137).

44
Fragment with a Quail,
late 5th – early 6th century

Linen and wool. 44.5 x 37

Museum of Art, Rhode Island School of
Design, Gift of Mrs. Henry D. Sharpe.
78.131

Isolated birds, particularly quail, are
common in this type of tapestry-woven
insert.[1] They can be executed in the
monochrome, modified monochrome,
or polychrome styles.[2] Their appearance
in textiles follows the general use of
birds as filler motifs in decorative compositions on walls and ceilings in floor
mosaics and other arts. Since specific
species of birds were also used as attributes of the Seasons, the choice of the
quail – a common migratory bird – may
have initially been motivated by such
seasonal associations.[3]

The present fragment comes from a
larger loop-pile linen cloth of a type
commonly used for blankets and other
household coverings (see also cat.
no. 38). When intact, it would have had
as many as four such panels. From
among many related fragments, a panel
depicting a quail in Haifa came from a
similar cover woven in the same workshop as the Providence piece.[4] Although
the simple shapes of the birds are too
ambiguous to help with the dating of
these two panels, the disk design of
the Providence border, which is definitely a later type of decorative motif,
supports their dating into the late 5th or
early 6th century.[5]

A.G.

Bibliography: Museum of Art Rhode
Island School of Design 1988, p. 50.

1. This tapestry square is woven into a linen
   loop-pile cloth. The design, mainly in dark
   purple wool and undyed linen, consists
   of a framing fillet with exterior crenellation
   followed by a wide band of dark disks
   containing six- or eight-petal white centers
   (these are filled with trefoils except for
   four axial ones that have rosettes). Technical information: tapestry-woven panel:
   warp: undyed linen (S-spun); weft: undyed
   linen (S-spun), red, purple, green and
   yellow wool (S-spun). Tapestry over 2–3
   warps; ca. 10 group warps per 1 cm; weft
   count varies. An inner square has an
   inscribed roundel with a quail. The bird is
   executed in purple wool and linen with
   red wool used for its legs and beak. The
   ground around is filled with three green
   and yellow branches. The design is dominated by the dark silhouette of the main
   motifs. The flying shuttle was used only to
   a limited extent. Even in the portrayal of
   the quail, details such as the eye, wing,
   and breast plumage are suggested rather

   than naturalistically depicted. The touches
   of red, yellow and green enliven what is
   otherwise a very simple design.
2. E.g., Victoria and Albert Museum, inv.
   654.1886, 1266.1888, both from Akhmim,
   and 2148.1900 (Kendrick 1920, nos. 174,
   168, 172, pp. 95–6, pls. 24–5); also
   Louvre, inv. x4133 and x4140 (du Bourguet
   1964, a8 and a9, p. 52).
3. Pliny, *Natural History* X.xxxiii.65–69; also
   Parrish 1984, pp. 27–8.
4. Haifa Museum, inv. no. 6041 (Baginski
   and Tidhar 1980, no. 11, pl. 1, p. 41). A
   similar piece is in the Staatliche Museen,
   Berlin, inv. 9136 (Wulff and Volbach 1926,
   p. 22, pl. 52).
5. E.g., Louvre, inv. x4981 and x4584 (du
   Bourguet 1964, c20–c21, pp. 90–1); also
   Vatican Museum, inv. nos. t63, t66, t67
   (Renner 1982, nos. 54 and 66, pp. 93–4
   and 107–8, pls. 36 and 42).

Color plate, page 16

45
Loop-pile Cloth with a Tapestry Panel, first half of 6th century

Possibly from Akhmim or Saqqara

Linen and wool. 54.5 × 47.5

Metropolitan Museum of Art, Funds from Various Donors. 89.18.123

Provenance: Purchased from Theodor Graf, Vienna

Tapestry panels like this colorful example are known in large numbers, almost always with some loop-pile cloth still partly attached. The complete piece would have been decorated with two or four such tapestry-woven panels in addition to end stripes (see cat. no. 38). It must have been used as a bed cover or blanket since loop-pile is unusually long and thick, making the original piece quite heavy and warm.

The panel is woven into the cloth in dark purple, yellow, green, and red wool and undyed linen.[1] The central frame is filled with a large lotus blossom. The corners contain dark purple leonine and canine creatures; spaces in between carry flower baskets. The design is executed completely in a tapestry of color surfaces; only the animals have a few inner details made with a flying shuttle. All motifs are executed in a stylized manner indicating that the present example belongs among the later rather than earlier versions of the design.[2] Although the original motifs may have had some specific meaning, here and in analogous examples the function only as appealing, colorful decoration.

Circumstantially, these textiles have been identified as coming from Akhmim and Saqqara.[3] Since the present panel was acquired from Theodor Graf of Vienna, known for his holdings of Saqqara and Akhmim textiles, it is most likely that it was also found in one of these sites.

A.G.

1. A continuous scroll forming medallion-like frames – the largest in the center with four smaller ones in the corners – is one of the most frequently used compositions for square tapestry inserts in linen loop-pile textiles. The frames are often filled with common motifs: hunters, warriors, playing putti, animals and fantastic creatures (see also cat. no. 183), but also rosettes and very frequently baskets of fruit and flower petals. The framing scrolls and the majority of the filler motifs are executed in dark purple woowarl, although red, green, and yellow wool are also used to various degrees. If colored wool is used, it forms distinct surface areas within the design; color gradation or mixing of shades is nonexistent. Outlines of the motifs are very important since these textiles represent only a modification of the monochrome silhouette style where the outlines represent one of the characteristic features. The weaving of the majority of the pieces is quite coarse. Technical information: loop-pile cloth: warp and weft in undyed linen (S-spun). Tapestry panel: warp: undyed linen (S-spun); weft: undyed linen (S-spun); purple, red, orange, yellow, green wool (all S-spun). Tapestry over 2–3 warps; ca. 6 group warps per 1 cm.

2. Related examples: Victoria and Albert Museum, nos. 712.1886, 842.1886, 1266.1888 (Kendrick 1920, no. 168, p. 95, pl. 25); Prague, Arts and Crafts Museum, inv. 2231 (Kybalova 1967, pl. 45, p. 93); Louvre, inv. X4787 and X4282 (du Bourguet 1964, D132 and D133, pp. 169–70); Pushkin Museum, inv. 354 (Šurinova 1969, no. 88).

3. See cat. no. 38.

46
Weaving with Dionysus and Labors of Heracles, 6th century

Possibly from Akhmim

Wool and linen. 22.5 × 22.5

Metropolitan Museum of Art, Funds from Various Donors. 89.18.244

Provenance: Theodor Graf, Vienna

Probably from a blanket or cover, this scene is an abbreviated version of the triumphal procession of the Greek god, Dionysus, which often included figures of the hero Heracles.[1] Heracles's twelve labors are depicted as a compact and uninterrupted figural frieze, starting clockwise from the top left: killing the Nemean lion, the golden apples of the Hesperides, the Erymanthean boar, cleaning of Augeas's stables, capture of the Cretan bull, killing of Kyknos, Cerberus, Diomedes's mares, shooting of the Stymphalian birds, the Larnaean hydra, capture of the Cerynean hide, and Hippolyte the Queen of the Amazons. Heracles, both bearded and beardless, is portrayed performing his tasks in a short-hand but intelligible manner in accord with the established iconographic tradition. For example, in the cleaning of Augeas's stables (top right), he is shown wielding a two-pronged hoe as in the floor mosaic from Volubilis.[2] And he is armed with a bow in the shooting of the Stymphalian birds (bottom center left) with birds falling around him, as on another floor mosaic from Liria in Spain.[3] The considerable stylization of the figures in the frieze as well as in the central medallion may be due either to workshop copying or to the use of a more abstract model from another artistic medium. Whichever is the case, the appearance of the panels agrees with a 6th century stylistic phase of Early Byzantine art.

This panel and its companion piece in Leningrad[4] could have been used as tunic ornaments, but more likely were applied to a domestic textile, such as a blanket or a cover. Similar Herculean imagery was employed on floors, walls, and household objects such as furniture and tableware throughout the Early Byzantine period.[5] It is another example of the popularity of mythological themes as decoration in the sphere of domestic art at this time.

Although not documented, the panels must have been found in Akhmim since their early owners, Theodor Graf in Vienna and Wladimir Bock in Leningrad, had considerable holdings of Akhmim textiles.

A.G.

Bibliography: Friedländer 1945, p. 41, pl. 14; Ostoia 1969, no. 10, pp. 23–33; Metropolitan Museum of Art 1979, no. 136, pp. 159–60; Brown University 1987, no. 9, pp. 44–5.

1. For iconographic parallels see, e.g., sarcophagi in the Vatican (Museo Chiarimonti) and the Museo Torlonia in Rome, inv. T iv-3 (Turcan 1966, p. 473, pls. 36C, 37A). This fragment of a linen cloth with an attached tapestry panel is another example of applied textile decoration. The panel is woven in linen and wool on woolen warps, as is frequently the case with appliqués (as in cat. no. 37). The design of the panel is executed in purple in the monochrome silhouette style with inner details carried out with a flying shuttle. Technical information: Plain (tabby) cloth: warp and weft: undyed linen (S-spun). Applique: warp: undyed wool (S-spun); weft: undyed linen (S-spun), purple wool (S-spun), undyed light wool for flying shuttle; tapestry weave over 1 warp. An identical but better preserved panel from the same textile is in Leningrad (Hermitage, inv. 11377; Mat'e and Ljapunova 1951, no. 35, pp. 98–9, pl. 18.3). The designs of both panels consist of a wide border with the twelve labors of Heracles framing a central square containing an inscribed medallion with Dionysus, Ariadne, and Heracles. Dionysus and Ariadne sit in a chariot drawn by three panthers and driven by a charioteer putto; Heracles is trotting along.

2. Parrish 1984, pls. 92–3.

3. Now in Madrid (Brommer 1953, pl. 31).

4. See n. 1.

5. E.g., on a silver plate in the Bibliothèque Nationale in Paris (Cabinet des Médailles, inv. 2879; Metropolitan Museum of Art 1979, no. 139, pp. 162–3); on ivory plaques in the Walters Art Gallery in Baltimore, inv. 71.11 and 71.12 (Metropolitan Museum of Art 1979, no. 206, pp. 229–30).

47

Hanging with Meleager and Atalanta, late 6th–7th century

Wool. 106 × 80

The Textile Museum, Washington, D.C. 71.90

Provenance: Paul Mellon Collection, Paris

This large decorative hanging demonstrates the difficulties in working with archaeological textiles. Its fragmentary condition precludes a more precise indentification of its decoration than a hunt. A restoration of this type of textile is difficult, since there is no way of assuring that the tens of small fragments now constituting many of them can be assembled with accuracy.

The figures appear to be an Amazon-like armed female on a horse, possibly a huntress, and an armed standing nude male, with wild game scattered throughout. Based on the presence of the huntress, the scene has most often been identified as the Calydonian Boar Hunt with Atalanta and Meleager, a classical myth frequently depicted in Greek and Roman art.[1] While the male figure corresponds to standard portrayals of Meleager, the huntress, with a sword in her raised hand, deviates from the common depiction of Atalanta, who is more typically shown hunting with a bow and arrow.[2] The game animals also pose a problem, since none is clearly a boar. (Two sets of clawed feet, one in the center top and the other at the lower right, belong to a lion and a leopard; the leg of the third animal, in the upper right, might be a boar's.) Nevertheless, animals other than boars are known from late Roman depictions of the Calydonian hunt.[3]

This hanging illustrates how infiltration of new motifs and a lax adherence to the original myth increased in late Roman times, along with a preference for less structured designs in which individual motifs could be placed almost at random on a neutral background.[4]

The weaving is perpendicular to the design,[5] a fact which may account for some of the distortions of the motifs, although their overall simplification and almost abstract forms are the result of the abandonment of naturalistic representation common in the art of the late 6th and 7th centuries, the date also suggested for this textile. At the same time, this hanging, together with other works of art, confirms that even in the 7th century, subjects from Classical mythology and literature continued to be used for the decoration of private homes.[6]

A.G.

Bibliography: Thompson 1975, p. 210; Metropolitan Museum of Art 1979, no. 142, pp. 164–5; Trilling 1982, no. 21, p. 43.

1. Daltrop 1966.
2. Apollodorus *Bibliotheca* I, viii, 2–3.
3. E.g., a lion hunt is included on a floor from the Constantinian Villa in Antioch-Daphne (Levi 1947, I. pp. 237–8; II. pl. 56b).
4. Lavin 1963.
5. The hanging is woven with polychrome woolen wefts on undyed woolen warps. See Trilling 1982, no. 21, p. 43. The dominant colors are red, for the background and other details, and blue and green for the costumes
6. Cf. the depiction of the Calydonian boar hunt with Meleager and Atalanta in an early 7th century silver plate now in Leningrad. See Metropolitan Museum of Art 1979, no. 141, pp. 163–4.

48
Fragment of a Hanging with Riderless Horse, 6th century

Wool. 39.6 × 44.8

The Walters Art Gallery, Baltimore. 83.461

This fragment with a riderless horse is one of several that survive from a larger textile, probably a wall hanging.[1] The hanging was made from white woolen cloth with woven-in tapestry roundels with horses, probably arranged in staggered rows as on an Antinoopolis textile in Lyons.[2] The red roundel of this fragment is bordered with pairs of symmetrically placed chains of white hearts on a dark blue background. The roundel contains a stylized plant in blue, green, and beige rising behind a galloping white horse, saddled but riderless. The white ground around the roundel is filled with fruit baskets with leaves and blue birds with red beaks and feet.

The complete hanging would have had a carpet-like appearance, with the main field containing staggered rows of roundels and interstitial baskets and birds surrounded by a narrow border. Hangings of this type became popular in the late 5th and early 6th century.[3]

The individual design elements of the repeat patterns used in these textiles can be either traditional or, as is often the case, new to the textile design and the other decorative arts of the Mediterranean. The most frequently copied foreign motifs are the unusual composite designs of Sassanian silks being imported into Byzantine territory (cat. no. 191).[4] The growing popularity of silks, both domestic and imported, which as a rule employed continuous repeat patterns, may also be behind the use of similar compositions in other textiles, including wall hangings like the Walters fragment. Except for the chains of white hearts and the stylized tree motif that may have been inspired by Sassanian art, the other motifs of the this fragment – the horse, the birds and the baskets – are taken from the traditional decorative repertory. Similar horses, for example, had been appearing in Egyptian textiles since the 5th century. The limited modeling along its back and legs is indicated through the traditional hatching technique of Egyptian weavers. The more unusual motif of baskets and leaves is a domestic version of the more exotic composite arrangements found in imported

silks. This familiarity with foreign motifs as well as the blending of the new and the traditional suggest that this piece was made later rather than earlier in the 6th century.
A.G.

Bibliography: The Brooklyn Museum 1941, no. 240, p. 76; Weibel 1952, no. 14, p. 79.

1. Cleveland Museum of Art, inv. 48.27 (Weibel 1952, no. 13, p. 79).
2. Musée historique des Tissus (Volbach 1969, no. 27, pp. 60–61).
3. These textiles were discussed as a group by Kitzinger 1946.
4. Guimet 1912; Geijer 1963; Martiniani-Reber 1986, pp. 36–60.

49

Woolen Cover with a Tapestry Decoration, second half of 6th century

Wool. 98.4 × 56 (tapestry roundel D. 27.6)

Museum of Fine Arts, Boston, Frederick Brown Fund. 47.382

Although the household textiles and clothing of Late Roman and Byzantine Egypt were made mainly of linen, natural or brightly dyed woolen cloth was used as well. Like their linen counterparts, woolen fabrics were decorated with tapestry-woven ornaments. This fragment of a green woolen cloth might have been used as a mantle, shawl, or even a cover. Parts of its left selvage and the corded bottom edge are preserved, as are some of its decoration, two beige stripes, and a large, woven-in tapestry roundel.[1]

The colorful design of the roundel consists of a border frieze framed by a running wave and a central medallion framed by a beaded band. Both frames are executed in red and white. The frieze contains four axially placed red-ground disks enclosing animals (a winged horse, two ibexes, and a leopard), and four vignettes of Nilotic scenes in the fields between the disks. A boating putto, crocodile, water birds, and in the lower left segment a large pale creature (most likely a stylized hippopotamus or water buffalo common to this subject) are represented on the dark blue ground in the midst of green leaves, pink and red lotus blossoms, and swimming fish. A bust of a winged youth clad in a chlamys is shown in three-quarter view against the yellow background of the central medallion. The face, framed by thick curly hair in dark blue and red, is simply drawn with a long nose, small mouth, and enormous eyes. Even without any obvious attribute, the figure either directly represents or is derived from a male personification of one of the Seasons. Although not as common as female personifications, male youths and putti are an important iconographic group of representations of the Seasons.[2]

In spite of the large range of colors, the motifs of the roundel are executed not through modeling but as outlined colored surfaces. Here and there additional yarn is used to articulate some detail. With the exception of limited horizontal hatching over the bodies of the two ibexes, there is no suggestion of volume or relief.

It is immediately apparent that two distinct groups of motifs and to some extent also styles have been combined in the design of the roundel. The central bust and the Nilotic scenes are traditional motifs of Graeco-Roman and Byzantine art in Egypt and elsewhere in the Empire. Used together or separately, in textiles and other decorative arts, they were commonly understood as allegories of well-being and prosperity.[3] The portrayal of the Nilotic fauna and flora, including the classical motif of boating putti (see also cat. no. 36), is especially successful here. It compares well with such fine examples of this theme as the decorative panels of the Shawl of Sabina (late 5th–early 6th century) or the carving on the ceiling beams of the Justinianic church at Mount Sinai (A.D. 550–565).[4] The omission of any specific iconographic details on the bust is mainly due to the late 6th century date of this weaving (cf. cat. nos. 37 and 187).

The animals of the four disks betray awareness of an altogether different artistic tradition, that of Sassanian Iran. All four are related to animals that decorate tapestry weavings inspired by patterned silks. The silks are believed to have been made in Iran but found in Egyptian graves of the Byzantine period in Antinoopolis (see cat. nos. 191 and 48).[5] The ibexes, the leopard and the winged horse of the Boston roundel look exactly like Egyptian imitations of imported motifs that bcame fashionable in the Byzantine world from the late 5th century onward.[6] In the Boston textile, they even appear to be intruders compositionally, superimposed on what would otherwise have been an uninterrupted Nilotic frieze.[7] The textile was certainly made in Egypt. It is an important example of the enrichment of a very traditional repertory with new, more exotic motifs. In this case, the new motifs not only enhance the decorative effect of the design, they also may have expanded the iconographic meaning of the roundel by alluding to the terrestrial sphere, as a counterpart to the aquatic one represented by the Nilotic subjects.[8] Like other large textiles of this kind, this piece was decorated with at least one but more probably three such tapestry roundels.[9]

A.G.

Bibliography: Abdel-Malek 1986.

1. Technical information: plain (tabby) cloth: warp: green wool (S-spun), weft: green and off-white wool (S-spun); ca. 12 warps per 1 cm, ca. 16 wefts per 1 cm. Tapestry: warp: green wool (S-spun); weft: several tones of undyed wool, blue, red, green, yellow, pink, tan wool (all S-spun); tapestry over 1 warp, ca. 12 warps per 1 cm; weft counts vary.
2. Parrish 1984, pp. 22–4.
3. Foucher 1965a.
4. The Metropolitan Museum of Art 1979, no. 112, pp. 134–5; Forsyth et al., 1973, pls. 68 and 69.
5. Geijer 1963 and Martiniani and Reber 1986, pp. 35–60; see also Kitzinger 1946.
6. Next to the textiles from Egypt, see also the Phoenix mosaic from Antioch (Baratte 1978, no. 44, pp. 92–9) and much of the sculpture from the church of St. Polyeuktos in Istanbul (Strube 1984, especially pp. 61–77).
7. Cf. the frieze of the Shawl of Sabina (Metropolitan Museum of Art 1979, no. 112, pp. 134–5).
8. Abdel-Malek 1986, p. 33 and *passim.*
9. As, for example, on a large tapestry hanging now in the Nelson-Atkins Museum of Art, inv. 35.2 (Kitzinger 1946, fig. 47).

50
Cushion Cover (?),
late 6th–early 7th century

Wool and linen. 75 × 63.5

Museum of Art, Rhode Island School
of Design. Gift of Jesse H. Metcalf.
39.126

Provenance: Dikran Khan Kelekian
Collection

Woolen textiles, including works like
this cover, have not been sufficiently
studied.[1] In spite of the overwhelming
evidence of the papyri where weavers
and merchants of woolen cloths and
woolen cloths and clothing are mentioned all the time, there is a general
perception that wool was rarely used
in Egypt before the Arab conquest of
640/1.[2] All-wool cloths, including tapestry-woven ones, were found in the 4th
and 5th century archaeological context
in Karanis.[3] Sturdy woolen and linen
tapestry-woven cloth would have been
ideally suited for such heavy uses as
cushion and mattress covers. The size
and compact weave of this piece suggest
that it may have served this purpose.
Similarly striped colorful seat cushions
are often represented in Early Byzantine painting in Egypt and elsewhere in
the Empire.[4]

This tapestry cover should be
assigned a late 6th and 7th century date,
a date which would agree with the very
two-dimensional, stylized forms of its
decorative motifs.

A.G.

Bibliography: Museum of Art, Rhode
Island School of Design 1988, p. 53.

1. This small cover is almost complete.
   Although some areas of the surface have
   been lost, both selvages as well as both
   corded warp endings remain. The piece is
   executed entirely in tapestry weave in
   undyed linen and colorful wools on undyed
   woolen warps. The design consists of two
   sets of decorative bands: two outer ones
   are filled with a loose three-strand guilloche in red, blue, and yellow with dotting
   between the strands; two wider inner
   bands contain symmetrically arranged
   pairs of feather-like pattern in blue, red,
   yellow, and orange. Smaller imbrication
   patterns fill these bands along the selvages.
   The feather patterns meet at central,
   lozenge-shaped panels, one enclosing a
   rooster and the other a hen. The space
   around the birds is filled with grape clusters and other fruit. The four patterned
   bands are separated by three linen fields,
   each decorated alternatingly with four-
   petal rosettes (either red or purple) and
   birds (in blue, orange, and yellow with
   brightly colored tail feathers). The rosettes
   and birds are arranged symmetrically
   inside each field while observing a staggered diagonal oaganization with respect
   to the composition of all three linen fields.
   Technical information: warp: undyed wool
   (S-spun); weft: undyed linen (S-spun),
   blue, red, green, yellow, purple, orange,
   and black wool (all S-spun); tapestry
   weave over 1 warp; ca. 8 warps per 1 cm;
   weft counts vary.
2. See the introductory essay; cf. Baginski
   and Tidhar 1980, p. 9.
3. Wilson 1933, nos. 100, 103, 105, 109,
   pp. 39–41, pl. 9.
4. As, e.g., in Bawit and Saqqara (Badawy
   1978, figs. 4.25–6, 4.37–8, pp. 253
   and 263).

51
Lampstand: Aphrodite,
5th–6th century

Probably from Egypt

Bronze. H. 50.2

The Nelson-Atkins Museum of Art,
Kansas City, Missouri (Nelson Fund).
58–5

A standard Late Antique lampstand
design – with tripod base, pricket (to fit
a sinking in the base of a bronze lamp;
cf. cat. no. 81), and pan (to catch dripping oil) – has been transformed into an
elaborate presentation piece through the
inclusion of Aphrodite on the shaft and
sea creatures and Nereids on the base.
The goddess holds a mirror in one hand
and a perfume applicator in the other.

Citing contemporary descriptions of
weddings and comparable iconography
on the lid of the famous Projecta casket,
Marvin Ross has argued that this lamp
was a wedding present; thus, Aphrodite
is the bride preparing for the ceremony
and the Nereids are bearers of wedding gifts.[1] On another level, the light
from the lamp would have illuminated
the boudoir of the bride as she made
her toilette.
G.V.

Bibliography: Ross 1959, *passim*;
Metropolitan Museum of Art 1979,
no. 318.

1. Ross 1959, *passim*.

Color plate, page 17

Personal Adornment

52
Pectoral Cross: Christ,
6th–7th century

Gold. 8 × 5.3

Dumbarton Oaks Collection,
Washington, D.C. 37.24

This is one of the few Early Byzantine
pectoral crosses to bear an image of
Christ; a near twin is preserved in the
Cairo Museum.[1] A youthful Christ,
wearing a *colobium*,[2] stands with arms
outstretched to reveal the wounds of the
Passion; beyond that, and the very shape
of the object, there is little to suggest the
physical reality of crucifixion. Above his
head is the inscribed plaque, and from
beneath his feet flow the Rivers of
Paradise, evocative of the life-giving
powers of the cross. In the medallions at
the end of the arms are (above and
below) the Virgin Mary and St. John the
Baptist, and (left and right) two saints.

Necklaces and pendants in sumptuous
materials were a salient feature of Late
Antique fashion. During the 5th and 6th
centuries jewelry that had formerly
borne pagan or religiously neutral imagery was gradually Christianized.
G.V.

Bibliography: Ross 1965, no. 15;
Metropolitan Museum of Art 1979,
no. 301.

1. Werner 1936, *passim*.
2. A colobium is a long, full, belted garment
   typically worn by Christ in Christian art
   of Syria-Palestine.

Color plate, page 18

53
Three Rings, Roman period

From Karanis

Bronze and silver (no. 23018).
D. 1.8 (no. 23018); D. 0.7 (no. 23054);
D. 1.6 (23064)

Kelsey Museum of Archaeology,
The University of Michigan. 23018,
23054, 23064

Because of their utilitarian role in sealing
(locks and documents), rings were the
most common form of jewelry in antiquity. Most were, therefore, seal rings,
with incised devices in their bezels.
Others, however, were simply decorative, and might rely on semiprecious
stones or colored glass for their effect.
And finally, some bore quasimagical
devices, like striding lions.
G.V.

54

Three Pairs of Earrings; and Three Individual Earrings,
3rd–4th century (gold earrings);
6th–7th century (bronze earrings)

From Terenouthis (Kelsey)

Gold; bronze (11.1514).
D. 1.4 (26264, 26265), D. 2 (26313, 26314); L. 5.4 (26289, 26290), L. 9.4 (11.1513), L. 6.8 (11.1514)

Kelsey Museum of Archaeology, The University of Michigan 26264, 26265; 26313, 26314; 26289, 26290; Museum of Fine Arts, Boston, Gift of Miss Mary S. Ames, 11.1511, 11.1513, 11.1514

This assortment of earrings covers a broad range, from simple gold wire hoops, to hoops with granulation, to elaborate pendant examples with glass beads. There is, moreover, a single open-work bronze specimen with a cross at its center. Abundant parallels for most of these specimens have been discovered in Egypt.[1] As a group they attest to the extent to which self-adornment had penetrated all strata of society and, in the case of the bronze earring, how the cross had come to dominate all aspects of decoration in private life.
G.V.

Bibliography: Museum of Fine Arts, Boston 1976, nos. 242, 243.

1. Strzygowski 1904, pl. XXXVIII, and Petrie 1927, pls. VIII-X.

55
Necklace with Ducks,
4th–6th century

Said to be from Nazareth
Gold and glass. Cir. 57.5

Walters Art Gallery, Baltimore. 57.1727

This necklace is composed of simple, toylike ducks separated by glass beads on twisted gold wires. The links contain little precious metal since they are stamped out of thin gold foil in two halves and joined. The clasp is formed of two oval plates of gold stamped with concentric circles and ending in hooks.

The circles with punched centers used for the animals' eyes and on the clasp plates appear commonly in the art of Early Byzantine Egypt. Furthermore, the ducks recall those on the edge of the standing bronze censer from the Brooklyn Museum (cat. no. 125).
G.V.

Bibliography: Walters Art Gallery 1979, no. 436.

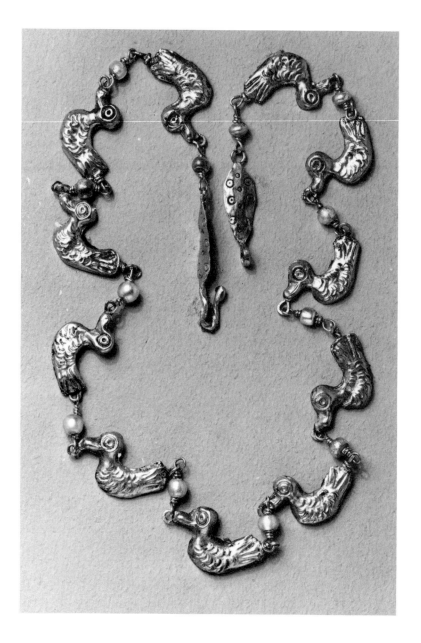

56
Cosmetic Box,
1st century B.C.–4th century A.D.

From Karanis

Wood. 5.5 × 6 × 8.5

Kelsey Museum of Archaeology,
The University of Michigan. 3327

Provenance: Excavated in 1926

Small boxes without locks of any sort
were used to hold a variety of everyday
items. Inside this dark brown wood box
with sliding lid (note the wooden pegs
used in the construction) were found
some papyri and cloth. Such containers
were also used to store an assortment of
inexpensive cosmetic utensils, like hairpins and kohl sticks[1] (cat. no. 55). The
incised circles decorating the surface of
this box are typical of much Late Roman
and Early Byzantine patterning.
G.V. and F.D.F.

1. Gazda et al. 1983, p. 26; cf. fig. 44, p. 27.

57
Cosmetic Aids (Hairpin and Spoon),
Roman period

From Karanis

Bone. L. 11 each

Kelsey Museum of Archaeology,
The University of Michigan. 21790,
21867

Thousands of hairpins in bronze, iron,
ivory, and bone survive from sites
throughout the Roman and Byzantine
world.[1] This delicate example was
fashioned on a lathe, as is indicated by
the shallow dot on its head. The round
shaft tapers gradually toward the tip and
slightly toward the head as well, from
which it is set off by incised lines and a
pair of disk bases. The relatively large
pinhead is oval in shape. Distinguished
by its fine workmanship and elegant
design, this hairpin is paralleled by many
examples excavated in Egypt.[2]

The spoon, which like the hairpin
comes from Karanis, has a long, tapering
handle. The other end is splayed and
flattened to form a bowl. Such spoons,
usually described as cosmetic applicators, survive in great numbers from
this region and period.[3] Along with the
hairpin, it attests to a sophisticated urban
culture capable of enhancing and appre-
ciating female beauty.
G.V.

1. Davidson 1952, p. 276.
2. Wulff 1909, pl. XXI; Petrie 1927, pl. XIX.
3. Ibid., pl. XXIIII.

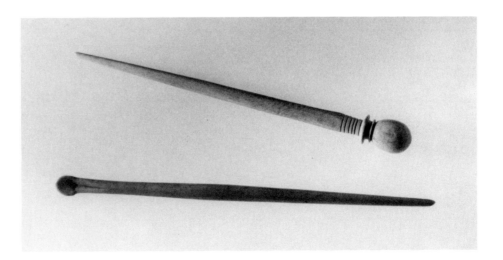

58

Comb, ca. 6th century

From Akhmim

Wood. 21 × 8

Museum of Fine Arts, Boston, Sears
Fund. 03.1628

Decorated combs are found in Egyptian
graves dating back to the predynastic
period (end of the 4th millennium), and
even in Late Roman and Early Byzantine
times they continue to be found in burials.
At Antinoe examples were found placed
on the chest of the dead.[1] But combs
certainly had utilitarian use during life,
as evidenced by frequent signs of wear.
Their practical design with two rows of
teeth was a feature introduced to the
Mediterranean world by the Greeks.
The larger, wider teeth, as shown here,
were used for combing out the hair,
while the smaller ones were used for
touching up and smoothing out the
coiffure.[2] The rectangular panel separating the teeth was typically decorated
with animals or geometric designs, a
feature illustrated here by the openwork
design with a profile of a bird amidst
foliage. Groups of tiny incised circles
with interior dots decorate the border of
the band and the bird's tail. This is a form
of decoration found on many Egyptian
objects of this period (e.g., cat. no. 56).
F.D.F.

Bibliography: The Brooklyn Museum
1941, p. 30, no. 73; Museum of Fine
Arts, Boston 1976, no. 248, p. 208.

1. Rutschowscaya 1986, p. 26, citing
   Strzygowski 1904, pp. 144–7, nos.
   8826–8836.
2. Rutschowscaya 1986, p. 26.

59

Comb, ca. 6th century

Probably from Antinoopolis[1]

Wood. 10.3 × 12.6

The Brooklyn Museum, Charles Edwin
Wilbour Fund. 65.1

This orange-brown wooden comb has a
double edging of teeth like the previous
example. But the overall horizontal
design of this comb is quite different. It
bears ring handles and its central panel
is decorated with a peacock surrounded
by a dense background of foliage extending around the circular handles and even
flanking the teeth. The peacock, with
its colorful plumage, was understood in
the Early Byzantine world as a sign of
nature's splendor but was also frequently
used as a sign of immortality.[2] Some
combs were used in a liturgical context,[3]
and though it is usually impossible to
determine which ones were, this deli-
cately crafted example may have been
such a case.

F.D.F.

1. I thank Donald Spanel for the information
   on the site of origin.
2. Maguire 1987, p. 39 and *passim.*
3. Rutschowscaya 1986, p. 26.

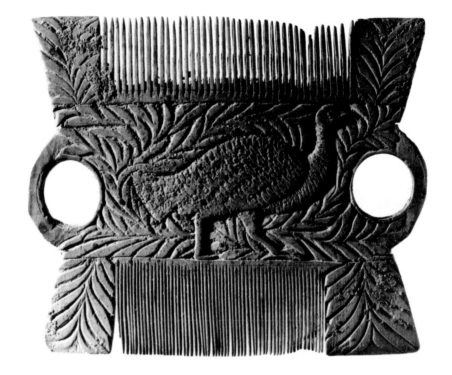

60

Roundel with a Head of Medusa,
first half of 4th century

Linen, wool, and gold leaf on linen core.
D. 31.7

The Textile Museum, Washington, D.C.
71.91

Provenance: Paul Mellon Collection,
Paris

Tunics were worn by all classes of Egyptians, and though most have not survived, many of their ornaments have. One purpose of this large tunic roundel may have been to magically protect the wearer. The rather complex interlace patterning is accented inside its central loop with a human head whose full face with large, upward-looking eyes is framed by a full crown of long and curly hair. In spite of the fabric losses due to the tear across the roundel, the head can be identified as that of the Gorgon Medusa, an image that appeared in the Hellenistic period and remained popular throughout Late Antiquity.[1] According to legend, a glance from the snake-haired Medusa could turn a person to stone. The Gorgon's traditional serpentine coiffure explains the unusual hairstyle here. Considering that Medusa's image was used for centuries as a powerful prophylactic emblem, often on such personal effects as amulets, necklaces, and metal costume appliqués,[2] its inclusion among woven tunic ornaments is to be expected. Medusa's head was only one of many types of decorative motifs used in textile and other arts precisely for their apotropaic and prophylactic functions and associations. The frequent use of these motifs can be viewed as an indication of the strength of magic and superstition in Late Antique culture (see also cat. no. 101).

The roundel is woven in dark purple wool on linen warps, with linen and gold thread used for the design (linen yarns for the interlace and gold thread for the head and occasional touches in the interstices of the interlace). Ancient gold-thread textiles are very rare and this fragment is one of a handful that have survived. As a group, gold-thread textiles are generally assigned to the period between the late 3rd and early 5th century; the earliest are considered to be those decorated with a central figural – usually mythological – motif enclosed within an interlace in the same

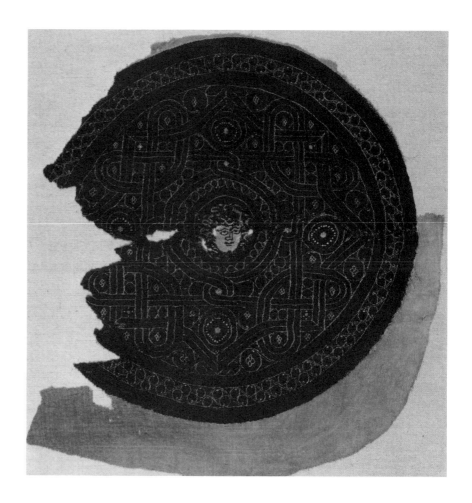

manner as in this roundel.[3] Although gold-thread textiles have been found in graves in various parts of the Roman world, the closest to the Textile Museum roundel are two pieces from Antinoopolis.[4] The direction of the warps and wefts in the Textile Museum roundel and its linen cloth frame indicate that originally this fragment must have been the shoulder decoration of a linen tunic. Monochrome roundels of similar size and ornamentation were fashionable embellishments of late 3rd and early 4th century clothing, especially tunics.[5]

A.G.

Bibliography: Beckwith 1959, p. 7;
Trilling 1982, no. 83, p. 81, color pl. 7.

1. Daremberg-Saglio, II/2, cols. 1615–1629.
2. E.g., British Museum, nos. 2886, 2736, 2737, 3078 and 3079 (Marshall 1911).
3. Orléans, Musée historique et archéologique (now destroyed); Coptic Museum, inv. 6714 (Renner 1981, p. 83, figs. 3 and 4; Daoud Girgis 1983, pl. 8).
4. See note 3 above.
5. Deckers 1979, esp. figs. 22 and 23 for the wall painting in Luxor; see also the Great Hunt mosaic in Piazza Armerina (Carandini et al. 1982, I, fig. 122, p. 217; II, pls. XXIX and XXX).

61
Neck Ornament of a Tunic,
5th century

Linen and wool. 35.5 × 13.

Cleveland Museum of Art, Gift of
George D. Pratt. 26.148

This decorative piece of very fine
linen is a fragment of a child's tunic. It is
made of thin linen cloth the fineness of
which matches that of the woven-in
tapestry neck-opening bands and shoulder panel.[1] These tapestries are woven
with dark purple wool yarns of exceptionally high quality and undyed linen.
The direction of the warps indicates that
the tunic was started at the hemline
instead of the sleeve, as was the more
usual practice.

The neck-opening bands are decorated with a narrow strip of interlaced
medallions filled alternately with human
heads and Solomon knots and finished
with a frieze of disk pendants. The
square shoulder panel has a border of a
plain vegetal scroll framing the center
with a bust. At present, the designs
appear only as a dark silhouette since
the fine surface detailing executed with a
flying shuttle is almost all gone. Usually
textiles of this fineness are dated quite
early, mostly into the 4th century. The
types of the head and bust motifs, however, point to a later date, not earlier
than the second half of the 5th century
(see also cat. no. 62).[2]

All the motifs employed in this fragment were commonly used in textiles as
well as in other arts. The heads and the
busts originally may have had some
iconographic meaning; here, however,
their function is mainly decorative. As
textile decorations, they may have been
inspired by their popularity as ornaments of necklaces and other jewelry.[3]
Such necklaces are imitated in tapestry-
woven neck-opening fragments in
Boston.[4]

A.G.

1. Technical information: warp: undyed linen
   (S-spun); weft: undyed linen (S-spun),
   purple wool (Z-spun, very fine). Tapestry
   weave over 2–3 warps; ca. 13 group
   warps per 1 cm; weft counts vary.
2. E.g. Österreichisches Museum für
   angewandte Kunst, T 370 (Egger 1967,
   pl. 36); Textile Museum, inv. 71.92 (Trilling
   1982, no. 81, p. 80); The Hermitage, inv.
   11291–11295 (Mat'e and Ljapunova 1951,
   nos. 48–52, pp. 102–3, pl. 22.1–6).

3. As on a gold pendant with busts in the
   Dumbarton Oaks Collection (Metropolitan
   Museum of Art, 1979, no. 276, p. 304) and
   on a marriage belt from the same collection (Ross 1965, no. 38).
4. Museum of Fine Arts, Boston, inv. 46.401
   and 46.402 (Ostoia 1969, no. 125,
   pp. 146–7).

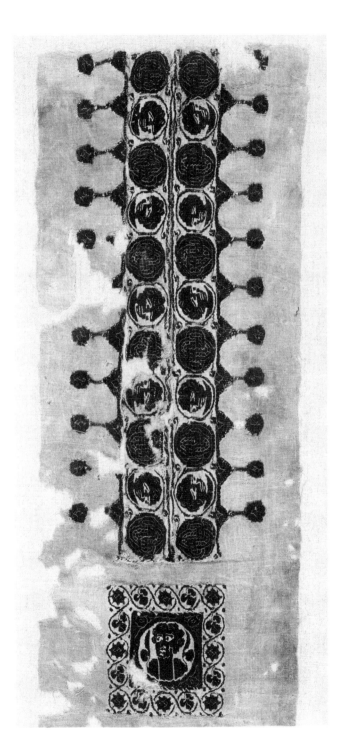

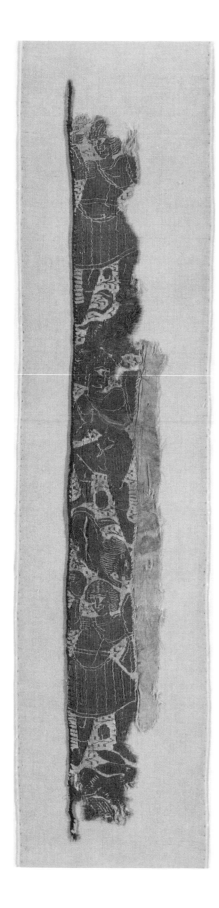

62
Ornamental Band of a Tunic,
late 5th century

Linen and wool. 44 × 5.9

Cleveland Museum of Art, John L. Severance Fund. 50.615

The vertical orientation of the design of this band indicates that it came from a type of tunic decoration known as a *clavus. Clavi* (the plural form) were vertical bands on the tunic descending from the shoulders. The band must have come from a tunic that was woven from the hemline, since the warps of the fragment run vertically with the band instead of perpendicularly, as would have been the case if the tunic was started with the sleeve, as was the most prevalent custom.[1] The band is filled with a dissassembled representation of a hunt: hunters holding shields and missiles are stacked one above another, interspersed with their prey. Minute foliate motifs indicate a landscape setting. Hunting was a popular theme in domestic and private art of Late Antiquity, particularly between the 3rd and 5th centuries. Decorative and compositionally adaptable to any surface, especially when rendered as a free assemblage of individual motifs, the hunt appears in a variety of compositions.[2] It was used for floor mosaics, bronzes, silver and glass vessels, jewelry, and, of course, textiles.[3] Iconographically it belongs to the repertory of subjects generally symbolic of prosperity and the good life. The execution of the hunt on this ornamental band shows a noticeable departure from a naturalistic representation of the figures. A similar style is found in much of late 5th century art, the probable date of this piece.
A.G.

1. This example is made of dark purple wool and undyed linen woven as a tapestry insert into a linen cloth. The fragment is a fine example of the monochrome silhouette style, with all design elements woven in dark wool into the light linen background. Typical of this technique are the inner details freely drawn in light yarns with a flying shuttle. Technical information: plain (tabby) cloth: warp and weft undyed linen (S-spun). Tapestry: warp: undyed linen (S-spun); weft: undyed linen (S-spun), purple wool (S-spun). Tapestry weave over 2–3 warps.
2. See Dunbabin 1978, pp. 46–64; also Lavin 1963.
3. For a review of these representations in general see Metropolitan Museum of Art 1979, pp. 83–92.

63
Tunic Fragment, 6th century

Linen and wool. 87 × 64

Metropolitan Museum of Art, Funds from Various Donors. 89.18.94

Provenance: Theodor Graf Collection

This large fragment is one of the bottom halves of a very finely woven linen tunic that could have been worn by a man or a woman. It is decorated with an angular hem band with spade-shaped finials on braided stems and two square panels woven-in tapestry technique in dark purple wool and linen.[1] Each panel, bordered with the same design, contains a medallion with a nude, cloaked male figure representing a hunter or a warrior. Around the male figures are scattered vegetal motifs.

Figures of hunters and warriors belong to the standard repertory of textile decoration. Here they are presented in a stylized manner, their propor-

tions considerably distorted. The inner details carried out with a flying shuttle and typical of the monochrome style are relegated to the geometric patterns of the borders. Similar representations of human figures are found in late 6th century art. An earlier and more naturalistic version of hunters is present in the tunic fragment from the Cleveland Museum of Art (cat. no. 62).

Friezes of paneling with geometric patterns are also known among extant textiles. The majority are without provenance but some are said to have come from Antinoopolis and Fustat.[2] All these textiles are exceptionally accomplished technically. Their similarities (fine yarns, dark purple wool, Z-spun wool) raise the possibility that this type of decorated tunic came from one center. While this tunic fragment was acquired from Theodor Graf, known for his textile holdings from Saqqara and Akhmim, the range of supposed find sites also includes Antinoopolis, Fustat, Saqqara and Akhmim. One must therefore caution against hasty acceptance of any one site as the workshop center.

A.G.

1. These angular U-shaped ornaments are often also called *clavi*. The actual hem is strengthened by a braid of wool and linen yarns. The decoration is executed in the silhouette monochrome style. All three tapestry inserts use a simple fillet and cresting as borders. The main design of the angular band is the frieze of small rectangles filled with guilloche and overlapping circle patterns. These patterns are executed with a flying shuttle in natural light woolen yarn. Technical information: plain (tabby) cloth: warp and weft: undyed linen (S-spun). Tapestry: warp: undyed linen (S-spun), weft: purple wool (Z-spun, very fine); natural light wool for flying shuttle. Tapestry weave over 2–3 warps, ca. 10 group warps per 1 cm, ca. 45 woolen and 24 linen wefts per 1 cm.
2. E.g., the Louvre, inv. X4428, X4455, AC168 (from Fustat), all three with Z-spun wool (du Bourguet 1964, D1–D3, p. 119); Musée de Cluny, Paris, inv. 14344, from Antinoopolis (unpublished); Museum of Fine Arts, Boston, inv. 90.245, Z-spun wool (unpublished); Metropolitan Museum of Art, inv. 90.05.321, Z-spun wool (unpublished); Pushkin Museum, Moscow inv. 335, Z-spun wool, from Upper Egypt (Šurinova 1967, no. 34).

64
Tapestry Panel with Orpheus,
6th century

Said to be from Akhmim

Tapestry weave in linen and wool.
8.4 × 9.5

Victoria and Albert Museum. 1290.1888

The main component of this panel, a tunic ornament, is an inscribed medallion containing a figure of Orpheus in the midst of figures and animals.[1] Orpheus appears frequently in Roman and Late Antique secular and religious funerary art, often in compositions very much like this weaving.[2] This Thracian poet and musician of ancient myth (his songs and music, played on a lyre given him by Apollo, charmed men, beasts, nature, and gods alike),[3] was also the deity of a mystery religion. He was one of the few pagan mythological figures adopted by the early Christians and represented in their art as an allegory of Christ.[4] The choice of Orpheus playing his music may have been motivated in Early Byzantine art by any of these reasons, although as a 6th century tunic ornament it most likely represents the Orpheus of mythology rather than the Orpheus of religion. As many other examples in Early Byzantine art illustrate, mythological subjects even at that date constituted the largest category of figural decoration in private domestic art, including clothing (see also cat. nos. 65 and 48).[5]

Although the composition of the panel follows the established tradition in the portrayal of Orpheus with the animals,[6] specific stylistic features of this weaving, such as the stylized forms of the figures with large heads and emphasized eyes and the crowding of the surface of the roundel, give an appearance that parallels the 5th and 6th century examples of the subject (for example, the ivory pyxis in Florence and the floor mosaics from Jerusalem).[7] Another likely 6th century feature of the panel is the use of red instead of purple wool for the design,[8] probably inspired by brightly colored silks that were beginning to be widely used just about that time.[9]

The London panel is said to be from Akhmim. A roundel in Leningrad displaying the same subject and executed in a very similar style may also have originated in Akhmim.[10]

A.G.

Bibliography: Kendrick 1920, no. 42, pp. 59–60, pl. 14.

1. Holding his lyre and clad in his customary Phrygian attire of a short tunic, trousers, high boots and a conical cap, Orpheus is portrayed in a three-quarter view turned to the left. Of the four figures surrounding him, the upper ones are winged putti. One carries a cornucopia and the other a bird. A lion, griffin, horse, and stag can be recognized among the animals. Additional animals and birds fill the corner spandrels of the panel. The design, which is densely organized, is executed in red wool on a background of undyed linen. The figures are internally articulated with considerable detail and heavily outlined externally with an extra linen yarn (2-plied and applied in soumac technique). The weaving proceeded perpendicularly to its design, suggesting that this may have been a hem *segmentum* of a linen tunic into which it was inserted in tapestry technique. Technical information: warp: undyed linen (S-spun); weft: undyed linen (S-spun), red wool (S-spun); undyed S-spun, 2-ply Z linen used for outlines. Tapestry weave over 1–2 warps, ca. 19 warps per 1 cm.

2. E.g., on a floor mosaic from the House of the Laberii at Oudna, late 3rd or early 4th century (Dunbabin 1978, Oudna 1.n, p. 266, pl. 134), and on a terracotta mold in the Römisch-Germanisches Museum in Cologne, inv. Ton 166 (Frankfurt am Main 1983–1984, no. 195, p. 587).
3. Apollodorus, *Bibliotheca*, I.iii.2.
4. Huskinson 1974, pp. 68–72; also Stern 1973.
5. For two different approaches to the use of mythological subjects in Early Christian art, cf. Brandenburg 1969 and Huskinson 1974.
6. See above n. 2.
7. As, e.g., on an ivory pyxis in Florence, Bargello (Volbach 1976, no. 92, pp.70–1, pl. 51); the Orpheus mosaic from Jerusalem is now in the Archaeological Museum in Istanbul (Grabar 1967, fig. 119, p. 113).
8. For some related textiles see Hermitage, inv. 13.217 (Mat'e and Ljapunova 1951, no. 39, p. 100, pl. 25.5); Louvre, inv. x4378, x4339, x4311, x4129 (du Bourguet 1964, C35, C36, D36 and D37, pp. 97–8, 132).
9. See cat. no. 192.
10. The Hermitage, inv. 13.217 (Mat'e and Ljapunova 1951, no. 39, p. 100, pl. 25.5).

65

Medallion with Pasiphaë and the Bull, 6th century

From Antinoopolis

Wool and linen. 11 × 10

The Brooklyn Museum. Gift of
Col. Robert B. Woodward. 15.429

Provenance: Excavated by the Egypt
Exploration Society, 1913–4.

The decoration of this small roundel,
a costume ornament, most likely depicts
an abbreviated version of the myth
of Pasiphaë. The wife of King Minos
of Crete, Pasiphaë was punished by
Poseidon who caused her to fall in love
with a bull. The offspring of this unusual
union was the Minotaur.[1] The scene,
bordered by a blue and yellow running
wave, focuses on nude Pasiphaë in a
green cloak, embracing the pale bull.
Another nude figure, probably an attendant, holds a cup and another object
while witnessing the encounter from the
left. The space above the figures is filled
with an abstract foliate motif.[2]

The roundel should be assigned a 6th
century date. Other works of this period,
especially ivory carving, small bronze
sculpture, jewelry and textiles, employ
the same stylistic features, including the
disproportionately large heads with
large, hollowed eyes.[3] The roundel was
woven into a white woolen cloth, probably decorating a tunic or a mantle. Even
in the 6th century, subjects taken from
classical mythology often decorated
costume and other objects for private
domestic use.

Excavated in Antinoopolis, this piece
belongs to a sizable group of small-scale
tapestries, many of which are roundels,
their provenance, however, is mostly
unknown. The group is characterized
by its use of red ground, running-wave
borders, abbreviated figural compositions, and linear style.[4] All appear to
have been costume ornaments.[5] Ever-
increasing use of brightly colored silks
for clothing and decorative touches, a
fashion that was well underway already
in the 5th century, may be responsible
for the popularity of such brightly
colored tapestry-woven ornaments for
wool and linen garments as well. This

popularity outlasted Byzantine rule in
Egypt. Polychrome tapestry-woven
costume ornaments continued to be
made long after the Arab conquest
of 640/1.[6]

A.G.

Bibliography: The Brooklyn Museum
1941, no. 215, p. 69; Beckwith 1959,
pp. 13 and 17; Wessel 1965, p. 218,
pl. 127; de Francovich 1963, pp. 147–8,
p. 84; Thompson 1971, no. 19, pp. 48–9.

1. Apollodorus *Bibliotheca,* III.xv.8.
2. The roundel is woven in tapestry technique in wool and linen on the warps of
fine white wool. The textile is dominated
by the red ground and dark blue outlines
of the design elements. The figures are
articulated with a certain amount of inner
detail and communicate with each other
with convincing gestures. Although
modeling of the figures is absent, some
foreshortening, as in the three-quarter-
view presentation of the attendant and in
Pasiphaë's lower body, give the scene an
appearance of volume and movement in
space. Technical information: tapestry:
warp: white wool (S-spun); weft: undyed

linen (S-spun), red, yellow, blue, green,
orange, tan, pink, pale green-gray wool
(all S-spun). Tapestry weave over 1 warp,
ca. warps per 1 cm, ca. 35–40 wefts per
1 cm (Thompson 1971, p. 48).
3. As, e.g., on an ivory plaque in Trieste
(Volbach 1976, no. 82, p. 63, pl. 45) and
on a pyxis in Wiesbaden (Volbach 1976,
no. 105, p. 75, pl. 56).
4. E.g., Österreichisches Museum für
angewandte Kunst, T.10.048 (Egger 1967,
pl. 17); Victoria and Albert Museum inv.
2149.1900 (Kendrick 1921, no. 389, p. 37;
Beckwith 1959, pp. 13 and 16); the
Louvre, inv. x4125, x4313, x4121, x4356,
x4126 (du Bourguet 1964, D39, D40, D44
D45 D47, pp. 133–4 and 136–7). See also
cat no. 66.
5. As, e.g., on a tunic fragment from Akhmim
now in Brussels, Musées Royaux d'Art et
d'Histoire (Errera 1916, no. 241, p. 109).
6. See also cat nos. 66 and 64 and other red-
ground tunic ornaments in the exhibition.

66
Roundel with the Judgment of Paris,
6th century

Linen and wool. 13 × 12

Museum of Fine Arts, Boston. 55.577

This roundel[1] and its companion piece in the Hermitage[2] are examples of small-scale tapestry weavings, probably costume ornaments characteristic for their use of abbreviated figural, often mythological, scenes executed on a red ground and enclosed in running-wave borders.[3] The two-tier composition of this roundel contains Zeus, Hermes, and Paris in the upper half and the three goddesses in the lower half. The figures are identified either by their specific iconographic types or by their attributes: a bearded Zeus is represented as a seated ruler, Hermes has winged feet, and Paris is clad in a Phyrgian costume; the standing nude is Aphrodite, while the matronly demeanor belongs to Hera (on the left), and the helmet-wearing figure (on the right) is Athena. An effective use of dark and light outlines (many are executed with extra yarns over the surface of the weaving in soumac technique) presents the small figures in considerable detail even though the modeling is absent and the colors are restricted to mainly beige, yellow, green, purple, and blue.

The roundel should be assigned a 6th century date, based on the fact that other works of this period, especially ivory carvings, small bronze sculptures, jewelry, and, of course, textiles employ the same stylistic features, including the disproportionately large heads with large, hollowed eyes.[4] Many of these objects are also decorated with similar mythological subjects, which continued to be used on objects of private use throughout the Early Byzantine period.

Concerning the popularity of brightly colored tapestry-woven costume ornaments, this fashion was mostly likely inspired by the ever-increasing use of brightly colored silks for clothing and for decorative touches. Polychrome tapestry-woven costume ornaments outlasted the Byzantine rule in Egypt and continued to be made long after the Arab conquest.

A.G.

1. Technical information: warp: linen (S-spun); weft: wool and linen. Tapestry weave.
2. Leningrad, Hermitage, inv. 11507 (Mat'e and Ljapunova 1951, no. 37, p. 99, pl. XX.4; also Kybalovà 1967, p. 76, pl. 25).
3. See also cat. nos. 64 and 65.
4. As, e.g., on a pyxis with the Judgment of Paris, Walters Art Gallery, inv. 71.64 (Metropolitan Museum of Art 1979, no. 115, pp. 137–8) and on an ivory plaque in Trieste (Volbach 1976, no. 82, p. 63, pl. 45) and on a pyxis in Wiesbaden (Volbach 1976, no. 105, p. 75, pl. 56); see also a painted reliquary lid in the Vatican Museum (Grabar 1967, fig. 205, p. 190).

67
Shoulder Panel from a Tunic,
6th–early 7th century

Silk, wool, and linen. 9.8 x 9.8

Museum of Fine Arts, Boston. 35.87

This tunic ornament and its related fragments are technically and stylistically significant, since they offer evidence of the technical excellence of weaving throughout the Early Byzantine period and of the responsiveness of textile art to ongoing stylistic changes.

This small panel is a shoulder ornament of a linen tunic,[1] and bears an inscribed roundel in the central square with a rider on a white horse. The rider, dressed in a beige cloak and a beige belted tunic, is shown in three-quarter view, his right hand raised back as if discharging a missile. In spite of the small size of the panel, the motifs are executed with precision and attention to minute detail. They are either interwoven in differently shaded yarns, as is the case with the fish and the birds, creating an almost naturalistic appearance, or they are carried out in outlines often executed in an extra yarn with a flying shuttle, as in the case of the fruit and flower motifs and the horseman. Some details are now gone.

The quality of the weaving of this panel (and its companion pieces) is exceptionally high. All yarns, even traditional linen and wool, are extremely fine. The quality, fine materials, and especially the presence of silk indicate that the tunic was costly. Although silk fabrics were produced in the Early Byzantine world from the late 4th century onward, the use of silk for tapestry weaving appears a novelty, since so few silk tapestries have survived. The fineness of the fabric and the delicacy of the weaving suggest an earlier date for this tunic than indicated by the stylistic execution of the motifs, which agrees with a late 6th and early 7th century phase of Byzantine art.[2]

The modeling of the birds and the fish approximates an earlier illusionistic style (as in cat. no. 35), but other motifs, especially the rider and horse, follow a different stylistic mode. Their forms are simple and stylized and composed of clearly outlined surface areas without any effect of three-dimensional relief. This same stylistic approach is found in other 6th and 7th century textiles, such as the riderless horse (cat. no. 48), and

the horse and lion tapestry in Washington.[3] Thematically, the Boston horseman is isolated, without any relationship to the border design; also, his action appears uncertain, as if the motif were employed only as an ornamental filler (cf. cat. no. 183). This disjointed use of decorative motifs is one of the characteristic features of 6th and 7th century art. Contemporary art, for example, silver plate, offers instances, however, of the coexistence of naturalistic and abstract styles.[4]

A.G.

Bibliography: The Brooklyn Museum 1941, no. 201, p. 66.

1. Two additional fragments from the same tunic are in London: Victoria and Albert Museum, inv. nos. 334.1887 and 335.1887 (Kendrick 1920, no. 62, p. 66, pl. 14; Beckwith 1959, pp. 13, 19). All three are executed in tapestry weave in silk, wool, and linen, and all three have a pale blue ground with motifs in white, brown, beige, red, and blue. The Boston panel has a narrow border filled with red pomegranates and white, beige and blue ducks, ibises, and fish between red corner flower petals, and the identical composition is

used in the London panel. Technical information for the Boston panel: warp: linen (S-spun); weft: beige, brown, and red wool (Z-spun), beige, white and blue silk (S- and Z-spun). Tapestry over 2 warps, ca. 20 group warps per 1 cm.

2. Beckwith 1959, pp. 13, 19.

3. Volbach 1969, no. 28, pp. 60–2; Kitzinger 1946, figs. 30, 40.

4. E.g., the Nereid jug in the Hermitage, A.D. 641–651/2; inv. w-256 (Effenberger 1978, Dok. no. 21, pp. 171–176, figs. 97 and 99).

68

Fragment of a Clavus with Hunters,
6th or early 7th century

Tapestry weave in linen and wool.
26.8 × 11.9

Virginia Museum of Fine Arts,
Richmond, The Glasgow Fund. 64.56.3

This colorful tapestry-woven fragment
is part of a tunic *clavus* decorated with a
hunt scene. A tip and pendant stem of a
clavus, it is decorated with a border of
stylized flowers and a central field displaying two hunting horsemen and their
prey.[1] The hunting theme was inspired
by the great popularity of this subject in
Late Antique and Early Byzantine art
(see also cat. nos. CMA 50.615, BMFA
1985,829). The clavus belonged to a set
of tunic ornaments that also included
segmenta and cuff-bands.[2] The decorative
motifs, color scheme, and even their use
as applied decorations are derived from
silk weavings.[3] This piece employs the
same border and a similar color scheme
as, for example, the silk roundels with
the Annunciation and Nativity scenes in
the Vatican Museum, and two silk roundels with mounted hunters in London.[4] It
is useful to discuss these parallels.

As in this *clavus,* the London hunter
moving to the right is a spearman, and
the one moving to the left is an archer.
Such close dependence of the Virginia
textile on the silks of the Vatican and
London group can be explained only by
a familiarity of the weaver with these
silks; this *clavus* must, therefore, be more
or less contemporary with these silks.
Although the Vatican silks in particular
have been variously dated from the
6th century to as late as the second half
of the 9th century and have been
considered examples of Alexandrian,
Syrian, or Constantinopolitan art, many
of their stylistic and decorative, even
iconographic features, can best be
explained in the context of 6th and early
7th century art.[5]

Because of their technical and artistic
excellence, the Vatican and London silks
had to be made in major artistic centers;
at the same time, the Virginia Museum
textile and other similar tapestry deriva-
tions indicate that silk weavings were
readily available to tapestry weavers in
Egypt. The weavers could observe and
imitate them in their own more traditional technique of weaving using linen
and wool instead of very expensive silk.

Copying patterned silks, especially the roundel designs of the Vatican and London type, was a common practice in Egypt, judging from the number of tapestry weavings with these designs.[6] This easy accessibility of silk models suggests that the tapestries were also woven in Egypt, most likely in Alexandria. It can be assumed that the complex design with Christian subjects, such as the Vatican Museum Annunication and Nativity, had to be invented and introduced into the highly specialized silk weaving before the Arab conquest of Egypt in 640/1.

The choice of the hunting theme for the Virginia *clavus* and its silk models was inspired by the great popularity of this subject in Late Antique and Early Byzantine art (see cat. nos. 62 and 183).

A.G.

Bibliography: Gonosová and Kondoleon forthcoming.

1. The figures are placed on a red ground in a vertical column, one above the other. They are outlined in dark blue and articulated with considerable detail; the hunters are dressed in tunics and cloaks and wear leggings; their white horses are richly caparisoned with saddles, red bridles, and trappings. Even the beasts of prey woven in brown are detailed with touches of white. The fragment is an example of a tunic appliqué woven in tapestry on plied linen warps. Technical information: warp: undyed linen (S-spun, 2-plied Z); weft: undyed linen (S-spun), red, yellow, ocher, green wool (Z-spun), buff, dark blue and brown and violet-purple wool (S-spun). Tapestry weave over 1 warp; ca. 14–15 warps per 1 cm; ca. 34–40 wefts per 1 cm. Some use of soumak wrapping.
2. For well-preserved examples of tapestry-appliqué sets, see two tunics in the Victoria and Albert Museum, inv. 136.1891 and 291.1891 (Kendrick 1922, nos. 619–20, pp. 6–7, pls. 3–4).
3. Victoria and Albert Museum, inv. 820.1903 (Kendrick 1922, no. 794, p. 75, frontispiece).
4. Grabar 1967, figs. 391–2, pp. 334–6; Kendrick 1922, nos. 822 and 823, pp. 82–3, pl. 27.
5. von Falke 1913, I, pp. 48–52; Volbach 1976, nos. 51 and 52, pp. 111, 115, 118; Beckwith 1971, pp. 347–8. For a recent review of these silks see also Trilling 1985, pp. 56–61, fig. 3.
6. E.g., Victoria and Albert Museum, inv. 2070.1900, 2165.1900 (Kendrick 1922, nos. 621–2, p. 8, pl. 5); Berlin, formerly in the Kaiser Friedrich Museum, no. 9270 (Wulff and Volbach 1926, p. 147, pl. 133), to mention a few.

69
Roundel with the Story of Joseph,
7th century

Wool and linen. 26 × 26.7

Metropolitan Museum of Art, Gift of Mr. and Mrs. Charles K. Wilkinson, 1963. 63.178.2

The present roundel was originally sewn onto a tunic as a shoulder or skirt *segmentum*,[1] in a manner illustrated by a well-preserved tunic in London.[2] It belongs to a large group of tunic ornaments decorated with scenes from the life of the Old Testament figure Joseph.[3] All are tapestry woven in separate sets consisting of small and large roundels, shoulder bands, and sleeve bands, and all were appplied. They also share the same color scheme: a red ground with figures executed in beige, green, blue and ochre. Also the selection of the scenes, usually from the 37th chapter of the Book of Genesis, relates the group.

In this roundel, a cycle of nine events (Genesis 37.9-36) is represented, starting with Joseph's second dream in the central medallion and continuing with eight other scenes from the top left counterclockwise in the main field (Joseph leaves Jacob for Shechen; he is directed toward the town of Dothan, is placed in a well, his stained coat is found, and he is sold to the Ishmaelites; Reuben laments Joseph; Joseph is brought to Egypt, and sold to Potiphar). The ground around the figures is filled with scattered floral motifs, birds and animals, and also some letters. A triple border of colorful, stepped, scrolled, and bead-and-reel bands frames the piece.

It is certain that the overall appearance of the New York roundel and the entire group of Joseph tapestries – especially their color scheme and ornamental borders – was inspired by silk weavings such as the Annunciation and the Nativity silks in the Vatican that were made sometime in the course of the 6th century.[4] Otherwise, the Joseph tapestries are the product of Egyptian tapestry weavers. The narrative sequence and the wealth of descriptive detail in these tapestries is without parallel among extant silks. The source for the original design of these tapestries may have been a manuscript,[5] or, as is even more likely, a painted resist-dyed curtain. Such curtains often employed extensive Old and New Testament narrative cycles profusely inscribed with names and biblical and scriptural quotations.[6] The lettering that is still recognizable in many Joseph tapestries may be a remnant of such titles. Difficult to execute in the tapestry technique, these minute inscriptions soon became distorted and even garbled.

Considering the size of this group of tunic ornaments, it is particularly regrettable that not more is known of their origin. They seem to have been found mainly in Upper Egypt in the area around Akhmim. However, it is not known whether they came from one or several locations, or from how many graves, and whether these were poor or rich burials. Even if the particular reverence for Joseph found among the Christians and the Jews in Egypt would explain the general popularity and demand for this subject, the possibility remains that some special circumstance lies behind the invention of the original set of these extraordinary tunic ornaments. Stylistic comparison with other textiles suggests that the Joseph tapestries were originally designed in the late 6th and early 7th century. They continued to be made for some time, those made later becoming more and more stylized. The New York roundel dates to a relatively early, 7th century phase of this process.

Bibliography: Metropolitan Museum of Art 1979, no. 412, pp. 460–2; Vikan 1979; Abdel-Malek 1980, no. 6.

1. Technical information: warp: linen (S-spun, 2-plied Z); weft: red, blue, green, yellow, black wool (all S-spun), linen (S-spun). Tapestry weave over 1 warp.
2. Victoria and Albert Museum, inv. 136.1891 (Kendrick 1922 no. 619, 6–7, pl. 3)
3. At least 54 tunic ornaments decorated with the Story of Joseph have been identified (Abdel-Malek 1980); see also Vikan 1979 and Nauerth 1978, pp. 24–31, figs. 44–6.
4. See also cat no. 63
5. Especially Vikan 1979.
6. For the overview see Kendrick 1922, pp. 60–8.

Color plate, page 19

70
Tapestry Roundel with Alexander,
7th century

Wool and linen. 33.5 × 31.5

The Textile Museum, Washington D.C.
11.18

This roundel and its companion piece
in the Cleveland Museum of Art[1] further confirm the richness of the thematic
repertory of Early Byzantine textiles.
The main motif of the roundel is a double portrayal of a horseman attired in an
imperial costume of the cuirass and the
chlamys. Each figure, his sword drawn,
is being crowned by a pair of winged
erotes. An animal is shown below each
of the two horses. A stylized plant
establishes the central axis of the composition. An inscription ΠΜΑΚCΤΟΠ
ΑΛΕΚCΑΝΤΕΡΟC (Alexander of Macedon)
spans the central caesura between the
two riders. While the forms in the design
are identical, their coloristic rendering
differs, most notably in the horses; the
left horse is yellowish, the right horse is
black. The roundel is framed by a triple
border filled with conventional ornamental motifs: steppes, a scroll, and a heart
chain. At the lower center, the roundel
terminates with a triangular pendant.

The textile is executed on plied linen
warps in the tapestry technique in multicolored wools; the red of the ground
is most pronounced. The roundel was
woven separately and applied on a tunic.
Its weaving is very fine with a considerable amount of articulation, especially in
the horsemen and the horses which are
shown with minute details of clothing in
the former, and the elaborate trappings
in the latter.

The overall appearance of the roundel
with its triumphant riders indicates that
this tapestry was modelled on a silk
weaving. The axial duplication of the
motifs repeats the point-return patterning common to drawloom textiles (see
cat. nos. 192 and 193). The figures are
clearly based on the portrayal of Roman
and Byzantine emperors.[2] A theme of a
triumphant emperor, as shown here and
known from official art, would have
been a most appropriate design for silks
since silk fabrics were particularly used
by emperors and other privileged persons. The name of Alexander could have
been added to the design when a silk
model was copied into a tapestry-woven
costume ornament.

A surprising resemblance between
the Textile Museum roundel and two
ivory carvings[3] also from Egypt can be
explained by a reliance on a similar silk
textile for a model. This silk must have
originated in Constantinople, probably
in the early 7th century following the
victory of Emperor Heraclius over the
Sassanians. This date is supported by
the specific saddle and stirrups depicted
in this textile, which were used by the
Sassanian cavalry at that time.[4] Careful
rendition of the figures of the roundel
would indicate a close dependence on a
silk model, thus supporting a 7th century
date for its manufacture.
A.G.

Bibliography: Berliner 1962; Shepherd
1971, Villa Hügel 1963 (no. 355, pl. II);
Metropolitan Museum of Art 1979 (no.
81 p. 91); Kajitani 1981, no. 68, p. 52.

1. Cleveland Museum of Art 59.12 (Shepherd
   1971, fig. 1)
2. Metropolitan Museum of Art 1979,
   pp. 60–62.
3. One ivory is in the Aachen cathedral
   and the other in the Walters Art Gallery
   (inv. 71.1144; Shepherd 1971, figs. 5 and 6.
4. Bivar 1972, pp. 287–8.

71
Tunic Fragments, 7th–8 century

Wool and linen. 13 × 13; 49 × 9

Field Museum of Natural History. 31538

These two textiles – a *clavus* with a pendant and a skirt *segmentum* – belong to a set of applied tunic ornaments. Their main surfaces, in blue, are covered with a diagonal diaper pattern with animal and foliate fillers framed by a delicate palmette scroll in white on a red ground. The *clavus* is also decorated with a standing haloed figure enclosed in a separate panel. As is usual with this type of appliqué costume ornament, they are woven in tapestry technique on plied linen warps. The colored woolen wefts are very fine and the quality of the weaving is very high (see also cat. no. 69).

The diagonal diaper designs were commonly used in Late Antique and Early Byzantine art. Simple versions of the design began appearing in textiles, especially silk and woolen compound weaves, as early as the late 4th century.[1] Growing in complexity by the 6th century they became one of the most characteristic designs employed for patterned silks (see cat. no. 192). It is probably these patterned silks that were then imitated in tapestry-woven tunic ornaments. The version of the diaper pattern with more elaborate foliate and animal fillers seen in the Chicago weavings, is frequently used from the late fifth century onwards. These two textiles, however, represent a later, most likely late 7th or even 8th century rendition of the design.[2].

A.G.

1. E.g., such a simple diagonal diaper design decorates a shoulder ornament of Emperor Theodosius's tunic on the silver missorium in Madrid (A.D. 388).
2. One of the most striking examples is the Mosaic of the Striding Lion from Antioch, ca. 500 (now in the Baltimore Museum of Art; Levi 1947, pp. 321–2, pl. 74). Related examples include textiles in Berlin, formerly Kaiser-Friedrich-Museum, inv. 9085 (Wulff and Volbach 1926, p. 116, pl. 35); Brussels, Musées Royaux d'Art et d'Histoire (Errera 1916, no. 297); Jerusalem, Meyer Memorial Museum, T473-73 (Baginski and Tidhar 1980, no. 144, p. 104); Louvre, inv. AC 327, said to be from Akhmim (du Bourguet 1964, F 51, pp. 266–7).

72

Sleeve Ornament, 7th–8th century

Wool and linen. 16 × 23

Metropolitan Museum of Art, Rogers Fund. 09.50.1053

One of the characteristics of textile art from Byzantine and Early Islamic Egypt is its continued use of a traditional repertory of motifs established in decorative arts as far back as the 2nd and 3rd century. The decoration of this cuff band, which can be assigned to the 7th and 8th centuries, illustrates this dependence. This fragment from a woolen tunic is tapestry-woven on brown woolen warps with variously dyed woolen wefts.[1] Several green, orange and brown bands filled with ornamental motifs (fish, birds, floral and abstract motifs) form a border for the wider three-part frieze in the middle of the cuff band. The central panel of this frieze contains a stepped

purple-and-black frame around a red field with a female bust (?) holding a chalice or a flower. The side panels have a teal-green ground covered with scattered figural and floral motifs: on the left a cloaked figure reclines on a sea-monster, surrounded by other creatures, and on the right, a naked putto, also in a cloak, pursues a lion.

All these motifs are among the most frequently used in textiles and other arts (cat. nos. 186 and 187),[2] yet their rendition in this textile differs considerably from their antecedents. Through centuries of use, these motifs lost much of their descriptive clarity and became primarily colorful surface designs, even abstract patterns. This process of "patternization," begun in the 6th and early 7th century, accelerated considerably

following the Arab conquest of Egypt in 640/41.

A.G.

Bibliography: Kajitani 1981, no. 51, p. 39.

1. Technical information: warp: brown wool (S-spun); weft: blue, red, orange, purple, green wool (all S-spun), linen (S-spun). Tapestry weave over one warp; ca. 5 warps per 1 cm, ca. 14 wefts per 1 cm.
2. E.g., Louvre, inv. x4387 (du Bourguet 1964, F141) and the Haifa Museum, inv. 6760 (Baginski and Tidhar 1980, no. 107, p. 84).

73
Sleeve Ornament,
late 7th–8th century

Linen and wool. 25 × 8.5

Metropolitan Museum of Art, Rogers Fund. 09.50.969

Provenance: Fischbach Collection

Although this cuff band was made after the Arab conquest of Egypt its technical and to some extent also stylistic links are with the Byzantine period. Woven on plied linen warps in a tapestry technique in linen and brightly colored wool it was applied (see also cat. nos. 68–71).[1] The five-part design consists of a large red central panel with a bust (female?) in a roundel between two pairs of superimposed white friezes with scrolls filled with birds and animals. Bands of interlocking stylized leaves form exterior borders. Such five-part decorative compositions, very popular from the 6th century onward in silk sleeve appliqués,[2] were adopted by tapestry weavers and became one of the most popular types of sleeve decoration, as this and many other examples illustrate.[3]

This piece is executed in a two-dimensional style with the distinct dark outlines and solid color surface characteristic of the 7th and 8th centuries. The bust, for example, although presented in a three-quarter view implying volume and surface relief, is perceived only as a two-dimensional design. Other motifs of the cuff band are also more abstract than on earlier textiles. The vegetal scroll of the lateral friezes are rendered

only as figure-eight-shaped loops, and the single white waves with dots on narrow red stripes separating them are actually late versions of the running wave motif. Only the birds and other animals filling the scroll retain some of the natural forms of the earlier phases of the design. The borders of interlocking leaves, however, already belong to the sphere of Islamic, specifically, Umayyad, ornament. The newest motif of the cuff band, they demonstrate the susceptibility of textile art to change and an expansion of the repertory of the motifs.

A.G.

1. Technical information: warp: linen (S-spun, 2-ply Z), weft: linen (S-spun), beige, red, apricot, green, olive, blue, black, brown wool (all S-spun); tapestry weave over 1 warp, ca. 10 warps per 1 cm; weft counts vary.
2. E.g., on a tunic in the Victoria and Albert Museum, inv. no. 820.1903 (Kendrick 1922, no. 794, p. 75, frontispiece).
3. E.g., inv. no. 922.1886 in the Victoria and Albert Museum, from Akhmim (Kendrick 1922, no. 747, p. 48, pl. 14); also two cuff bands at the Louvre, inv. x4788 and x4135 (du Bourguet 1964, F168 and F168, pp. 308–9), and a cuff band in the Field Museum of Natural History, Chicago, inv. 173544 to illustrate the commonality of this type of composition.

74
Sandals

Probably from Hawara in the Fayum

Leather. 13.8 × 4.8

The Petrie Museum, University College London. UC28348

Throughout most of Egyptian history people went barefoot except for the more well-to-do who could afford sandals. This pair of leather sandals was made for a child, probably of a comfortable middle or upper middle class home in the Fayum. The design of the footwear, with straps and thongs, is not unlike that of ancient pharaonic footwear. The construction of the left sandal shows evidence of the wearer's extremely high instep.[1]
F.D.F.

1. I thank Miss Rosalind Hall for this information.

75
Dolls, 4th–8th century

From Akhmim (Boston)

Bone. (1) (with human hair) 11.2 × 5 (Boston); (2) 7.4 × 3.2 (Kelsey)

Kelsey Museum of Archaeology, The University of Michigan. 66-1-119; Museum of Fine Arts, Boston, Sears Fund. 04.1949

Provenance: Albert M. Lythgoe Collection (Boston)

Hundreds of such nude female dolls survive from Late Antique Egypt. They are characteristically of bone, with incised schematic features and stubby arms; more elaborate examples are cylindrical, echoing the shape of the bone, and some, like the Boston example, have real hair.

Many of these dolls were found in graves, and as a group they generally evoke the ancient Egyptian dolls of various materials that were buried with the deceased. Though some scholars believe that they served as concubines [1] or fertility amulets,[2] it seems more likely that they were simply toys.[3]
G.V. and F.D.F.

Bibliography: Museum of Fine Arts, Boston 1976, no. 249, p. 208.

1. Badawy 1978, p. 339.
2. Wulff 1909, p. 131
3. Cf. Gazda et al. 1983, fig. 52, p. 29.

Letters

76

Inventory, 7th–8th century

Place of origin in Egypt unknown

Papyrus. 16 × 23.5
Written in Coptic (Sahidic)

The Beinecke Rare Book and Manuscript Library, Yale University. P.CtYBR inv. 1809

Provenance: Bought from dealer (Nahman), Cairo, 1964

This inventory of utensils and clothing items is headed "With God. The furnishings which Sarapammon took." It includes a hat, a pillow, an item of harness for a camel, a censer, three knives and "a large knife," a goatskin shirt, a nail clipper, and perhaps a hair shirt. It is not certain from the context whether Sarapammon was a monk or a lay person. (Note that censers were used in houses and buildings as air fresheners, as well as in Christian liturgy.) On the other side is an account of amounts of grain paid to people named George, John, Colluthus, a shepherd, and "for taxes." It is from lists of simple items like this that we can reconstruct the everyday world that ordinary Copts lived in in late antiquity.
L.S.B.M.

Bibliography: MacCoull 1986a, no. 5, pp. 38–9.

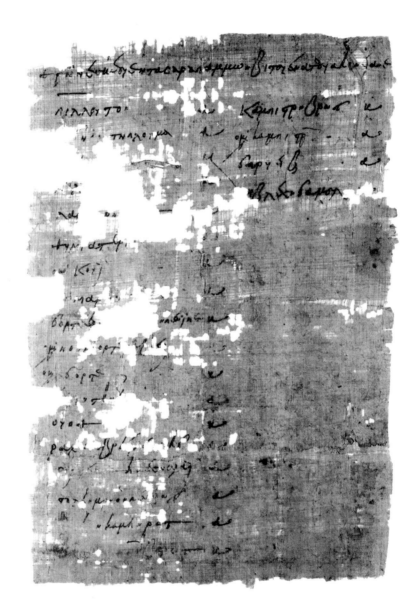

77
Writing Implements (three styli and one pen),
Graeco-Roman

From Gurna, Upper Egypt (bone implement); Karanis (wood and reed implements)

Left to right: wood, L. 12.6; wood, L. 8.2; bone, L. 13.5; reed, L. 13.2

Kelsey Museum of Archaeology, The University of Michigan. 23922, 23986, 10750, 23981

The thin reed pen (far right) is polished and unblemished; the tip is narrow and slit, and the top is narrow and squared. Both ends have been cut on opposing diagonals. Such pens, which survive in some abundance from Egypt but are otherwise, because of their material, rare, were used with ink and papyrus.[1]

The other three implements are probably styli for writing on wax-covered tablets;[2] they are distinguished by a pointed tip and a square end for making erasures.[3] Styli and hairpins are much alike, and it is possible that the bone implement falls into the latter category. In either case, the "Z" on its head is probably a magical "ring sign."[4]
G.V.

1. Davidson 1952, p. 186; Petrie 1927, pl. LVIII.
2. Ibid., pl. LIX.
3. Davidson 1952, p. 185.
4. Vikan 1984, p. 76. Ring signs, like eight- and five-pointed stars, and sideways Z-signs, have their roots in astrological magic; they are characteristic of amulets and much so-called "Gnostic" jewelry. Their precise meaning, however, is not clear.

78
Inkwell, 2nd–4th century

From Karanis

Clay. H. 4.4 to 4.9; rim D. 4.5; bottom D. 3.2

Kelsey Museum of Archaeology, The University of Michigan. 120617

Provenance: Excavated by the University of Michigan, 1924–5

Among the locally made pottery found in Karanis homes were two inkwells, one of which is shown here. Presumably it once had a cover with a narrow opening at the top to restrict evaporation.[1] A reed pen (e.g., cat. no. 77) would have been dipped into the ink for writing on papyrus or other material. The concave rim around the opening of the container collected excess ink.[2] A variety of similarly shaped containers in other media were used both at home and in church for holding things other than ink.[3]
G.V. and F.D.F.

Bibliography: Johnson 1981, pp. 11, 56, pl. 45, no. 319.

1. Petrie 1927, fig. 299.
2. Johnson 1981, p. 11.
3. Walters Art Gallery 1986, no. 70.

79
Writing Box, 8th century

From Hamouli

Wood, bronze, and lead. 17.2 × 8.3 × 3.8

The Pierpont Morgan Library. Hamouli
pen case 1

This is one of only a few surviving writing boxes from the period,[1] presumably used by the scribe who was responsible for writing the 8th century gospels found with it. It is further distinguished by the elaborate bronze fittings of its sliding lid, and by the delicate intertwining floral motifs that decorate both its lid and its inner deck, into which is set an inkwell. A set of reed pens would have been kept in the long trough at the right, and powdered colors in the compartments beneath the deck.

Structurally, this writing box has much in common with weight boxes (cat. no. 85) and with boxes designed for medical tools and ointments.[2] Although dateable to the 8th century by the Gospel book with which it was discovered, its basic decorative motifs are anticipated by Kom Eschkaw wood carvings of around 600.[3]

G.V.

Bibliography: The Newark Museum 1977, no. 91.

1. Petrie 1927, pl. LVIII.
2. Ibid., pl. XXXIII.3.
3. Strzygowsky 1904, no. 7211.

80

Reading Stand, Roman period

From Karanis

Wood. 17.5 × 26.5 × 33.3

Kelsey Museum of Archaeology,
The University of Michigan. 3343

This dark brown carved reading stand,
one of several found at Karanis, has two
rectangular "legs" with a narrow cross-
piece. The top consists of two boards slanting toward the center; four wooden pegs
on each side hold the top to the legs. The
upper surface bears an incised diamond
pattern. The slanted surface was apparently
designed for holding an unrolled papyrus,
for literacy was apparently not common
in the Fayum in this period.[1]
G.V. and F.D.F.

1. Gazda et al. 1983, p. 25.

81
Lamp and Lampstand,
6th–7th century

Bronze. H. 32.3

The Brooklyn Museum, Charles Edwin Wilbour Fund. 41.086A, B

Both the tripod stand, with its wide, flat cup and pricket (small spike), and the lamp, with its pear-shaped body and hinged seashell cover, are of a common sort used for public and domestic lighting in Late Antiquity. The Evangelist in the Rabbula Gospels reads by just such a lamp.[1] What is noteworthy here is the substitution of a large Latin cross for the shaft or column of the stand, and the presence of a small Greek cross on the lamp's ring handle.[2] Together they attest the extent to which the cross had come to dominate the decoration of objects in all aspects of life.

G.V.

Bibliography: The Brooklyn Museum 1941, no. 89.

1. Florence, Laur. Lib., cod. Plut. I, 56, fol. 9v. On the lamp, see Hayes 1984, no. 224.
2. For such cross-lampstands from Egypt, see Strzygowski 1904, no. 9126, and Wulff 1909, no. 994.

Marketplace

82
Steelyard and Bust Weight in the Form of an Empress,
5th–6th century (bust),
5th–6th century (steelyard)

Bronze. Bust 20.3 × 10.2, steelyard
L. 57.1

The Malcove Collection, University of
Toronto. M82.395a (bust), b (steelyard)

Provenance: Purchased from J. J.
Klejman, New York, January 1966 (bust)
and from Blumka Gallery, New York
(steelyard).

This once lead-filled bronze bust takes
the form of a Byzantine empress with
jeweled diadem and necklace and a
tightly wrapped mantle. The figure's
face is smooth and fleshy, her eyes wide
and staring, and her hands almost doll-
like in their anatomical simplicity. The
more strictly utilitarian scale, embellished by only a few incised lines, terminates in a stylized dog's head.

The Romans introduced the *stratera*
or "steelyard," so called because it was
used in more recent times to weigh steel
on the banks of the Thames; it is still in
common use in the Near East.[1] With it
the Romans, and later the Byzantines,
often employed lead-filled bronze
weights molded in the form of animals
or portrait busts. Early examples, for
the most part of 1st or 2nd century
date, are usually in the form of pagan
gods, particularly Mercury and Mars.
Later examples, which tend to cluster in
the 5th and 6th centuries, exhibit greater
uniformity; most popular were bust
portraits of Athena and Byzantine
empresses – whose attributes are so
generalized as to preclude specific
identification. Very likely this second
category – the so-called imperial busts –
were employed to connote official and
therefore honest weighing.

The *stratera*'s main component is a
balance beam consisting of two sections
that are unequal in length; the shorter
section is equipped with two or more
suspension hooks and the longer section
is calibrated on two or more of its facets
with scales corresponding to the possible

fulcra (hooks) opposite. A merchant,
after lifting the *stratera* with the hook
appropriate to the relative heft of the
load, slid the counterpoise along the
calibrated scale until it balanced with
whatever was being weighed. The item
weighed would be suspended (by hooks
or in a pan) from a chain fitted over the
collar at the extremity of the short end.
This implement was intended for trans-
actions involving such heavy commod-
ities as cheese and produce, whereas the
balance scale (see cat. no. 83), typically
smaller and more delicate, was designed
for more precise exchanges involving
precious metal, cosmetics, medicines,
and coins. Both were in general use
throughout the Early Byzantine empire.
G.V.

Bibliography: Metropolitan Museum of
Art 1979, no. 327 (bust); Campbell
1985, nos. 90, 91.

1. For a full discussion of this implement, see
   Vikan forthcoming 1989, ch. 8.

83
Folding Balance and Weights in a Wooden Box, 6th century (?)

Bronze balance, wooden box, probably boxwood. Box: 16.4 × 3 × 6.3–6.5; Balance: beam L. 11, pan D. 3

Collection of The Newark Museum. 78.78

Portable balances of this type were widely used by merchants, money changers, and jewelers for checking the weights of gold coins and small quantities of precious metals.[1] The bronze weights that came with the box conformed to government standards. A bronze *scrupulum* weight in one of the lower compartments may have belonged with the box.[2]

The rectangular box that contains the balance is carefully made with a sliding lid decorated with a carved cross. It is ingeniously divided into compartments, three lidded ones on the bottom layer for storage of the weights,[3] and fitted spaces on the top layer for the beam and scale pans of the folding bronze balance. S.A.

1. Skinner 1967, pp. 72–3; Johnson and West 1949, p. 173. A number of these balances in fitted wooden boxes have been found in Egypt. They were used elsewhere as well, as finds from Corinth in Greece show (Davidson 1952, nos. 1672–4, pp. 208, 216–7, n. 117, pl. 99).
2. See Kisch 1965, p. 132 for *scrupulum* weight. Bronze, and some glass, weights were used in Egypt at this time.
3. There are now three coins in the bottom compartments: a *dodechanumian* of the early 6th century from the mint of Alexandria; a *dodechanumian* of earlier date than the first one, and a coin of Constantine, mint uncertain, 330–335 A.D. (Michael Bates, of the American Numismatic Society, identified the coins). There is also a small round bronze piece with the dot-in-circle sign used on the *scrupulum* weight, the smallest division of the Roman pound.

84
Flat Weights, 6th century

Said to have come from the eastern Mediterranean

Bronze inlaid with silver.
WB25: 2.2 × 2.2; WB26: 5.8 × 5.5

The Menil Collection, Houston.
WB25, WB26.

Flat weights like these survive in abundance from all areas of the Early Byzantine empire.[1] Earlier examples (of the later 4th and 5th centuries) sometimes bear generic imperial portraiture or various personifications of abundance or city *tyches*; their propagandistic intent was to equate honest weighing and its resultant economic prosperity with imperial authority and the will of the people. Later, "Christianized" specimens like these substitute the cross, and link the prosperity of the marketplace with the "Grace of God," the phrase incised on the larger weight. The monogram on the reverse of the smaller example probably identifies the state official who issued the weight.

In contrast to bust weights, which are typically quite heavy and were used with steelyards to weigh such things as produce (see cat. no. 82), flat weights are generally light (under one Roman pound, 12 ounces) and were used with balance scales to weigh precious metal (see cat. no. 83). These two examples are clearly part of a single set which would have been stored and transported in a wooden weight box of the sort attested by numerous examples preserved by the dry climate of Egypt (see cat. no. 85).

G.V.

Bibliography: Vikan and Nesbitt 1980, p. 36 (WB26); Vikan forthcoming 1989, ch. 6 (WB25, WB26).

1. The larger of these two weights, WB26, shows a large cross with flaring arms beneath a round arch flanked by a pair of steeply pointed arches supported on two columns each; flanking the cross is the abbreviated notation for "one pound" (*lambda* and *tau* conflated at the left, for litra, "pound") and an alpha ("1") at the right. The cross and value mark are highlighted with inlaid silver, and above is incised the pious phrase *Theou charis* ("Grace of God"). The smaller weight, WB25, bears, on its obverse, basically the same design, although its value mark for "one ounce" (*gamma* for *oungia,* "ounce," and *alpha,* "1") is set between the lateral pairs of columns, and there is more inlaid silver; again, "Grace of God" appears above. In addition, the reverse of this example shows a monogram set within an eight-pointed star (comprised of two off-set squares) which is in turn enclosed by a wreath. See Vikan forthcoming 1989, ch. 6.

85

Weight Box: Cross Beneath Arch,
6th–7th century

Said to have come from Egypt

Wood and copper. 39 × 16 × 7

The Menil Collection, Houston. 83–25 DJ

This weight box consists of two elements: a sliding lid with turning-key lock and the box proper. The bottom panel of the box bears a series of geometric sinkings to accommodate a balance pan and a series of round bronze flat weights. The wood is covered with a zigzag pattern and punched circles and dots. The central panel of the lid bears the remains of a cross atop steps and set beneath a compound arch; the raised section above is inscribed "Grace of God." A monumental cross with the same biblical inscription appear together on contemporary weights and suggest that it is "By the Grace of God" (1 *Cor.* 15:10) that honest

weighing and thereby commercial prosperity were ensured.[1]

The box's lock suggests the weights it once contained were valuable and should not be tampered with. The alignment of the small copper brackets on the lid and the remains of what may be a handle on the lock plate suggest that the box was carried vertically, as we know similarly designed doctors' surgical boxes of the period were. Although weight boxes were certainly in use throughout the Byzantine Empire, only the dry sand of Egypt has preserved them in significant numbers.[2]

G.V.

Bibliography: Vikan forthcoming 1989.

1. Vikan forthcoming.
2. Rutschowscaya 1979, pp. 1 ff.

86
Coarse-Ware Amphora, 5th century

From Karanis

Pottery. H. 40, neck H. 16,
D. at shoulder 16

Kelsey Museum of Archaeology,
The University of Michigan. 8130

Although this shape of amphora (storage jar) is common in Egypt, this one was made of a non-Egyptian type of clay.[1] Amphoras like this may have been imported from the Antioch region of North Syria or from Cyprus.[2] The exterior has pronounced horizontal ridges with evidence of a join a third of the way up the body. There are two sturdy strap handles, a narrow outflaring rim, and a rounded base with a vestigial knob. Traces of red writing in a cursive Greek script survive on the shoulder, probably a notice of the capacity of the amphora and the origin of the wine or oil that it contained.[3] The interior of this amphora is coated with pitch, a technique used to waterproof the vessel and protect its contents from deterioration during shipping.[4] This custom is still in use in Greece today.

S.A.

1. Peacock and Williams 1986, p. 185, as determined from petrological studies.
2. Peacock and Williams 1986, pp. 186–7.
3. These inscriptions are very hard to decipher (Egloff 1977, p. 111; Bourriau 1981, p. 244). A similar form found at Kellia, form 166, is dated to the mid-5th–mid-6th century (Egloff 1977, I p. 112; II, pl. 57, 6. Cf. pl. 21, 2).
4. I am indebted to Nigel Pollard for this information and references on amphoras. Mr. Pollard is studying the entire collection of *amphorae* in the Kelsey Museum for a doctoral dissertation at the University of Michigan.

87
Stamp, 6th century

Said to have come from the eastern Mediterranean.

Clay. D. 8.7 cm.

The Menil Collection, Houston. 79-24 DJ

The back of this terracotta stamp bears a cylindrical handle; its matrix consists of an equal-armed cross highlighted by dots and flanked above and below by stylized birds. Around its circumference is the invocation: "May the Lord of Sion bless you."

This is one of a large group of Early Byzantine commercial stamps; most are clay, although stone and bronze specimans are also known.[1] All are round, range between 6 and 12 centimeters in diameter, and bear an inscription invoking divine blessing; many, like this specimen, have a cross at the center. Their dating, generally to the 6th century, is suggested by their cross designs, and their function as seal matrices for the plaster stoppers of wine amphorae, is indicated by their close correspondence (in size, design, and wording) to extant stoppers – most of which have been discovered in Egypt. Here, the invocation of the blessing of the "Lord of Sion" may have been simultaneously applicable to the buyer of the vessel and the liquid it contained – which was in danger of turning sour.[2]

G.V.

Bibliography: Vikan forthcoming 1989, no. s1981.

1. For a general treatment of this object type, see Vikan forthcoming 1989, no. s190.
2. Note Julius Africanus's prescription for keeping wine from spoiling: write the words of Psalm 34.8 ("O taste and see that the Lord is good") on an apple and throw it into the cask. See Vikan 1984, p. 70, note 29.

88

Stamp, 5th–7th century

Wood. D. 7.5

The Malcove Collection, University of Toronto. M82.307

Provenance: Purchased from Royal Athena Gallery, New York 1963

One side of this stamp bears a cross with flaring arms set within a circle; at least two Greek letters are identifiable between the arms, a *chi* and an *eta*, suggesting (in reverse) "Jesus Christ," or perhaps (direct) "Christ" (in the vocative case). The edge of the other face is marked by deep circles that enclose seven Greek letters which may be read as the name "Theodore." The protrusion along the disk's side may be the remains of a shaft handle or of an attachment for a rope handle.[1]

Stamps of this size, material, and general design survive in abundance from Early Byzantine Egypt;[2] moreover, many closely related specimens in terracotta have been found here as well.[3] Their general dating to the Byzantine period is assured by their letter forms and iconography, and their function as stamps for clay or gypsum amphorae stoppers is assured by their close correspondence to the surviving seals themselves.[4] The cross, often with accompanying letters, is a common motif, and private names appear quite frequently, usually as monograms but occasionally, as here, spelled out in full. The name probably identified the manufacturer, shipper, or owner of, most likely, wine or oil.[5]

G.V.

Bibliography: Campbell 1985, no. 79.

1. See Petrie 1927, nos. 200, 222.
2. See Petrie 1927, pls. LXI, LXII.
3. See Strzygowski 1904, pl. XXII.
4. See Kaufmann 1910, pl. 102, and Winlock and Crum 1926, fig. 33.
5. For a full treatment of this object type and its function, see Vikan forthcoming 1989.

89
Small Bottle in Basket, 3rd century (?)

Pale blue bubbly blown glass, palm fiber wrapping. 11

Kelsey Museum of Archaeology, The University of Michigan. 5351

Provenance: Purchased in Cairo in 1927

This very small bottle, which must once have held perfume, is protected by its original basket cover.[1] Egypt is one of the few places in the ancient Mediterranean world with a climate conducive to the preservation of such covers, and they were probably more widely used than appears in the archaeological record. Such an insignificant type of glassware would have been protected, in shipment or, more probably, during everyday use, because of its expensive contents.
S.A.

1. See Harden 1936, p. 222 Bil for some examples of glass in basket containers, including an example from Karanis: fig. 4d, 45766, p. 315, now in the Egyptian Museum, Cairo. See also the purple jar in a lidded basket holder in Loudmer and Kevorkian 1985, no. 453, p. 181.

90
Statuette of Camel with Panniers, 1st–3rd century

Molded clay. 11 × 8.5

Collection of The Newark Museum. 81.20

Although camels are commonly associated with Egypt, they were not used until quite late, when desert caravan routes made camel transport an important feature of foreign trade.[1] This camel, which is carrying two panniers of grapes, is a farmer's beast of burden, much as in Egypt today. The statuette was made in a two-part mold of which the joins are clearly visible along the back. All of the known Egyptian statuettes of camels have been found in the Fayum region, perhaps a reflection of their use in the agriculture of the area.[2]
S.A.

1. Forbes 1955.
2. For statuettes of the same type, see Berlin 11670 in Weber 1914, no. 434, pl. 39; Perdrizet 1921, no. 403.

91
Fragment of a Statue or Bust: Imperial Portrait,
late 3rd–early 4th century

From Upper Egypt (?)

Porphyry. 16.5 × 10.4 × 10.5

Anonymous Lender

In the early Byzantine period, as in antiquity, portraits were powerful images that not only bore a person's likeness but also contained and represented his or her essential character. Imperial portraits set up in public places, such as markets, theaters, and hippodromes, reminded those gathered there of the emperor's authority over all aspects of their public and civic lives. Christian emperors, however, questioned how much homage was appropriate to imperial portraits.[1] One early Byzantine law reflects these Christian concerns:

"If at any time, whether on festal days, as is usual, or on ordinary days, statues or images of Us are erected, the judge [any official acting in a judicial capacity] shall be present without employing the vainglorious heights of adoration, but so that he may show that his presence has graced the day, the place, and Our memory. Likewise if Our images are shown at plays or games, they shall demonstrate that Our divinity and glory live only in the hearts and secret places of the minds of those who attend. A worship in excess of human divinity shall be reserved for the Supernal Divinity."[2]

Porphyry, a deep purple stone with flecks of white, is not only hard and difficult to carve, but also absorbs light so that the carved shapes must be strongly defined. The hardness of the stone did not necessarily influence carving style, however, since we find it variously treated both before and during the early Byzantine period.[3] The abstract style of this portrait is found in all materials and media during the late 3rd and early 4th centuries, especially on official monuments. In this case, the generalized features make an identification of the individual especially difficult.[4]

The Egyptian provenance of porphyry (from Jebel Dokhar in the eastern desert) was generally known, as was the significance of its color. Purple had imperial connotations, and imperial restrictions were established concerning who had the right to use it.[5] In spite of the symbolic importance of its color, individual motifs on sculptures in porphyry were sometimes polychromed.[6]

T.K.T.

1. See the discussion of iconoclasm in the essay on sculpture for a general discussion of the significance of statuary and the Christian theology of images, and to the last quotation in the last footnote of the essay for an example of how imperial portraits fit into this controversy.
2. Pharr 1952, p. 432, *Theod. Code* 15, 3, 4 (A.D. 425).
3. See, for example, Delbrueck 1932 on the female torso in Hellenistic style of the 3rd–4th centuries, Abt. 30.
4. Other problems in identifying this figure stem from the fact that in this early period there was more than one ruler at a time, all of whom were given similar features in their portraits. For confirmation of this dating and suggested attribution, compare this portrait to the statues of the tetrarchy from Ptolemais and the bust from Athribis (ME 7257), both dated to the first quarter of the 4th century, wherein stylistic characteristics for works in porphyry are defined by hair modeled as a close-fitting cap, eyelids, and eyebrows plastically rendered as convex rolls, drilled pupils, strong planes, and curves.
5. All remaining works, however, are not strictly imperial: there are portraits of generals as *chlamydati*, architectural elements, furnishings, and sarcophagi.
6. Delbrueck 1932, pp. 84–5 describes the polychromy of details in the statues of the tetrarchy from Ptolemais: paint and gilding are found on their caps, fibulae, hair, whites of the eyes, and jewels on belts, shoes, and sword cases. Different color stones and other materials were also used for polychromatic effect. For example, in some portrait statues porphyry was used for drapery but the head and arms were carved from marble (polychromed?). In others, where the intended effect was clearly not realistic, a head of porphyry was completed with teeth of white marble.

Religion

92
Isis Nursing Harpokrates,
2nd – 3rd century

From the Fayum

Terracotta. H. 22.2

Royal Ontario Museum, Gift of Walter Massey. 910.108.364

The Egyptian goddess Isis, dressed in a fringed himation, sits cross-legged on a wicker basket suckling her nude child, Horus, called Harpokrates. One of the most popular subjects for Roman-Egyptian terracottas, the piece was probably used as a votive offering or placed in a wall niche in the home for protection of and worship by the household.

The most important mother goddess in the Egyptian pantheon, Isis was also magician par excellence. She protected her son Harpokrates (and resurrected her brother-husband Osiris) through her magical power, and was therefore called upon by her devotees for similar protection. A line from Apuleius, the 2nd century Roman writer, says of Isis, "To the troubles of people in misfortune you bring the sweet love of a mother" (dulcem matris affectionem miserorum casibus tribuis).

While images of Isis suckling Harpokrates surely influenced later depictions of the Virgin and Child, it is difficult to know to what extent Isis and the Virgin were blended in the popular imagination at this time. In the 2nd to 3rd century, when this statuette was made, Christianity was just becoming a recognizable force in Egypt, and any association with Mary, Mother of God (a notion discussed in the 3rd century by Origen but fully articulated in church dogma only in the mid-5th century), is doubtful.

F.D.F.

Bibliography: Tran Tam Tinh 1973, fig. 186, pp. 24, 39, and especially 184–5.

Frontispiece

93
Lamp Handle with Isis and Harpokrates, 1st–2nd century

Probably from the Fayum

Terracotta. 13.6 × 6.7 × 3.9

Kelsey Museum of Archaeology,
The University of Michigan. 7024

Provenance: Purchase from
D.L. Askren, 1935

Lamps with plastic handles with relief decoration were common in Roman Egypt, though less common than simple clay containers with wicks. The lamp portion of this piece has not survived. The remaining handle is decorated with an image of Isis suckling Harpokrates, a subject found on many similar handles, though the extent of Hellenization in the treatment of the figures varies.

Unlike the Newark bronze Harpokrates (cat. no. 114), these figures face front in the ancient Egyptian sculptural tradition. Stylistically, however, they are clearly Hellenistic despite Egyptian iconography. Isis sits on a throne ("throne" is the original Egyptian meaning of her name), draped in a Greek tunic and mantle knotted with the "Isis knot," an Egyptian fertility symbol. (Such long knotted gowns were also worn by the priestesses of Isis.) She wears a degenerate form of the Isis crown (the cow's horns and sundisk), originally the ancient attribute of Hathor, and holds in her right hand a sistrum, the ritual rattle also originally Hathor's. Ears of corn, a Graeco-Roman reference to the earth's fertility, and a feather are additions to the standard Egyptian iconography of the crown. There is little modeling of the bodies, except for Isis's facial features and carefully articulated ringlets of hair. The child does not suckle; instead, Isis carries his hand to her breast. Her gesture, as opposed to the act of nursing, makes the subject clear. Isis was extremely popular in her role as protectress of children.
F.D.F.

Bibliography: Kelsey Museum 1977, no. 6, p. 24,

94

Plaque with Isis as Uraeus: Isis-Thermouthis, 1st–2nd century

From the Fayum

Terracotta. H. 17.6

Royal Ontario Museum, Walter Massey Collection. 916.1.430

Provenance: Walter Massey Collection

The Egyptian mother goddess Isis is portrayed here in terracotta relief with the face and breasts of a woman, while the rest of her body is a coiled snake on a pile of folded drapery. Little winged Hellenistic sphinxes flank each side, and a torch lies to the right. Just the head of the goddess extends above the back of her flat throne, which provides the surface for the relief decoration.

Isis as uraeus (i.e., royal cobra) was inspired by an association, dating back possibly to the New Kingdom, of Isis with Renenutet, the ancient Egyptian cobra goddess of grain, the harvest, and general fertility of the land. Renenutet, also spelled Ernutet and pronounced by the Greeks as Thermouthis,[1] sometimes bore the crown of cow horns and sun disk also attributed to Isis. In harvest scenes, Renenutet was depicted by the ancient Egyptians as a snake, but in her aspect of mother and mortuary deity, she assumed human form or a female body with the head of a snake.[2] The Greeks, worshiping Isis as a form of Renenutet, always gave her a human head, however, as on this plaque.

Besides the agrarian association, Isis as uraeus was also correlated with the funerary aspect of the god Sarapis in his form of Sarapis-Agathodaimon.[3] Thus as uraeus she incorporates and reconciles the opposites of life (the associations with Renenutet) and death (the associations with Sarapis-Agathodaimon). Reconciling life and death in this way is a function common among fertility deities. Her agrarian character connected to the fertility of the fields, however, was predominant,[4] as one would expect in a country where most people made their living by farming. Numerous terracottas of this type were produced in Roman Egypt, most of which showed Isis with a full human torso and serpent tail. In the Fayum, statuettes of Isis-Thermouthis, like this example, were used in household shrines.

F.D.F.

Bibliography: Illustrated in Vanderlip 1972.

1. Beinlich-Seeber 1984, col. 232.
2. Ibid., col. 233.
3. Dunand 1979, p. 64 and n. 112; see especially pl. XXI, 30 for parallel.
4. Ibid., p. 65.

95
Harpokrates on Horseback,
ca. A.D. 100

From Egypt
Terracotta. H. 17.3

Museum of Fine Arts, Boston, Gift of
Horace L. Mayer. 58.1324

The name Harpokrates is the Greek
version of the Egyptian for "Horus the
Child" (Hr-p3-ḥrd), one aspect of
Horus, son of Osiris. In Graeco-Roman
Egypt Harpokrates assumed the form
of a chubby child, and was sometimes
shown nude with one finger to his
mouth, standard ancient Egyptian features for "child." This gesture was misunderstood by the Romans, however,
who thought Harpokrates was guarding
a secret connected with his mysteries,
and the child thus became a god of
silence. Here he is shown clothed and on
horseback, like standard images of the
Thracian god Heron and other military
rider gods (see cat. no. 98) whose
images gave rise to later depictions of
rider saints. One of the most popular
deities among the lower classes in
Graeco-Roman Egypt, Harpokrates
was also protector of children.
F.D.F.

Bibliography: Museum of Fine Arts,
Boston 1976, no. 41, p. 30.

96

Fragmentary Vase with Molded Relief Decoration of Isis, Sarapis/Zeus-Ammon, and Harpokrates, 1st–2nd century (?)

Possibly from Memphis or the Fayum or the vicinity of Rome

Clay with volcanic intrusions.
12.2 × max. D. 14.6

Royal Ontario Museum. 965x9.1

Roman Egypt's favorite gods were Isis, Sarapis, and Harpokrates, the Graeco-Roman version of the pharaonic family triad of Isis, Osiris, and their child Horus. There are numerous representations of the triad at the temples of Philae near Aswan, a cult center of Isis. Rulers ranging from the late Ptolemaic king Nectanebo I to the 2nd century A.D. emperor Hadrian appear on the temple walls making offerings and pouring libations to Isis, Osiris, and Harpokrates.[1] As savior deities, Isis and Sarapis had cult centers not only in Egypt but throughout the Hellenistic and Greek worlds.

This mended fragment, the base of a large ceramic vase made in a two-part mold, is decorated with high-relief busts of Sarapis/Zeus-Ammon on the left, Isis on the right, and the child Harpokrates in the center. Sarapis as Zeus-Ammon is shown with the kindly bearded face of the chief god of the Greek pantheon, Zeus, who in turn was conflated with the chief Egyptian god, Amon (so spelled by the Egyptians). Despite their Egyptian origins, these figures are depicted with Hellenistic features and dress. Just above their heads are the possible remains of an inverted egg-band, a classical decorative motif. Underscoring the non-Egyptian style of the piece are fragments of what appear to be two standing putti (not visible in this photograph) flanking the heads of Sarapis and Isis.[2]

This vase, made in Egypt or possibly the vicinity of Rome, may have been made as a New Year's gift, a usage known from inscribed Gallo-Roman vases with Isiac (i.e., pertaining to Isis, Sarapis, and Harpokrates) decoration.

F.D.F.

Bibliography: Tran Tam Tinh 1972, pp. 321–40, with a number of parallels from Egypt; Hayes 1976, pp. 35–6, no. 170, pl. 21.

1. Tran Tam Tinh 1972, p. 336.
2. Cf. also Aegyptisches Museum 1967, no. 1015.

97
Statuette: The Goddess Nephthys,
4th century

From Upper Egypt (?)

Terracotta, plaster ground, paint.
22 × 7.5 × 10

The Malcove Collection, University of Toronto. M82.338

Small terracotta statuettes such as this pagan example were deposited in household shrines and in burials. In the funerary setting they had a variety of functions, as servants to the deceased, and as representations of the divinities necessary for a safe entry into the afterlife.

This figure represents the ancient Egyptian funerary goddess Nephthys. She wears a large round headdress, necklace and bracelets, and a tight-fitting dress, but is most readily identified by the colored cloth she holds over her knees. This is an attribute of Nephthys who, as an official mourner in the entourage of Anubis, the Egyptian god of embalming, carried a cloth impregnated with natron, a substance used in mummification.[1]

This statuette has been broken and repaired, particularly in the area of the face and headdress, and the polychromy is only partially preserved.[2]

T.K.T.

Bibliography: Campbell 1985, no. 125.

1. McCleary first identified this figure as the goddess Nephthys by the 'cloth of natron' in Campbell 1985, pp. 98–9. The markings on the back of the figure that he identified as indecipherable letters are, in fact, numbers in Arabic.
2. Helpful in reconstructing the statuette's original appearance is a similar statuette in Guiry en Vexin where different parts are broken and preserved. See also Breasted 1948 and, as noted by McCleary 1987, Quibell 1903, pp. 87–8, pl. 2.

98
Votive Panel:
The God Heron, A.D. 210–220

Probably from the Fayum

Tempera (?) on five wooden slats.
52.4 × 42.5

Museum of Art, Rhode Island School of
Design, Museum Works of Art. 59.030

Provenance: From a private collection,
Cairo, then art market

This votive panel painting depicts the
god Heron with frontal face and large,
staring eyes, much like the early Byzantine icons of saints.[1] Remarkably, the
panel bears its original 4th-century
wooden frame; it would have been hung
on the wall by a string wrapped around
the corners of the frame. In view of the
size and quality of the work, it was probably owned by a well-to-do Roman-
Egyptian or Greek-Egyptian. The Greek
inscription (even among the Romans,
Greek was the language of the educated
elite) at the upper right is from the donor
and states: On behalf of Pantophemmios
for good.

As a military god, Heron is usually
shown on horseback.[2] Here, however,
he is depicted in Roman cuirass and
military mantle, marching to the left. He
pours a libation over an incense burner
at the lower left. Barely visible, a snake,
often associated with Heron, curls
upwards to drink the offering. A servant,
on a smaller scale, stands to the right;
above sits the griffin goddess, Nemesis,
with one paw on a wheel. Nemesis, a
goddess of destiny in griffin form
and in Egypt associated with Isis, was a
popular deity in the Roman army (cf.
cat. no. 169).

Heron was especially popular in
the Fayum, with temples at Magdola,
Tebtynis, and Theadelphia.[3] In a house
painting from Karanis,[4] also in the
Fayum, he appears on horseback, a pose
that served as the model for later depic-

tions of Christian rider saints. As a further correlation with later Christian notions, Heron was believed able to confer immortality on his followers.[5] Since Karanis houses had wall niches to hold household statuettes of gods, the present writer thinks it possible that the Heron panel may have hung in one of the more elaborate of these niches. The Pantophemmios mentioned in the inscription was perhaps a deceased soldier of the area.

Probably of Thracian origin, Heron was quickly blended with other gods in Graeco-Roman Egypt.[6] Due to the sun's rays typically depicted about his head (note the nimbus in this image), he was associated with the Egyptian solar gods Horus (Greek Apollo) and Amon-Re; as a military god he was correlated with the Greek gods Ares and Herakles.[7]

F.D.F.

Bibliography: Winkes 1973, pp. 14–5; Winkes 1982, pp. 68–9.

1. Winkes 1973, p. 7.
2. See Wadsworth Atheneum 1934.6
3. Bonnet 1952, p. 296.
4. Boak-Peterson 1931, p. 34, pl. 24.
5. Lewis 1973, p. 43. I thank Susan Auth for this reference.
6. Most scholars contend that Heron's cult as rider god derived from Thrace in northern Greece, though others have argued for a Near Eastern origin, e.g., Winkes 1973, p. 15 for sources.
7. Bowman 1986, p. 176 for sources.

99
Statuette of a Horseman, 3rd century

Molded clay. 11 × 8.5

Collection of The Newark Museum. 85.292

Despite what seems to us to be a toy-like naiveté, this horseman figurine may be an image of the powerful Thracian rider god Heron,[1] who was believed to assure immortality to his followers.[2] His assimilation in Egypt to the god Horus may explain the similarity of this statuette to images of Harpokrates, the Hellenized version of Horus, on horseback.[3] A statuette such as this might have been placed in a burial, or in the niche of a household shrine.

This statuette was molded in two parts, the front in three-quarter relief on a high plinth, the back plain. There is a circular back vent. The rider wears a V-necked short tunic and a triangular hat or helmet, and carries a shield and short sword.[4] The clay was originally covered with paint, of which faint traces of blue and red remain.

S.A.

1. Lewis 1973, pp. 33, 34, and 36 indicates the role of the Thracian cavalry recruited by the Ptolemies in bringing this foreign rider god to Egypt. Other rider gods were also worshiped in Egypt, and without an inscribed title the identification is tentative.
2. Lewis 1973, p. 43.
3. Kelsey Museum 6978 and 6504 are similar. Breccia 1934, pls. 11–2, nos. 42–7 shows a range of Harpokrates-on-horseback types from a naturalistic example to more schematic types similar to this one. I am indebted to Dr. Marti Lu Allen of the Kelsey Museum for helpful information on the Harpokrates-on-horseback terracotta types and the problems connected with their dating. A more detailed discussion can be found in her University of Michigan dissertation, Allen 1985, nos. 50, 51, pp. 352–5.
4. Lewis 1973, p. 43 notes that this costume and attributes are among those found in images of the Thracian rider god both in Egypt and in other parts of the Roman Empire.

100
Female Orant Figure, 4th century

From Karanis

Plaster-covered painted clay. 13.3 × 8

Kelsey Museum of Archaeology,
The University of Michigan. 3768

This stylized figure of a woman may be
praying with arms outstretched. A solid
lump of clay was roughly shaped by
hand into a figure with a spade-shaped
head, pinched-out nose and breasts, and
rudimentary arms and feet. On the white
plaster that completely covers the figure,
black paint outlines the eyes, the neck,
clavus, and sleeve bands of the woman's
dress and an amulet worn around the
neck. Matte red paint further emphasizes
the garment decorations and the face.
There are holes for earrings at the sides
of the head.[1] Earlier terracotta funerary
figurines of women with elaborate hair-
dos are often called "brides of the dead"
from the ancient Egyptian tradition of
including such figures in tombs. This
figure, however, seems closer to the
more stylized praying terracottas such
as cat. no. 138.

S.A.

1. Bronze(?) and leather dangle earrings
   still survive on the comparable figure
   from Behnasa in the Icon Museum,
   Recklinghausen; Kybalová 1967, pl. p. 16.

101

Two Pendant Amulets:
Evil Eye(?) and Medusa Head(?),
4th–6th century

Steatite (and jet?). 4.9 × 2.7; D. 4

Detroit Institute of Arts, Gift of Frederick
Stearns. 90.1S.12698, 90.1S.12943

The lighter-colored of these two small,
simple pendants is shaped like a broad,
pointed leaf; it has a loop at the top
for suspension and bears a series of
concentric circles with drilled centers.
That its intent was magical is suggested
by its shape, which parallels that of
some Late Antique amulets bearing the
so-called Holy Rider.[1] Its prominent
decoration may have been intended to
evoke the Evil Eye (and thereby repel
the malevolent forces of the envious
glance), as suggested in a recent analysis
of comparable steatite pendants.[2]

The black stone pendant bears a
stylized face distinguished by full cheeks,
a hatlike band of hair(?), and prominent
eyes with drilled pupils. Many other such
pendants have been found in Egypt.[3] In
size, material, and format, they bear
comparison with Roman period (jet)
pendant amulets with Medusa heads,[4]
whose intent was clearly to ward off
evil. This black pendant may also represent Medusa.

G.V.

1. Campbell 1985, no. 198.
2. Maguire 1987.
3. Strzygowski 1904, no. 8766.
4. Toynbee 1962, no. 137.

102

Amulet: Holy Rider, 6th–7th century

Haematite. 3.1 × 2.4

Kelsey Museum of Archaeology,
The University of Michigan. 26092

Provenance: Purchased in 1932

The Holy Rider was one of Late Antiquity's most popular amuletic images
(see cat. nos. 104 and 105), and one of
its most characteristic appearances is on
the obverse of a distinctive genre of
intaglio haematite amulets represented
by this example. Here a mounted warrior
in military garb impales a prostrate,
nude female demon.[1] Typically, as here,
the rider is labeled "Solomon," and the
object's reverse bears the words *sphragis*
theou, "seal of God." According to the
Testament of Solomon, probably the
most popular magic treatise of Late
Antiquity, King Solomon was able to
control and exploit the forces of evil,
and thereby build the temple (of Solomon), due to God's having given him a
"little seal ring" with which he could
"lock up all the demons." Solomon's
identification with the Holy Rider–a
generic emblem of victory–evokes in a
graphic but symbolic way his victory
over demons, and the inscription on the
reverse simply identifies the vehicle of
that victory, the "seal of God."

That this amulet type developed out
of a Graeco-Egyptian gem amulet tradition is clear from its design and medium,
and from details of its iconography.
Indeed, it closely parallels the popular
Chnoubis amulet type, and probably
fulfilled the same basic function, that of
controlling blood flow from the uterus.
Thus, like the Chnoubis (a magical
lion-headed snake), Solomon was
believed capable of protecting the womb.
Haematite (the material of both amulet
types) was believed capable of absorbing
blood. And the key on this example's
reverse–which appears as well on earlier
Chnoubis amulets–was believed capable
of controlling (i.e., blocking up) the
opening to the uterus.

G.V.

Bibliography: Bonner 1950, no. 294;
Vikan 1984, pp. 79 ff; Brown University
1987, no. 50.

1. For a complete discussion of this object
type and of the thesis presented in this
entry, see Vikan 1984, pp. 79 ff.

103

Amulet: Holy Rider and Evil Eye,
5th–7th century

Said to have come from Asia Minor

Copper. 5.0 × 4.0

The Walters Art Gallery, Baltimore.
54.2628

Two thin oval sheets of embossed copper, once attached back-to-back, are now detached, and the reverse sheet, with the Evil Eye, has partially broken away. The obverse (the front) shows the Holy Rider impaling with his lance a female(?) figure who lies prostrate beneath the hooves of his galloping horse; beneath is a running lion. At the center of the reverse is the Evil Eye being attacked from below by various wild beasts (snake, scorpion, lion, etc.), and from above by a pair of sharp weapons (lance and knife). At the top center is the inscription

"Lord, Help," and slightly below and to the sides are a pair of crosses.

The front and back of this amulet were meant to complement one another. The so-called Holy Rider was one of Late Antiquity's most potent apotropaic images; it was a generic evocation of the force of good, whereas the creature it vanquishes was generically evocative of evil.[1] The Evil Eye was more specific in its power in that it was designed to repel the destructive force of the envious glance which, once directed toward something good in one's life (e.g., a newborn child), would allow access to demons.[2] It was commonly believed that by showing the "much-suffering eye" attacked by various pointed instruments (e.g., the scorpion's claws, the knife), envy would be reminded of the inherent reciprocity of its evil – that greed consumes the greedy party; thus its evil would be repelled.

Many incised bronze pendant amulets, cruder in execution but with basically the same magical imagery,

have been found at various sites around the eastern Mediterranean, including Egypt.[3] Indeed, there is the well-known magical fresco from Bawit where the Holy Rider (inscribed Sissinios) and the Evil Eye are juxtaposed.[4] Especially close in technique and quality to this amulet is the front (Holy Rider) of a two-sided amulet preserved in Berlin.[5] A similar though less finely executed two-sided specimen was recently excavated at Anemurium;[6] like this one, it combines a Christian invocation with the pre-Christian apotropaic imagery of the Holy Rider and the Evil Eye.

G.V.

1. Vikan 1984, pp. 79 ff.
2. Dunbabin and Dikie 1983, pp. 7 ff.
3. Bonner 1950, nos. 294 ff.
4. Clédat 1904, pl. 55.
5. Wulff 1909.
6. Russell 1982, pp. 540 ff.

104
Amulet:
Holy Rider and Evil Eye,
6th–7th century

Said to come from the vicinity of
Nazareth

Bronze. 6.1 × 3.0

The Art Museum, Princeton University,
Museum purchase. 31–34

On the obverse of this crudely incised
bronze pendant is a mounted warrior
impaling a prostrate figure who lies
beneath the hooves of his horse (see cat.
no. 103); it bears the inscription: Heis
Theos ho nikon ta kaka, "One God conquering Evil." The reverse shows the
Evil Eye (see cat. nos. 101 and 103)
attacked by a trident, lion, ibis, snake,
scorpion, and dog (leopard?); it bears
the inscription *Iao Sabaoth.*

This amulet was common in the eastern Mediterranean during the Early
Byzantine period (5th to 7th centuries).[1]
Its powers were thought to derive from
the Holy Rider, from the apotropaic
acclamation that accompanies it (invoking the power of the monotheistic god),
and from the names Iao and Sabaoth on
the reverse. And finally, there is the Evil
Eye – or, more properly, the "much-
suffering eye of envy," which by virtue
of showing the inevitable pain to be
expected by the source of the envious
glance acted as a powerful antidote
against it.[2]

G.V.

Bibliography: Baltimore Museum of Art
1947, no. 325; The Art Museum, Princeton University 1986, no. 64; Brown
University 1987, no. 51.

1. See Bonner 1950, pp. 211 ff.
2. See Bonner 1950, pp. 96 ff. and Russell
   1982, pp. 539 ff.

105

Amulet: Entry into Jerusalem and the Three Hebrews in the Furnace,
6th–7th century

Said to have come from Egypt

Lead. 2.06 × 2.54

Museum of Art, Rhode Island School of Design. Lownes and Kimball Funds. 1987.081

Provenance: Purchased from L'Ibis Gallery, New York

The suspension loop of this crudely cast lead amulet has broken away, obscuring the fact that it was originally a pendant. On one side appear the three Hebrews from the Old Testament Book of Daniel. Dressed in tunics, mantles, and Phrygian caps, they stand frontally, with arms raised in the fiery furnace into which King Nebuchadnezzar had them cast for refusing to worship a gold-plated image of a deity. The Hebrews were saved from the flames by the power of God. On the other side of the amulet is a simplified version of the entry into Jerusalem on Palm Sunday, consisting of Christ on a long-eared donkey with one hand raised in blessing and the other holding a cross staff.

This object is identifiable as an amulet through both its design and its iconography. Specifically, it is a simplified, solid-cast lead version of an unusual sort of folding copper capsule that seems to have been designed to enclose an amuletic papyrus text and bore relief amuletic imagery on its two faces: one example, probably intended to keep wine from spoiling, shows the Miracle of Cana on one of its faces and encloses a papyrus fragment describing that biblical event.[1] The Entry into Jerusalem, which appears on another such amuletic capsule,[2] was a common Early Byzantine magical image for two reasons: the acclamation that accompanied the event, "Blessed is He who comes in the Name of the Lord," was thought to be apotropaic, and Christ atop the donkey was the paradigm of one of early Christianity's most powerful magical images, the Holy Rider.[3] Similarly and for more obvious reasons, the three Hebrew youths being saved by God from a fiery death was commonly taken as a model of divine salvation.[4]

G.V.

Bibliography: Friedman 1988a, p. 10.

1. Papyrorum 1894, pp. 124 ff. And for other such amulets, see Wulff 1909, nos. 825, 827.
2. Wulff 1909, no. 825.
3. See Vikan 1984, p. 75, n. 57, and pp. 79 ff.
4. See, for example, Metropolitan Museum of Art 1979, no. 415.

106

Casting Mold for Amulet: Veneration of the True Cross,
6th–7th century

Steatite. 7.3 × 3.9

The Brooklyn Museum, Gift of the Estate of Charles Edwin Wilbour. 16.233

Provenance: Acquired in Egypt by Charles Edwin Wilbour, 1886

Many casting molds survive from Late Antiquity and most, like this example, are of steatite, a soft stone that can be easily carved and yet produces a precise matrix. Typically they were designed for the manufacture of inexpensive crosses, earrings, or pendants in lead for a mass market. Their two halves would be aligned by matching dimples and depressions; any casting irregularities or leakage would simply be broken off or filed away.

This mold is especially interesting because of its iconography, which shows on the obverse a cross surmounted by a bust of Christ and flanked by the two crucified thieves. It reproduces, in highly simplified form, a compositional formula developed in the later 6th century for the decoration of small metal ampullae (pilgrim flasks) (like cat. nos. 139 and 140) issued to pilgrims at the Shrine of the Holy Sepulcher in Jerusalem.[1] It is not, properly speaking, a portrayal of the Crucifixion but rather of the Veneration of the True Cross – an act of pilgrim piety commonly practiced at the Holy Sepulcher. The two schematic forms flanking the base of the cross represent (from comparison with more detailed ampullae) kneeling pilgrims reaching forward to touch (i.e., venerate) the True Cross relic.

From the inscriptions that appear on the ampullae, it is clear that they functioned as amulets for the pilgrims who wore them, that is, as protection in travel or as instruments for miraculous cures. Specifically, their supernatural power was thought to derive from the holy oil they contained, which had been sanctified by contact with the True Cross.[2] In this mold it is clear that the image itself (i.e., the "icon" of the Veneration) was thought to be a conveyor of power as well, since there is no association with sanctified oil nor is there any direct connection with the Holy Land.[3]

G.V.

Bibliography: The Brooklyn Museum 1941, no. 143.

obverse

reverse

107
Amuletic Armband:
Virgin and Child, Women at the
Tomb, Holy Rider, 6th century

Said to have come from eastern Anatolia

Silver. D. ca. 7.8

Royal Ontario Museum, Gift of the
Government of Ontario and ROM
Membership. 986.181.93

Provenance: J. Spier collection,
New York

The circumference of this armband bears
the opening words from the apotropaic
90th Psalm: "He that dwells in the help
of the Highest. . . . " It is highlighted
by four crudely incised medallions. One
shows a frontally seated Virgin and Child
surrounded by the invocation "Theotoke,
help Anna" and the word "Grace";
another shows the Women at the Tomb
wherein Christ's tomb appears as a
simple aedicula and just one Mary (and
the Angel) take part; another has the
Trisagion; and the final medallion, which
bears the word "Health," shows a Holy
Rider carrying a long cross-staff.

This is one of more than a dozen
surviving examples of a type of amuletic
armband produced in the eastern Mediterranean, including Egypt and Syria-
Palestine, in the 6th and 7th centuries.[1]
That its iconographic roots lie substan-
tially in the pilgrimage trade is clear
from such scenes as the Women at the
Tomb, which includes architectural
details of the Holy Sepulcher shrine in
Jerusalem, and from the striking compositional parallels that exist between the
more richly embellished examples (with
up to eight medallions) and the well-
known Palestinian pilgrimage ampullae
preserved in Monza and Bobbio. Their
intent was specifically amuletic, as is
clear from such characteristic inscriptions as Psalm 90 and the word "Health,"
and from the recurrent appearance of
the magical Holy Rider. But more reveal-
ing both for the armbands' origins and
their function is the presence on some of
the traditional Graeco-Egyptian figure
of Chnoubis – a lion-headed snake
thought to be efficacious in the control

1. On this genre of object see Grabar 1958,
   passim, and Vikan 1982, pp. 20 ff.
2. For the ritual of sanctification, see Vikan
   1982, p. 11 (Piacenza Pilgrim, ca. 570).
3. A comparable though more elaborate
   copper pendant is preserved in the Cabinet
   des Médailles in Paris (see Vikan 1982,
   pp. 40 ff.); its upper half shows the Veneration of the Cross, much as here, and its
   lower half the Women at the Tomb (again,
   as taken over from the ampullae). Significantly, it is inscribed: "Cross, help
   Abamoun" – confirming its amuletic
   function.

or protection of the uterus (which would explain the invocation for "Anna").

Such a combination of magical motifs – pagan, Christian, and Jewish (the Holy Rider as Solomon) – is eloquent testimony to the rich mixture of beliefs and traditions in Early Byzantine Egypt.

G.V.

Bibliography: Vikan 1984, pp. 75 ff; Walters Art Gallery 1986, no. 94.

1. See Vikan 1984, pp. 75 ff. for a full discussion of this object type, its iconographic origins and its function.

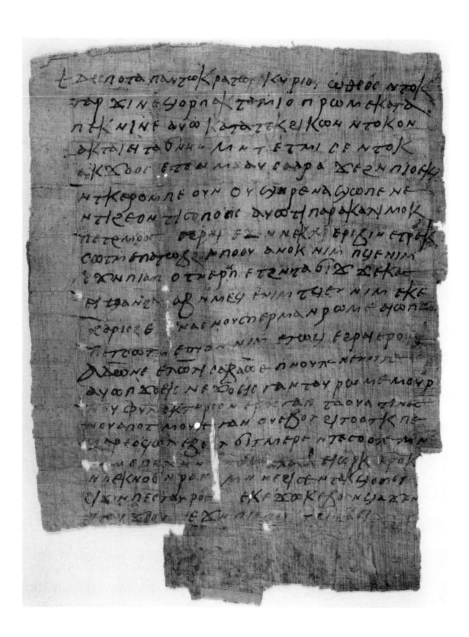

108
Prayer for Pregnancy, 7th century (?)

From Upper Egypt (?)

Papyrus. 28 × 21.8
Written in Coptic (Sahidic)

The Pierpont Morgan Library.
M662 B 22

Provenance: Bought from a dealer (Nahman), Cairo, 1920

This charm is a prayer to be used by a man, to ask that a woman become pregnant: it is a sample form, with the names to be filled in at the blanks marked N I M (= "N.") (lines 9, 11). The phraseology is strongly biblical. God is invoked as the one who made man in his own image (Genesis 1:26), who promised "our mother Sarah" (line 5) that she would have a child (Genesis 18:10, 14; 21:1–2), who "sits upon the Cherubim" (line 8) (Psalm 99:1). He is called Adonai Elohim Sabaoth, God of Gods, and Lord of Lords (lines 14–15), and invoked by "the sufferings you bore upon the Cross" (lines 20–21). No ancient Egyptian or Gnostic supernatural powers are named in this text. Apparently the charm is to work by the man's giving the woman a cup of wine to drink, over which the prayer has been said: this will cause her to be "graced by the seed of man" (line 12). On the other side is an account of amounts of wine.

L.S.B.M.

Bibliography: MacCoull 1982b, pp. 10–12.

109
Magical Text, early 2nd century

From Oxyrhynchus

Papyrus. 29.2 × 16.5
Written in Late Egyptian, transcribed
in Greek and Demotic letters

The British Museum. BM 10808

This papyrus leaf contains a complete
three-part magical text (col. 1), plus
remnants of another magical text (col. 2)
of which too little is preserved for com-
ment. The text preserved in col. 1 is
unique in that it evidently reflects an
attempt to transcribe an Egyptian hieroglyphic text using the Greek alphabet,
with Demotic characters used for sounds
not occurring in Greek.[1]

The original hieroglyphic prototype
of this text (col. 1) was presumably
quite ancient. It consists of three magical
spells to ward off fever. The spells are
pronounced against three demons, Sro,
Kai, and Tepie,[2] thought to be responsible for attacks of fever. The victim of
fever is identified in the text with the
Egyptian god Osiris-Onnophris,[3] and
mythological references and allusions
abound in the text.

The first four lines of text can be translated thus:[4] "O [demon] Sro, enemy of
Onnophris [i.e., the victim of fever],[5] /
Adversary of Osiris, the First of the
West, / You who are deeply entrenched
on account of the Flame [i.e., fever]
which he [the victim] has swallowed, /
And you who have launched an attack
against the Consort of Hathor, the Great
Goddess, / As the Flame became deeply
entrenched in painful Fire! / He (Osiris)
did not plunge into the water / Until
Thoth came to him / As the one who
grabbed you and protected him against
your provocation, / For which the great
magical spell was suitable, which is to
be pronounced with efficacy / On the
occasion of your furious assault and
spread of provocation. / Back! Desist
from the oppression of the Great God."
The spell ends (lines 16–17) with :
"You [i.e., the demon of fever] shall fall,
you whom I have bound by oath, / On
this day, for I have divested you of your
great evil."[6]

B.A.P.

Bibliography: Crum 1942; Osing 1976;
Shisha-Halevy 1980.

1. The so-called "Old Coptic" manuscripts, in
contrast, are attempts to transcribe Demotic
Egyptian texts in Greek letters.
2. These are probably made-up names. "Sro,"
"Kai," and "Tepie" seem to be related to
words meaning, respectively, "sheep," "ape"
or "bird," and "snake." Cf. Osing 1976,
pp. 50, 86.
3. "Onnophris" is an epithet of Osiris. The god
Osiris is the paradigm in ancient Egyptian
mythology and religion of victory over violence and death.
4. The following is based on Osing's German
translation, though his interpretation is con-
troversial; for a critical review see Shisha-
Halevy 1980.
5. See n. 3 above.
6. The second spell begins on line 17 ("Kai,
enemy of Onnophris, adversary of
Osiris..."). The third begins on line 39
("Tepie, enemy of Onnophris, adversary
of Osiris...").

110
Magical Text, 6th or 7th century

Papyrus. 32.4 × 24.1
Written in Coptic (Sahidic)

The Beinecke Rare Book and
Manuscript Library, Yale University.
P. Ctybr inv. 1800

Provenance: Purchased from Hans
P. Kraus in New York, May 1, 1964.

This is a piece of black magic in which
three angels named Psateel, Ennael,
and Asaroth are invoked for the purpose
of bringing upon an intended victim
"suffering, and [sickness], and illness,
and rheum, and fever, and pain, and
weariness, and depression, and chills,
and tumors, and [demonic] madness,
and seventy different diseases."[1] At the
end of the text, the demons Asmodeus,
Phelloth, and Athes are also adjured.
The incantation includes the provision
that "no sorcerer or sorceress can help it
or heal it away from my clutches until I
myself, so-and-so,[2] have mercy upon it."
B.A.P.

Bibliography: Petersen 1964, pp. 48–9;
MacCoull 1975, p. 219.

1. From an unpublished translation supplied by Stephen Emmel of The Beinecke
   Rare Book and Manuscript Library, Yale
   University.
2. The person performing the spell would
   supply his or her name here.

III

Magical Text, 6th or 7th century

Egypt, exact site unknown

Papyrus. 9.1 × 15.9
Written in Coptic (Sahidic)

The Beinecke Rare Book and
Manuscript Library, Yale University.
P. CtYBR inv. 882

Provenance: Purchased from Phocion J.
Tano in Cairo by Michael Ivanovich
Rostovtzeff and Charles Bradford
Welles, 1931

This unpublished papyrus contains a
magician's invocation of an angel to aid
him in conjuring up someone, presumably a dead person. Translation:[1] "Come
to me today! The one mighty in his
power, Shafriel, the angel, has worked
changes today until he deprived himself
of his peace. I beseech and I entreat you,
I, so-and-so (insert name of magician),
so that you might come to me, voice of
so-and-so (insert name of person to be
conjured up)."

B.A.P.

1. Translation supplied by Stephen Emmel of
the Beinecke Library.

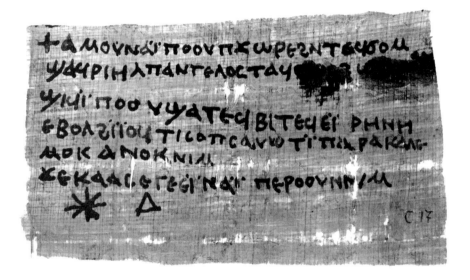

112
Magical Text, 6th or 7th century

Papyrus. 13.5 × 20.9
Written in an unknown language

The Beinecke Rare Book and Manuscript
Library, Yale University. P. CtYBR
inv. 1795

Provenance: Purchased from Hans P.
Kraus in New York, May 1964

This odd text, apparently a sort of magical amulet, features crude drawings of
three figures, with undeciphered symbols inscribed beneath them. The central
figure is a rooster; the flanking figures
are anthropoid, holding up their arms in
a gesture of worship. The rooster was
a solar symbol in the ancient Mediterranean world, and was often used as a
sacrificial animal in magical rituals.
B.A.P.

Bibliography: Petersen 1964, pp. 45–6.

113
Votive Plaque(?) with Cross,
6th–7th century

Wood. 22.9 × 10.5

The Walters Art Gallery, Baltimore.
61.300

This crudely but expressively carved
wooden plaque, probably used in the
home, has as its main design a cross
beneath an arch. The arms of the cross
consist of triangles and its center is
marked by a large circle with a smaller
incised circle and punched center; similar
small circles with punched centers fill
the plaque's background. The cross is
set atop a raised rectangle bearing three
faintly incised lines of Coptic inscription.[1] Flanking it are two small equal-
arm crosses, above which are the simple
bases for the columns. The columns are
covered with an incised chevron pattern
and terminate in crude capitals, which in
turn support an arch ornamented with
diamonds. Within the arch is a schematic
shell motif. This basic design is common
in the art of Early Byzantine Egypt,
most notably on grave stelae (cf. cat. no.
177), but also on wooden lintels and box
covers.[2] The general intent seems to
have been to evoke the victory of the
cross and thereby its redeeming and
resurrecting powers.
G.V.

1. The inscription remains undeciphered,
   although it seems to begin like that of the
   "Hanna" stele in Strasbourg. Villa Hügel
   1963, no. 98.
2. See, respectively, Duthuit 1931, pl. LXV,
   Strzygowski 1904, no. 8781, and the
   weight box in this exhibition, cat. no. 85.

114

Harpokrates on Lotus, ca. 1st century

From Egypt

Bronze. H. 15

Collection of The Newark Museum.
75.102

Harpokrates, Horus the Child, is seated atop a lotus, ancient Egyptian symbol of rebirth. His pose recalls that of the pharaonic sun god Nefertum who squats as a child on a lotus blossom that emerged from the primordial waters at creation. While the iconography of this piece is Egyptian, the style is Hellenistic. The child is dressed in a chiton, while all Egyptian Harpokrates were nude. His legs swing to the right, his head turns to the left, displaying none of the strict frontality characteristic of Egyptian sculpture for millennia. The sidelock of youth, a pharaonic convention denoting a child, is visible on the figure's right side, but unlike an Egyptian Harpokrates, the child also has a full head of hair. And the attempted double crown of Upper and Lower Egypt on the child's head is a ludicrous misunderstanding. The finger to the mouth, an Egyptian convention denoting a child, was also misunderstood by the Romans, as noted above. A fully Graeco-Roman feature is the cornucopia, symbol of abundance, a fragment of which the child holds in his right hand.

The original function of this very attractive bronze is puzzling. From its size, weight, and high level of craftsmanship, it is unlikely that it was a scepter handle, as was the function of similar pieces. It may have been an attachment to a large cult statue of the syncretistic goddess Isis-Aphrodite.[1] Such statues sometimes held a small, separately cast Harpokrates in one hand. Susan Auth, who raised this possibility,[2] suggests that this bronze may have come from a large cult statue in an Alexandrian temple. But since Alexandrian coinage does not feature this image as it does other famous cult statues of the city, Auth further suggests it may instead have been modeled on such an attachment.
F.D.F.

1. For parrallels see Roeder 1956, pl. 18a, p. 117; Breccia 1934, pl. 29, nos. 131–6, p. 21; Williams 1979, especially p. 98; cf. also The Brooklyn Museum 44.224 and Aegyptisches-Orientalische Sammlung 762A.
2. I thank Susan Auth for her comments, suggestions, and references in written correspondence.

115

Horus as a Roman Emperor, ca. 150

Probably from Egypt

Bronze. H. 10.2

Museum of Fine Arts, Boston, Arthur Mason Knapp Fund. 1974.415

The ancient god Horus, son of Osiris, is shown here as Pharaoh of Egypt, wearing the royal double crown of Upper and Lower Egypt. Following Egyptian custom, he is shown as a man with the head of a falcon; with typically Graeco-Roman gesture, however, he pours a libation. Most un-Egyptian is his Roman armor. (Armed soldiers were ubiquitous in Roman Egypt, and Roman armor, worn by the legionnaires and depicted on images of the Emperor, was a common sight.) In Graeco-Roman Egypt, Horus, as Harpokrates, wore armor in his mythological role as avenger of his father's death, and he was especially characterized as a warrior in the Roman period, especially in his role as an avenger god who could intercede in men's affairs.[1] The Roman cuirass and paludamentum (military cloak) are also used here to identify Horus, Pharaoh of Egypt, with the Roman Emperor. As pharaoh had been considered divine, so now was the Emperor.
F.D.F.

Bibliography: Museum of Fine Arts, Boston 1976, no. 22; Brockton Art Center 1975, no. 91, p. 59, fig. 30.

1. Bianchi in The Brooklyn Museum 1988, p. 246.

116
Bust of Sarapis, 4th century

From Alexandria
Bronze. H. 18

Museum of Fine Arts, Boston,
Harriet Otis Cruft Fund. 60.1450

Provenance: New York art market

Although probably known as early as the time of Alexander the Great,[1] the god Sarapis really rose to prominence under Ptolemy I (305–282 B.C.), and by the 3rd century B.C. had gained a devoted following in Egypt, Greece, and Asia Minor. Contrary to previous belief, however, many scholars now agree that Sarapis was not a mere political invention of the Ptolemies meant to unite the Greek and Egyptian populations,[2] but, rather that his popularity was probably due to a genuinely spontaneous, albeit varied, response by each group.[3]

Sarapis is an excellent example of the religious syncretism of Graeco-Roman Egypt. His Egyptian prototype was Osiris, Egyptian god of the underworld and the earth's fertility (thus the corn measure on Sarapis's head). This aspect of the god was in turn conflated with the dead and deified Apis bull at Memphis, who in death was believed to absorb the qualities of Osiris. The linguistic conflation of Osiris and Apis produced "Oserapis," which then resulted in the single god's name "Serapis," also spelled Sarapis. The god's cult spread throughout Egypt, with major cult centers at Memphis and Alexandria. This bronze bust came from a private chapel or shrine to the god.[4]

Because of his Egyptian origins Sarapis was always considered an Egyptian god by the Greeks, despite the Hellenistic appearance given him (draped himation over a chiton, full beard, and curly locks). Due to his Egyptian funerary and fertility aspects, he was identified by the Greeks with their gods Dionysus (death, renewal, and fertility) and Pluto (god of the underworld). In his role as universal king, Sarapis also absorbed the identities of Zeus, king of the Greek gods, and Helios, the sun god. He was sometimes invoked as Zeus Helios Great Sarapis. A god of life and death, he was thus worshiped as a transcendent, omnipotent, and all-seeing god. But unlike the remote deities Osiris or Pluto, he was a loving god who personally cared about the health and well-being of his devotees. Prayers are known from all strata of Egyptian society to Sarapis, who was said to appear in dreams and grant healings.

By the late 4th century paganism was declining in the face of triumphing Christianity. In 391 the Serapeum (the cult center of Sarapis) at Alexandria, one of the most visible bastions of paganism, was destroyed by a host of Christians and armed soldiers led by the imperial prefect. The Abbot Shenoute (see cat. no. 148), foremost figure in Coptic Christianity, was among the group.
F.D.F.

Bibliography: Comstock and Vermeule 1971, no. 125, p. 118; Vermeule 1962a, pp. 150–1, fig. 7; Vermeule 1962b, no. 243; Vermeule 1966a, p. 31, fig. 18a; Jucker 1969, p. 79, fig. 3.

1. Vidman 1970, p. 22; Stambaugh 1972, p. 11.
2. Stambaugh 1972, pp. 12–3; and see Heyob 1975, pp. 8–9 for discussion of the relevant works on the subject.
3. Lewis 1986, pp. 69–70. Lewis, however, subscribes to the idea that Sarapis was a political invention of Ptolemy I.
4. Comstock and Vermeule 1971, p. 118.

117
Pantheistic Deity on a Couch,
A.D. 150–250

From Alexandria (?)

Bronze. 10.2 × 8.2 × 13.75

Museum of Fine Arts, Boston,
Harriet Otis Cruft Fund. 65.100

Provenance: New York art market

This votive bronze illustrates the type of syncretistic deity characteristic of religious and philosophical thought in Roman Alexandria. Modeled on images of Isis and Harpokrates, this mother goddess, dressed in Near Eastern Phrygian cap and Graeco-Roman chiton and flowing himation, nurses her child. The serpent and other beasts suggest the Nilotic setting appropriate to Isis.

The goddess is related to a host of Greek deities through an abundance of iconography. As noted by previous scholars,[1] there are Hermes's purse and caduceus, Zeus's thunderbolt, Dionysiac cymbals, Cybele's tambourine, Pan's pipes, and Tyche-Fortuna's (or Justitia-Moneta's) balances. While the ceremonial couch on which the pantheistic deity reclines is Alexandrian in style, this type of couch also appears on Roman-Egyptian terracottas elsewhere in Egypt.[2]

F.D.F.

Bibliography: Comstock and Vermeule 1971, no. 118, p. 111; Museum of Fine Arts, Boston 1976, no. 23; Vermeule 1965, p. 67; Idem 1966b, p. 108f, fig. 20; Mitten and Doeringer 1968, no. 274, p. 281.

1. Comstock and Vermeule 1971, no. 118, p. 111.
2. Ibid.

118

Nilus, 2nd or early 3rd century

From Karanis in the Fayum

Travertine marble. 42.2 × 28.3 × 19

Kelsey Museum of Archaeology,
The University of Michigan.
25747/25869

Provenance: Excavated by the Kelsey
Museum

The Egyptians did not personify the river that was their life source. Instead they deified the most important aspect of the Nile, its annual inundation, which they identified with the god Hapy. Shown as a male with pendulous female breasts, Hapy alternately carried the heraldic plants of Upper and Lower Egypt. His androgynous appearance incorporated male and female fertility; his Upper and Lower Egyptian attributes encompassed Egypt; and his fleshy appearance referred to the abundant gifts of the Nile.

Unlike the Egyptians, the Greeks and Romans regularly personified rivers and represented the Nile as a classical reclining god called Nilus, shown here. On mosaics and textiles, a figure of Nilus is often surrounded by nymphs and a personification of Abundance. This statuette may have included a small sphinx at the base of the shaft against which the bearded god rests.[1] Despite the god's wholly un-Egyptian appearance, Egyptian tradition survived in the popular Roman cult of the Nile. Like Hapy, Nilus was the benevolent force behind the inundation. And, following pharaonic tradition, Roman officials made sacrifices to the Nile, and Roman prefects avoided sailing on the river during inundation.[2]

The statue's marble was not indigenous to Egypt and must have been imported. The figure was carved by an artist trained in Graeco-Roman sculptural traditions, probably in the late 2nd century, i.e., Antonine period.

F.D.F.

Bibliography: Gazda et al. 1978, no. 26, p. 36; Gazda et al. 1983, p. 42, fig. 73.

1. Gazda et al. 1978, p. 36.
2. Bowman 1986, p. 183.

Christian Church

119
Architectural Relief from an Ecclesiastic Setting: Fragment of a Double-Sided Screen, 5th–6th century

From Bawit?

Limestone, traces of red. 29.2 × 31.8 × 7

Metropolitan Museum of Art, Rogers Fund. 10.175.18

This small, fragmentary screen was originally placed in a church or chapel. In early churches of the eastern Empire, including Egypt, screens were set up as altar enclosures and barriers. Waist-high, free-standing screens divided the nave, where the congregation gathered, from the sanctuary, where only clergy were allowed. Sanctuary screens did not block the congregation's view of the sanctuary or their communication with the clergy within: the lay faithful in the nave were allowed to see, touch, and press against the sanctuary barrier, but not to pass beyond it. Behind the screen was the holiest part of the church, oriented to face the rising sun. There, at the altar, priests performed one of the mysteries of Christian worship, when the bread and wine are transformed into the body and blood of Christ to be taken by the faithful in communion.[1]

The nave and sanctuary sides of this screen have decoration appropriate to their original placement and audience. On the side that would have faced the congregation is a general reference to the sacramental wine of communion: in an interlaced vine rinceau, birds drink the juice of grapes. (One wonders whether there was another panel referring to the sacramental bread.) On the side originally facing the clergy and the altar is a two-part composition alluding to the mystery of the sacraments and Christ's resurrection. Below are peacocks flanking a chalice on a cloth within an architectural setting, and in the center above is a bird with outstretched wings and spread tail feathers in a wreath. The chalice is a symbol of the sacraments, the peacocks represent officiating clergy in the church, and the bird in the wreath is an image of the ascended

Christ. Similar two-zoned compositions representing the earthly church below and the majesty of the kingdom of heaven above are found in the painted decoration of church sanctuaries in early Byzantine Egypt.[2]

The relief bears traces of a red color on the grapes, but no traces of the necessary layer of ground. There are similar examples of color on bare stone, in red and black, which may have been either guides for the painters or the remains of pigments that leached through the ground before it was lost. That this relief was originally polychromed is indicated by the rough surface and the

lack of detail in the carving. The relief was broken along a diagonal line through its center, but has been repaired.

T.K.T.

Bibliography: Duthuit 1931, pl. LXI c.; Gayet 1902, p. 210 and ill. before reconstruction; Strzygowski 1904, p. 85 (ME 7368a, b); Dalton 1911, fig. 27.

1. Refer to Grossmann's essay on church architecture. For a vivid discussion of the liturgical functions of church buildings, see Mathews 1977.
2. For a discussion of these wall paintings and their liturgical references, see van Moorsel 1978, p. 325.33.

120

Composite Capital: Crosses,
6th–7th century

From Upper Egypt or Nubia

Granite. 77.5 × 80 × 78.7

The University Museum, University of
Pennsylvania. E15222

Although there is no evidence for the
original architectural setting of this
capital, its large size, the expense of
working in granite, and the symbolism
of the jeweled crosses indicate that it
belonged to a large Christian structure.

The Upper Egyptian granite from
which it is carved is pinkish in color
with white, grey and black specks. In
general, granite is extremely difficult to
carve because it is very hard and compact. But it is also durable and valued
for the permanence of its polish. The
physical characteristics of the granite
have contributed to the excellent preservation of this capital: its vulnerable
corners are still intact and its surface is
smooth. The hardness of the stone,
however, did not dictate the linear style
of carving. In the softer sandstones of
Upper Egypt, there are many examples
of this style where forms are outlined by
convex lines giving the impression of
having been applied in tubular rolls of
clay. These stylistic conventions are
particular to Upper Egypt.[1]

The form of the capital has two distinct parts. Around the circular bottom is
a row of half-circles, perhaps a convention abstracted from curling acanthus
leaves. The volutes at the four upper
corners are clearly schematic renditions
of curling leaves. On each of the four
faces of the body of the capital is a cross
with wedge-shaped arms decorated with
beads. The crosses stand on long thin
pedestals supported by the central half-
circle at the bottom. There is a small
circle on either side of each pedestal and
in each cross arm.

T.K.T.

Bibliography: Badawy 1978, fig. 3.171,
p. 204.

1. No evidence exists on whether Early
   Byzantine granite sculpture would have
   been polychromed. In spite of the rich
   colors of the stone, some granite sculptures were polychromed in earlier periods.

121

Intarsia Glass Picture with St. Thomas, late 4th century

From Egypt

Cut glass sheets, rods, and millefiori canes in a resin matrix on terracotta backing. L. 79

The Corning Museum of Glass, Corning, New York. 86.1.1

Provenance: Galerie Nefer, Zurich

It is known that early Christian churches were ornamented with fine mosaics, paintings, and even textile hangings. However, it is a surprise to see the medium of glass intarsia (large flat pieces of glass glued to a backing) used in this fashion. This fragmentary picture comes from what was once a large panel, part of a continuous frieze band or perhaps a rectangular panel. The thin glass pieces have been attached to a coarse terracotta tile backing for attachment to a wall.

The surviving portion of the picture shows the profile head of a man identified as "Thomas" in Greek letters. Although he is not haloed, the context makes it likely that he is a saint or the Apostle of that name.[1] He is facing a very large *crux monogrammatica* symbol of shimmering gold-glass[2] surrounded by a circle of yellow and red glass. Thomas's head is fashioned of carefully cut pieces of opaque pinkish-beige glass with dark brown eyes and brows, purple-and-white streaked glass hair, and a beard of small "curls" formed of cut millefiori canes of purple and white.[3] Behind Thomas is an Ionic column capital in red, green, and yellow cut-glass, and white and red millefiori glass. The top border of the panel is formed of wide and narrow bands of red, brown, beige, and yellow glass. The background is of thin cut slabs of dark blue glass.

At Rome and Ostia, wall decorations have been found that use colored stone slabs for intarsia designs.[4] In Egypt, glass seems to have been preferred to stone. For example, two small fragments of rather crudely cut glass intarsia show-

ing figures of Coptic style survive from Antinoe.[5] The best comparison to the Thomas panel is a series of large glass intarsia wall panels with Graeco-Roman and Nilotic scenes found in the courtyard of the temple of Isis at Kenchreai in Greece[6] that formed a complete scheme of room decoration. The Kenchreai panels, found still in their ancient packing crates, were most probably exported from Egypt; an earthquake prevented their installation.[7] These panels are very close to the Thomas panel in technical excellence, chemical composition of the glass, and type of glue and backing – so close, in fact, that they could have been made in the same workshop.[8]

Millefiori and brilliantly colored glass of the type used in the Thomas panel was produced in the luxury-glass workshops of Alexandria in the Ptolemaic period and the early years of Roman rule. Lack of evidence had led scholars to think that this very elaborate type of glass and the market for it had disappeared by the Coptic period in Egypt. It is now evident that in the 4th century

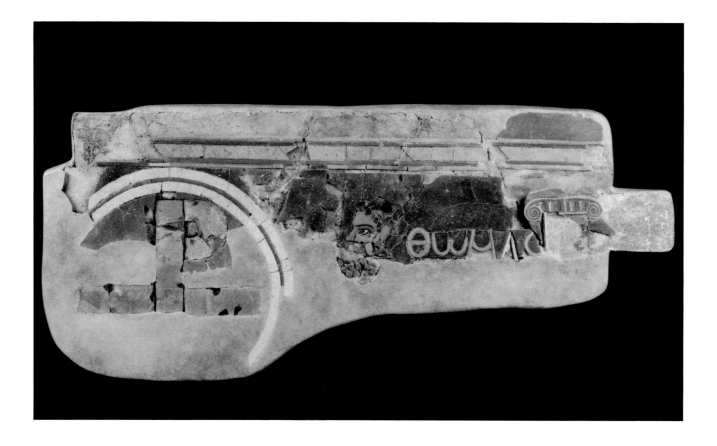

glass craftsmen were still capable of turning out elaborate, ambitious designs and adapting them both to more conservative Egyptian cult buildings and to the newly monumental churches of the Christian religion.

S.A.

Bibliography: Auth forthcoming; Grose 1984, pp. 32–3. Corning Museum of Glass 1987, no. 11, p. 34; Whitehouse and Brill 1988, pp. 34–50.

1. In the library of gnostic religious writings found at Nag Hammadi (see essay on Gnosticism) was a heretical secret gospel of Thomas, attributed to the Apostle of that name. The 4th century Coptic version was translated from a Greek manuscript at least two centuries older, of which fragments were found at Oxyrhynchus. This Gospel was among the many non-canonical writings circulating in Egypt in the early period of Christianity before Gnosticism and its writings were declared heretical. The Apostle Thomas received greater importance among this sect than is given to him in the familiar canonical gospels. Given this background, it is intriguing to speculate whether the Thomas of the intarsia panel represents this apostle.

2. On the history and technique of gold-glass see Auth 1979, *passim*.

3. For the techniques of millefiori or "mosaic" glass, see Auth 1976, p. 17; Goldstein 1979, pp. 29–33 with illustration; Grose 1983, p. 42 with illustration.

4. As at the basilica of Junius Bassus at Rome: see Beccati 1969, pls. 81–3, pp. 181–215; and Dorigo 1971, pp. 153–5, color pl. 13, fig. 113. Panels from late 4th century building at Ostia are discussed in Metropolitan Museum of Art 1979, no. 340, pp. 363–4; no. 468, p. 523 is a head of Christ in stone intarsia.

5. Müller 1962, pp. 13–8.

6. See Scranton et al. 1976, pp. 1–3 (Isis temple), drawing 54 (suggested room decoration scheme), drawings 3–4 and figs. 6–12 (packing crates).

7. See Scranton et al. 1976, pp. 262–6 for a thorough discussion of the origin of the panels and pp. 268–9 for the earthquake of A.D. 375.

8. The similarities are summarized in Corning Museum of Glass 1987, no. 11, p. 34. Brill has presented a more detailed survey of the scientific analyses that led to these results: see Whitehouse and Brill 1988. See most recently Auth forthcoming.

122
Two-Handled Chalice,
5th century

Pale green glass with opaque blue handles; knocked-off rim; applied twisted hollow knopped stem, lopsided. H. 18; rim D. 13.4; base D. 7.5; base H. 4.2–4.5

Kelsey Museum of Archaeology, The University of Michigan. 5361

Provenance: Purchased in Cairo, 1927

This chalice gives an idea of the more elaborate glassware used in Late Antique Egypt. Such glasses might have formed part of a church set imitating more expensive metalware.[1] The indented body pattern was produced by blowing into a pattern mold whose design was enlarged and softened by sub-sequent free-blowing. To form the handles, threads of hot blue glass were applied and shaped out into square handles with long tails pressed to make a horizontally crimped surface.[2] The rippled surface of the vessel itself may have been intended to simulate the hammered texture of silver. Though almost intact, the chalice lacks one piece at the rim. The body is broken and mended with no weathering.

S.A.

1. See, Pottery and Glass, n. 17.
2. For a smaller chalice of similar shape from Kellia, see Egloff 1977, p. 174, pl. 91, 4; it was found with African red-slip pottery of the 5th–6th century. Harden 1936, p. 170, n. 4 cites older references to the glass chalice shape.

123

Fish Plate, early 5th century

Found in the Fayum

Painted clay, pale buff with orange-red
slip. 2.6–3.4 × 38.2

Royal Ontario Museum. 910.165.446

This very large and impressive red-
slipped plate (with pitting on the interior
surface, the paint rubbed in places, and
some chipping at the rim) is an Egyptian
imitation of North African fine pottery.
It is an Egyptian innovation to substitute painted decoration for the stamped
and rouletted designs of North African
ceramics. The manufacturing marks of
the potter's wheel are clearly visible on
the underside of this plate, which is
slightly bowed up in the center and
slopes slightly to the broad flat rim.

A very large fish with water weed in
its mouth is depicted in black outline.
White slip is used on the fish, on the
black-banded circle that frames it, and in
the faint lines on the rim. Fish are common motifs on these very large plates,
of which few survive.[1] The large size,
careful manufacture, and fish motifs of
these plates suggest a usage other than
ordinary tableware. They may have
been used instead of silver as liturgical
patens for communion bread.[2]
S.A.

Bibliography: Hayes 1976, no. 107,
p. 24, pl. 14.

1. A plate with five fishes is described in
   Winlock and Crum 1926, pl. 33B; a plate
   with one fish with water weed is described
   in Mond and Myers 1940, pl. 75, Hayes
   1976, no. 108, Bourriau 1981, no. 185,
   pp. 93–4. Brunner-Traut, Brunner, and
   Zick-Nissen 1984, no. 156, color pl. p. 189
   show a plate with fish, hare, grapes, lotus,
   and water weed.
2. For the form and symbolism of the paten,
   see Elbern in Metropolitan Museum of Art
   1979, pp. 592–3; for the symbolism of
   fish, see Lowrie 1965, pp. 55–6.

124
Frog and Cross Lamp,
3rd–4th century or later

From Karanis

Molded clay. H. with handle 8.
Body: 4.8 × 14 × 9.4

Kelsey Museum of Archaeology,
The University of Michigan. 22369

This lamp of coarse, light red clay has a
reddish slip. The long pear-shaped body
is ornamented with a frog outlined by
rays and circles. The frog was associated
with Heket, the ancient Egyptian goddess
of birth, and the frog-shaped hieroglyph
also signified rebirth and resurrection.[1]
The Christian cross motif on this lamp
emphasizes this significance. Another
type of cross and frog lamp actually
includes the Greek inscription, "I am the
resurrection."[2] Here the ancient Egyptian frog with implications of rebirth
was assimilated to ideas of Christ as the
resurrection.
S.A.

Bibliography: Shier 1978, no. 437,
pp. 47, 147, pl. 46. Gazda et al. 1983,
p. 44, fig. 75.

1. Shier 1972, pp. 356–8.
2. Shier 1972, p. 357.

125

Censer, 5th century

Bronze. 28.3 × 14

The Brooklyn Museum, Charles Edwin
Wilbour Fund. 41.684

Provenance: Acquired in Cairo

This handsome bronze censer, used for
incense, was cast in three sections: a
flaring bowl with ventilating rings surmounted by a row of ducks, a short but
richly profiled baluster, and a broad
tripod base with finely detailed clasp
feet. Both baluster and base have abundant parallels in Coptic Egypt,[1] although
their termination is usually not a bowl
but a pricket for a lamp. Stationary censers are also attested from the period,
however, both in texts and in art,[2] though
they are much less common than those
to be carried on a chain.

Incense in Late Antiquity at first
carried a strong connotation of pagan
worship, but it eventually became very
popular among Christians, both in
church and at home. It was used as an
honorific accompaniment to prayer.[3]
The bowl of this censer bears two lines
of a pointillé inscription (an inscription
composed of little dots), which to judge
from its simplicity may have been a later
addition (though only slightly later, since
its letter forms are still of the period).
The first line ("In fulfillment of a vow of
Auxanon") is marked by a menorah,
suggesting use in Jewish worship.[4]
G.V.

Bibliography: Metropolitan Museum of
Art 1979, no. 353.

1. Wulff 1909.
2. Vikan 1982, p. 30, fig. 6.
3. Atchley 1909, pp. 117 ff.
4. Metropolitan Museum of Art 1979, no. 353.

126

Censer, 6th–7th century

Said to have come from Egypt

Bronze. 20

Dumbarton Oaks Collection,
Washington D.C. 40.56

Provenance: Purchased from Brummer,
October 1940

The tall, pyramidal lid of this censer has
a clasp in the front and a hinge in the
back, and is topped by a simple cross
with a loop for suspension. Its openwork
decoration consists of grapevines, and
crosses flanked by stylized birds. The
cubelike body is decorated with circles
and dots, some arranged in cruciform
pattern, and by two roughly engraved
crosses on the front. The feet are in the
form of balls.

In both shape and decoration this
incense burner, said to come from Egypt,
bears comparison with known Egyptian
objects of the Early Byzantine period.[1]
While possibly for private use, it may
also have been used in a church. By the
6th century incense was in common use
throughout the Christian Mediterranean, along with candles and lamps, as a
means of paying homage to emperors,
bishops, saints, and icons, and as an
accompaniment to intense prayer. On
the one hand, the sweet-smelling smoke
was pleasing to the honored party, and
on the other, the rising fumes evoked
the rising prayers of the supplicant.[2]
G.V.

Bibliography: Ross 1965, no. 49.

1. Ross 1965, no. 49.
2. Atchley 1909, pp. 117 ff.

127
Fragment of a Sanctuary Curtain (?),
late 5th–6th century

Linen and wool. 138.5 × 70

The Minneapolis Institute of Arts.
83.126

The practice of using curtains in doorways and in between the columns of colonnades of Late Roman architecture was continued in Early Christian churches. In Egypt and in Syria curtains were also used to separate the sanctuary area from the rest of the church's interior.[1] This fragmentary textile carrying a large Latin cross adorned with a wreath may be an example of such an early sanctuary curtain. The orange and yellow cross with slightly flaring arms and a design imitating a setting of jewels and pearls, is shown fitted into a base. The head of the cross is further emphasized by the fruit and foliate wreath. The surface of the curtain must have been filled with floral buds and blossoms similar to the ones that still flank the cross. The curtain is made of a plain linen cloth, and the cross, the wreath and the floral motifs are executed in tapestry technique and directly woven into the ground fabric as was customary for this type of curtain.[2]

The cross of the Minneapolis curtain belongs to a group of crosses whose monumental form and jeweled appearance were most likely inspired by the large bejewelled cross erected at Golgotha in the 4th century and which is known from Theodosius II's restoration of 420.[3] Similar crosses are known to have decorated apse and sanctuary areas of churches and several of these still exist.[4] The choice of the jeweled cross for the sanctuary curtain would only have followed this practice. Like the apse and sanctuary crosses, the jeweled cross of the curtain symbolizes Christ's triumph over death and his resurrection. This meaning with its promise of man's salvation is further strengthened by the presence of the fruit wreath. While the wreath was used to symbolize victory, the fruit refers to the rich offerings of Nature and thus regeneration. Both motifs, widely used in Roman – especially imperial – art, were eventually appropriated by the Early Christians.

Although curtains like these must have been made as early as the 5th century, the style of the fruit, floral buds and blossoms suggests that the curtain was made in the late 5th and 6th century.
A.G.

Bibliography: Stack 1984

1. Schneider 1936. Various types of hangings and curtains are mentioned in a 5th–6th century church inventory from Ibion in Egypt (Hunt and Edgar 1932, no. 192, pp. 432–35).
2. Technical information: linen tabby cloth; tapestry weave in wool and linen (Stack 1984, p. 14, n. 1).
3. Coüasnon 1974, pp. 50 ff.
4. E.g., in the S. Pudenziana and in S. Stefano Rotondo in Rome; and in S. Apollinare in Classe outside Ravenna.

Color plate, page 21

128

Icon of a Saint (St. Theodore?),
6th century

Said to be from Akhmim

Wool. 48 × 37 (a); 31.8 × 44.1 (b)

Harvard University Art Museums
(Arthur M. Sackler Museum), Gift
of Mrs. John D. Rockefeller, Jr.
1939.112.1 and 2

In the 6th century much art, including textiles, was made for the use of the Church, but very little has survived. The St. Theodore fragment is one of only a handful of such large-scale tapestries known, the best-preserved example of which is the seated Virgin and Child with angels in the Cleveland Museum of Art.[1] Like other religious images, these hangings were icons that served not only as alternatives to other media, especially painting and mosaics, but were important vehicles of intercession on behalf of the pious.

In its present condition, this textile is an assemblage of several fragments mounted together. The largest piece shows a bust of a dark-haired, bearded saint wearing a *chlamys*, his head framed by a pale halo, his large eyes gazing into the distance. Other fragments mounted around the saint include a hand holding a staff, an arm, another staff, a jeweled cross from a staff, and some vegetation, all on a red background. Now separate, but originally mounted with other fragments, are a vine-scroll border and a triangular field in blue outlined by a jeweled band and inscribed O ΑΓΙ⟨OC⟩ ΘEOΔO⟨POC⟩, Hagios Theodoros or St. Theodore. All fragments are woven in an identical tapestry technique in wool on undyed woolen warps,[2] and could well have belonged to the same textile, probably a large hanging with at least two but probably several standing saints holding cross-headed staffs. The only extant figure resembles 6th century representations of St. Theodore,[3] the popular soldier saint named in the inscription.

The St. Theodore fragment is an important example of 6th century art. As in contemporary paintings and mosaics (e.g., in the mid-6th century church of San Vitale in Ravenna), the figure and other motifs are defined by distinct outlines, while at the same time subtly shaded yarns are blended and interwoven to evoke volume, surface modeling, and texture. The weaving proceeded perpendicularly to the direction of the design, causing slight distortions in the figure of the saint.

The textile is said to have been found in Akhmim.[4] Although it is superficially related to other 6th century tapestry weavings,[5] it is particularly close to a hanging with the Hestia Polyolbos, the Goddess of the Hearth, in Washington, D.C.[6]

A.G.

Bibliography: Tyler 1939, pp. 2–13; Shepherd 1969, pp. 105–8, fig. 14.9; Zaloscer 1974, p. 166, fig. 80; Metropolitan Museum of Art 1979, no. 494, pp. 549–50.

1. Shepherd 1969.
2. Technical information: warp: undyed wool (S-spun); weft: red, blue, brown, green, tan, apricot, all wool (S-spun); tapestry over in warp, ca. 11 warps per 1 cm; weft count varies.
3. E.g., an apse mosaic in SS. Cosmas and Damian, Rome (Wilpert and Schumacher 1976, pls. 105–6; an icon at Mt. Sinai (Weitzmann 1976, cat. B3, pp. 18–21, pl. IV), and a mosaic icon in St. Demetrius, Thessaloniki.
4. Tyler 1939, p. 1.
5. Especially Shepherd 1969.
6. Dumbarton Oaks Collection, inv. no. 29.1 (Volbach 1969, no. 32, pp. 68–70; Friedländer 1945, pp. 1–26, frontispiece).

Cover

a

b

129
Weaving with Ankh-Crosses,
6th or 7th century

From Akhmim

Wool and linen. 30.5 × 35.5

Victoria and Albert Museum. 258.1890

The ankh – the *crux ansata* or looped cross – is an ancient Egyptian sign for life that began appearing as an Egyptian version of the Christian cross sometime in the late 4th century.[1] One of its many early appearances is the finispiece of the Acts of the Apostles in New York, variously dated from the very early 5th through the 6th century.[2] The use of ankh crosses seems to accelerate in the 6th and 7th centuries, judging from their frequent presence in funerary stelae and other arts.[3] It is tempting to associate their more frequent, even exclusive use, with objects made specifically for Egyptian Coptic Christians rather than Egyptian Greek Christians. Although this may be so, the complex religious and cultural situation in Byzantine Egypt does not permit such clear-cut identification of artistic patronage.

This type of decoration, and the size of fragments like this one, suggest that such weavings may have been used as altar cloths.[4] They can be assigned to the 6th or 7th century when decorated altar cloths are well documented.[5] The design elements are commonly used in Late Antique and Early Byzantine art. The braid motif is ubiquitous: the colorful and well-executed braids in these fragments could have been woven any time before the end of the 7th century. The cross and its many types employed here are also in use from the 4th century onward.[6]

A.G.

Blbliography: Kendrick 1921, no. 399, pp. 12–3, pl. 4; Cramer 1955, p. 24, pl. 14, fig. 30.

1. Cramer 1955, pp. 46–7.
2. Pierpont Morgan Library, William C. Glazier Collection G.67 (Leroy 1974, pp. 15–17, pl. 2, fig. 1).
3. See Badawy 1978, pp. 210–21; also Daoud Girgis 1983, pl. 2.
4. The left selvage and the corded edge indicate that this piece is the lower left corner of a larger textile. It is all tapestry-woven in linen and wool on undyed woolen warps. Technical information: all tapestry cloth; warp: yellow wool; weft: undyed linen and blue, red, green and pink, purple wool. Tapestry over one warp. The design consists of a series of *ankh*-crosses, four in the lower and two in the upper field (of the last two the larger one is very fragmentary), separated by horizontal stripes with braided pattern in graded tone of red and blue and green with white dotting. The smaller *ankh* in the upper field and the second *ankh* from the left in the lower field are red; the other *ankhs* are purple. The loops of the *ankhs* are filled with various types of crosses, including the XP monogram in the red *ankh* of the lower field. An analogous but larger fragment (46 × 30 cm.) in Paris, which even may be the top portion of the same textile, is preserved from selvage to selvage. Its design shows a row of five *ankhs*, the central one in red with a XP monogram in its loop; the lateral *ankhs* are purple, as in the London fragment. In the Paris fragment, the lower part is fragmentary with a partially preserved loop of the central purple *ankh* flanked by λ and ω. The braided pattern of the two stripes is blue and red (Paris, the Louvre, inv. x4237) (du Bourguet 1964, E107, pp. 228–9).
5. As, e.g., in the presbytery mosaics of S. Vitale in Ravenna (ca. A.D. 547).
6. Cabrol and Leclercq 1948, III/2, cols. 3045–3131.

130
Fragment of a Clavus,
7th–8th century

Wool and linen.

103 × 24

The British Museum. 30806.

Although this *clavus* dates into the 7th, or even the 8th century, its technique of execution and the style of its decoration were established already in the 6th century. Its Christian subject matter, however, may reflect still an earlier, 5th century tradition. The *clavus* is decorated with densely arranged scenes from the life of Christ stacked one above the other and framed by delicate scrolled borders. The scenes can no longer be identified precisely but the grouping of figures, their gestures and details such as a cross-halo, indicating Christ, and bed-like objects next to the figures suggest the scenes represent the Miracles and the Ministry of Christ. Costume ornament of this sort was mentioned in the writings of an early 5th century bishop, Asterius of Amaseia:

> You may see the wedding of Galilee with the water jars, the paralytic carrying his bed on his shoulders, the blind man healed by means of clay, the woman with an issue of blood seizing [Christ's] hem, the sinful woman falling at the feet of Jesus...."[1]

In its present condition, the British Museum *clavus* consists of two separate pieces that may have come from any section of the two tunic *clavi*.[2] The *clavus*, woven in the tapestry technique on plied linen warps, was applied. The figures are executed in an abstract style common to 7th and 8th century weaving, which evolved from a more descriptive 6th century style (cat. nos. 68 and 70). The heads, arms, and colorful clothing of the figures have been reduced to plain tan, green, blue, and brown surfaces. Each inner division is distinctly outlined. The brownish ground of the *clavus* is barely visible. It is filled here and there with vegetal motifs and lettering, probably remnants of the titles that accompanied the scenes in earlier phases of the design. As a matter of fact, the lettering suggests that the design was originally based on a painted source, either a manuscript or a painted resist-dyed textile (see also cat. no. 69).[3]

A.G.

1. Mango 1972, p. 51.
2. Two very similar fragments are in the National Museum in Copenhagen (Koefoed-Peterson 1944, p. 63).
3. E.g., Cleveland Museum of Art, inv. 51.400 (Metropolitan Museum of Art 1979, no. 390, pp. 433–434); London, Victoria and Albert Museum, inv. 722.1897 and 1103.1900 (Metropolitan Museum of Art 1979, nos. 391–392, pp. 434–436).

detail

131
Silk Fragment, 7th–8th centuries

From Akhmim

Silk 18 × 6.5

Philadelphia Museum of Art, Given by Howard L. Goodhart. 33.83.1

This small fragment of a drawloom silk must have been used as a tunic ornament, either as a cuffband or as a *clavus*.[1] It is woven in purple and cream-colored silk with the design of a standing saint in the lower panel and a bird of prey attacking an animal in the upper panel. The band is framed by floral borders.

The saint is the most distinctive motif of the design. He carries a cross in his left hand, and attacks the dragon at his feet with a spear held in his right hand. His identification has, however, been problematic. He has been variously described as the triumphant Christ trampling on a serpent, as Archangel Michael, and as St. George.[2] The lack of a halo and the dress argue against the identification as Christ, just as the absence of the wings argues against Archangel Michael. The identification as St. George or another warrior saint seems most plausible. The figure holds a cross, the symbol of faith and martyrdom customary for saints, and like warrior saints, he wears a tunic and a military cloak (see also cat. no. 128). The dragon at his feet allows for even more precise identification as St. George.[3] The choice of a saintly figure for a costume ornament would not have been accidental in the Early Byzantine period. The presence of a holy image was not only a statement of the wearer's faith but also an instrument of the saint's protective powers.

The design of the Philadelphia fragment is known from other silks, some showing the same composition repeated four times in one piece in a mirror-image style common to the point-return patterning of drawloom weaving. It is obvious that this silk is a fragment from such a larger textile.[4] These silks were found in Akhmim. Their ornamental motifs and the figural style are found in other weavings of the 6th through the 8th centuries. Because of the high degree of stylization in the floral borders and animal motifs, the whole group should be dated to the 7th or possibly the 8th century (see also cat. no. 193).

A.G.

Bibliography: The Brooklyn Museum 1941, no. 258, ill., p. 82; Baltimore Museum of Art 1947, no. 761, p. 150, pl. 115.

1. Technical information: weft-faced compound twill.
2. Martiniani-Reber 1986, pp. 91–2.
3. Braunfels-Esche 1976.
4. Forrer 1891, p. 23, pl. III.2; Geneva, Musée d'Art et d'Histoire, no. D739 (from the Forrer Collection); Lyons, Musée historique des Tissus, inv. 910.III.1 (Martiniani-Reber 1986, no. 75, pp. 91–3); Athens, Museum of Greek Handcraft, inv. 1370 (Apostolakis 1932, pp. 184–5); Berlin, formerly Kaiser-Friedrich-Museum, no. 9283 (Wulff and Volbach 1926, p. 150, pl. 134); London, Victoria and Albert Museum, inv. T34.1917 (Kendrick 1922, no. 819, p. 81, pl. 25).

132
Old Testament Apocryphon,
7th century

Possibly from Hou (Diospolis Minor)

Papyrus. 12.6 × 11.8 (fol. 2, smallest);
15.5 × 18.9 (fol. 1, largest)
Written in Coptic (Sahidic)

The Pierpont Morgan Library, Amherst
Collection. Coptic Theological
Texts, no. 3

These fragments, together with five
others not exhibited here, are from a
papyrus codex containing an apocryphal
story featuring the biblical patriarch
Enoch (cf. Genesis 5:18–24). In the
story, an angel of God (probably
Michael) appears to Enoch and proph-
esies Enoch's future role in the Judgment. Enoch, as the righteous scribe,
will record people's sins and good deeds.

Part of the beginning of the story is
found in Folio 2, introducing Enoch as a
righteous man who was taken up to
heaven for special revelations. Folio 8
preserves material featuring Enoch's
sister, Sibyl. Folios 1 and 7 have parts of
Enoch's vision of the Judgment, featuring "the balances of righteousness." An
"angel of mercy" (Michael?) tips the
scales in favor of God's elect. The judgment scene in this text is somewhat
reminiscent of the judgment of the dead
in ancient Egyptian religion. Enoch the
scribe plays a role analogous to that of
the ibis-headed god, Thoth.

B.A.P.

Bibliography: Crum 1913, pp. 3–11;
Pearson 1976.

133
Synaxary for Epiphi 20, 844

From Hamouli, found on the site of the
monastery of St. Michael in the Fayum
in 1910

Manuscript on vellum. 35.6 × 27.3
Written in Coptic (Sahidic)

The Pierpont Morgan Library. M586

Provenance: acquired by Pierpont
Morgan in 1911

A synaxary (or *synaxarion*) is an account
of the life of a saint, read as a lesson in
public worship, or a collection of such
accounts. This manuscript comprises
Sahidic texts of the Martyrdom of St.
Theodore Stratelates, Martyrdom of Sts.
Cosmas and Damian, and prophecies
concerning spiritual laxity in the community of Pboou by Apa Tsharour. There is
some text missing from the first two
texts. There are interlaced headpieces,
paragraph marks of scrolls and birds
marking the divisions of the book, and
small crosses marking the quires. The
codex retains its original binding, tooled
with a geometrical design. This synaxary was made for the Monastery of St.
Michael by the calligrapher Zacharaias
of Kalamon, who also made the related
Synaxary M588, dated 842, for the
Monastery of Samuel of Kalamon.

This frontispiece (fol. 1v) prefaces the
first text, which is the reading for the
20th day of the 11th month of the Coptic
calendar (July 8–August 6). An interlace
cross dominates the page, comprised of
interwoven colored bands, stepped
evenly on all four sides. Inscribed above
and below the arms, it represents the
salvation of the crucifixion. Appropriate
to its position opening a Synaxary, the
cross functions as a call to prayer, the
liturgical aspect implied by the hanging
lamps, suspended from the arms and
between the tops and sides. This frontispiece differs from that of cat. no. 135,
then, in not depicting the saint referred
to in the text, but is consonant with the

liturgical context. Cross frontispieces
(and finispieces) are common in Syriac
as well as Coptic manuscripts with various texts, where they are suggested to
have a talismanic function as well as
providing an initiation into prayer. But
such interlaced frontispieces are not
exclusive to the oriental Christian tradition, and their appearance in Celtic
manuscripts betokens the widespread
use of such non-figurative imagery in
the early medieval world.
L.A.H.

Bibliography: Buchthal and Kurz 1942,
p. 48, no. 223; Petersen 1954, p. 312;
Leroy 1974, p. 59, pl. 3(1).

134
Synaxary: Pseudo-John Chrysostom, Eulogy of the Four Incorporeal Animals, 893

From Hamouli

Manuscript on vellum. 33.5 × 26
Written in Coptic (Sahidic)

The Pierpont Morgan Library. M.612

This miniature (fol. 1v), preceding the text in Sahidic Coptic, depicts the Virgin suckling the Child, a subject known in Latin as Maria Lactans and in Greek as Galaktotrophousa. They are enthroned between angels. Inscriptions label the Virgin and Christ in monogram form. Below the Virgin's feet is a signature of Isaac the priest, whose name is given elsewhere in the manuscript as Apa Isaac of Ptepouhar. The colophon of the manuscript (one of six folios now detached from the manuscript) gives the name of the donor for whom Michael made the manuscript, the monk Papostolos, son of John the archimandrite of the monastery of St. Michael of Fayum. This John was the donor to St. Michael's of another manuscript from Hamouli (Pierpont Morgan Library M.574) with a very similar miniature of the Virgin Lactans between angels, a servicebook dated 897/8 which must share the same model as the present miniature. This overlap explains the inclusion here of an image of the Virgin and Child rather than one of the four Beasts of Revelation (Revelation IV. 6–8) commented on in the text but not found in Coptic manuscript illumination. M.612 also includes two anthropomorphic capital letters, knotted crosses, paragraph marks and zoomorphic imagery, as in folio 2r. The manuscript is detached from its original binding, now in the Coptic Museum in Cairo. The miniature has suffered some damage.

The image of the Virgin Lactans is not in itself exclusively Coptic. However, the Virgin holding her breast offered to the grown Christ child on her knee is Egyptian, derived from Isis-Horus iconography. It is paralleled in wall painting as well as manuscript illumination, including a niche painting from the monastery of Jeremiah at Saqqara of the 6th–7th century now in the Coptic Museum in Cairo. The cross-nimbed Christ bears a scroll in his left hand and gestures with his right towards the Virgin. He thus endorses the Virgin as the Mother of God, a tenet of Monophysite Christian theology, with its unequivocal belief in the indivisibility of the human and divine natures of Christ. The pair is seated on a cushioned, elaborately carved wooden throne, the front of which is shown in perspective. Painted directly onto the parchment, the garments of both the Virgin and Christ are vividly colored. Adoring angels that flank the figures present the group as an icon, their hands extended in appropriate gestures while their unfurled inner wings offer protection. They look front while their bodies are in profile. An interlace frame encloses the icon-image, representative of the cult of the Virgin in Christian Egypt.

L.A.H.

Bibliography: Buchthal and Kurz 1942, p. 48, no. 223; Petersen 1954, p. 316; Leroy 1974, pp. 94–96, pls. 31, 23(2).

135
Synaxary: St. Stephen Between Two Angels, 895

From Hamouli, found on the site of the monastery of St. Michael in the Fayum in 1910

Manuscript on vellum. 33 × 25.4
Written in Coptic (Sahidic)

Pierpont Morgan Library. M577

Provenance: acquired by Pierpont Morgan in 1911

The manuscript comprises texts of the Life of St. Stephen the Protomartyr, Death of the Patriarch Isaac, Reverential Homily on Luke VII, 37 ff. by St. John Chrysostom, and Discourse by Athanasius of Alexandria on Luke XI, 5 ff. Texts are marked with geometric headpieces and paragraph marks, including zoomorphic imagery. The codex retains its original binding, with geometric tooling.

The first text begins with an exhortation by St. Stephen, followed by events of his life, including his marriage, the birth of his daughter, his adoption of the eremitical life, the appearance of the Virgin Mary to him exhorting him to visit his daughter and accept her death, his conversion of three robbers and his election as one of the seven deacons by the twelve disciples, as described in Acts VI. 1–8. This miniature (folio 1v) prefacing this first text is therefore appropriate to the text in illustrating St. Stephen performing the Liturgy. St. Stephen, deacon and protomartyr, (**CTЄΦANOC**) is shown flanked by two angels (each inscribed **AΓΓЄΛOC**). His white hair and beard signal old age in deference to his martyrdom, in contrast to the usual depiction of him in youth, as in the wall painting in the north church at Deir al-Chohada' of the second half of the 12th century. His embroidered deacon's garb – a chasuble worn over an alb or tunic with a stole around the neck and suspended down the front – is unusual in medieval art. The compelling gaze of St. Stephen draws the viewer into the liturgy over which he presides. He stands in an apse, shaped by the rounded area of pink background behind him, and presents the chalice. The assisting angels hover on either side, against a lighter background, the left bearing a long-handled flabellum and the right a jug. Their sidelong gaze, segmented draperies, and patterned wings offset the austere frontality of the central saint. Foliage at the feet of the saint, matched by that at the top of the frame, refers to the salvation in Paradise, anticipated by the saint through his martyrdom and prepared for through the practice of the Church liturgy. The miniature can be interpreted as a prayer by the donors, specified in the colophon as Peter and Nimna of the Fayumic town of Narmoute, who had the manuscript made for the convent of St. Michael.

L.A.H.

Bibliography: Buchthal and Kurz 1942, p. 47, no. 214; Petersen 1954, p. 318; Abd Al-Masih 1957; Leroy 1974, pp. 97–99, pl. 33.

136
Letter, early 7th century

From Hermonthis (Thebes),
Upper Egypt

Limestone ostrakon. 12.7 × 17.8
Written in Coptic (Sahidic)

The British Museum. 32782

Provenance: Egypt Exploration Society
excavation

This is a highly rhetorical pastoral letter
from the famous Bishop Abraham of
Hermonthis, superior of the monastery
of St. Phoibammon at Thebes around
600 A.D. He declares that he has been
informed that a certain Psate has been
oppressing the poor. Anyone who would
do this, says the bishop, is like all the
worst people in the Old and New Testaments: like Judas Iscariot, the mockers
of Christ, the mercenary Gehazi, the
murderers Cain and Zimri, the idolator
Jeroboam, those who falsely accused
Daniel and Susanna, the mob who
demanded Christ's blood, and the soldiers who spread the lie that the disciples
had stolen away Christ's body to fake a
resurrection. Anyone who oppresses the
poor, says Bishop Abraham, is to be
excommunicated.

This letter shows to what extent the
local bishop in Egypt became the champion of the little man, the downtrodden,
the "underclass," and could back up
his power with ecclesiastical sanctions.
The strongly repetitive Biblical style
in which it is composed (characteristic
of all Abraham's letters) is a typical
example of the extent to which Coptic
language, thought, and behavior were
completely and naturally interwoven
with quotations from the Scriptures.
When something happened in the life of
the ordinary person, the first response
was to describe it by using a Biblical
parallel. Bible stories were the prime
fabric of Coptic folklore.
L.S.B.M.

Bibliography: Crum 1902a, no. 71.

137
Marriage Contract, 6th to 7th century

From Upper Egypt (?)

Papyrus. 36.1 × 11.2
Written in Coptic (Sahidic)

The Pierpont Morgan Library. M662 B 12

Provenance: Bought from a dealer
(Nahman), Cairo, 1920

This is the marriage contract of a cleric
in minor orders, probably a subdeacon,
who promises "in the presence of the
Blessed Trinity" never to take another
wife, nor to fornicate, nor to consort
with wandering monks ("Sarakote"),
nor to celebrate more than one liturgy in
one sanctuary per day. He swears that
his bride is a virgin and is not his near
relative (aunt or niece). The names of
the signer and of any witnesses have not
been preserved.

The "Sarakote" with whom it is said
to be wrong to associate or to eat may
be Meletians. Meletians were a sect of
rigorists, surviving into the late 6th
century, who did not readmit to the
church those who had capitulated to the
Decian persecution. On the other hand,
"Sarakote" may simply have referred
to non-Pachomian monks.[1]

L.S.B.M.

Bibliography: MacCoull 1979a,
pp. 116–23.

1. See Alcock 1987, p. 189.

138
Praying Figure,
possibly 6th–7th century

Orange clay with white slip and traces
of painted decoration in red and black.
H. 14.6

Collection of The Newark Museum.
Gift of John D. Rockefeller Jr. 38.161

Although this statuette is even more
schematic than cat. no. 100, it is readily
recognized as a praying woman. It is
hand-built in two pieces joined at the
sides to form a hollow tube with
upraised arms and a curious triangular
headdress. The eyes, nose, and breasts
are formed of added clay lumps, while
incised lines indicate hair. There are
traces of vertical and horizontal red and
black painted lines on headdress and
body.[1] This crude yet expressive figure
seems almost like a hieroglyph of
prayer as shown in Coptic textiles,
sculptures, and wall paintings with
Christian subjects.[2]

S.A.

1. For the same type cf. Perdrizet 1921,
   pl. VI, lower left; p. 6. Perdrizet notes that
   there are a dozen examples of this type of
   figure in the Fouquet Collection, all coming from the Fayum region. Cf. also Weber
   1914, pl. 23, nos. 235 and 236, and The
   Brooklyn Museum 1941, nos. 126–7. For
   the progression of this figure from earlier
   types, see Badawy 1978, p. 346.
2. Textile examples include a loop-weave
   textile from Akhmim (ancient Panopolis)
   in the Abegg-Stiftung, Bern; see du
   Bourguet 1971, color pl. p. 55. Sculpture
   examples include tombstone of Rhodia,
   Staatliche Museen zu Berlin 1.966; tombstones with orant figures, Beckwith 1963,
   no. 114, pp. 26, 55–6; nos. 116–8, p. 55.
   Paintings to note are Chapel B and Cell A
   at Saqqara. Badawy 1978, figs. 4.43 and
   4.44, pp. 267 and 268.

139
St. Menas Flask, ca. 450–550 [1]

Pale beige clay made in two-part mold.
13–13.5 × 10.3

Collection of The Newark Museum.
85.46

Pilgrims to the international Christian shrine of St. Menas in the Maryut desert west of Alexandria returned with flasks such as this filled with holy water from the miraculous spring at the site. The indistinctly stamped design on each side shows St. Menas in soldier's costume, his name written in Greek, standing between a pair of camels. On one side a retrograde inscription in Greek reads,

"Blessing of St. Menas," while on the other the same circular design is surrounded by a stylized garden border. [2]

St. Menas was a Christian Egyptian recruit in the Roman army who was martyred for his beliefs. According to legend, his body was carried through Egypt for burial on the back of two camels. When they reached the future site of the saint's shrine in the desert, in the manner of camels they refused to go any further. [3] A spring of water on this spot acquired miraculous properties from the presence of the saint's relics. Its healing powers attracted the patronage of the Byzantine emperors in erecting lavish buildings [4] and a wide international following among pilgrims, making it the Lourdes of ancient times. [5]
S.A.

1. Dated on the basis of the Polish stratigraphical excavations at Kom el-Dikka, Alexandria; see Kiss 1969, pl. 165. Cf. also Müller-Wiener 1967, pp. 216–7, the recent German excavations at Abu Mena itself. The 4th century date for the start of these flasks given by Kaufmann, the original excavator of Abu Mena in 1905–7, is now seen to be too early.
2. The original publication of the St. Menas flasks, Kaufmann 1910, details the many variants of the designs, of which this is just one.
3. Kiss 1969, pp. 155–6, nos. 13–7 gives a good discussion of the sources and variant versions of the St. Menas legend. See also Metropolitan Museum of Art 1979, no. 512, pp. 573–4.
4. Metropolitan Museum of Art 1979, no. 591, pp. 662–4 gives a summary with references by Alfred Frazer. See also Grossmann 1977, pp. 237, 240 and fig. 68 with references.
5. This comparison is made in du Bourguet 1967, p. 82. The exceptionally wide distribution of the St. Menas flasks throughout the Mediterranean area suggests the many places from which the pilgrims came.

140
Pilgrim Flask:
Sts. Menas and Thekla,
6th –7th century

Terracotta. D. 17.7

The British Museum. EA69839

Crude clay flasks like this were used by early pilgrims to take sanctified water home from the shrine of St. Menas at Abu Mena, near Alexandria.[1] The water was drawn from great cisterns in an elaborate architectural complex housing the saint's relics. Indirect contact with the relics was the source of the water's reputed miracle-working properties.

Typically, as here, an orant portrait of Menas between two bowing camels appears on one side of the vessel; it is believed to match a large relief image at the shrine. Somewhat unusually, however, St. Thekla appears on the other side, tied to a stake amid two steers, a bear, and a lion.[2] According to legend, Thekla was converted by St. Paul during his travels through Asia Minor. For this she was condemned to the arena, but the wild beasts refused to touch her. By the 6th century the cult of St. Thekla had spread throughout the eastern Mediterranean.

G.V.

Bibliography: British Museum 1987, p. 27.

1. Kaufmann 1910, *passim*.
2. Nauerth and Warns 1981, ch. 6.

141
Pilgrim Token: St. Menas,
6th–7th century

From Abu Mena

Clay. D. 7.0

The Malcove Collection, University of Toronto. M82.260

At the center of this crudely stamped clay disk – half of whose border molding has broken away – is an orant portrait of St. Menas who, as was customary in the period, is portrayed in military garb flanked by kneeling camels (see cat. nos. 139 and 140). Among the most popular pilgrimage shrines in Late Antiquity was that of St. Menas at Abu Mena, southwest of Alexandria.[1] Renowned for its miracle-working holy waters, the shrine is now known primarily through the many clay "Menas flasks" that survive in museum collections throughout the world.[2]

This unusual "Menas token" matches the stamped center section of such flasks in size, medium, and iconography. But its design is different from that of the flasks, and instead conforms to a very common sort of pilgrim souvenir known from other Early Byzantine holy sites, namely the sanctified (i.e., miracle-working) earthen token.[3] One may guess that this Menas clay token was probably molded with water drawn from the famous shrine.

G.V.

Bibliography: Campbell 1985, no. 104.

1. See Kaufmann 1910, *passim*.
2. In addition to Kaufmann (preceding note), see Metzger 1981, pp. 9 ff.
3. On such tokens see Vikan 1982, pp. 11 ff.

142
Niche Decoration From a Monastic Setting with Eagle, 4th–6th century

From Bawit

Limestone, originally polychromed. 50.3 × 77.5 × 32.0

Cincinnati Art Museum, Museum Purchase. 1953.123

At the monastery of Apa Apollo at Bawit, this relief would have been inserted into the crown of a niche in the wall in one of the monastery's several churches.[1] The main scene has been deliberately damaged, like many other figural reliefs from Bawit. Carved from a rectangular block of stone, the decoration is in three parts: a bird, probably an eagle, with outstretched wings and tail feathers (body and head partially destroyed) sits in a rounded cavity at the bottom; framing the scene is a border composed of interlaced vines; outside of the border, at the sides, are palmette acroteria, and in the spandrels are crosses in circles (partially destroyed).[2]

The eagle was a common motif in Early Christian art. Especially popular in the Christian arts of early Byzantine Egypt, eagles often decorate apses and niches in church buildings. Allegorical references to eagles in the Scriptures are based on their physical characteristics: their swiftness of flight, their ability to soar high into the air (Isaiah 40: 31), their strength and vigor, their tendency to nest in high places, and as symbols of powerful empires (Ezek. 17: 3,7; Dan. 7: 4). In Christian texts contemporary with this niche, the eagle is also interpreted as a symbol of Christ.[3]

T.K.T.

Bibliography: Detroit Institute of Arts 1954, p. 179.

1. See Grossmann's essay on the multiplication of niches in Egyptian church architecture during the early Byzantine period. Refer also to this phenomenon in 6th century Constantinople at the church of St. Polyeuktos where polychromed marble niches were decorated with peacocks and framed with vine-scroll borders.

2. Compare this relief, for example, to a niche head with the same format in the Louvre (inv. no. x 5101) which is in better physical condition since its decoration is nonfigural: the main scene is a shell. It bears traces of red polychromy. In addition to formal and stylistic similarities, the Louvre niche is also an interesting iconographic parallel in that the eagle and shell are often counterparts in early Byzantine apse decoration. Sometimes the two images are conflated, so that the head of the eagle becomes the hinge of the shell.

3. See, for example, Ephrem the Syrian in Beck 1957, p. 53, line 15.4.

143
Fragment of an Engaged Column: Geometric and Vegetal Motifs,
5th–6th century

From Bawit

Limestone, traces of plaster ground, paint. 87 × 27 × 40

Metropolitan Museum of Art, Rogers Fund. 10.175.77

This fragment was once part of a matched pair of columns flanking a doorway to one of the buildings in the monastery of Apa Apollo at Bawit.[1] Technical points of the column decoration are especially interesting. Traces of the original polychromy, for example, reveal how color would have heightened the decorative effect of the carved motifs. Curving around the lower portion are rows of lobes radiating diagonally from a central band at the bottom. Around the middle is a thin band decorated with a rounded and convex bead and chevron pattern. The upper portion contains acanthus leaves in triangular patterns above which are rows of chevrons. On the side is an interlaced vine in a rectangular frame.

The same type of decoration was also found on an engaged column in a doorway at the Coptic monastery of Apa Jeremias at Sakkara. In fact, the present piece was once attributed to Sakkara, but similarly decorated columns from Sakkara are busier and even more ornate. Clearly, this decoration from Bawit is not an isolated instance of untrained artistic inspiration, but rather one example of a specific type of column decoration.[2]

T.K.T.

1. Excavation reports record a number of these ornate columns. See Chassinat 1911, t. 13 pl. *24, 36, 69. Duthuit 1931, pl. XXXVII and c, pl. XXXVIII and d, and screen in pl. lviii (also frieze with jeweled cross in pl. LV c). Refer also to Grossmann's essay on the Early Byzantine trend toward grandiose decoration of church entrances.

2. See figure 10 in essay and Quibell 1905–8, vol. 3, pls. vi and xiv, 2. At both sites this type of column was paired with the same type of elongated acanthus capital, indicating the consistent use of types and decorative systems in Early Byzantine Egyptian architecture. These columns from Bawit and Sakkara have been dated to the 6th century, but other highly ornamented columns from around the Early Byzantine Empire indicate that this work is an example of an international trend begun in 4th century architectural decoration. See, for example, the columns in the tetrapylon of Theodosius in Constantinople, and those of the baldacchino in St. Peter's in Rome as represented on the ivory casket from Pola (Krautheimer 1965, figs. 73 and 23).

144

Architectural Relief: Fragment of a Cornice, 5th–6th century

From Bawit

Limestone. 38 × 18 × 16

Metropolitan Museum of Art, Rogers Fund. 07.228.39

This cornice fragment from the monastery at Bawit is shaped like a hinge, as if the main section and thin band at top were flaps that could move around a central pivoting pin. It is noteworthy for its style. The three sections are decorated with motifs found elsewhere at Bawit. Their patterning is based on the repetition of the following elements: in the main section, separated by simple frets, are an eight-petaled rosette, a four-leafed square-shaped rosette, a round rosette with jagged-edged petals, and two crossed acanthus branches. Above are a string of two beads to one reel, and at top a row of concentrically outlined squares. When painted, the patterns formed by these motifs would have been highlighted by the repetition of colors. The colors would have made the narrow bands more jewel-like and the vegetal motifs in the main sections more clearly defined.[1]

T.K.T.

1. See the corner block from Bawit (cat. no. 145) for an example of the same carving style, as well as similar motifs and the principle of patterning based on the repetition of these motifs.

145
Architectural Relief,
Corner Block Decorated with
Rosettes in a Meander Pattern,
5th–6th century

From Bawit

Limestone. 38 × 18 × 6

Metropolitan Museum of Art, Rogers
Fund. 07.228.38

This corner block, attributed to one of
the buildings at the monastery of Apa
Apollo at Bawit, offers a telling example
of the Early Byzantine architectural
aesthetic in which the tectonic functions
of walls were obscured by their richly

decorated surfaces. As is evident in this
relief, the same patterns continued around
corners onto the walls of adjacent rooms
in unified decorative schemes.

The carving of this well-preserved
relief presents a repeating pattern based
on geometrical shapes: in octagons are
six-petaled circular rosettes; in elongated
hexagons are six-branched rosettes
stretched and shaped to fit their frames;
and in squares are four-petaled square-
shaped rosettes. The octagons, hexagons,
and squares are outlined and connected
by an angularly interlaced meander pattern based on horizontal, vertical, and
diagonal lines. All elements have been
fused into one harmonious pattern.

The elements of this repeating pattern were part of the repertory of the
decorative scheme at Bawit, and were
combined differently in other reliefs
from the monastery (as seen, for example, in cat. no. 144). The original paint
of these reliefs would have made the
visual effect of the interrelated designs
more resonant and colorfully complex.
T.K.T.

Bibliography: Duthuit 1931, p. 55,
pl. LXI, fig. b.

146
Composite Capital, 5th–6th century

From Sakkara

Limestone. H. 43; abacus 52 × 43

Metropolitan Museum of Art, Rogers Fund. 10.175.29

The fantastic composite form of this capital – using papyrus and acanthus elements – and the minimal attention to detail in its carving indicate that verisimilitude was not the main artistic concern.[1] Instead of the exact reproduction of natural elements, the capital presents an imaginative hybrid. The original polychromy would also not have been realistic in its depiction of detail. Capitals of this type that retain their paint use the unnatural colors of red and orange for both sets of leaves. This same use of vivid, unexpected colors is found on early Byzantine capitals of other types, both in Egypt and throughout the Empire. These architectural elements evoked nature but did not copy it. In fact, the columns supporting these capitals were often decorated with polychromed relief or painting in abstract designs.[2]

T.K.T.

Bibliography: Metropolitan Museum of Art 1919, fig. 65.

1. The form of this capital combines two separate types of capitals: papyrus (a variant on the ancient pharaonic papyrus capital) and acanthus. At the bottom, curling acanthus leaves are boldly rendered in symmetrical arrangements placed at regular intervals. Above, the flaring bell of the capital is covered by flat, shallowly carved papyrus leaves. The abacus or cushion at top is flatly finished without embellishment. The basic shapes of the vegetal ornament are carved without detail.
2. See the essay on sculpture and cat. no. 143. This capital may have been engaged rather than freestanding; one side has been cut back.

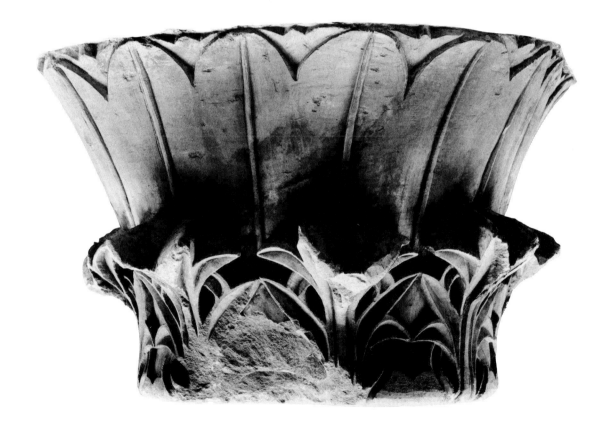

147
Cabinet Doors, 5th–7th century

Wood. Two wings, 44.5 × 34.2 (total)

The Walters Art Gallery, Baltimore.
61.303

Although a significant amount of Late
Antique carved wood has survived in
the dry climate of Egypt, these richly
carved double doors, probably from a
monastery, are among the finest and
most complete of the few extant doors.
Each wing bears three medallions
formed of interlacing bands; those at top
and bottom are rosettes, while those at
the center, now defaced, are eagles.
Floral motifs fill the interspaces, and
there are simple trefoils in the corners. A
thick column with Corinthian capital
covers the seam between the wings; its
shaft bears flutes below, and barklike,
overlapping edges above.

The precision of the carving of these
panels and especially their finely sculpted rosettes recall wooden beams now in
Berlin;[1] their overall decorative richness
evokes in a more general way the limestone choir screen fragment from Bawit
in Cairo.[2] Among surviving wooden
doors, comparison should be made to a
single small wing with an eagle in Cairo,
which is much cruder in execution, and
to the huge multipanel 6th century doors
still in place at the monastery church of
St. Catherine at Mount Sinai.[3] Although
technically less sophisticated than the
Walters cabinet doors, the Sinai doors
are similarly rich and full of detail; there,
too, are frontal eagles and decorated
columns masking the seams between
the panels.
G.V.

Bibliography: Ross ed. 1947, no. 85.

1. Wulff 1909, nos. 254–7.
2. Duthuit 1931, pl. LVIII c.
3. See, respectively, Strzygowski 1904, no.
   8766, and Forsyth and Weitzmann n.d.,
   pls. LVI ff.

Color plate, page 20

Life of Shenoute, 6th or 7th century

Probably from the White Monastery
at Sohag

Papyrus. 2 leaves, 20.4 × 14.2 (each)
Written in Coptic (Sahidic)

The British Museum. 71005

These leaves from a papyrus codex are
part of a set of six leaves and a fragment of a seventh that has only recently
been catalogued by the British Museum,
though it has been in the Museum's
possession for over 150 years. An
interesting story surrounds this manuscript. It was last studied by an English-
man, the Rev. Henry Tattam, author of a
number of works on Coptic subjects
including a grammar (1830) and a lexi-
con (1835). In a letter dated February
1837, Rev. Tattam says that he is returning the manuscript after having copied
and translated what he could. He identifies it as "part of a Life of St. Shenuti in
Sahidic," and concludes his letter with
the remark, "The Manuscript does not
appear to be of value except for its age."[1]
On this last point he was fortunately
mistaken.

Shenoute of Atripe (ca. 348–466)
is a monumental figure in the history of
the Coptic Church, though (unlike
Pachomius, Antony, and others) he
plays virtually no role at all in Christian
tradition outside of Egypt. He entered
his uncle Pjol's monastery in ca. 370,
and became its abbot in ca. 385. Under
his leadership the White Monastery
became a powerful institution in Upper
Egypt and attracted hundreds of monks.
The only complete Coptic *Life of
Shenoute* we have is that of Shenoute's
disciple, Besa, preserved in Bohairic
Coptic.[2] The leaves shown here, however, are from a different version of
the *Life,* a Sahidic version that is only
partially preserved and is very different
from the much younger Bohairic version.

The readable portions of this text
include several miracle-stories that illustrate the spiritual powers of the saint:
1) flour ground by the monks yields
more bread than expected; 2) Shenoute
reveals his clairvoyance by exposing a
person who had disparaged him; 3) a
poor steward unable to pay what he
owes his master in taxes is rescued from
his plight; 4) a rich man dies on the
road, is resuscitated, and then gives

away his property and joins the monastery; and 5) the bread supply is miraculously increased to feed a multitude of
visitors.[3]

B.A.P.

Bibliography: unpublished, but see
Leipoldt 1906; Bell 1983.

1. The German scholar Moritz Schwartze
   transcribed the manuscript in 1848; his
   transcription is included among the papers
   of W. E. Crum in the Griffith Institute,
   Ashmolean Museum, Oxford. (Information on this transcription was supplied by
   Stephen Emmel.)
2. Edition: Leipoldt 1906. English translation: Bell 1983.
3. The first story resembles an event
   recorded in the Bohairic Life, chapter 20;
   the second resembles a story found in
   chapter 74; the third is a version of a story
   found in chapters 27–8 (cf. 141–3); the
   others are absent from the Bohairic version. The pages exhibited here (7 and 10)
   contain the last part of the second story
   and the first part of the third. The numbers
   assigned by the British Museum to the
   glasses that now encase the leaves do not
   correspond to the original order of the
   pages in the manuscript.

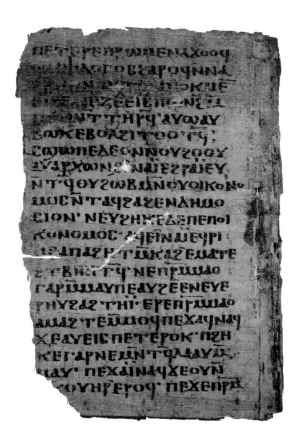
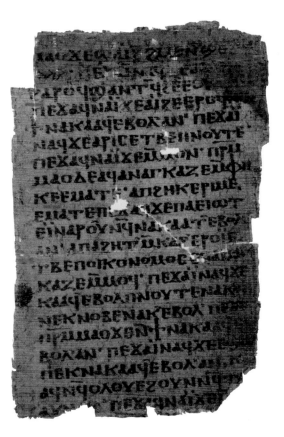

149

Coptic Codex of Biblical and other Texts, 8th or 9th century

Monastery of Apa Jeremias, Saqqara

Vellum. 106 leaves, averaging 9.5 × 8
Written in Coptic (Sahidic)

Department of Rare Books and Special
Collections, The University of Michigan.
N.B. Ms166

This is a small codex, inscribed by three
different scribes, and contains the following texts: Letter of Christ to Abgar, an
apocryphal text in which Christ is
responding to the Letter of King Abgar
to Christ; two epistles of Paul of Tamah
(an obscure monastic leader); Letter of
Abgar to Christ, in which King Abgar
invites Christ to send an apostle to
preach to the Edessenes (this apocriphal
correspondence is part of the founding
legend of the Syrian church); the Old
Testament Book of *Ecclesiastes*, the *Song
of Songs*, and the *Book of Ruth*. The codex
is open here at folio 3 verso – folio 4
recto, (i.e., the back side of the third leaf
to the front side of the fourth), with the
hair sides of each vellum leaf showing.
These pages provide an interesting
insight into monastic life, especially the
scribal activity. The back side of the
third leaf, 3v, contains the explicit of the
text that ends on 3r, the front side of that
leaf. (An explicit, placed at the end of
the text, is a sentence that identifies the
previous material.) In the case of the
letter whose contents were on the previous pages, the explicit reads: "The letter
of our Lord Jesus Christ which he sent
to Abgar, king of Edessa. Amen." The
colophons, scribal notations at the end,
identify the text from which this one
was copied and (in bad Greek) the scribe
who wrote it: "The book of my brother
Phoibammon. Remember him. Amen."

"Lord, preserve your servant, Antonios
Mikkos, calligrapher. Amen. The
(spiritual) son of Abba Apollon and
Abba Jeremias."

4r, the front side of the fourth page,
contains the first page of Paul of Tamah's
first letter, which ends later on 5v, the
back of the fifth leaf. Addressed to an
unnamed monk, it exhorts him to pursue
the monastic virtues of poverty and
solitude. The text has recently been
edited by T. Orlandi.

B.A.P.

Bibliography: Worrel 1942, pp. 25–32;
van Lantschoot 1929, vol. 1, pp. 139–40;
Orlandi 1988, pp. 86–7.

150
Pages of a Psalter, 9th–11th century

Origin unknown

Paper. 27 × 19
Written in Coptic (Sahidic)

The University Museum, University of Pennsylvania. E16261

Provenance: purchased for the University Museum by W. Max Müller from a Professor Moritz in Cairo in 1910.

These pages, numbers 66 and 67 in the psalter, contain verses 27 through 34 of Psalm 18. Verse 29 of this manuscript is notable for its divergence from other texts. It reads, "Lord, my God, enlighten my darkness." The King James Version following the Hebrew of the Masoretic text has "The Lord, my God, will enlighten my darkness," and another Sahidic Coptic psalter in the British Museum has "You enlighten." These variations illustrate the problems which occur in the translation and transmission of texts.

It is not known exactly where in Egypt this particular psalter was used, because it was purchased from a dealer rather than excavated. However, portions of other psalters have been excavated from desert monasteries. If it is indeed from a monastery, there are three possible uses for a psalter. First, the 4th century monastic rule of Pachomius specifies the use of the Psalms in the weekly gatherings of the monks as part of the liturgy. Second, the Pachomian monastery included a library, and the rule allows monks to borrow codices for one week for personal use. Finally, private ownership can not be ruled out, as one of the *Sayings of the Fathers* specifically encourages "the ownership of Christian books." Thus, even assuming the psalter is from a monastery, it is not clear if it was for liturgical, communal or private use.

The psalter was discovered in damaged condition. Water had caused both the disintegration of parts of the pages and the fusing of some pages together. Part of the binding materials was preserved, which consist of leather and linen. The fused pages were separated by submerging them in water and then peeling the layers from one another. The next step was to reconstruct the pages and the order of the original codex. Once reconstructed, the preserved portion was found to consist of 12 signatures of 12 folios each, extending from Psalm 1 to the beginning of Psalm 49. B.P.M.[1]

1. I have received considerable assistance on this entry from J. Noel Hubler.

151
Ostrakon with Psalm Verses,
7th or 8th century

From the Thebaid

Pottery. 13.2 × 10
Written in Coptic (Sahidic)

The British Museum. 14030

This pottery ostrakon is inscribed with verses from Old Testament Psalms, mostly psalms featuring Zion, city of David. An ostrakon of this sort was a mnemonic device that would have been used by a monk as an aid to his meditations: the first line of the psalm would trigger his memory of the entire psalm. A translation of the first five lines is provided below, with identification of the psalm verses quoted. Citations are from the Greek Septuagint (the basis of the Coptic Bible), with the equivalent Hebrew and English psalms in parentheses:

"And give salvation with your right hand, and . . . ," Ps. 59(60):5.

"The glory of the daughter of the king of Aise," Ps. 44(45):13.

"Very blessed is he in the city of (our God)," Ps. 47(48):1.

"Zion heard and rejoiced," Ps. 96(97):8.

"Zion which is exalted, which is the city of the Great King," Ps. 47(48):2.
B.A.P.

Bibliography: Hall 1905.

152

Biblical Text: Proverbs,
4th or 5th century

Parchment. 8.5 × 16.8
Written in Coptic (Sahidic)

The Beinecke Rare Book and Manuscript
Library, Yale University. P. CtYBR
inv. 2118

This sheet from a parchment codex is
also the center of a quire, flesh side up
(pp. **PNΓ-PNA**, 153–4 of the manuscript),
and bears part of the Old Testament Book
of Proverbs. It is not part of any of the 22
other Sahidic manuscripts in which the Old
Testament Book of Proverbs is preserved,
however. The sheet contains Proverbs
20:28–21.4 and 21.6–16. The text (on
p. 153) begins at Proverbs 21:2: "It is God
who knows the hearts...." Presumably,
the codex contained one or more texts
beside Proverbs, and was probably part
of a monastic library.
B.A.P.

Bibliography: Emmel 1989.

front

back

153

Bookbinding, 7th or 8th century

From Hamouli in the Fayum

Goatskin over papyrus boards.
38.5 × 29.5

The Pierpont Morgan Library. M569

This pair of covers constitutes what is reputed to be the finest Coptic bookbinding in existence. On each cover is a background panel of gilded leather, over which was applied a cut-out pattern made from red-dyed leather. The intricate ornamentation on these covers, though differing in detail, has as its main feature a Coptic cross within a rosette. Sewn to the inside of the upper cover is an *ex libris*: ⲠⲀⲢⲬⲀⲄⲄⲈⲖⲞⲤ ⲘⲒⲬⲀ, "The Archangel Michael." The *ex libris* indicates that the book was owned by the Monastery of the Archangel Michael. However, the manuscript associated with the binding, a parchment codex of the four gospels dated to the 8th century, is inscribed with a colophon indicating ownership by the Church of the Holy Mother of God at Perkethoout, not far from the Monastery of the Archangel Michael. This binding seems thus to have been used originally for a different codex and later reused for the gospels with which it is now associated.
B.A.P.

Bibliography: Needham 1979, pp. 13–6.

154
Bookbinding, 4th century

From Jabal al-Tarīf (near Nag Hammadi)

Leather (sheepskin). 33.9 × 42.7
(opened)

The Institute for Antiquity and
Christianity, Claremont Graduate School

This rather humble leather binding is
important largely because it originally
held the 70 inscribed leaves (140 pages)
of Nag Hammadi Codex I. This codex
was one of thirteen discovered in 1945
beneath the cliff of the Jabal al-Tarīf in
Upper Egypt, near the city of Nag Hammadi. Codex I has also been referred to
as the "Jung Codex." A large part of the
manuscript, smuggled out of Egypt in
1949, was acquired in Belgium for the
Jung Institute in 1952 and presented to
C. G. Jung as a birthday present. The
binding, however, had been separated
from its contents, and was eventually
acquired by the Institute for Antiquity
and Christianity in 1973, with the permission of the Egyptian authorities. The
binding also originally contained cartonnage, scraps of discarded papyrus glued
to the inside (flesh side) as a stiffener.
The cartonnage has been removed, and
the Greek and Coptic papyri that comprised it, dating from the 3rd and early
4th centuries, have been published. The
bindings of the Nag Hammadi Codices
are among the oldest leather bookbindings in existence.
B.A.P.

Bibliography: Robinson et al. 1977,
pp. vii–xix, plates 1–2; Robinson 1984,
pp. 71–86.

155

Letter, 6th to 7th century

From Middle Egypt (?)

Papyrus. 9 × 20
Written in Coptic (Sahidic)

The Beinecke Rare Book and Manuscript
Library, Yale University. P.CtYBR inv.
1853

Provenance: Bought from a dealer
(Nahman), Cairo, 1964

One priest (unnamed) is writing to
another, Phoibammon, described as
"his beloved brother who serves God
and is good." He asks his fellow to give
him some bread "from the deacon,"
two measures of oil, and two measures
of wine. Such a short, practical message
(continued on the back) illustrates the
provisioning of village clerics, both for
their own sustenance and, presumably,
for the celebration of the liturgy.
L.S.B.M.

Bibliography: MacCoull 1986a, no. 17,
p. 46.

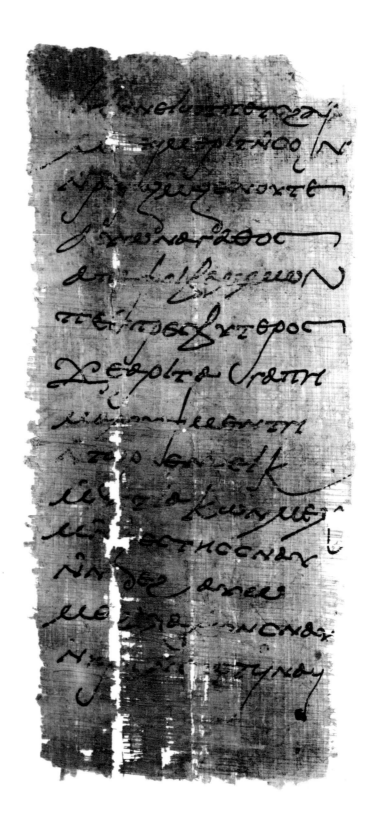

156

Apocryphal Narrative of the
Dormition of the Virgin, 7th century

Place of origin unknown

Papyrus. 30 × 23
Written in Coptic (Sahidic)

The Beinecke Rare Book and Manuscript
Library, Yale University. P.Ctybr inv.
1788

Provenance: Bought from a dealer
(Nahman), Cairo, 1964

This bifolium[1] from a papyrus codex
preserves part of a Coptic story of the
Dormition (the "falling asleep," i.e.,
death) of the Virgin, in which the Virgin
expresses sadness at her approaching
death and then praises her Son, Jesus.
Christ comes to take her to heaven with
words of comfort, saying "My mother's
going forth from the body . . . is also a
birth." The Virgin is surrounded by
angels and apostles. These elements are
shared with later Coptic Dormition
narratives, but in this text they are not
interwoven with motifs from ancient
Egyptian mythology such as the underworld, called Amenti.[2] The hand is
elegant, that of an accomplished literary scribe.

L.S.B.M.

Bibliography: MacCoull forthcoming a;
Emmel, unpublished typescript, New
Haven.

1. A bifolium is two leaves formed by the
   folding of a single sheet.
2. Robinson 1896, p. 58.

157

Letter, 6th to 7th century

From Middle Egypt (?)

Papyrus. 17.5 × 13
Written in Coptic (Sahidic)

The Beinecke Rare Book and Manuscript
Library, Yale University. P.CtYBR inv.
1856

Provenance: Bought from a dealer
(Nahman), Cairo, 1964

The writer, identified as Philemon,
writes to a monk and scribe named
David, addressing him as "your beloved
brotherhood." He says that he has made
arrangements for the Nile inundation
and for providing barley as camel fodder.
He then asks how much wheat is in the
storehouse, and closes with the usual
Coptic phrase "Farewell in the Lord,"
preceded by a cross. An abundance of
such monastic letters are preserved in
Coptic, attesting to the monks' activities
in agriculture and livestock raising.
L.S.B.M.

Bibliography: MacCoull 1986a, no. 20,
p. 48.

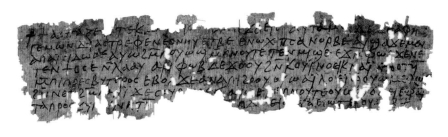

158

Letter, 6th–7th century

From Middle Egypt (?)

Papyrus 31.3 × 7.6
Written in Coptic (Sahidic)

The Pierpont Morgan Library,
New York. Inv. M622 B18

Provenance: Bought from a dealer
(Nahman), Cairo, 1920

The writer of this letter, an unnamed
monk, informs his correspondent
that he has heard that the *hegemon*
(superior) has been making trouble for
the brothers on account of one Enoch
the wafer-seller. The writer has, however, spoken to Apa (Father) Isidore and
settled the dispute. He also asks for
bread, since it is up to him to provide
food in his house (presumably he is
the sub-superior of a dormitory in the
Pachomian system). A private document
like this allows us to see into the day-
to-day workings of a Coptic monastic
community, with its concerns for the
provisioning of foodstuffs and for peace-
ful relationships among its members.
Monastic bakeries were of course of basic
importance to community support:
Enoch may have been an outside trader
trying to impress the superior with his
competing goods, and a compromise had
to be reached to let the monks' kitchen
keep on functioning.
L.S.B.M.

Bibliography: MacCoull 1982b, pp. 8–9.

front

back

159

Letter, 6th to 7th century

From Middle Egypt (?)

Papyrus. 29 × 15
Written in Coptic (Sahidic)

Department of Rare Books and Special
Collections, The University of Michigan.
6858

Provenance: Bought from a dealer
(Nahman), Cairo, 1936

The writer, Anouti, greets Apa Macarius,
Apa Apollo, and Brother Joseph, thank-
ing them for their prayers and asking
them to remember him. He says that he
has acted according to their advice in
a previous letter, and helped to bring
about a settlement in a legal matter
concerning the revenue of a vineyard
and shares of a house. This illustrates
the role of Coptic monks as advisors
and arbitrators in people's everyday
affairs. The writer concludes by asking

to be sent "a little water of the feet of
the holy men," that is, as a kind of relic,
some of the water in which the monks
had washed their feet. The water was
thought of as having and conferring a
blessing thanks to its contact with the
living bodies of the holy men. Such a
detail tells much about the reverence in
which saints, living and dead, were held
in the minds of the people.

L.S.B.M.

Bibliography: Worrell 1942, no. III 8,
pp. 188–90.

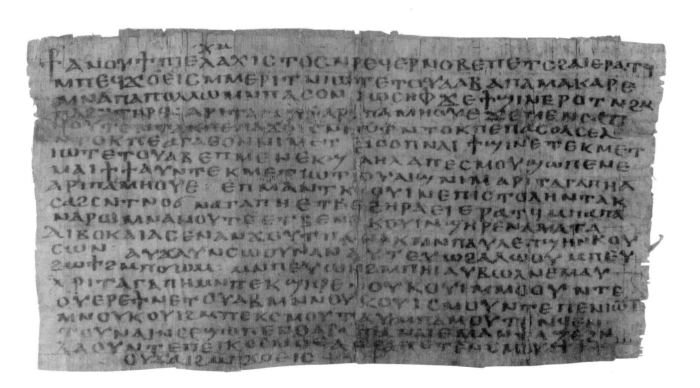

160

Canopic Jar Fragment with the Drawing of an Angel,
Jar, Ptolemaic Period, 3rd century B.C.; drawing, ca. 6th century A.D.

From Deir el Bahri

Alabaster. 17.1 × 11.4

The British Museum. 41416

Provenance: Egypt Exploration Fund

Ancient Egyptian funerary ritual required that the internal organs (liver, lungs, stomach, and intestines) be removed from the corpse, embalmed, and often deposited in containers known today as canopic jars. This alabaster fragment is clearly part of such a jar, identified by the remaining columns of incised prayers/spells standard for the containers. It was originally part of someone's tomb equipment, which was apparently dismantled. What is remarkable is that this jar fragment was probably lying about in the cliffs of Deir el Bahri like so many pottery sherds today, and was picked up and reused by a Coptic monk. He must have been a member of the monastery of St. Phoibammon located among the ruins of Hatshepsut's 18th Dynasty temple (early 15th century B.C.).[1] Using it as a sketch pad, just as his Egyptian predecessors had used limestone and pottery flakes, the artist-monk drew an angel. In stark contrast to Egyptian figure drawing, the winged angel has a typically Hellenistic stance with the weight shifted onto one leg, and is draped in a toga-style garment.
F.D.F.

Bibliography: Naville 1913, p. 21 and pl. XXXIV, no. 9.

1. On the monastery of St. Phoibammon, see Godlewski 1986. I thank Donald Spanel for supplying me with a copy of this publication.

Death

161
Mummy Mask of a Woman,
1st century

From Egypt

Polychromed plaster (stucco).
23.5 × 18.5 × 11.9

Museum of Art, Rhode Island School of
Design, Gift of Mrs. Gustav Radeke.
17.056

The ancient Egyptian practice of mummification and the use of associated funerary equipment were adopted by some Greeks and Romans living in Egypt and were only discontinued in the 4th to 6th centuries A.D. under the influence of Christianity. Unlike Egyptian religion, which required preservation of the body, Christianity focused on the immortality of the soul, and mummification thus became irrelevant. This plaster mummy mask, an expensive item in its day, was probably purchased for or by a well-to-do lady of the Greek-Egyptian middle class. It would have been placed over the face of her bandaged mummy; some examples bear holes through which a cord secured the mask to the head.

This type of mask derived from earlier Egyptian funerary masks that fit like a hood over the entire head and down to the chest (see cat. no. 162), a type still in use in the 1st century and later. The masks reflect the ancient Egyptian notion that the essence of the personality and intelligence lay in the head, most notably in the face. This plaster example, with its large eyes, small mouth, full face, and curly black hair, has idealizing features and is not to be considered a portrait; the masks were mass-produced, though a few specific features could be added after purchase.

F.D.F.

Bibliography: Ridgway 1972, no. 5,
p. 23; Winkes 1973, p. 9.

162
Roman- (Greek-) Egyptian Mummy Mask, end of 2nd century

Probably from Tuna el Gebel

Plaster with inserted glass eyes.
37.2 × 25.2 × 30.1

Museum of Art, Rhode Island School of Design, Museum Appropriation. 40.155

Like the terracotta mask of a woman (cat. no. 161), this mask, which extended over head and chest, was placed on the reclining mummy. Some masks of this type include a further extension down to the chest, over which the hands of the deceased are depicted in relief. Since notions of sleep and death naturally coalesce, it is understandable that the sloping base takes the form of a sort of pillow on which the elevated head rested. A portion of a mantle appears to cover the shoulders.[1]

The Roman features of the face – curly beard and hair – contrast with stock[2] Egyptian features. A panel at the back of the bust depicts the mummy of the deceased flanked by Isis and Nephthys, the two sisters of Osiris who are traditionally shown kneeling and weeping beside their brother's corpse; since every deceased is identified with Osiris, the two goddesses grieve for him as well. One cannot tell, of course, whether the owner of this mask actually believed in the ancient gods or was simply purchasing standard funerary equipment made for the local trade.
F.D.F.

Bibliography: Ridgway 1972, no. 6.

1. Ridgway 1972, p. 24, citing Parlasca 1966, pl. c.
2. For a slightly different opinion, see Ridgway 1972, p. 24; cf. Staatliche Kunstsammlungen Dresden, no. 48, inv. Aeg. 790 for an interesting parallel showing a clearly aged face.

163
Mummy Shroud,
late 1st–early 2nd century

Probably from Thebes[1]

Painted linen. 225 × 71.5

Museum of Fine Arts, Boston, Gift of C. Granville Way. 72.4723

In the Roman period, shrouds continued to be used to wrap bandaged mummies or their cartonnage (plastered layers of linen or papyrus) coverings,[2] as in pharaonic times. But the linen shrouds that wrapped pharaonic mummies were rarely decorated. This shroud, in contrast, depicts a full-length image of a deceased woman whose mummified corpse would have lain beneath it. The figure is painted directly on the textile, as opposed to being woven into the fabric, the standard technique found in later textiles and illustrated throughout this exhibition.

The woman is shown in Egyptian style, with long, full, curly hair tied with a fillet, a wide Egyptian collar, snake bracelets (some actual examples of these survive), and a decorated sheath dress with sleeves. Flanking her sandaled feet are seated jackals, representing the god of embalming and guide of the dead, Anubis (see also cat. no. 168 and 170). Jackals appear in this position after the Trajanic period and are thus a means of dating the shroud.[3] A close parallel to this shroud figure, even bearing the vine scrolls on the shoulder straps,[4] appears on the inside of a Louvre coffin lid[5] and testifies to the borrowing of coffin decoration for shrouds in this period. The two may actually be from the same workshop. The Louvre example shows the hieroglyphic sign for the sky goddess Nut (identified as an embodiment of the coffin since the 5th Dynasty), and it is possible that the same sign that would have appeared in the missing area on the shroud above this woman's head. However, the deceased on the shroud is probably being equated with the mother goddess Hathor, as indicated by the vine motif, which refers to a tree association with this deity.[6]
F.D.F.

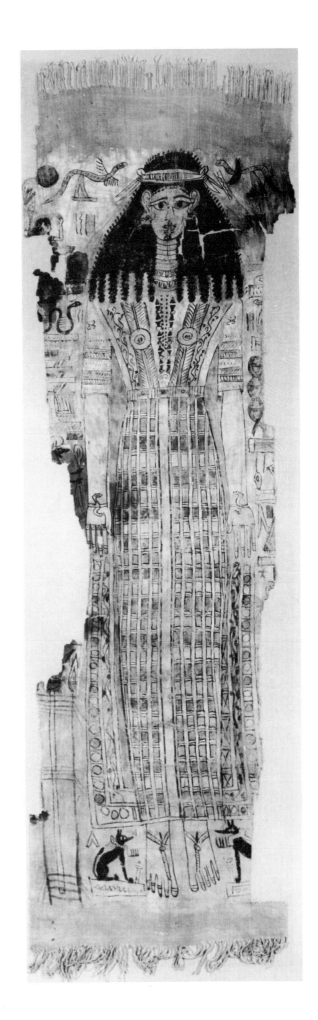

1. On the basis of Grimm 1974, p. 118 with coffin parallels (pl. 138, no. 3, pl. 139, no. 1) the shroud can be assigned to a Theban provenance.
2. Morenz 1963, p. 58 notes that early Christian monks were sometimes mummified and even included tomb offerings and texts in some of their burials.
3. Grimm 1974, pp. 117–8. I thank Lorelai Corcoran for this reference and for discussing the shroud with me.
4. For mention of the design on the straps, see Smith 1960, p. 189.
5. Cf. Louvre inv. E13048 Schmidt 1919, no. 1329, p. 231.
6. There may be some syncretism present here, however, between Nut and Hathor, as Ms. Corcoran noted in conversation.

164
Mummy Portrait:
Head of a Young Man,
first third of the 2nd century

From El Rubiyat in the Fayum
Encaustic on wood. 29 × 18.4

The University Museum, University of
Pennsylvania. E16213

Provenance: Theodore Graf Collection

In some homes of wealthy Greek- and
Roman-Egyptians, the outfitted mummy
of a family member was sometimes kept
on view for a time before burial. But
instead of using a mask with stock features to cover the mummy's face, some
used a wooden panel with a painted
likeness of the decased. These so-called
mummy portraits, used from the 1st to
4th centuries in the Fayum and El Sheikh
Ibada, among other sites, were most
often painted in encaustic (hot beeswax).

Unlike the idealizing masks also in
use at this time (cf. cat. nos. 161 and
162), the more expensive panels appear
to be dramatically realistic, for example,
in their use of light and shade and the
slight turn of the sitter's head evidenced
in this example. The paintings were
apparently done from live models, and,
according to many scholars, were hung
in the home until death when they were
inserted into the bandages around the
mummy's face. Indeed, the buyer could
choose which stage of life he wanted
captured for eternity. Some of these
so-called portraits (they are probably
idealizing likenesses) have been redrawn
to give the sitter a more youthful appearance. The ancient Egyptian desire to be
youthfully immortalized was not lost on
the Greek and Roman settlers.

The curly hair, small beard and mous-
tache suggest a date in the reign of the
Emperor Hadrian (117–138), though it
should be noted that the fashions in
Egypt often lagged considerably behind
those in Rome.
F.D.F.

Bibliography: Graff n.d., no. 68, p. 30.

Color plate, page 12

165
Funerary Stela: Portrait of the Deceased in Prayer, 2nd–3rd century

Possibly from Terenouthis
Limestone. 20 × 22

Field Museum of Natural History. 31284

The carving of this pagan stela is in good condition, although all traces of polychromy have disappeared. Abrasion at the bottom of the stela, however, has erased much of the inscription, so that it is possible to determine only that the name was based on the stem Apollo-.

The deceased is dressed in a himation over a chiton, and has long hair parted in the middle and tucked behind the ears, falling in neat curly locks on either side. Since men and women at this time wore the same types of clothing, the long hair is the only indication that this figure represents a woman. Her upraised arms indicate that she is praying. With her weight on the left leg, her right leg slightly bent at the knee, and her right foot turned out as if stepping forward, she appears to be about to emerge from the entrance to a temple. Papyrus capitals support its triangular pediment. Because there are no overtly Greek or Egyptian religious motifs, it is impossible to determine to which divinities she addresses her prayers.[1]

T.K.T.

Bibliography: unpublished

1. For examples of Egyptian motifs on this type of stela, cat. nos. 166 and 168.

166

Funerary Stela:
Family Portrait, 2nd–3rd century

Said to be from Akhmim

Limestone, plaster ground, paint.
35 × 42

The Walters Art Gallery, Baltimore. 26.3

The Greek inscription commemorates five deaths from a family: "Didymis, 40 years old, Theodora, her daughter, 19, Athas, a baby of one year, Dionysarin, 45, Athur 10. First year of the indiction. Farewell." Only four figures are shown, however: two women holding *phialai* (libation bowls) and reclining on a funeral bed, another woman (or girl) standing in an attitude of prayer with her arms upraised, and

an infant sitting in a chair and praying. While the women wear chitons and himations, and their hair falls in rows of curls with short bangs across their foreheads, the infant, dressed in a simple tunic, wears his hair in the sidelock typical of Egyptian representations of children.[1]

The carving and polychromy on this pagan stela are well-preserved. Some abrasion of the edges and bottom obscure the shallowly incised representations of food offerings, jackals, and the inscription. The polychromy, which relies on blocks of color and precise lines to fill in the carved details, and the carving technique in 'sunk' relief hark back to older Egyptian artistic traditions, as do the jackals representing the ancient Egyptian god and guide of the dead, Anubis. Yet

the clothing, the Greek inscription, and the primarily Greek names indicate that this family was culturally Hellenized, if not Greek. While the use of local materials and the poor quality of the inscription may be taken as indications of a middle-class setting, the use of one stela to commemorate numerous individuals (but lacking one of them) is more likely an indication of a disastrous year in the history of this family.[2]
T.K.T.

Bibliography: The Brooklyn Museum 1941, no. 34.

1. For a brief discussion of the meanings associated with the sidelock, see cat. no. 168.
2. For a discussion of this type of funerary stela, see the essay on Sculpture regarding the stela from Terenouthis.

167
Funerary Stela:
Portrait of the Deceased,
Aurelia Artemis, 3rd–4th century

Said to be from Akhmim

Marble, plaster ground, paint. 41 × 34

The Walters Art Gallery, Baltimore. 26.2

This stela presents a portrait of the deceased reclining on her funeral bed. The composition, drawn from Greek models and in continuous use on Greek stelae since the 5th century B.C., represents figures reclining at ritual funerary banquets. Using this compositional type here testifies to the importance of ancient Greek artistic traditions within the Greek communities of Egypt.[1] There

is also a corresponding emphasis on Hellenism in the style of carving and painting. The Greek inscription reads: "Aurelia Artemis, daughter of Pasion, the sweetest, beyond comparison above all, farewell."

The patron must have been fairly wealthy to afford such a sumptuous grave marker made of marble, a stone which had to be imported.[2] And in fact her appearance stresses her well-to-do background: Aurelia (which is a title) Artemis is every inch the upper middle-class matron dressed in an elaborately embroidered chiton and himation, and coiffed as was fitting for a mature, respectable woman.

T.K.T.

1. For a broad discussion of the origins of this type of funerary composition, see Thonges-Stringaris 1965, pp. 1–99. Ancient Egyptian funerary reliefs, in contrast, show seated rather than reclining banqueting figures.
2. This type of stela probably would have marked a tomb similar to the type found at Terenouthis. See McCleary 1987, pp. 1–8 and illustration in this catalogue essay.

168
Funerary Stela: Portrait of the Deceased, C. Julius Valerius, 3rd century

From Egypt

Limestone, traces of plaster ground, paint.
35 × 28

The Brooklyn Museum, Gift of the Estate of Charles Edwin Wilbour. 16.105

This pagan stela, like those from Terenouthis, was originally placed at the front of a small tomb.[1] Jagged edges are traces of its removal. The rare Latin inscription, largely illegible due to abrasion, identifies the figure as C. Julius Valerius. The well-preserved carving would originally have been completely polychromed.

The composition is framed by an architectural setting of columns topped by papyrus capitals supporting a rounded pediment. On column brackets are images of the Egyptian gods Anubis and Horus in their animal forms as jackal and hawk. The goddess Nemesis is shown at the lower right in the form of a griffin with one paw on a wheel. The central figure, the deceased Valerius, is shown with a child's physique – large head, chubby limbs and bulging belly – wearing a boy's short tunic with a belt; around his neck is a *bulla* (the round pendant worn by free-born Roman boys until they reached maturity), and his hair is caught up in a sidelock. With his right hand Valerius holds a *patera* (offering bowl) over offerings of food placed on a small altar, and in his left hand he carries a *situla* (ritual container).

The images of the gods and the boy making a sacrifice are appropriate to this particular funerary setting and testify to a Roman following of Egyptian religious cults. Nemesis was the protectress of the dead who oversaw human fate, as symbolized by the wheel under her paw. Anubis guided the dead on their journey in the afterlife. Horus was the life-giving solar god in whose ship they traveled through the afterlife. Harpokrates, the god Horus as a child symbolizing the rising sun, was traditionally shown as a chubby infant with his hair bound in a sidelock. The *situla* (which would have contained Nile water) and the offerings of food represent young Valerius's needs in the afterlife.[2]

T.K.T.

Bibliography: Herbert 1972, pp. 45–7.

1. See the illustration and discussion of this type of stela in the catalogue essay on sculpture.
2. The inscription, iconography, and polychromy of this relief are thoroughly discussed in Herbert 1972, pp. 45–7.

Color plate, page 14

169
Nemesis, late 1st–2nd century

Limestone. 20.3 × 10.2

Jack A. Josephson Collection

This sculpture in the round depicts a Roman-Egyptian deity in the form of a griffin. A fabled composite beast in antiquity,[1] the griffin was represented with the head and wings of a bird and the body of a lion. In Roman times the male griffin was associated with Nemesis, a goddess of retribution, whose origins lay in Egyptian religion (despite the Greek name), and who, like ancient pharaohs and other gods, could intervene in human affairs.[2] Through Greek influence Nemesis, as a griffin, was feminized through the addition of teats and breasts as shown here,[3] and she was also correlated with Isis, mistress of fate.[4] What is remarkable in this figure is that male genitalia are also represented, thereby combining original male and later female characteristics. The figure was originally on a plinth, a portion of which remains beneath the beast's hindquarters. Its right paw once lay on a wheel, the wheel of fortune, and the left paw rested on the plinth.[5] Like the Egyptian god Anubis, Nemesis was also a funerary god and guide of the dead, and appears on Roman Egyptian funerary stelae in company with the deceased (cat. no. 168).[6]

The carving of this Nemesis ranks among the finest Late Roman sculpture in Egypt. The careful detailing of the mane and wings and the modeling of the taut muscular haunches are particularly beautiful. Also noteworthy is the treatment of the feathers. Instead of the more flamboyant swirls of some examples, these are distinguished by their restrained Egyptian style. The low relief detailing of the bands of pointed feathers is reminiscent of the crisply carved and painted feathering of pharaonic winged sun disks. Examples of the latter, which often decorated the lintels of Egyptian temple gates, were still visible in Late Roman times.

F.D.F.

1. Earliest examples derive from 4th millennium Mesopotamia, from which country the motif was imported by Egypt, where it appears on late predynastic slate palettes.
2. Quaegebeur 1983.
3. Flagge 1975, p. 117.
4. Quaegebeur 1983, p. 48.
5. For a similar but larger example, see the 2nd–3rd century Nemesis (H. 50 cm.) in the Israel Department of Antiquities and Museums, discussed in Leibovitch 1958, pp. 141–8, pls. 25–9. Cf. also The Brooklyn Museum 1956, no. 47. See also Lichochka forthcoming. Flagge 1975, p. 118 notes that the griffin as winged sphinx with its paw on the wheel first appears on coins under the Emperor Domitian (81–96).
6. Flagge 1975, p. 120.

Color plate, page 15

170
Funerary Stela:
Portrait of the Deceased,
3rd–4th century

From Oxyrhynchus

Limestone, plaster ground, paint.
98.5 × 42 × 19.6

Royal Ontario Museum. 972.379

This pagan funerary stela portrays the deceased woman in dark red chiton and mantle standing in an aedicula (niche) on the lintel of which is a row of uraei (cobra heads). One hand is wrapped in the mantle, and the other holds a hand-garland of flowers. Painted jackals flank her head.[1]

While both the manner of representation and the costume of this figure are Greek, other iconographic details are Egyptian. The hand-garland, for example, was traditionally carried by devotees of the goddess Isis in their funeral portraits; the uraei were identified with the eye of the sun god Re; the jackals represent the divine guide of the dead, Anubis. The woman therefore is to be understood as looking out from a gate (the aedicula) to the afterlife under the protection of the Egyptian gods of the dead.

Other examples of this type of stela attributed to Oxyrhynchus represent women with different dress and attributes, as well as men and children. The varied iconography of these figures apparently reflects the different gods to whom they appeal and differences in the status of the deceased.[2]

T.K.T.

Bibliography: Parlasca 1978, pl. 38.

1. The face, hands and feet, and uraei may have been recarved. For a discussion of the widespread recarving of this type of funerary stela, see Vikan and Boyd 1981.
2. Two recent publications discuss different examples of this type of funeral portrait. Parlasca 1978, pp. 115–120, groups a wide range of examples in North America, Europe, Egypt, and Australia. Schneider 1982 discusses the large collection of these stelae in the Rijksmuseum van Oudheden in Leiden. See also Heyob 1975.

171

*Frieze Fragment from a Tomb:
Nereid on a Sea Monster,*
4th–5th century

From Herakleopolis Magna

Limestone. 28.6 × 60.3

Columbus Museum of Art, Ohio:
Gift in Memory of Dr. Edward B.
Titchener. 42.11

An elaborately coiffed nereid clad in a
cestus (marriage belt)[1] and holding a
veil rides on a sea monster whose tail
grows branches of laurel in a scroll pattern. The billowing veil indicates that
both figures are moving quickly. At the
left, a hound (probably a hyena) runs
away over background vegetation. All
three figures – hound, sea monster, and
nereid – are extraordinarily small in
comparison to the laurel branches in
the background.[1]

This scene represents the pagan Greek
themes of metamorphosis in death and
the fertile paradisical abode of the dead.
The deceased, upon her death, has
become a nereid. The Greek origin of
these motifs and their meanings indicate

that the relief must have decorated the
interior of the tomb of a pagan Greek or
Hellenized Egyptian.[2] Iconographic
details, such as the marriage belt and
rampant growth of vegetation from the
monster's tail, must have been inspired
by the fact that the deceased was a mature
woman of childbearing years, who was
married or engaged to be married.[3]

Although the carving of this tomb
frieze is in excellent condition, preserving a variety of crisply rendered chisel-
ing techniques, the relief no longer retains
its polychromy and broken edges indicate that the composition is incomplete.
T.K.T.

1. The *cestus* was the elaborately ornamented
   marriage belt of Aphrodite that made its
   wearers irresistibly attractive. Aphrodite
   sometimes gave it to women who wished
   to make themselves desirable. The 5th
   century Graeco-Egyptian poet Nonnos of
   Panopolis recounts a number of such
   instances in his epic poem *The Dionysiaca*.
   As an article of clothing in everyday life, it
   functioned as a brassiere. J. Boardman has
   described the development of the iconography of the Greek sea monster (*ketos*) in
   its traditional service of water divinities
   and proposes Egyptian influences on
   some of its earliest representations; see
   Boardman 1987, pp. 73–84. Refer to cat.
   no. 173 for a discussion of the motif of
   small animals in a large vine-scroll.

2. An extraordinarily touching Graeco-
   Egyptian interpretation of this subject is
   found in the 2nd century tomb of Isidora
   in the cemetery of the Greek city of
   Hermopolis Magna, where inscribed
   poems laud the deceased girl's metamorphosis into a nymph upon her death and
   the abundant paradisical setting of which
   she becomes a part.

3. See Roscher 1894–7, vol. 2, pp. 3121 ff.
   for a discussion of similar subjects in
   Graeco-Roman funerary monuments,
   especially concerning the fertility of soil,
   and women represented as nereids and
   nymphs. Nereids and nymphs, however,
   also had particularly Egyptian associations
   by this time. That some were daughters of
   the Nile (rather than Oceanos or Acheloos,
   as in classical Greek mythology) is mentioned in the poems commemorating
   Isidora (see note 2). See also Hani 1974,
   pp. 212–224.

172

Fragmentary Niche Decoration from the Interior of a Tomb: Portrait of the Deceased,
5th–6th century

From Herakleopolis Magna

Limestone, plaster ground, paint.
42 × 40 × 27

The Malcove Collection, University of Toronto. M82.314

This niche decoration, part of the interior architectural decoration of a monumental tomb, was originally inserted in the tomb wall so that the figure faced down.[1] Thus the figure appeared to the original viewers, those relatives who conducted the appropriate rituals at the tomb, to emerge from the space of the niche and from the mandorla.

The main scene is clearly identifiable as a female figure holding a scroll and emerging from a mandorla composed of two concentric circles. The surviving colors transform the carving style and adds definition to the scene. On the mandorla there is an effective interplay between the carved layers and their painted decoration of a red background overlaid with a gray scroll pattern.[2]

Bejeweled and clothed in a tightly fitted embroidered and pleated garment, and wearing a small decorated cap, the deceased appears in the garb of a noblewoman of the 5th and 6th centuries.[3] Yet the mandorla, an ancient convention indicating an appearance from another reality, informs us that the figure does not belong to this world despite her dress: this is a portrait of the deceased in the afterlife. The scroll she holds also suggests that she is represented as a muse or a philosopher.[4]

T.K.T.

Bibliography: Campbell 1985, no. 133.

1. The piece is largely intact and retains most of its original polychromy. The head was broken off cleanly at the neck but has been reattached. The nose and scroll have been chipped recently. The sides of the niche decoration have been cut away, destroying all but the smallest traces of the vegetal ornament in the bottom corners. Some portions, especially noticeable on the garment, have been recently abraded to impart a smooth surface, and the etched outline of the figure at bottom is also recent.

2. All elements are outlined in black, including decorative motifs, drapery folds and facial features. Gray or brown alternates with yellow or ocher on the bead and reel ornament. The vine rinceau has a yellowish or ocher stem and red veining. Squares of the necklace are painted alternately black, bluish green, and brown. The paint on the face has been abraded, but seems to have been a light brown. There are stray traces of a spurious pink (it fluoresces white under ultraviolet light) on the mouth and necklace.

3. When first published in Campbell 1985, p. 106, this figure was identified as an angel. But she is not clothed as an angel would be in a blousy peplos. For a description and illustration of a variant on this costume see Houston 1947, pp. 132–8 and fig. 144b.

4. Portraits of the deceased with the attributes of the muses are common in pagan and Christian funerary arts of the Late Roman and Early Byzantine periods. See, for example, discussions of earning one's place in the afterlife by one's life on earth and earning the cultural right to use such symbols of status whether pagan or Christian, in Murray 1981. In this example, however, there are no iconographic clues to the religious background of the patron.

173
Fragment of a Frieze: Animals in a Vine Rinceau,
5th–6th century

Limestone, plaster ground, paint.
22 × 20

The Malcove Collection, University of Toronto. M82.313

The frieze consists of a narrow border decorated with an interlaced band, and, in the main section, a running ram, looking back over its shoulder, against a background of relatively enormous scrolled vines. This fragment was part of a repeating pattern and would have shown other animals fleeing and hunting. The motif of animals in vine-scrolls first gained widespread popularity during the Roman period in architectural relief, wall-paintings, mosaics and textiles. During the early Byzantine period the motif was used in both pagan and Christian settings, and was especially common in funerary decorations, where it has been interpreted as representing the lush setting of paradise.[1]

The carving of this frieze fragment is in excellent condition, and the relief retains most of its original polychromy, although the colors of the paint have faded.[2] The carving, in a medium depth of relief, is sharpened by the surviving painting. The contours of all carved shapes are further defined by black lines covering both the front and the side edges. Details, such as the striations on the horns, are also emphasized by black outlines. The hide of the ram, the vines, and the background were all painted in lighter colors.

T.K.T.

Bibliography: Campbell 1985, no. 127.

1. See, for example, Peterson 1974. For an example of this motif in a clearly pagan context, see cat. no. 171.
2. In its first publication, this work was described as unfinished, apparently because the painted details were not visible from a distance, and because painted lines followed the carved shapes. The small size of this relief, however, suggests that it was not meant to be seen from a distance. Moreover, the painting is over the layer of ground known to have been applied after carving was completed, and the carving here never cuts through the polychromy.

174
Funerary Stela: Paradisical Motifs,
6th–7th century

Said to come from Armant

Limestone, traces of plaster ground, paint. 14.5 × 20.5

Metropolitan Museum of Art, Rogers Fund. 36.2.6

The composition of this Christian funerary stela has two parts. Below is an architectural frame defined by two columns, the bases of which stand on representations of fish. Above, resting on the capitals, is a highly decorated apse described by an arching vine scroll and interlace patterns following the semicircular shape of the stela. At the center of the concentric arches is a rosette. The polychromy adds details not found in the carving; there are, for example, red and green sections in the striated columns and, between the columns, small black circles ornament the frame that surrounds an inscription in Coptic: "To the memory of the deceased, Taeiam, who departed from this life on the 18th of Choiak (December) of the 7th indiction. She sleeps in Christ." That the deceased was not dead but simply asleep was widely believed by early Christians and is referred to in many funerary inscriptions. "Taeiam 'sleeps in Christ'" is an avowal that her soul has ascended to the kingdom of heaven. As if in confirmation, the composition represents a vision of the kingdom of heaven in the form of a tabernacle, where the pious Taeiam will sojourn until the second coming of Christ.[1] Her hopes are also expressed in the Coptic liturgy for the dead:

"And these, O Lord, and all those names we have recited... who have fallen asleep and have gone to their rest in the faith of Christ, vouchsafe to grant rest to all their souls in the bosom of the holy fathers... nourish them in a place of pasturage beside the waters of comfort in the paradise of joy, whence sorrow and sighing and weeping have fled away in the light of thy saints...."[2]

T.K.T.

Bibliography: Cramer 1957, pp. 4–5.

1. Many Christian texts of visions of paradise describe this structure. In his *Christian Topography*, the 6th century monk known as Cosmas Indicopleustes wrote that "...the righteous will enter into the upper heaven beyond this visible heaven, where is the kingdom of the heavens – the second Tabernacle called the Holy of Holies..." (Book II, p. 114). Cosmas's text and contemporary visions of paradise also describe rivers in paradise. The fish beneath the columns here may allude to those waters, which were paralleled in the paradisical "waters of comfort" referred to in the liturgical passage quoted in the text.
2. Brightman 1896, pp. 170–1.

175
Funerary Stela: Cross in Wreath,
6th–7th century

From Esna

Limestone. 56 × 40

Museum of Fine Arts, Boston, Sears
Fund. 04.1846

This Christian funerary relief lacks its
original polychromy, but the strong,
self-assured carving is well preserved.
Represented inside a leafy wreath with
berries is a cross with wedge-shaped
arms decorated with beads. The spaces
between the cross arms are filled with
branches. Surrounding this circular composition is an inscription in Coptic:
"There is one god, the helper, Samuel."[1]

Images of the crucifixion are rare in
the Christian arts of Early Byzantine
Egypt, but the cross is ubiquitous as a
sign of Christ's passion and triumph
over death. Glorifying the cross with
jewels and branches in this representation makes it clear that it is used here
as a victorious symbol of Christ's resurrection. The cross was also a reference
to man's salvation through Christ's
suffering that resulted in man's entry
into the kingdom of heaven. If the (for-
mulaic) inscription alludes to the divinity
of Christ and his seemingly contradictory death on the cross, then this composition could express a specifically
Monophysite statement. Monophysites
like the Copts viewed the crucifixion
only as the crucifixion of God and thus
refused to portray the body of the
crucified Christ.[2]

T.K.T.

Bibliography: Cramer 1957, p. 13 and
fig. 23.

1. Cramer 1957, p. 23.
2. Compare this composition to that of cat.
   no. 176, which makes a different statement
   based on overtly paradisical allusions to
   the cross.

176
Funerary Stela: Paradisical Imagery, 6th–7th century

From Esna

Limestone. 58.5 × 42

Museum of Fine Arts, Boston, Sears Fund. 04.1845

Provenance: Formerly in Albert M. Lythgoe Collection

This Christian round-topped stela represents paradise within the vault of heaven as seen from the outside looking in. The composition has three zones. The outermost circumscribes the scene by two columns that carry an arch decorated with an interlace motif, and inside that frame, at the bottom, are two arches resting on two pairs of decorated columns. Inside each small arch is a cross. In the third section, resting on the two lower arches, are two decorated columns supporting a pitched roof with an interlace design on its cornice. Inside the triangular space of the pitched roof is a bird with outstretched wings, probably an eagle, wearing a pendant. Flanking this, below, are two deer, and above are two other birds with wings at their sides. Animals, crosses, and the tripartite architectural setting are common elements on the later funerary stelae of Early Byzantine Egypt and are also described in contemporary accounts of visions of paradise and in funerary inscriptions.[1]

No polychromy remains. Thus, all details depicted in the painting and all patterns created by color have been lost.
T.K.T.

Bibliography: The Brooklyn Museum 1941, no. 39; Museum of Fine Arts, Boston, 1988, no. 168, p. 218.

1. For example, the Coptic text known as "The Revelation of St. Paul" describes Paul's visit to paradise and mentions three concentric walls surrounding the paradise of heaven and three eagles at its door. Moreover, at the entrance to paradise stand the Tree of Knowledge and the Tree of Life, both widely associated with the cross.

177
Stela Fragment,
6th–7th century

Limestone. 63 × 44 × 37

The Royal Ontario Museum,
the Walter Massey Collection.
910.108.151

Provenance: Acquired by Dr. Currelly
in the Fayum

The funerary stelae (gravestones) of
Early Christian Egypt, like those of
pharaonic times, were placed near the
grave and offered a site where the living
and dead could meet.[1] This stela is a
fragment of a larger composition,[2] perhaps originally bearing an inscription
that was to be read by the passer-by on
behalf of the deceased. Though restored
in several places, the piece displays sure,
crisp carving. The main design is a large
cross in the form of the ancient Egyptian *ankh* (crux ansata), the sign for eternal life that had been used as a substitute
for the cross since the 4th century.[3] Its
arms are filled with foliate decoration,
and in its loop is a wreathed cross,[4] symbol of the triumph and glory of Christ
(cf. cat. 178) and of the deceased's
Christian faith. The whole piece would
originally have been painted.
F.D.F.

1. Badawy 1978, p. 210.
2. Possibly of the type found in Badawy
   1945, fig. 1, p. 3, Cf. also Beckwith 1963,
   pl. 30.
3. Cf. also Crum 1902b, no. 8518, pl. 21, and
   no. 8531, pl. 22.
4. This is a Maltese cross, of the same type
   used on either side of the upper edge of
   the piece.

178
Panels with Birds and Crosses,
5th century

Wool and linen. 21.5 × 16 and 22 × 22

The British Museum. 22867 and 22868

These panels from a large linen cover or
hanging show birds, which were common
motifs in Late Antique and Early Christian
art. They were typically used as neutral
decorative fillers but also with more specific
meaning. In Roman and Late Antique art
they often accompany the Seasons and
nature imagery (e.g., cat. nos. 35 and 50),
but for the Early Christians some species
soon became symbols of saints and the
blessed dead.[1] The inclusion of the wreathed
crosses in the panels makes their Christian
content obvious. One of the crosses is an
ankh, an ancient Egyptian sign for life used
from the late 4th century onward by Egyptian Christians as an alternative form of the
cross (see also cat no. 129). The wreathed
cross was a sign of the triumph and glory
of Christ and the Christian faith, and was
used mainly in formal religious or funerary
settings. These panels may therefore have
decorated a textile made for use in a church,
or even more likely in a funerary chapel.[2]

Textiles made of plain cloth were commonly decorated with sets of applied tapestry ornaments, but such sets are only rarely
preserved. The two pieces shown here are
two of a complete set of four panels.[3] The
two birds facing right would have been
matched by two others to the left. The
tapestry weaving of the panels, executed in
variously shaded woolen yarns, is very
fine. The birds and the wreaths are simple
and somewhat stylized, although the use of
modeling gives their shapes a distinct volume and surface texture.

A.G.

1. For the most recent discussion of this and
   other interpretations of birds in Early
   Byzantine art, see Maguire 1987, especially
   pp. 57–66.
2. For a similar panel with an ankh and a parrot
   see Lyons, Musée historique des Tissus, inv.
   24.566/6.
3. British Museum, inv. nos. 22.869 and 22.870.
   Each panel contains a blue-gray bird in a dark
   blue field framed by a red and beige fillet.
   Three birds are dove-like with wing and
   tail-feathers markings; the fourth lacks tail
   feathers but has breast markings.

179
Court Proceedings of a Murder Trial, probably A.D. 542-3

From Aphrodito

Papyrus. 73 × 30; 49 × 30
Written in Greek and Latin

Department of Rare Books and Special Collections, The University of Michigan. 6900–6901

Provenance: Bought from Prof. Thomas Whittemore, 1943

These two papyri record the testimony of witnesses in a hearing on a double case of murder. Maria, the widow of Heraclius, is accusing some village officials of having come to where her husband was jailed and having killed him with swords and burned his body. And the brother of the late Victor, the priest, accuses one Menas of having beaten his brother to death with a club. Both sets of defendants claim innocence and point the finger at a magnate, "the illustrious" Sarapammon, who is supposed to have hired murderers for money. Sarapammon in his turn says it was all a conspiracy by some other people, and that he was elsewhere at the time.

Of interest is the fact that, while the testimony is in Greek, the court clerk's narration ("X said...") is in Latin. Unfortunately the texts break off before it can be discovered who actually committed the murders.

L.S.B.M.

Bibliography: Sijpesteijn 1977, nos. 660 and 661; MacCoull forthcoming b.

6900 (left)

6900 (right)

6901

Textiles: Technique and Style

180

Head of a Woman ca. 300 A.D.

Wool. 17 × 12

Detroit Institute of Arts, Gift of
the Founders Society, Octavia W. Bates
Fund. 35.103

Provenance: Ex-collection Marguerite
Mallon-Nadaud

This haloed head probably represents a
female deity or personification. While
only a fragment of a larger textile, it is
an excellent example of the illusionistic
style of tapestry weaving. The head is
shown in a moderate three-quarter view
with a slight bend towards a bare right
shoulder, of which only a trace is visible.
The oval face is framed by a crown of
dark brown curly hair partly falling to
the shoulder and partly held up by a
gold headband; the features are grace-
fully proportioned and carefully executed. The downcast, sidelong glance of
its large eyes gives it a lively, engaged
expression. The figure must have been
richly adorned with gold jewelry, for
even in this fragment she wears a pendant earring (cf. cat. no.54), collar necklace, and possibly a breast chain, in
addition to the headband.[1]

The small size of the fragment allows
only a tentative identification of the
figure. The hairstyle and the use of the
halo suggest a female deity or a personification. Mythological figures since
Classical Antiquity are shown with
similarly arranged hair kept in place
with a headband or a diadem, while it
was mostly divinities and only occasionally personifications and lesser mythological figures that were portrayed with
a halo. The thorough illusionism and its
complete adaptation to tapestry technique, as well as the specific rendering
of the head, make this textile a masterful
example of late 3rd and 4th century art.
Although it has been suggested that this
may be a 6th or even 7th century work[2]
instead of a Late Antique one,[3] neither
its stylistic nor its technical aspects
support this reassignment.
A.G.

Bibliography: Weibel 1948, pp. 106–7,
fig. 1; Weibel 1952, no. 1, p. 75; Beckwith
1959, pp. 13, 18; Villa Hügel 1963,
no. 262, p. 305; Shepherd 1969, p. 113,
fig. 21; Volbach 1969, pp. 27–28, no. 10;
Zaloscer 1974, p. 164, fig. 79.

1. The tapestry is executed in wool in a wide
   range of tans and browns, with touches of
   yellow, red, and blue. It is traditionally
   identified as tapestry in wool on linen
   warps (Weibel 1952, p. 75), although this
   type of weaving is done most frequently
   on woolen warps. Skillful interweaving of
   tan and brown yarns produces an image
   evoking both the overall volume and the

subtleties of facial modeling and texture.
The play of light and shadow over the face
is consistent with the position of the head.
Although the weaving was done at right
angles to the direction of the design, the
distortions that often result from this
technique were avoided, at least in the
facial features (cf. cat. nos. 42 and 128).

2. Beckwith 1959, p. 13; Shepherd 1969,
   p. 113.
3. Weibel 1952, p. 75; Volbach 1969,
   pp. 27–28.

181
Linen Cloth with Tapestry Ornaments, ca. middle of 4th century

Possibly from Akhmim

Linen and wool. 78.75 × 68

Metropolitan Museum of Art, Funds from Various Donors. 89.18.151

Provenance: Purchase from Theodor Graf

Textiles of this type were used for many purposes, such as clothing, curtains, covers, bed sheets, and eventually shrouds for the dead.[1] From a technical point of view, fragments of plain linen cloths with ornaments in tapestry weave, like this example, are the largest group of surviving textiles. The majority of the ornaments are variously shaped panels and horizontal and vertical bands woven in purple wool and linen. They are decorated internally with foliate and geometric patterns executed with a flying shuttle. Although the origin of the present piece is not known, circumstantial evidence points to Upper Egypt, specifically Akhmim, as its possible provenance. It was acquired from Theodor Graf, who is known to have had many Akhmim textiles.[2] Related fragments in other collections said to have come from this site exhibit many of the same decorative patterns.[3] The similarities between them are such that they must be considered works from the same place.

Comparative material from other media, especially painting, helps with the broad dating of this group of textiles. Similar large roundels are painted on late 3rd-century mummy wrappings from Antinoopolis[4] and can be found in wall paintings of the late 3rd and 4th centuries.[5] The complexity of the interlace in the roundel of this piece and in the tapestry ornaments of the related group suggests a date not earlier than the middle of the 4th century for their manufacture.

A.G.

Bibliography: Kajitani 1981, no. 13, p. 13; Trilling 1982, p. 107, fig. 4.

1. The present example is made of a fine linen cloth decorated with a woven-in tapestry roundel and two horizontal stripes in dark purple wool and linen. The stripes are filled with a simple scroll of heart-shaped leaves; the scroll includes two birds placed on an axis with the large roundel. The roundel (D. 35.5 cm.) has a running wave border and a main field filled with an interlace pattern inside an eight-point-star frame. The intertwining of the interlace is tightly interlocked into medallion-like motifs with centers consisting of four coils. A variation of this pattern is used in the roundel of the loop-pile cover also from the Metropolitan Museum (cat. no. 38). Technical information: tabby cloth: warp and weft: undyed linen (S-spun). Tapestry: warp: undyed linen (S-spun); weft: undyed linen (S-spun) and purple wool (S-spun); tapestry over 2–3 warps, ca. 8 group warps per 1 cm; ca. 30 wefts per 1 cm. Undyed wool (S-spun) used with flying shuttle.

2. Egger 1967, p. 3.

3. E.g., Victoria and Albert Museum, inv. nos. 726.1886, 365.1887; (Kendrick 1920, nos. 12 and 191, pp. 12 and 101, pl. 27); Metropolitan Museum of Art, inv. 89.18.203 (unpublished, also from the Graf collection); Pushkin Museum, inv. 345-A (Šurinova 1969, no. 29).

4. Guimet 1912, nos. 72 and 74; pl. 46 and 45, p. 38; also Renner 1982, cat. 1, pl. 1, pp. 31–6.

5. Deckers 1979, esp. figs. 22 and 23.

182
Textile Fragment, 4th century

Linen and wool. 110 × 58.5

Metropolitan Museum of Art, Gift of
Miss Lily Place. 21.6.22

This fragment, another example of a
Late Antique decorative household
textile, illustrates a number of interesting
technical points. With one selvage and
one edge preserved, as well as its ornamental composition consisting of two
stripes, a roundel and a corner panel, its
size suggests that it is a corner piece of
either a curtain or a bed cover. It is made
of a linen cloth finished with an à-joured
(openwork) and fringed edge. The decoration is in a tapestry weave in dark
purple wool and linen with much of the
patterning done with a flying shuttle.[1]
The two horizontal stripes carry a stylized scroll with fruit and leaf motifs
between scalloped borders. Another
scroll fills the border of the roundel.
More can be seen in the fragmentary
L-shaped panel that was once the largest
decorative element, serving as either
a corner *gammadion* (in the shape of
the Greek letter gamma) or an angular
U-shaped ornament applied across the
width of the textile. At present, the composition consists of two main parts: one
is an L-shaped center framed by a vegetal scroll and filled with three fields of
an elaborate interlacing; the other is a
pointed oval tip covered with a design of
overlapping circles enclosed by a simple
border of connected disks.

All four tapestry elements of this
piece were made separately following
different practices and then applied over
reserved unwoven areas in the linen
cloth instead of being woven-in as
inserts, as is the case with most of the
domestic textiles exhibited (cat. nos. 181
and 38). Otherwise, patterning of these
ornaments contains the same repertory
of motifs as observed on many monochrome tapestry decorations, but especially those circumstantially associated
with the finds from Upper Egypt and
Akhmim, and to some extent with those
from Saqqara in Lower Egypt (cat. nos.
181 and 38). In this respect the similarity
between the L-shaped panel of the Metropolitan Museum piece and the interlace
designs of a wide neckband with *clavi* on
a tunic fragment in Leningrad is important, since the tunic almost certainly
came from Upper Egypt.[2] Representations of tunics decorated with similar
large panels, either as *segmenta*, neck-
bands, or *clavi* in several early- to mid-4th
century monuments such as the Tomb of
Aelia Arisuth in Gargaresh,[3] the tomb of
Trebius Justus in Rome,[4] and a silver
plate with Constantius II from Kerč,[5]
help to date the Leningrad tunic as well
as this and other related textiles to the
middle of the 4th century.

A.G.

1. Technical information: Tabby cloth: linen
(S-spun), ca. 16 warps per 1 cm. ca. 15
wefts per 1 cm. Tapestry appliqués: warp:
undyed linen (S-spun), weft: undyed linen
(S-spun), dark purple wool (S-spun);
tapestry over 2–3 warps, ca. 10 group
warps per 1 cm, ca. 30 wefts per 1 cm.
2. Leningrad, Hermitage, inv. no. 11620
(Mat'e and Ljapunova 1951, cat. 8, p. 92,
pl. 9).
3. Bianchi-Bandinelli 1971, p. 95, fig. 87.
4. Grabar 1968c, p. 222, fig. 244.
5. Leningrad, Hermitage, inv. 1820/79;
Effenberger et al. 1978, cat. 1, pp. 78–81.

183
Fragment of a Tapestry Panel,
second half of the 5th century

Linen and wool. 32.2 × 28.6

Museum of Fine Arts, Boston, Gift of
Marion D. Campbell. 1985.829

This fragment of a square panel is
typical of a group of tapestry-woven
inserts of large, usually loop-pile cloths.
These inserts have related compositions, many of which include mounted
hunters inside wide ornamental borders.
They are woven mainly in the monochrome silhouette style of purple wool
and undyed linen, although other colored
yarns are used for details (see cat. no.
45).[1] The border of the present panel
consists of interlaced medallions with
floral baskets, busts, and game animals.
The inner square has an inscribed roundel
with the hunter on horseback holding a
missile in his left hand. The horse is
shown in profile; the man, dressed in a
tunic and a red cloak, is in a slight three-
quarter view. The design is executed
primarily in purple wool and undyed
linen; red, yellow, and green wool were
used for the baskets, interstitial palmette
leaves of the border and some details of
the figures. The flying shuttle technique
was used for much of the inner articulation of the figures and for the outlines.
The central roundel and all but four
corner border medallions have a hatched
background in purple and white.[2]

The Boston panel can be assigned
to the second half of the 5th century. A
similar combination of a more naturalistic style shown in the accurate and
energetic images of the rider and the
horse with the more stylized forms of the
busts and the floral baskets is often found
in the monuments of this period. Other
5th century stylistic features include
enlarged heads and large eyes. In this
textile version they are executed with
their characteristically prominent whites
(see also cat. nos. 61 and 62). Representation of the hunt through isolated motifs
also agrees with the 5th century date of
the panel. Hunts are shown frequently in
Roman and Early Byzantine art. Sometimes they represent a myth (see cat. no.
47), but from the late 2nd century onward
they often strive for realistic portrayals of
contemporary activity.[3] Earlier depictions of the hunt take place in a landscape
setting, but from the late 4th century
onward they are increasingly rendered as
freer compositions of isolated motifs

placed on neutral backgrounds. In this
form, they appear on floor mosaics of
private homes, on table utensils, jewelry
and in textiles (as decorations of both
clothing and household furnishing, as is
the case with this panel, which must have
come from a blanket or some other kind
of cover).[4] By the 5th century, the hunting
motifs and the floral baskets, besides
being purely decorative in function, also
became associated with prosperity and
well-being in general (see also cat. nos.
61 and 62).

A.G.

1. E.g., Leningrad, Hermitage, inv. 12959
   (Mat'e and Ljapunova 1951, no. 129,
   p. 122, pl. 31.3); Victoria and Albert
   Museum, inv. 745.1886 and 1260.1888
   (both from Akhmim), and 282.1891
   (Kendrick 1920, nos. 68, 70, 71, pp. 67–8,
   pls. 16 and 17); Pushkin Museum, inv.
   5180 (Šurinova 1969, no. 86, pl. 64);
   Museum of Arts and Crafts, Prague,
   inv. 2248 (Kybalova 1967, pl. 51, p. 100).
2. Technical information warp: undyed linen
   (S-spun); weft: undyed linen (S-spun),
   purple, red, green, yellow, ochre and pink
   wool (all S-spun); tapestry over 2–3
   warps, ca. 7 group warps per 1 cm.,
   ca. 16–26 wefts per 1 cm.
3. Aymard 1951; Lavin 1963; Dunbabin
   1978, pp. 46–64.
4. The Metropolitan Museum of Art 1979,
   pp. 83–92. For a different interpretation
   of the Boston panel and its group of
   textiles see Lewis 1973, pp. 27–63.

184
Tapestry Panel from a Blanket: Hare Eating Grapes,
late 5th century

Linen and wool. 11.5 × 11

The Tellalian Collection.

Provenance: Purchased from Charles D. Kelekian, February 7, 1979.

This fragment of a panel displays a hare, enclosed in a loop of grapevine, eating grapes. The panel is framed by a band of simple interlacing with an exterior cresting of heart-shaped leaves. It is woven in tapestry weave on linen warps in linen and dark purple and red wool (the latter color's the hare's tongue).[1] Several loop-pile textiles with similar tapestry ornaments suggest that this panel originally belonged to a larger piece, possibly a blanket, cushion, or curtain (in which case it would have been woven into a plain cloth).[2] Ornamental panels like this were used in homes in sets of two or four; a pair of related panels said to be from Saqqara is in Leningrad.[3] The image of a hare or a rabbit feasting on grapes appears quite frequently as a motif of textile decoration. It could be used as one element in a larger composition or as the main theme, as with this panel. Sometimes the animals are woven in a painterly, illusionistic style of tapestry weaving;[4] others, like this panel, are done in the silhouette monochrome style, with or without additional color touches.[5] This very popular image became one of the favorite motifs of Islamic art. The present panel should be assigned a late 5th century date, as suggested by its simply rendered hare and ornamentalized leaf pattern that conform to others in late 5th century art.

This subject was popular because the grapevine and the hare alluded to renewal and a prosperous life. The hare was a well-known symbol of fecundity often used in seasonal and Dionysiac iconography,[6] and thus functioned as a kind of protective charm for assuring life's blessings.

A.G.

1. Technical information: Tapestry weave in linen and wool, red embroidery, dark purple wool, undyed linen; ochre, red wool (S-spun). Warp: undyed linen (S-spun), ca. 13 warps per cm.; weft: undyed linen (S-spun), ca. 72 wefts per cm. Tapestry weave over 3 warps; ca. 18 warps per cm. Some use of soumac wrapping.
2. Musée historique des Tissus, Lyons, inv. 24.401/9 (Volbach 1969, no. 8, p. 25); Leningrad, Hermitage, inv. 11606 (Mat'e and Ljapunova 1951, no. 88, pp. 112–3), pl. 27.1).
3. Leningrad, Hermitage, inv. nos. 1160–11161 (Mat'e and Ljapunova 1951, nos. 89–90, p. 113, pl. 27.); see also another pair in the Museum of Fine Arts, Boston inv. 96.343a and b.
4. E.g., the panel in Lyons, above, note. 2.
5. E.g., London, Victoria and Albert Museum, inv. 770.1886 (Kendrick 1920, no. 138, p. 88, pl. 24); stylistically very close is also Leningrad, Hermitage, inv. no. 11606 (see above, note 2).
6. Pliny *Natural History*, XIII.lxxxi, 217–220. Also Bauer 1986, esp. cols. 663–671; and Turcan 1966, p. 574, n. 4.

185
Fragment of a Band with a Scroll Design, late 5th century

Linen and wool. 62 × 6

The Tellalian Collection.

Provenance: Purchased from Charles D. Kelekian, June, 7, 1979

Populated acanthus scrolls are among the most commonly used motifs of ancient art. These two fragments represent this motif in the monochrome silhouette style of tapestry weaving. The fragments are woven in wool and linen on linen warps. The design is executed in dark purple wool with minimal inner detail in linen and red wool. Parts of the design are executed with a flying shuttle.[1] The acanthus scroll is composed of juxtaposed pairs of luxurious leaves issuing from short stems. Interior loops are filled with birds, animals, fruit, and foliage. The decorative effect of the design depends on contrasts between the dark silhouettes of the motifs against the lightness of the background. The direction of weaving indicates that the fragments came from a horizontal strip of a larger textile. They are strikingly similar to several such bands still preserved with their loop-pile cloths attached, some of which are said to be from Akhmim.[2] The two fragments compare best with late 5th century examples of similar foliate and animal motifs in textiles and other arts, and should, therefore, be assigned this date.
A.G.

1. Technical information: warp: undyed linen (S-spun); weft: undyed linen (S-spun), ochre, red wool (S-spun). Tapestry weave over 3 warps; ca. 18 warps per cm., ca. 72 wefts per cm., some use of soumac wrapping.
2. E.g., Victoria and Albert Museum, inv. 754.1886, 1270.1888, 1271A.1888 (Kendrick 1920, no. 145, p. 90; Kendrick 1921, no. 300, p. 10); British Museum, inv. no. 21.791 (Badawy 1978, fig. 4.72, p. 293); also Österreichisches Museum für angewandte Kunst, inv. T.645 (Egger 1967, pl. 19).

186
Tapestry Panel with Nereids,
late 5th–6th century

Tapestry weave in wool and linen.
21.5 × 21.8

The Virginia Museum of Fine Arts, Richmond, Purchase, Glasgow Fund. 64.56.5

This colorful tapestry panel is decorated with nereids riding sea monsters, one of the most popular figural motifs in Late Antique art in Egypt and throughout the Early Byzantine Empire. The panel is divided into an outer field with the nereids and a central medallion with a rooster and a siren. Each part is framed by a narrow red band. The nude nereids and their blue-and-white aquatic mounts, two fish-like and two with canine foreparts, occupy the corners of the yellow ground of the outer field. They are separated by four green and red baskets filled with fruit and flowers. The purple, red and yellow rooster and the dark-haired siren with blue wings and one white bird leg with talons are placed on the orange ground of the central medallion. The motifs are emphasized by their distinct colors and outlines. The panel is woven in wool and linen on linen warps.[1]

A certain stiffness and distortion of the panel's figures may be attributed to the difficulties of executing polychrome tapestries on such a small scale. Their overall stylization, however, is also the result of the general tendency of the Late Antique period towards more abstract, less naturalistic art. A late 5th or early 6th century date seems appropriate for the stylistic phase represented by this panel. A characteristic feature of this phase of Late Antique art is the representation of an iconographic theme through the assemblage of separate, often even random motifs placed on a neutral ground such as we see here in the use of the yellow and orange grounds and the juxtaposition of marine and other seemingly unrelated motifs within the same composition. Two later stages of this style are represented by textiles from the Harvard University Art Museum (1975.41.19) and from the Allen Memorial Art Museum (cat. no. 187).

The Virginia panel is a companion piece to a textile in the same museum decorated with a Nilotic scene and a nereid seated on a sea-monster.[2] The pair was part of a larger textile, probably a linen cover that had four such tapestry ornaments. Customarily, these textiles were decorated with a set of polychrome tapestry inserts that contained either identical or, as in this case, only related motifs and compositions.[3] The provenance of the Virginia pieces is not known, but several textiles employing similar yellow backgrounds and strewn with similar motifs are associated with the textile finds from Antinoopolis.[4]

Marine scenes and nereids and sea-monsters have a long tradition of representation in the Mediterranean, including Egypt. From the Hellenistic through the Late Antique and the Early Byzantine periods these themes appeared in all forms of art. Together with related portrayals of the Nilotic scenes, they became not only popular genre subjects but also symbolic representations of regeneration and allegories for the abundance of life's blessings.[5] Their meaning explains their frequent use in domestic art, including textiles. Even the baskets of fruit and flowers, in the context of this panel, are an extension of this meaning, as is the presence of the rooster, another fertility motif of ancient art. The rooster and the baskets may also be a terrestrial counterpart to the aquatic motifs of the nereids and the Nilotic scene.

A.G.

Bibliography: Gonosová and Kondoleon forthcoming.

1. Technical information: Warp: undyed linen (S-spun); weft: undyed linen (S-spun), red, yellow, orange, blue, beige, violet, dark purple, green wool (all S-spun); tapestry over 2–3 warps, ca. 6 group warps per 1 cm.; ca. 20–30 wefts per 1 cm.
2. Acc. no. 64.56.4.
3. E.g., the Shawl of Sabina in the Louvre, inv. GU 1230 and GU 1231 (Metropolitan Museum of Art 1979, no. 112, pp. 134–5); a textile in the Coptic Museum, Cairo, inv. 8473 (Daoud Girgis 1983, pl. 9).
4. E.g., Louvre, inv. X4153 (du Bourguet 1964, C 77, p. 115; also Pfister 1932b, pl. 19).
5. Dunbabin 1978, pp. 109–10, 149–61.

187
Panel with Putti and Seasons,
late 6th–early 7th century

Tapestry weave in wool and linen.
20.4 × 19.1

Allen Memorial Art Museum, Oberlin
College, Gift of Oberlin Friends of Art.
42.44

Representations of aquatic-Nilotic putti
and the Seasons were commonly used
in textile decoration. Both refer to the
renewal of nature and are thus interpreted as allegories of prosperity and
the goodness of life. They appear frequently in private art, especially in floors
and wall and ceiling decoration. Their
use in textiles is further evidence of their
popularity as domestic images.[1] The
aquatic scene with playing putti displayed on this textile, woven in wool
and linen on linen warps,[2] is a late 6th
century rendition of the theme in polychrome tapestry weaving.[3]

Stylistically, this piece shows a loosen-
ing of the naturalistic tradition. An earlier
phase of this process can be observed in
the Virginia Museum panel (cat. no. 186).
The panel shown here is close to the Virginia textile. In both cases, the individual
motifs are placed on a neutral ground;
they are more important for their compositional role than for their representation of the subject. The greater degree of
stylization in this piece is due to copying
and the dependence on less naturalistic
models than those used for the Virginia
textile.[4]

A.G.

Bibliography: Allen Memorial Art
Museum 1964, p. 122.

1. Parrish 1984, pp. 12–14 and *passim*;
   Dunbabin 1978, pp. 109–10; Pfister
   1931–32.
2. Allen Memorial Art Museum 1964, p. 122.

3. The composition consists of an outer
   field and a central medallion. The outer
   field, framed by a narrow dark blue band,
   has a yellow background. Its corners
   contain four medallions with female busts,
   undoubtedly personifications of the Seasons. They alternate with four axially
   placed naked putti playing and holding
   birds and some other objects. The ground
   around them is strewn with blue-green
   leaves and fish. The central medallion has
   a red background with two putti also in
   red and outlined in a light yarn done with
   a flying shuttle.
4. See also the Louvre, x4154 and x4297
   (du Bourguet 1964, D 145 and D 156,
   pp. 178–9); and a panel in the University
   of Kansas Museum (Badawy 1978,
   fig. 4.90, p. 301).

188
Ornamental Tapestry Panel,
late 5th–early 6th century

Wool and linen. 14.6 × 16.5

Metropolitan Museum of Art, Funds
from Various Donors. 89.18.100

Provenance: Theodor Graf Collection

The decoration of most Late Antique
textiles is quite simple. This small tapestry panel in linen and wool is an example
of such restrained ornamental weaving.[1]
Originally woven into a larger textile, it
was possibly a shoulder ornament of a
tunic. Tunics often display discreetly
placed Christian crosses as part of their
decoration. The four small crosses hidden in the midst of the medallion foliage
may be considered unobtrusively placed
Christian symbols.[2]

The composition of the panel is dominated by the silhouette of the main design
executed in dark purple wool. It is outlined by a wide frame with an external
cresting. The square field in the center
contains an interlaced medallion with
four three-part sprays of stylized vine
leaves. Similar leaves fill the spandrels
of the square. The dominance of the
dark purple is somewhat muted by the
band of delicate guilloche executed over
the main frame with a flying shuttle in
fine yarns of undyed wool. Similar
touches of undyed wool were added to
the roundels of the cresting. Another
color accent is provided by yellow
crosses inside four small purple disks
between the leaves of the medallion.

As with almost all textiles from
Egypt, the provenance of this panel is
not known. Acquired from Theodor
Graf, like previous textiles, it could have
come either from Akhmim or Saqqara.[3]
The abstract, almost geometric shapes
and organization of the vine leaves
probably point to a late 5th or early 6th
century date.

A.G.

Bibliography: Dimand 1930, fig 12,
p. 244.

1. Technical information: warp: undyed linen
   (S-spun); weft: undyed linen (S-spun),
   purple and yellow wool (S-spun), white
   wool used for flying shuttle. Tapestry
   weave over 2–3 warps, ca. 10 group
   warps per 1 cm., ca. 30 wefts per 1 cm.
2. Dimand 1930(b), p. 244.
3. A tunic decorated with an almost identical
   shoulder panel is in the Victoria and Albert
   Museum, inv. 290.1887 (Kendrick 1921,
   no. 3, p. 41, pl. 2); see also a panel from
   Deir el-Dyk (Gayet 1900, no. 17, p. 97).

189
Ornamental Tapestry Panel,
late 6th–early 7th century

Wool and linen. 25.5 × 24

Metropolitan Museum of Art, Funds from Various Donors. 89.18.125

Provenance: Theodor Graf Collection

This panel demonstrates one of the characteristic features of textile art, namely its tendency to retain and continue motifs once they are introduced into the repertory. The panel was woven in tapestry weave with colored wools (purple, green, red, blue, and yellow) and bleached white linen on fine woolen warps.[1] The composition consists of a series of frames around a central square: a narrow exterior band followed by a wide one with a guilloche, followed by an interior one in purple decorated with variously colored lozenges. The central square contains an inscribed roundel with an inner field in the shape of an eight-pointed star filled with a continuous design of vases and vine-leaf sprays in blue. Blue stylized leaves also fill the spandrels of the central square. Additional color designs fill the lozenge-shaped interstices around the star field and in its center. The fine surface detailing throughout was done with a flying shuttle in wool.

All the individual ornamental elements in this panel had been used for a long time.[2] The majority of them figure prominently in monochrome weaving, where their decorative effect depends mainly on the contrast between the clear outlines of the motifs and the surrounding background. The same design principle was followed in this weaving, except here the restrained color scheme of monochromatic textiles was transformed into a composition of variously colored surfaces. Nevertheless, these colored portions continue the same relationship between the motif and the background that was obtained in the monochrome weaving (cat. no. 188).

The panel was acquired from Theodor Graf known for his extensive holdings of the Akhmim and Saqqara textiles. A panel identical to this piece was once in the Kaiser Friedrich Museum in Berlin.[3]

The strong chromatic effect as well as the stylization of the vase and the vine-and-leaf motifs of these two panels and of this group of textiles in general (cat. no. 190) places them in the late 6th and 7th century.

A.G.

1. Technical information: warp: undyed wool (S-spun); weft: undyed linen (S-spun), purple, green, yellow, rose, blue, gray wool (S-spun). Tapestry weave over 2 warps; ca. 8 group warps per 1 cm., ca. 30 wefts per 1 cm.
2. For the earlier versions of the vase and vine motif, see Louvre, inv. AC199 (du Bourguet 1964, B35, p. 80), Victoria and Albert Museum, inv. 1271.1888 (Kendrick 1921, no. 300, p. 10); Vienna, Österreichisches Museum für angewandte Kunst, T 620 (Egger 1967, pl. 22).
3. Wulff and Volbach 1926, no. 9644, pp. 29–30, pl. 62.

190
Ornamental Tapestry Panel,
late 6th–7th century

Possibly from Akhmim or Saqqara

Wool and linen. 18.2 × 15

Metropolitan Museum of Art, Funds
from Various Donors. 89.18.359

Provenance: Theodor Graf Collection

The most important aspect of this panel
is the novel use of traditional motifs
and compositions. It is an example of
the change through which a common
monochrome silhouette weaving of light
and dark contrasts was transformed into
a design of brightly colored surfaces. All
individual elements used in this piece
appear in other monochrome and polychrome tapestry weavings, often in greater descriptive detail. Here, however, they
are executed only as colorful silhouettes.
Internal detail is minimal, really nonexistent. The panel is compositionally united
by the use of purple for the exterior
crested border, for the frames of the
medallions of the main band and for the
ground of the central square. The green,
red, and yellow colors of the background
of the medallions and their fillers (hares,
lions, three-leaf sprays) are interchange-
able while the purple ground of the
central square is filled with a regularized
pattern of stylized orange, green, tan,
and yellow vine leaves. The panel is
woven in woolen warps in fine-textured
wool and linen.[1] An identical panel was
once in the Kaiser-Friedrich-Museum in
Berlin.[2] This type of weaving is an
example of both the survival of earlier
decorative motifs and compositions and
evidence of their continuous stylistic
change. The distinct silhouettes of the
individual design elements and their
brilliant colors may also have been
inspired by patterns and rich colors of
silk weaving, increasingly used from the
6th century onwards. This textile and its
Berlin counterpart should be assigned to
the late 6th and 7th centuries.

Since this textile was acquired from
Theodor Graf, it might have been found
in Akhmim or Saqqara since the majority
of textiles in the Graf collection came
from these two sites.

A.G.

Bibliography: Kajitani 1981, pp. 26–7.

1. Technical information: warp: wool
   (S-spun); weft: undyed linen (S-spun)
   purple, red, green, ochre, tan, orange wool
   (S-spun). Tapestry weave over 2 warps
   ca. 8 group warps per 1 cm.; ca. 30 wefts
   per 1 cm.
2. Wulff and Volbach 1926, no. 9675,
   p. 39, pl. 62.

191

Fragment of a Hanging, 6th century

From Antinoopolis (?)

Wool and linen. 30.5 × 47.5

Museum of Fine Arts, Boston. Purchased from the Francis Bartlett Donation. 27.566

Only a taste for the new and exotic can explain the unusual ornamentation of a group of colorful tapestry weavings, most likely wall hangings, many of which were found in Antinoopolis.[1] These weavings are typically decorated with narrow borders framing extensive main fields filled with orderly repeated motifs. While the continuous patterning of these textiles approximates the effect of mechanized patterned weavings, the unusual motifs that many of them employ were either inspired or taken directly from imported Sassanian silks, also found in Antinoopolis.[2] Since this city was known for its textile industry, it is quite likely that the silk inspired tapestries were woven right there.

Although the Boston Museum textile does not have a confirmed Antinoopolis provenance, its red woolen ground covered with paired crested and beribboned birds alternating with stepped bases supporting tree-shaped finials and half-length animals in green, ochre and white, are strikingly similar to the coloring and designs of the known Antinoopolis pieces.[3] Also the Boston textile's secondary motifs (capped and bearded human masks and abstract floral sprays) and the remains of an inner border of red cresting on a white ground between ochre and blue bands are found in other Antinoopolis weavings.[4] Since the Boston motifs are on the whole simpler than the motifs of other Antinoopolis tapestries this textile may have been copied from another tapestry and not directly from imported silks whose designs are generally more complex.

The appeal of Sassanian ornament is particularly noticeable in the late 5th and early 6th centuries. For example, an imported silk was copied on a late 5th century vault mosaic in the Church of St. George in Thessaloniki, and Sassanian motifs are found among the architectural ornaments in the Churches of St. Polyeuktos (524–527) and Sts. Sergius and Bacchus (before 536) in Constantinople, as well as on early 6th century mosaic floors from Antioch.[5] The main group of Sassanian-inspired tapestry weavings was made at that time. The second generation textiles, like the Boston fragment, should, however, be assigned a more advanced 6th century date.

A.G.

Bibiliography: Kitzinger 1946, p. 10 fig. 4.

1. This group of textiles is discussed by Kitzinger 1946.
2. Especially Guimet 1912; Geijer 1963; Martiniani-Reber 1986, pp. 36–60.
3. Technical information: warp: red wool (S-spun), weft; blue, red green, ochre wool (all S-spun), bleached linen (S-spun). Tapestry weave over 1 warp; ca. 7–8 warps per 1 cm.; weft counts vary.
4. Lyons, Musée historique des Tissus. inv. 28.929/118, 28.929/121 and 28.929/122.
5. E.g., in the House of the Rams' Heads and the Phoenix Mosaic, both ca. 500 (Levi 1947, pp. 350–3, pls. 133B and 134).

192
Silk Fragment with a Diagonal Grid Pattern, 6th century

Probably from Akhmim

Silk. 20 × 30.5

Museum of Art, Rhode Island School of Design, Mary B. Jackson Fund. 47.066

Patterned silks are the finest examples of compound weaves. Silk thread, which is very fine but strong, was particularly well suited to mechanized drawloom weaving. The decorative possibilities of textiles were further enhanced by the excellent dying properties of the silk. In this silk only two colors, red and cream, are used.[1] The design consists of a diagonal scroll grid filled with alternate round and eight-lobed medallions; the former contain a pair of birds facing each other across a stylized plant, and the latter contain a pair of birds, also separated by a plant, facing outward. This design with its symmetrical fillers exemplifies the repeat – here specifically point-return – patterning of drawloom weaving. Although diagonal grids are a staple of ancient ornament,[2] they began appearing in Roman and Early Byzantine textiles only in the late 4th century.[3] Vegetal scroll and floral grids are characteristic of the 5th and 6th century versions of the design in textiles as well as in other arts, while the stylized plants and the beribboned birds of the medallions belong to 6th century ornament.

This silk is known from several other fragments; the same design also appears in a purple and cream combination. Since several of these textiles come from Akhmim, the Providence textile probably originated there as well.[4] Some of these silks were used as applied shoulder bands (*clavi*), others as shoulder and skirt panels (*segmenta*) or as borders. Since silk textiles were made mainly from imported silk yarns until the end of the 6th century, all-silk clothing was expensive and affordable only by the most affluent. Even clothing with applied silk ornaments – certainly a less expensive alternative – must have been a luxury item.

Although most silks from the Early Byzantine period were found in Egyptian sites, not all were made there. Some, such as a group of silks from Antinoopolis now justifiably considered Sassanian, were imported, but the majority were produced domestically both in Egypt and in other centers of the Byzantine world. The extent of silk industry in Egypt, however, remains unknown, since the specific information available on the manufacture and trade of linen and wool textiles is lacking for silks.[5] Undoubtedly, Alexandria, like other major Byzantine artistic and commercial centers, was an important producer of silks, but the existence of provincial workshops in the 5th and 6th centuries, although assumed, needs to be more firmly established. Although this silk was found in Akhmim, it was not necessarily made there.

A.G.

1. Technical information: compound twill with five-span float; warp: cream silk; weft: red and cream silk.
2. See Levi 1947, pp. 436–53; Gonosová 1987.
3. E.g., on the tunic *segmentum* and the chlamys *tablion* of Emperor Theodosius of the Madrid Missorium (A.D. 388).
4. Forrer 1891, pl. VIII.5. See also Victoria and Albert Museum, inv. 300.1887, 291.1889 (Kendrick 1922, nos. 846–848, pp. 88–90, pl. 22); also Musée historique des Tissus, Lyons, inv. 910.III.5 (Martiniani-Reber 1986, no. 73, pp. 90–91; also no. 62, pp. 82–3 with the list of related textiles).
5. For recent discussion of the subject see Martiniani-Reber 1986.

193
Silk Panel, 7th–8th century

Silk. 34.3 × 36.2

Virginia Museum of Fine Arts, Richmond, Gift of an Anonymous Donor. 69.74

The decoration of this silk panel exemplifies 7th and 8th century ornament. The decorative motifs which are both classical and eastern – specifically Sassanian – in origin are by this date fully integrated. The main element of the design is a large medallion framed by a border of heart-shaped petals with sheath leaves between braid and heart-chain edgings. This medallion would have been connected to other medallions by the axially placed disks in the border. This interior of the medallion contains a symmetrical composition of a stylized tree-of-life motif with several tiers of leaves and palmettes to which were added two hares at the bottom, two peacocks on the sides, and two male figures with sickles flanking the floret finial at the top. The spaces between the medallions were filled with elaborate rosettes. The design is woven in blue-green and cream-colored weft yarns; the coloristic subtleties of this silk are enhanced by salmon colored warps.[1] This silk is a typical example of a point-return patterning commonly used in drawloom weaving. Both the medallion composition and the symmetrical tree-of-life motif are eminently suited for this type of patterning.

Although it cannot be confirmed, it is possible that the Virginia silk came from Egypt. A number of related silks were found in Akhmim and Lahun.[2] They share with the Virginia panel the same repertory of design elements and often also the overall composition, although none is completely identical to it. These silks were produced over a period of time; those of the group decorated with kufic inscriptions had to be made well after the Arab conquest of Egypt of 640/41.[3] Following a common practice for silk weavings, the Virginia panel was cut from a larger piece and used as an appliqué, probably on a tunic (see also cat. no. 192; cat. no. 131).

A.G.

Bibliography: Gonosová and Kondoleon (in preparation).

1. Technical information: weft-faced compound twill; warp: salmon colored silk; weft: blue-green and cream colored silk.
2. See esp. Victoria and Albert Museum, inv. nos. 820.1904, 301.1887, 355.1887, 2178.1900, 412.1890, 817.1903 (Kendrik 1922, nos. 794, 795, 798, 807–8, 810, pl. 25 and frontispiece, pp. 75–9); also Lyon, Musée historique des Tissus, inv. 900.III.8, 963.III.1 and 963.III.3 (Martiniani-Reber 1986, nos. 68, 76–77, pp. 86–7, 93–9).
3. E.g., Victoria and Albert Museum, inv. 768.1893 and 2150.1900 (Kendrick 1922, no. 806, p. 78, pl. 24). See also Grube 1962, pp. 76–81.

194
Compound Weave with Birds and Octagons, 5th century

Probably from Akhmim

Wool. 30.2 × 33.3

The Brooklyn Museum, Gift of John D. Cooney. 45.77.1

Provenance: Said to be from the Fouquet Collection.

While we do not know when and how the technique of compound weaving, with its continuous patterning that required a more complex loom of the drawloom type, was introduced to the Mediterranean area, the evidence of the textiles themselves suggests they were commonly manufactured from at least the late 4th and 5th centuries onwards.[1] Both wool and silk yarns were used for compound-weave fabrics (cat. no. 192; cat. no. 193; cat. no. 131). Compound woolen weaves were not merely decorative, however. Their double construction also made them heavier and sturdier and thus very suitable for household use, especially for blankets, cushion, and mattress covers. This fragment is an example of such a patterned compound weave. Woven in tan and brown wool, its design, consisting of octagons enclosing scrolls and birds with rosettes filling the spaces in between, is reversible. Additional color is provided by red and purple stripes running parallel to the warps on the left and right sides of the fabric. This textile is known from several other examples, including a completely preserved piece that may have been used as a cushion or seat cover, now in London, that is supposed to have been found in Akhmim.[3] It is possible that this entire group of textiles decorated with birds and octagons came from that site.

The relative simplicity of the design and the use of such common 4th and 5th century ornamental motifs as octagons and birds suggests that these textiles may have been made as early as the late 4th or early 5th century. However, since some pieces, for example, that in London, have an additional and distinctly later style of decoration and must therefore be dated accordingly, it can be assumed that the design continued to be employed for some time after its initial introduction. Because the London and Brooklyn pieces are exceptionally alike they are both assigned a late 5th century date.

A.G.

Bibliography: Baltimore Museum of Art, 1947, no. 785, p. 154; Thompson 1971 no. 6, pp. 22–23.

1. Compound weaves dated to the 4th and 5th century were found in Egypt in Karanis (Wilson 1933, nos. 16–19, pp. 17–18, pl. 20). See also Crowfoot and Griffiths 1939 and Bellinger 1952.
2. Technical information: warp: light brown wool (S-spun); weft: light brown, dark brown, red, and purple wool (all S-spun); compound tabby weave with one main and one binding warp; ca. 15 warps per 1 cm., and ca. 72 wefts per 1 cm. (Thompson 1971, p. 22)
3. Victoria and Albert Museum, inv. 243.1891 (Kendrick 1921, no. 537, p. 73, pl. 25); Jerusalem, Israel Museum, inv. 928/70a (Baginski and Tidhar 1980, no. 14, pp. 42 and 43).

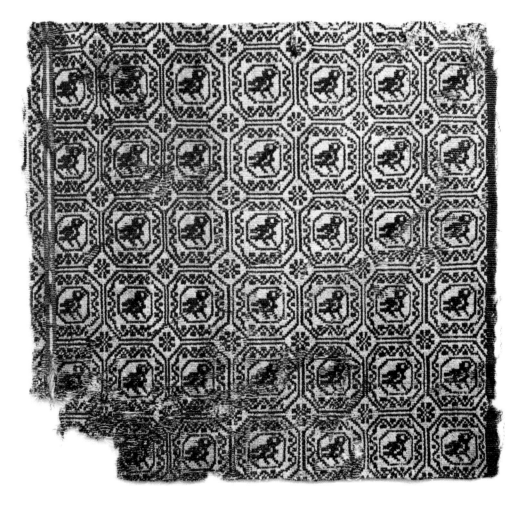

List of Abbreviations

AA	Archäologischer Anzeiger
Acta IRNorv	Acta ad archaeologiam et Artium Historiam pertinenta. Institutum Romanum Norvegiae.
AEE	Ancient Egypt and the East
AJA	American Journal of Archaeology
ASAE	Annales du Service des Antiquités de l'Egypte
Ath Mitt	Mitteilungen des (Kaiserlich) Deutschen Archäologischen Instituts. Athenische Abteilungen
BIFAO	Bulletin de l'Institut Français d'Archéologie Orientale du Caire
BMFA	Bulletin of the Museum of Fine Arts, Boston
BMMA	Bulletin of the Metropolitan Museum of Art
BSAC	Bulletin de la Société d'Archéologie Copte
BSFE	Bulletin de la Société Française d'Egyptologie
CdE	Chronique d'Egypte
CJ	The Classical Journal
Corso	Corsi di Cultura sull'arte ravennate e bizantina
DOP	Dumbarton Oaks Papers
Fasti A	Fasti Archaeologici
GRBS	Greek, Roman, and Byzantine Studies
IEJ	Israel Exploration Journal
JAC	Jahrbuch für Antike und Christentum
JÖB	Jahrbuch der Österreichischen Byzantinistik
JARCE	Journal of the American Research Center in Egypt
JCS	Journal of Classical Studies
JEA	Journal of Egyptian Archaeology
JDAI	Jahrbuch des Deutschen Archäologischen Instituts
JGS	Journal of Glass Studies
JHS	Journal of Hellenic Studies
JTS	Journal of Theological Studies
LÄ	Lexikon der Ägyptologie
MDAIK	Mitteilungen der Deutschen Archäologischen Instituts
MIFAO	Mémoires de l'Institut Français d'Archéologie Orientale du Caire
NARCE	Newsletter of the American Research Center in Egypt
PBSR	Papers of the British School at Rome
ZÄS	Zeitschrift für Ägyptische Sprache und Altertumskunde
ZDMG	Zeitschrift der Deutschen Morgenländischen Gesellschaft
ZPE	Zeitschrift für Papyrologie und Epigraphik

Bibliography

Abd Al-Masih 1957
Y. Àbd Al-Masih. "A Coptic Apocryphon of St. Stephen the Archdeacon," in *Le Muséon* 70 (1957), pp. 329–47.

Abdel-Malek 1980
L. Abdel-Malek. *Joseph Textiles and Related Coptic Textiles*. Ann Arbor, 1980.

Abdel-Malek 1986
L. Abdel-Malek. "Tapestry Roundels with Nilotic Scenes," in *Textile Museum Journal* 25 (1986), pp. 33–46.

Adams 1986
W. Y. Adams. *Ceramic Industries of Medieval Nubia*, 2 pts. Memoirs of the UNESCO Archaeological Survey of Sudanese Nubia. Vol. I. The University Press of Kentucky, 1986.

Adriani 1933–34
A. Adriani. "L'Architecture," in *Annuaire du Musée Gréco-Romain* (1933–5), pp. 67 ff.

Aegyptische Museum 1967
Aegyptische Museum. Staatliche Museen, East Berlin. *Aegyptisches Museum Berlin* (by W. Kaiser). Berlin, 1967.

Alcock 1987
A. Alcock. "Two Notes on Egyptian Monasticism," in *Aegyptus* 67 (1987), p. 189.

Allen Memorial Art Museum 1964
Allen Memorial Art Museum. *Bulletin of the Allen Memorial Art Museum* 22, part 2, (1964), p. 122.

Aly 1953
Z. Aly. "More Funerary Stelae from Kôm Abou Bellou," in *Bulletin de la Société d'Archéologie d'Alexandrie* 40 (1953), pp. 101 ff.

Amelinéau 1895
E. Amelinéau. *Histoire des Monastères de la Basse-Egypte*. Paris, 1895.

Apostolakis 1932
A. Apostolakis. *Ta Koptika Huphasmata tou an Athēnais Mouseiou Kosmetikōn Technōn*. Athens, 1932.

The Art Museum, Princeton University 1986
The Art Museum, Princeton University. *Byzantium in Princeton*. Princeton, 1986.

The Art News 1939
The Art News. "Coptic Art Survey in a New Gallery," in *The Art News* XXXVII (1939), p. 10.

Assmann 1985
J. Assmann. "Gibt es eine 'Klassik' in der ägyptischen Literaturgeschichte? Eine Beitrag zur Geistesgeschichte der Ramessidenzeit," in *ZDMG*, Supplement 6, (1985), pp. 35–52.

Atchley 1909
E. G. C. F. Atchley. *A History of the Use of Incense in Divine Worship*. London, 1909.

Atiya 1968
A. Atiya. *A History of Eastern Christianity*. London, 1968.

Auth 1976
S. H. Auth. *Ancient Glass at the Newark Museum from the Eugene Schaefer Collection of Antiquities*. Newark, N.J., 1976.

Auth 1979
S. H. Auth. "A Fragmentary Christian Gold-Glass at The Newark Museum," in *JGS* 21 (1979), pp. 35–38.

Auth 1983
S. H. Auth. "Luxury Glasses with Alexandrian Motifs," in *JGS* 25 (1983), pp. 39–44.

Auth 1988 forthcoming
S. H. Auth. "Intarsia Glass Pictures in Coptic Egypt," in *Annales du 11e Congrès de l'Association internationale pour l'Histoire du Verre*. Basel, 1988 (forthcoming).

Auth forthcoming
S. H. Auth. "Coptic Glass," in A. S. Atiya ed., *The Coptic Encyclopedia*. New York.

Aymard 1951
J. Aymard. *Essai sur les chasses romaines des origines à la fin du siècle des Antonins (Cynegetica)*. Paris, 1951.

Bacht 1983
H. Bacht. *Das Vermächtnis des Ursprungs* II. Würzburg, 1983.

Badawy 1945
A. Badawy. "La stèle funéraire copte à motif architectural," in *BSAC* XI (1945), pp. 1–25.

Badawy 1953
A. Badawy. *Guide de l'Egypte chrétienne: Musée copte, églises, monastères*. Cairo, 1953.

Badawy 1976
A. Badawy. *Coptic Art and Archaeology: the Art of the Christian Egyptians from the Late Antique to the Middle Ages*. Cambridge, Mass., 1976.

Badawy 1978
A. Badawy. *Coptic Art and Architecture*. Cambridge, Mass., 1978.

Baerlocher 1983
M. Baerlocher. *Grundlagen zur systematischen Erfassung koptischer Textilien*. Basel, 1983.

Baginski and Tidhar 1980
A. Baginski and A. Tidhar. *Textiles from Egypt 4th–13th Centuries C.E.* Jerusalem, 1980.

Bagnall 1985
R. S. Bagnall. *Currency and Inflation in Fourth-Century Egypt*. Atlanta, 1985.

Bagnall 1988a
R. S. Bagnall. "Late Roman Egypt," in *Dictionary of the Middle Ages* 10. New York, 1988 (pp. 453–456).

Bagnall 1988b
R. S. Bagnall. "Greeks and Egyptians: Ethnicity, Status, and Culture," in The Brooklyn Museum 1988 (pp. 21–27).

Bagnall and Worp 1981
R. S. Bagnall and K. A. Worp. "Christian Invocations in the Papyri," in *CdE* 56 (1981), pp. 112–33, 362–65.

Bailey 1984a
D. M. Bailey. *Ashmunein (1983)*. British Museum occasional papers 53 (1984), pp. 29–49.

Bailey 1984b
D. M. Bailey. Review of Johnson, *Pottery from Karanis*, in *JEA* 70 (1984), pp. 185–7.

Baines and Malek 1980
J. Baines and J. Malek. *Atlas of Ancient Egypt*. Oxford and New York, 1980.

Balestri and Hyvernat 1980
I. Balestri and H. Hyvernat. *Scriptores Coptici* versio series tertia. Tomus I. Paris, 1908.

Baltimore Museum of Art 1947
Baltimore Museum of Art. *Early Christian and Byzantine Art at the Walters Art Gallery* (ed. by M. C. Ross). Exhibition held at the Baltimore Museum of Art. Baltimore, 1947.

Baratte 1978
F. Baratte. *Catalogue des mosaïques romaines et paléochrétiennes du Musée du Louvre*. Paris, 1978.

Barnes 1981
T. Barnes. *Constantine and Eusebius*. Cambridge, MA, 1981.

Barns 1981
J. W. B. Barns, G. M. Browne and J. C. Shelton. *AG Hammadi Codices: Greek and Coptic Papyri from the Cartonnage of the Covers* (NHS 16). Leiden, 1981.

Bauer 1986
J. B. Bauer. "Hase," in *Reallexikon für Antike und Christentum* 13 (1986), cols. 662–77.

Bauer 1977.
W. Bauer. *Orthodoxy and Heresy in Earliest Christianity*. Philadelphia, 1977.

Beccati 1969
G. Beccati. *Edificio con opus sectile fuori Porta Marinna. Scavi di Ostia* pt. 6. Rome, 1969.

Beck 1957
E. Beck ed. *Hymnen contra Haereses*. CSCO, CLXIX, Scriptores Syri 76. Louvain, 1957.

Beckwith 1959
J. Beckwith. "Coptic Textiles," in *CIBA Review* 12,133 (1959), pp. 2–27.

Beckwith 1963
J. Beckwith. *Coptic Sculpture 300–1300*. London, 1963.

Beckwith 1971
J. Beckwith. "Byzantine Tissus," in *Actes du XIVe Congrès internationale des études byzantines*. vol. I. Bucharest, 1971.

Beilleux 1986
A. Beilleux. "Monasticism and Gnosis in Egypt," in Pearson and Goehring 1986 (pp. 271–306).

Beinlich-Seeber 1984
C. Beinlich-Seeber. "Renenutet," in *LÄ* 5 (1984), cols. 232–6.

Bell 1983
D. Bell. *Besa: The Life of Shenoute*. Cistercian Publications 73. Kalamazoo, 1984.

Bell 1944
H. I. Bell. "An Egyptian Village in the Age of Justinian," in *JHS* 64 (1944), pp. 21–36.

Bell 1948
H. I. Bell. *Egypt from Alexander the Great to the Arab Conquest*. Oxford, 1948.

Bell 1951
H. I. Bell. *Cults and Creeds in Graeco-Roman Egypt*. Chicago, 1951.

Bellinger 1952
L. Bellinger. "Textile Analysis: Early Techniques in Egypt and the Near East," in *Textile Museum Workshop Notes*, Paper no. 2, 1952.

Bergman 1968
J. Bergman. *Ich bin Isis*. Uppsala, 1968.

Bergman 1969
J. Bergman. "Beitrag zur Interpretatio Graeca. Aegyptische Götter in griechischer Übertrang," in S. S. Hartman ed., *Syncretism*. Stockholm, 1969 (pp. 207–27).

Bergman 1970
J. Bergman. *Isis-Seele und Osiris-Ei*. Uppsala, 1970.

Berliner 1962
R. Berliner. "A Coptic Tapestry of Byzantine Style," in *Textile Museum Journal* 1 (1962), pp. 3–22.

Bianchi 1988
R. S. Bianchi. "Ptolemaic Egypt and Rome: An Overview," in The Brooklyn Museum 1988 (pp. 13–21).

Bianchi-Bandinelli 1971
R. Bianchi-Bandinelli. *Rome: The Late Empire, Roman Art A.D. 200–400*. New York, 1971.

Biedenkopf 1983
A. Biedenkopf-Ziehner. *Untersuchungen zum koptischen Briefformular*. Würzburg, 1983.

Bivar 1972
A. O. H. Bivar. "Cavalry Equipment and Tactics on the Euphrates Frontier," in *DOP* 26 (1972), pp. 271–91.

Boak and Peterson 1931
A. E. R. Boak and E. E. Peterson. *Karanis: Topographical and Architectural Report of Excavations During the Seasons 1924–28*. Ann Arbor, 1931.

Boardman 1987
J. Boardman. "'Very Like a Whale' – Classical Sea Monsters," in A. Farkas, P. Harper, and E. Harrison eds. *Monsters and Demons in the Ancient and Medieval Worlds: Papers Presented in Honor of Edith Porada*. Mainz, 1987 (pp. 73–84).

Bonner 1950
C. Bonner, *Studies in Magical Amulets, Chiefly Graeco-Egyptian*. Ann Arbor, 1950.

Bonnet 1952
H. Bonnet. *Reallexikon der ägyptischen Religionsgeschichte*. Berlin, 1952.

du Bourguet 1951
P. du Bourguet. "Saint-Antoine et Saint-Paul du Desert," in *BSFE*, 1951.

du Bourguet 1964
P. du Bourguet. *Catalogue des Etoffes coptes*. Paris, 1964.

du Bourguet 1971
P. du Bourguet. *The Art of the Copts*. New York, 1971.

du Bourguet 1983
P. du Bourguet. "Le Mot 'Copte,'" in *BSAC* 25 (1983), pp. 101–6.

du Bourguet 1988
P. du Bourguet. *Les Coptes*. Paris, 1988.

Bourriau 1981
J. Bourriau. *Um-el-Gaab. Pottery from the Nile Valley Before the Arab Conquest*. Cambridge, England, 1981.

Bowman 1986
A. K. Bowman. *Egypt After the Pharaohs*. Berkeley, 1986.

Brandenburg 1969
H. Brandenburg. "Bellerophon christianus?" in *Römische Quartalschrift* 63 (1969), pp. 49–86.

Braunfels-Esche 1976
S. Braunfels-Esche. *Sankt Georg*. Munich, 1976.

Breasted 1948
J. Breasted, Jr. *Egyptian Servant Statues*. Princeton, 1948.

Breccia 1930–34
E. Breccia. *Monuments de l'Egypte gréco-romaine II, 1–2: Terracotte figurate greche e greco-egizie del Museo di Alessandria*. Bergamo, 1930–34.

Bresciani 1981
E. Bresciani. "Dall'Egitto ellenistico all'Egitto cristiano: l'eredita faraonica (Riassunto)," in *Corso* 28 (1981), pp. 21–30.

Brightman 1896
F. Brightman ed. *Liturgies, Eastern and Western*. Reprint 1965. Oxford, 1896.

British Museum 1977
British Museum. *Wealth of the Roman World. Gold And Silver A.D. 300–700* (ed. by J. P. C. Kent and K. S. Painter). London, 1977.

British Museum 1987
"Recent Acquisitions," in *British Museum Society Bulletin* 54 (March, 1987), p. 27.

Brockton Art Center 1975
Brockton Art Center. *The Ancient Mediterranean* (by S. K. Morgan). Brockton, Mass., 1975.

Bröker 1970
G. Bröker. *Umetnost Kopta*. Narodni Muzej, Beograd; Državni Muzej, Berlin, Belgrade, 1970.

Brommer 1953
F. Brommer. *Herakles*. Münster, 1953.

Brommer 1971–76
F. Brommer. *Denkmälerlisten zur griechischen Heldensage*. Marburg, 1971–76.

The Brooklyn Museum 1941
The Brooklyn Museum. *Pagan and Christian Egypt* (by J. D. Cooney). Brooklyn, 1941.

The Brooklyn Museum 1957
The Brooklyn Museum. *Five Years of Collecting, 1951–1956* (by J. D. Cooney). Brooklyn, 1957.

The Brooklyn Museum 1988
The Brooklyn Museum. *Cleopatra's Egypt: Art of the Ptolemies, 305–30 B.C.* (by R. S. Bianchi). Brooklyn, 1988.

Brown University 1987
Brown University. *Survival of the Gods: Classical Mythology in Medieval Art.* Department of Art, Brown University. Providence, 1987.

Brunner-Traut 1981
E. Brunner-Traut. "Pharao und Jesus also Sohne Gottes," in *Antaios 2* (1961), pp. 266–84; republished in *Gelebte Mythen. Beiträge zum alt-ägyptischen Mythos.* Darmstadt, 1981.

Brunner-Traut, Brunner and Zick-Nissen 1984
E. Brunner-Traut, H. Brunner, and J. Zick-Nissen. *Osiris, Kreuz und Halbmond, die drei Religionen Ägyptens.* Mainz am Rhein, 1984.

Bruxelles, Musées Royaux d'Art et d'Histoire 1916
Bruxelles, Musées Royaux d'Art et d'Histoire. *Collection d'anciennes Etoffes égyptiennes* (by I. Errera). Brussels, 1916.

Bryer and Herrin 1977
A. Bryer and J. Herrin eds. *Iconoclasm: Papers Given at the 9th Spring Symposium of Byzantine Studies, University of Birmingham, March 1975.* Birmingham, 1977.

Buchthal and Kurz 1942
H. Buchthal and O. Kurz, *A Hand List of Oriental Christian Manuscripts.* Reprint Nendeln, 1968. London, 1942.

Budge 1934
E. A. W. Budge. *The Wit and Wisdom of the Christian Fathers of Egypt.* London, 1934.

Butler 1929
H. C. Butler. *Early Churches in Syria.* Reprint 1969. Princeton, 1929.

Cabrol and Leclercq 1907–53
F. Cabrol and H. Leclerq. *Dictionnaire d'archéologie chrétienne et de liturgie.* Paris, 1907–53.

Calderini 1946
S. Calderini. "Ricerche sull'industria e il commercio dei tessuti in Egitto," in *Aegyptus 26* (1946), pp. 13–83.

Campbell 1985
S. Campbell. *The Malcove Collection.* Toronto, 1985.

Carandini et al. 1982
A. Carandini et al. *Filosofiana, la villa di Piazza Armerina: immagine di un aristocratica romano di tempo di Costantino.* Palermo, 1982

Chaîne 1960
M. Chaîne. *Le manuscrit de la version copte en dialecte sahidique des "Apophthegmata Patrum"* (Bibliothèque d'Etudes coptes, 6). Cairo, 1960.

Charleston 1978
R. J. Charleston. "Glass Furnaces Through the Ages," in *JGS* 20 (1978), pp. 9–33.

Chassinat 1911
E. Chassinat. "Fouilles à Baouît," *MIFAO* 13. Cairo, 1911.

Chitty 1966
D. Chitty. *The Desert a City – An Introduction to the Study of Egyptian and Palestinian Monasticism Under the Christian Empire.* Crestwood, N.Y., 1966.

Clairmont 1977
C. W. Clairmont. *Benaki Museum. Catalogue of Ancient and Islamic Glass.* Athens, 1977.

Clairmont et al. 1975
C. W. Clairmont et al. *Excavations at Salona, Yugoslavia (1969–1972).* Park Ridge, N.J., 1975.

Clédat 1904–16
J. Clédat. *Le Monastère et la Nécropole de Baouît.* Cairo, 1904–16.

Comstock and Vermeule 1971
M. Comstock and C. Vermeule. *Greek, Etruscan and Roman Bronzes in the Museum of Fine Arts.* Boston, 1971.

Cooney 1943
J. D. Cooney. *Late Egyptian and Coptic Art: An Introduction to the Collections of The Brooklyn Museum.* Brooklyn, 1943.

Cooney 1944
J. D. Cooney. Foreword to *Coptic Egypt: Papers Read at a Symposium.* Brooklyn, 1944.

Coptic Museum 1984
Coptic Museum. *The Coptic Museum Handbook.* Cairo, 1984.

The Corning Museum of Glass 1987
The Corning Museum of Glass. *Glass of the Caesars* (by D. B. Harden et al.). Milan, 1987.

Coüasnon 1974
C. Coüasnon. *The Church of the Holy Sepulchre in Jerusalem* (translated by J.-P. B. and C. Ross). London, 1974.

Cramer 1955
M. Cramer. *Das altägyptische Lebenszeichen im christlichen (koptischen) Ägypten.* Wiesbaden, 1955.

Cramer 1957
M. Cramer. *Archaeologische und epigraphische Klassifikation koptischer Denkmäler des Metropolitan Museum of Art, New York und des Museum of Fine Arts, Boston, Mass.* Wiesbaden, 1957.

Crowfoot and Griffiths 1939
G. M. Crowfoot and J. Griffiths. "Coptic Textiles in Two-Faced Weave with Pattern in Reverse," in *JEA* 25 (1939), pp. 40–47.

Crum 1902a
W. E. Crum. *Coptic Ostraca.* London, 1902.

Crum 1902b
W. E. Crum. *Coptic Monuments. Catalogue Général des Antiquités Égyptiennes du Musée du Caire.* Cairo, 1902

Crum 1913
W. E. Crum. *Theological Texts from Coptic Papyri.* Oxford, 1913.

Crum 1942
W. E. Crum. "An Egyptian Text in Greek Characters," in *JEA* 28 (1942), pp. 20–31.

Dalton 1911
O. M. Dalton. *Byzantine Art and Archaeology.* Oxford, 1911.

Daltrop 1966
G. Daltrop. *Die kalydonische Jagd in der Antike.* Hamburg, 1966.

Daoud Girgis 1983
G. Daoud Girgis. "Coptic Textile Decorations from the 4th to the 7th century A.D." in *ASAE* 65 (1983), pp. 129–33.

Daremberg and Saglio 1881–1929
C. Daremberg and E. Saglio. *Dictionnaire des antiquités grecques et romaines, d'après les textes et les monuments.* 5 vols. Paris, 1881–1929.

Darlton 1925
O. M. Darlton. *East Christian Art: A Survey of the Monuments.* Oxford, 1925.

Dart 1976
J. Dart. *The Laughing Savior.* New York, 1976.

Davidson 1952
G. R. Davidson. *Corinth: The Minor Objects.* The American School of Classical Studies at Athens, vol. 12. Princeton, 1952.

Deckers 1979
J. G. Deckers. "Die Wandmalerei im Kaiser Kultraum von Luxor," in *JDAI* 94 (1979), pp. 600–52.

Deichmann 1937
F. W. Deichmann. *Versuch einer darstellung der grundrisstypen des kirchenbaues in frühchristlicher und byzantinischer zeit im Morgenland auf Kunst geographischer grundlage.* Halle, 1937.

Deichmann 1938
F. W. Deichmann. "Zum Altägyptischen in der koptischen Baukunst," in *MDAIK* 8 (1938), p. 34–7.

Deichmann 1969
  F. W. Deichmann. *Frühchristliche Bauten
  und Mosaiken von Ravenna. Ravenna.
  Haupstadt des spätantiken Abendlandes*,
  III. 2nd edition. Wiesbaden, 1969.
Deichmann 1975
  F. W. Deichmann. *Die Spolien in der
  spätantiken Architektur*. Munich, 1975.
Delbrueck 1932
  R. Delbrueck. *Antike Porphyrwerke*.
  Berlin and Leipzig, 1932.
Delattre and Derchain 1964
  A. Delattre and P. Derchain. *Les
  intailles magiques gréco- égyptiennes*.
  Paris, 1964.
Demisch 1984
  H. Demisch. *Erhobene Hände,
  Geschichte einer gebärde in der bilden den
  Kunst*. Stuttgart, 1984.
Descoeudres 1983
  G. Descoeudres. *Die Pastophorien im
  syro-byzantinischen Osten*. Wiesbaden,
  1983.
Detroit Institute of Arts 1954
  Detroit Institute of Arts. *The Art
  Quarterly*. XVII, 2 (1954), p. 179.
Dimand 1924a
  M. S. Dimand. *Die Ornamentik der
  ägyptischen Wollwirkereien*. Leipzig,
  1924.
Dimand 1924b
  M. S. Dimand. "A New Coptic Vase,"
  in *BMMA* 19 (1924), pp. 123–24.
Dimand 1924c
  M. S. Dimand. "A New Coptic Vase in
  the Metropolitan Museum of Art,
  New York," in *Burlington Magazine*
  XLV (1924), pp. 269–73.
Dimand 1930
  M. S. Dimand. "Coptic Tunics in the
  Metropolitan Museum of Art," in
  Metropolitan Museum Studies. Vol. 2,
  Part 2 (1930), pp. 239–352.
Donadoni 1974.
  S. Donadoni. *La necropoli meridionale.
  Antinoe (1965–1968)*. Rome, 1974.
Dorigo 1971
  W. Dorigo. *Late Roman Painting*. New
  York, 1971.
Drioton 1950
  E. Drioton. "De Philae à Baouît," in
  M. Malinine ed., *Coptic Studies in Honor
  of W. E. Crum*. Boston, 1950 (pp. 443–
  48).
Dunand 1973a
  F. Dunand. "Le Syncrétisme isiaque à
  la fin de l'époque hellénistique," in
  *Les Syncretismes dans les religions grecques
  et romaines*. Paris, 1973 (pp. 79–93).
Dunand 1973b
  F. Dunand. *Le culte d'Isis dans le bassin
  oriental de la Méditerranée. I: Le culte
  d'Isis et les Ptolemées*. Leiden, 1973.

Dunand 1979
  F. Dunand. *Religion populaire en Egypte
  romaine: les terres cuites isiaques du Musée
  du Cairo*. Leiden, 1979.
Dunbabin 1978
  K. M. D. Dunbabin. *The Mosaics of
  Roman North Africa*. Oxford and New
  York, 1978.
Dunbabin and Dickie 1983
  K. M. D. Dunbabin and M. W. Dickie.
  "Invida rumpantur pectora: The
  Iconography of Phthonos-Invidia in
  Graeco-Roman Art," in *JAC* 26 (1983),
  pp. 7–37.
Duthuit 1931
  G. Duthuit. *La Sculpture Copte.
  Statues – Bas Reliefs – Masques*. Paris,
  1931.
Effenberger 1975
  A. Effenberger. *Koptische Kunst:
  Ägypten in spätantiker, byzantinischen und
  frühislam*. Reprint. Vienna, 1976. 1st
  edition Leipzig, 1975.
Effenberger et al. 1978
  A. Effenberger et al. *Spätantike und
  Frühbyzantinische Silbergefässe der Staat-
  liche Ermitage, Leningrad*. Staatliche
  Museen, East Berlin. Berlin, 1978.
Egger 1967
  G. Egger. *Koptische Textilien.*
  Österreichisches Museum für
  angewandte Kunst. Vienna, 1967.
Egloff 1977
  M. Egloff. *Kellia: la poterie copte: quatre
  siècles d'artisanat et d'échanges en Basse-
  Egypte*. Geneva, 1977.
Elbern 1979
  V. H. Elbern. "Altar Implements and
  Liturgical Objects," in Metropolitan
  Museum of Art 1979 (pp. 592–640).
Emmel n.d.
  S. Emmel. Unpublished typescript,
  New Haven.
Emmel 1978
  S. Emmel, "The Nag Hammadi
  Codices Editing Project: A Final
  Report," in *NARCE* 104 (Spring 1978),
  pp. 10–32.
Emmel 1989
  S. Emmel. "Coptic Biblical Texts in
  the Beinecke Library," in *JCS* 1 (1989).
Equipe Archéologique Canadienne à
  Carthage 1933–78
  Equipe Archéologique Canadienne à
  Carthage. *Carthage* (by P. Senay).
  Montreal, 1933–76.
Errera 1916
  I. Errera. *Collection d'anciennes étoffes
  égyptiennes*. Brussels, 1916.
Evetts 1948
  B. Evetts. *History of the Patriarchs of the
  Coptic Church of Alexandria*. Paris, 1948.

Fakhry 1951
  A. Fakhry. *The Necropolis of al-Bagawat
  in Kharga Oasis*. Cairo, 1951.
von Falke 1913
  O. von Falke. *Kunstgeschichte der
  Seidenweberei*. Bd. 1. Berlin, 1913.
von Falke et al. 1930
  O. von Falke et al. *Die Sammlung Dr.
  Albert Figdor*. Vienna and Berlin, 1930.
Federn 1949
  W. Federn. "Review of H. Frankfort's
  *Ancient Egyptian Religion: An Interpreta-
  tion*," in *AJA* 53 (1949), pp. 316–20.
Fikhman 1965
  I. F. Fikhman. *Egipet na rubeže dvukh
  epokh. Remeslenniki i remeslennyj trud v
  IV – serdenine VII v*. Moscow, 1965.
Flagge 1975
  I. Flagge. *Untersuchungen zur Bedeutung
  des Greifen*. St. Augustin, 1975.
Fleming et al. 1980
  S. Fleming et al. *The Egyptian Mummy:
  Science and Secrets*. University
  Museum, University of Pennsylvania,
  Philadelphia, 1980.
Forbes 1955
  R. J. Forbes. "The Coming of the
  Camel," in *Studies in Ancient Technology*.
  vol II. Reprint 1965. Leiden, 1955
  (pp. 187–204).
Forrer 1891
  R. Forrer. *Römische und byzantinische
  Seiden-Textilien aus dem Gräberfelde von
  Achmim-Panopolis*. Strasbourg, 1891.
Forsyth and Weitzmann n.d.
  G. H. Forsyth and K. Weitzmann. *The
  Monastery of Saint Catherine at Mount
  Sinai: The Church and Fortress of
  Justinian*. Ann Arbor, n.d. (1973).
Foucher 1961
  L. Foucher. *Découvertes archéologiques à
  Thysdrus en 1960. Notes et Documents V.
  Institut d'Archéologie*. Tunis, 1961.
Foucher 1960
  L. Foucher. *Inventaire des mosaïques
  Sousse*. Tunis, 1960.
Foucher 1965a
  L. Foucher. "Les Mosaïques nilotiques
  africaines," in *La Mosaïque gréco-
  romaine. Colloques internationaux du
  Centre national de la recherche scientifique,
  Paris 1963*. Paris, 1965 (pp. 137–43).
Foucher 1965b
  L. Foucher. *La Maison des masques à
  Sousse. Fouilles 1962-3*. Tunis, 1965.
Fowden 1986
  G. Fowden. *The Egyptian Hermes*.
  Cambridge, 1986.

de Francovich 1963
G. de Francovich. "L'Egitto, la Siria e Constantinopoli, Problemi di Metodo," in *Rivista dell'Istituto nazionale d'archeologia e storia dell'Arte* 11/12 (1963), pp. 89–229.

Frankfort 1948
H. Frankfort. *Ancient Egyptian Religion.* New York, 1948.

Frend 1972
W. H. C. Frend. *The Rise of the Monophysite Movement.* Cambridge, 1972.

Friedländer 1945
P. Friedländer. *Documents of Dying Paganism.* Berkeley and Los Angeles, 1945.

Friedman 1986
F. Friedman. "ȝḥ in the Amarna Period," in *JARCE* 23 (1986), pp. 99–106.

Friedman 1988
F. Friedman. "Department of Antiquities," in *Museum Notes.* Museum of Art, Rhode Island School of Design (1988), p. 10.

Gabra 1941
S. Gabra. *Rapport sur les fouilles d'Hermoupolis Ouest.* Cairo, 1941.

Gabra and Drioton 1954
S. Gabra and E. Drioton. *Peintures à fresques et scènes peintes à Hermoupolis-Ouest (Touna el-Gebel).* Cairo, 1954.

Gardiner 1905
A. H. Gardiner. "Hymns to Amon from a Leiden Papyrus," in *ZÄS* 42 (1905), pp. 12–42.

Gascou 1985
J. Gascou. "Les grandes domaines, la Cité et l'Etat en Egypte byzantine," in *Travaux et Mémoires* 9 (1985), pp. 1–90.

Gascou and MacCoull 1987
J. Gascou and L. S. B. MacCoull. "Le cadastre d'Aphroditô," in *Travaux et Mémoires* 10 (1987), pp. 103–58.

Gayet 1900
A. Gayet. *Le Costume en Egypte du IIIe au XIIIe siècle.* Paris, 1900.

Gayet 1902
A. Gayet. *L'Art Copte.* Paris, 1902.

Gazda et al. 1978
E. K. Gazda et al. *Guardians of the Nile, Sculptures from Karanis in the Fayoum (c. 250 B.C.–A.D. 450).* Kelsey Museum of Archaeology, University of Michigan, Ann Arbor, 1978.

Gazda et al. 1983
E. K. Gazda et al. *Karanis, An Egyptian Town in Roman Times. Discoveries of The University of Michigan Expedition to Egypt (1924–1935).* Kelsey Museum of Archaeology. The University of Michigan. Ann Arbor. 1983.

Geijer 1963
A. Geijer. "A Silk from Antinoë and the Sassanian Textile Art," in *Orientalia Suecana* 12 (1963), pp. 3–36.

Geijer 1979
A. Geijer. *A History of Textile Art.* Totowa, N.J., 1979.

Godlewski 1986
W. Godlewski. *Le monastère de St. Phoibammon.* Warsaw, 1986.

Goehring 1986
J. E. Goehring. "New Frontiers in Pachomian Studies," in Pearson and Goehring 1986 (pp. 236–57).

Goehring and Pearson 1986
J. E. Goehring and B. A. Pearson eds. *The Roots of Egyptian Christianity.* Philadelphia, 1986.

Goldstein 1979
S. Goldstein. *Pre-Roman and Early Roman Glass in the Corning Museum of Glass.* Corning, N.Y. 1979.

Goldstein 1982
S. Goldstein. "Glass," in Museum of Fine Arts, Boston 1982 (160–62, nos. 172–94).

Gonosová 1981
A. Gonosová. *The Role of Ornament in Late Antique Interiors with Special Reference to Intermedia Borrowings of Patterns.* Unpublished dissertation, Harvard University, 1981.

Gonosová 1987
A. Gonosová. "The Formation and Sources of Early Byzantine Floral Semis and Floral Diaper Patterns Reexamined," in *DOP* 41 (1987), pp. 227–37.

Gonosová and Kondoleon forthcoming
A. Gonosová and C. Kondoleon. *Catalogue of Byzantine Art in the Virginia Museum of Fine Arts.* forthcoming.

Goyon 1988
J.-C. Goyon. "Ptolemaic Egypt: Priests and the Traditional Religion," in The Brooklyn Museum 1988 (pp. 29–39).

Grabar 1943/1946
A. Grabar. *Martyrium: recherche sur la culte des reliques et l'art chrétien antique.* 2 vols. Paris, 1946.

Grabar 1958
A. Grabar. *Ampoules de Terre Sainte (Monza, Bobbia).* Paris, 1958.

Grabar 1966a
A. Grabar. *Byzantium: Byzantine Art in the Middle Ages.* trans. B. Forster. London, 1966.

Grabar 1966b
A. Grabar. *Le premier Art chrétien (200–395).* Paris, 1966.

Grabar 1967
A. Grabar. *The Golden Age of Justinian, from the Death of Theodosius to the Rise of Islam.* New York, 1967.

Grabar 1968a
A. Grabar. *Synthronen, art et archéologie de la fin de l'Antiquité et du Moyen Age.* Paris, 1968.

Grabar 1968b
A. Grabar. *L'Art de la fin de l'Antiquité et du Moyen Âge.* Paris, 1968.

Grabar 1968c
A. Grabar. *Early Christian Art, from the Rise of Christianity to the Death of Theodosius.* New York, 1968.

Grabar 1968d
A. Grabar. *Christian Iconography: a Study of its Origins.* trans. T. Grabar. Princeton, 1968.

Graf n.d.
T. Graf. *Antique Portraits from Hellenistic Times.* Theodore Graf's Antike-Porträt Galerie. Vienna, n.d.

Graindor 1939
P. Graindor. *Terres cuites de l'Egypte gréco-romaine.* Antwerp, 1939.

Grant 1980
R. M. Grant. *Eusebius as a Church Historian.* Oxford, 1980.

Griffiths 1960
J. G. Griffiths. *The Conflict of Horus and Seth.* Liverpool, 1960.

Griffiths 1970
J. G. Griffiths ed. *Plutarch, De Iside et Osiride.* Cardiff, 1970.

Griffiths 1984
J. G. Griffiths. "Egyptian Influences on Athanasius," in F. Junge, *Studien zu Sprach und Religion Ägyptens, Band II: Religion.* Göttingen, 1984 (pp. 1023–37).

Grimm 1974
G. Grimm. *Die römischen Mummienmasken aus Ägypten.* Deutsches Archäologisches Institut. Wiesbaden, 1974.

Grose 1983
D. Grose. "The Formation of the Roman Glass Industry," in *Archaeology* 36, no. 4 (July-August 1983), pp. 38–45.

Grose 1984
D. Grose. "Origins and Early History of Glass," in Klein and Lloyd eds. *The History of Glass.* London, 1984.

Grossmann 1967
P. Grossmann. "Die Siedlung im kômring A," in *AA* (1967), 463–73.

Grossmann 1977
P. Grossmann. "Frühchristliche Baukunst in Ägypten," in *Propyläen Kunstgeschichte Supplementbände I*. Beat Brenk, *Spätantike und frühes Christentum*. Frankfurt, 1977, pp. 234–43.

Grossmann 1980
P. Grossmann. "Abu Mina. Neunter vorläufiger Bericht. Kampagnen 1977, 1978, und 1979," in *MDAIK* 36 (1980), pp. 203–29.

Grossmann 1982a
P. Grossmann, "Abu Mina. Zehnter vorläufiger Bericht. Kampagnen 1980 und 1981," in *MDAIK* 38 (1982), pp. 131–54

Grossmann 1982b
P. Grossmann. *Mitteralterliche Langhauskuppelkirchen und verwandte Typen in Oberägypten*. Glükstadt, 1982.

Grossmann 1983
P. Grossmann. "Die Zweischaligen spätantike vier Konchenbauten in Ägypten und ihre Beziehung zu den Gleicharpigen Bauten in Europa und Kleinasien," in "Das römisch-byzantinische Aegypten," *in Aegyptiaca Treverensia II*. 1983 (pp. 167 ff).

Grossmann 1984
P. Grossmann in *Le site monastique Copte des Kellia*. Actes du colloque de Geneve 13 au 15 août 1984. Geneva, 1986 (pp. 33 ff).

Grossmann 1987
P. Grossmann. "Madinat Madi - Die Kirche (1987)," in *Egitto e Vicino Oriente* 10 (1987), pp. 7–20.

Grossman forthcoming
P. Grossmann. Forthcoming in *ASAE* 72 (1987).

Grube 1962
E. J. Grube. "Studies in the Survival and Continuity of Pre-Muslim Traditions in Egyptian Islamic Art," in *JARCE* 1 (1962), pp. 75–97.

de Gruneisen 1922
W. de Gruneisen. *Les caractéristiques de l'art copte*. Florence, 1922.

Guimet 1912
E. Guimet. *Les Portraits d'Antinoe au Musée Guimet*. Paris, 1912.

Hall 1905
H. Hall. *Coptic and Greek Texts of the Christian Period from Ostraka, Stelae, etc. in the British Museum*. London, 1905.

Hall 1986
R. Hall. *Egyptian Textiles*. Aylesbury, 1986.

Hamelin 1953 and 1954
P. Hamelin. "Materiaux pour servir à l'étude des verreries de Begram," in *Cahiers de Byrsa* 3 (1953), pp. 121–8; (suite) *C. de B.* 4 (1954), pp. 153–83.

Hani 1974
J. Hani. "Les Nymphes du Nil," in *Antique Classique* 43 (1974), pp. 212–24.

Hanson 1976
A. E. Hanson ed. *Collectanea Papyrologica. Texts published in honor of H. C. Youtie*. Bonn, 1976.

Harden 1936
D. B. Harden. *Roman Glass from Karanis*. University of Michigan Studies. Humanistic Series 41. Ann Arbor, 1936.

Harden 1940
D. B. Harden. "Glass," in Mond and Myers 1940 (pp. 117–36)

Harden 1960
D. B. Harden. "The Wind Hill Hunting Bowl and Related Glasses," in *JGS*, II (1960), pp. 45–81.

Harden 1969
D. B. Harden, "Ancient Glass, II: Roman," in *The Archaeological Journal* 126 (1969), pp. 44–77.

Harden et al. 1987
D. B. Harden et al. *Glass of the Caesars*. The Corning Museum of Glass. Milan, 1987.

Hardy 1932
E. R. Hardy. *The Large Estates of Byzantine Egypt*. New York, 1932.

Harnack 1958
A. Harnack. *Geschichte der altchristliche Literatur bis Eusebius*. 2nd edition. Leipzig, 1958.

Hayes 1972
J. W. Hayes. *Late Roman Pottery*. The British School at Rome. London, 1972.

Hayes 1976
J. W. Hayes. *Roman Pottery in the Royal Ontario Museum*. Toronto, 1976.

Hayes 1980
J. W. Hayes. *A Supplement to Late Roman Pottery*. The British School at Rome. London, 1980.

Hayes 1984
J. W. Hayes. *Greek, Roman, and Related Metalware in the Royal Ontario Museum: A Catalogue*. Toronto, 1984.

Herbert 1972
K. Herbert. *Greek and Latin Inscriptions in the Brooklyn Museum*. Brooklyn, 1972.

Heyob 1975
S. K. Heyob. *The Cult of Isis Among Women in the Graeco-Roman World*. Leiden, 1975.

Hill 1949
D. Hill. *Catalogue of Classical Bronze Sculpture in the Walters Art Gallery*. Baltimore, 1949.

Honey 1946
W. B. Honey. *Glass: A Handbook*. Victoria and Albert Museum. London, 1946.

Horn 1985
J. Horn. "Kontinuität im Übergang, ein Beitrag zum Problembereich 'pharaonisches' vs. 'Christliches' Ägypten," in *ZDMG* Supplement 6 (1985), pp. 53–73.

Hornbostel 1973
W. Hornbostel. *Sarapis*. Leiden, 1973.

Hornbostel-Huttner 1979
G. Hornbostel-Huttner. *Studien zur römischen Nischenarchitektur*. Leiden, 1979.

Hornung 1982
E. Hornung. *Conceptions of God in Ancient Egypt*. Ithaca, 1982.

Houston 1947
M. Houston. *Ancient Greek, Roman and Byzantine Costume*. London and New York, 1947.

Hunt 1983
L.-A. Hunt. "Coptic Art," in *Dictionary of the Middle Ages* 3, New York, 1983 (pp. 585–93).

Hunt and Edgar 1932–34
A. S. Hunt and C. C. Edgar. *Select Papyri*. 2 vols. Reprint 1970. London and New York, 1932–34.

Huskinson 1974
J. Huskinson. "Some Pagan Mythological Figures and their Significance in Early Christian Art," in *PBSR* 42 (1974), pp. 68–97.

Illgen 1968
V. Illgen. *Zweifarbige reservetechnisch eingefärbte Leinenstoffe mit grossfigurigen biblischen Darstellungen aus Ägypten*. Mainz, 1968.

Jacquet-Gordon 1972
H. Jacquet-Gordon, *Les ermitages chrétiens du désert d'Esna, III*. Cairo, 1972.

Jansen 1950
H. L. Jansen, "The Coptic Story of Cambyses' Invasion of Egypt," in *Avhandlinger utgitt av det Norske Videnskaps Akademi i Oslo, II His.-Filos Klasse*, no. 2, 1950.

Jaritz 1980
H. Jaritz. "Abu Mina. Neunter vorläufiger Bericht. Kampagnen 1977, 1978 und 1979," in *MDAIK* 36 (1980), pp. 203–29.

Johnson and West 1949
A. C. Johnson and L. C. West. *Byzantine Egypt: Economic Studies.* Princeton, 1949.

Johnson 1981
B. Johnson. *Pottery from Karanis. Excavations of the University of Michigan. Kelsey Museum of Archaeology Studies 7.* The University of Michigan. Ann Arbor, 1981.

Johnson 1986
D. W. Johnson. "Anti-Chalcedonian Polemics in Coptic Texts, 451–641," in Pearson and Goehring 1986 (pp. 216–34).

Johnson 1986
J. Johnson. "The Role of the Egyptian Priesthood in Ptolemaic Egypt," in L. Lesko ed., *Egyptological Studies in Honor of Richard A. Parker. Presented on the Occasion of his 78th Birthday, December 10, 1983.* Hanover, New Hampshire and London, 1986.

Jonas 1963
H. Jonas. *The Gnostic Religion,* 2nd ed. Boston, 1963.

Jones 1959
A. H. M. Jones. "Were Ancient Heresies National or Social Movements in Disguise?" in *JTS* 10 (1959), pp. 280–98.

Jones 1960
A. H. M. Jones. "The Cloth Industry under the Roman Empire," in *The Economic History Review* 13 (1960), pp. 183–92.

Jones 1983
A. H. M. Jones. *The Cities of the Eastern Roman Provinces.* Amsterdam, 1983.

de Jonghe 1985
D. de Jonghe. "Koptische weefsels. Een technologische kunstgreep," in *Bulletin des Musées Royaux d'Art et d'Histoire* 56/2 (1985), pp. 5–23.

Jucker 1969
H. Jucker. "Die frühesten Reproduktione des Kanonischen Sarapistyps auf Alexandrinischen Münzen," in *Schweizer Münzblatter* 19 (1969), pp. 78–94.

Judge and Pickering 1977
E. Judge and S. Pickering. "Papyrus Documentation of Church and Community in Egypt to the Mid-Fourth Century," in *JAC* 20 (1977), pp. 47–71.

Junge 1979
F. Junge. "Isis und die ägyptischen Mysterien," in W. Westendorf ed., *Aspekte der spätägyptischen Religion.* Wiesbaden, 1979 (pp. 93–115).

Kahle 1954
P. Kahle. *Bala'izah: Coptic Texts from Deir el-Bala'izah in Upper Egypt.* 2 vols. London, 1954.

Kajitani 1981
N. Kajitani. "Coptic Fragments," in *Textile Art* 13 (1981), pp. 6–77.

Kaufmann 1910
K. M. Kauffmann. *Zum Ikonographie der Menas-Ampullen.* Cairo, 1910.

Kaufmann 1913
K. M. Kaufmann. *Ägyptische Terrakotten der griechisch-römischen und koptischen Epoche vorzugweise aus der Oose el Faijum.* Cairo, 1913.

Keenan 1984
J. G. Keenan. "Aurelius Apollos and the Aphrodite Village Elite," in *Atti del XVII Congresso internazionale di papirologia.* Naples, 1984 (pp. 957–63).

Kelsey Museum 1977
Kelsey Museum of Archaeology. *The Gods of Egypt in the Graeco-Roman Period.* The University of Michigan. Ann Arbor, 1977.

Kendrick 1920–22
A. F. Kendrick. *Catalogue of Textiles from the Burying-Grounds in Egypt.* Victoria and Albert Museum. vols. I–III. London, 1920–22.

Kisch 1965
B. Kisch. *Scales and Weights.* New Haven, 1965.

Kiss 1969
Z. Kiss. "Des ampoules de St. Menas découvertes à Kôm el-Dikka (Alexandrie) en 1967." *Travaux du Centre d'Archéologie Méditerranéenne de l'Académie Polonaise des Sciences, Vol. 8.* Etudes et Travaux III, 1969.

Kitzinger 1937
E. Kitzinger. "Notes on Early Coptic Sculpture," in *Archaeologia* 87 (1937), pp. 181–215.

Kitzinger 1946
E. Kitzinger. "The Horse and Lion Tapestry at Dumbarton Oaks: a Study in Coptic and Sassanian Textile Design," in *DOP* 3 (1946), pp. 1–72.

Kitzinger 1954
E. Kitzinger. "The Cult of Images in the Age before Iconoclasm," in *DOP* 8 (1954), pp. 83–150.

Kitzinger 1977
E. Kitzinger. *Byzantine Art in the Making.* Cambridge, Mass., 1977.

Koefoed-Peterson 1944
O. Koefoed-Peterson. *Koptik Kunst.* Copenhagen, 1944.

Krause 1974
M. Krause. "Die Koptologie im Gefüge der Wissenschaften," *ZÄS* 100 (1974), pp. 108–125.

Krautheimer 1965.
R. Krautheimer. *Early Christian and Byzantine Architecture.* Harmondsworth, 1965.

Kybalova 1967
L. Kybalova. *Die alten Weber am Nil. Koptische Stoffe. Ein Beitrag zur ästhetisch-technologischen Problematik.* Prague, 1967.

Labib 1956
P. Labib. *Coptic Gnostic Papyri I.* Cairo, 1956.

Lamm 1941
C. J. Lamm. *Oriental Glass of Medieval Date Found in Sweden and the Early History of Lustre Painting.* Stockholm, 1941.

van Lantschoot 1929
A. van Lantschoot. *Recueil des colophons des manuscrits chrétiens d'Egypte.* 2 vols. Louvain, 1929.

Lavin 1963
I. Lavin. "The Hunting Mosaics of Antioch and their Sources," in *DOP* 17 (1963), pp. 181–279.

Layton 1973
B. Layton. "The Text and Orthography of the Coptic *Hypostasis of the Archons,*" in *ZPE*, pp. 173–200.

Layton 1974
B. Layton. "The Hypostasis of the Archons," in *Harvard Theological Review* 67 (1974), pp. 351–425.

Layton 1976a
B. Layton. "The Hypostasis of the Archons (conclusion)," in *Harvard Theological Review* 69 (1976), pp. 31–101.

Layton 1976b
B. Layton. "Coptic Language," in *The Interpreter's Dictionary of the Bible, Supplementary Volume,* pp. 175–7. Nashville, 1976.

Layton 1977
B. Layton. "Editorial Notes on the 'Expository Treatise Concerning the Soul' (Tractate II6 from Nag Hammadi)," in *Bulletin of the American Society of Papyrologists* 14 (1977), pp. 65–73.

Layton 1987
B. Layton. *The Gnostic Scriptures.* Garden City, 1987.

Lazarus 1978
P. Lazarus. *The Cinzano Glass Collection.* London, 1978.

Leibovitch 1958
J. Leibovitch. "Le griffon d'Erez," in *IEJ* 3 (1958), pp. 141–9.

Leipoldt 1903
J. Leipoldt. *Schenute von Atripe und die Entstehung des nationalägyptischen Christentums.* Leipzig, 1903.

Leipoldt 1906
J. Leipoldt. *Sinuthii Vita Bohairice.* CSCO 41, Scriptores Coptici 1. Louvain, 1906.

Leroy 1974
J. Leroy. *Les manuscrits coptes et coptes-arabes illustrés.* Paris, 1974.

Lesko 1977
L. Lesko. *The Ancient Egyptian Book of Two Ways.* Berkeley, Los Angeles, and London, 1977.

Lesko 1987
L. Lesko. "Review of *Das Totenbuch in den Thebanischen Beamtengrabern des Neuen Reiche,* by Mohammed Saleh," in *JEA* 73 (1987), pp. 270–1.

Levi 1947
D. Levi. *Antioch Mosaic Pavements I.* London, The Hague, Princeton, 1947.

Lewis 1983
N. Lewis. *Life in Egypt Under Roman Rule.* Oxford, 1983.

Lewis 1986
N. Lewis. *Greeks in Ptolemaic Egypt.* Oxford, 1986.

Lewis 1973
S. Lewis. "The Iconography of the Coptic Horseman in Byzantine Egypt," in *JARCE* 10 (1973), pp. 27–63.

Lichocka forthcoming 1989
B. Lichocka. "Némésis dans l'Egypte Romaine," in *Aegyptiaca Treverensia, Trierer Studien zum griechisch-römischen Aegypten,* Bd. 5. 1989

Lichtheim 1976
M. Lichtheim. *Ancient Egyptian Literature II: The New Kingdom.* Berkeley, 1976.

Lichtheim 1980
M. Lichtheim. *Ancient Egyptian Literature III: The Late Period.* Berkeley, 1980.

Liebighaus Museum 1983–4
Liebighaus Museum. *Spätantike und Früheschristentum.* Frankfurt am Main, 1983–4.

Loudmer and Kevorkian 1985
Ancient and Islamic Glass. Formerly the Property of a Gentleman, Mr. D. Auction at the Hotel Drouot. Monday, June 3, 1985 and Tuesday, June 4, 1985. Guy Loudmer Auctioneer, Mrs. A. M. Kevorkian, expert. Paris, 1985.

Lowrie 1965
W. Lowrie. *Art in the Early Church.* 2nd revised edition. New York, 1965.

MacCoull 1975
L. S. B. MacCoull. "Coptic Papyri in the Beinecke Collection at Yale University," in *Proceedings of the XIV International Congress of Papyrologists,* Oxford, 24–31 July 1974. London, 1975 (pp. 217–19).

MacCoull 1979a
L. S. B. MacCoull. "A Coptic Marriage Contract in the Pierpont Morgan Library," in *Actes du XVe Congrès international de papyrologie II.* Brussels, 1979 (pp. 116–23).

MacCoull 1979b
L. S. B. MacCoull. "Child Donations and Child Saints in Coptic Egypt," in *East European Quarterly* 13 (1979), pp. 409–15.

MacCoull ed 1979c
L. S. B. MacCoull ed. *Coptic Studies Presented to Mirrit Boutros Ghali.* Cairo, 1979.

MacCoull 1981
L. S. B. MacCoull. "The Coptic Archive of Dioscorus of Aphrodito," in *CdE* 56 (1981), pp. 185–93.

MacCoull 1982a
L. S. B. MacCoull. "The Coptic Cambyses Narrative Remembered," in *GRBS* (1982) pp. 185–88.

MacCoull 1982b
L. S. B. MacCoull. "Documentary Texts from the Pierpont Morgan Library," in *BSAC* 24 (1982), pp. 10–12.

MacCoull 1986a
L. S. B. MacCoull. *Coptic Documentary Papyri from the Beinecke Library.* Cairo, 1986.

MacCoull 1986b
L. S. B. MacCoull. "Coptic Documentary Papyri as a Historical Source for Egyptian Christianity," in Pearson and Goehring 1986 (pp. 51–81).

MacCoull 1988a
L. S. B. MacCoull. *Dioscorus of Aphrodito: His Work and His World.* Berkeley, 1988.

MacCoull 1988b
L. S. B. MacCoull. "Dioscorus and the Dukes: an Aspect of Coptic Hellenism in the Sixth Century," in *Byzantine Studies / Etudes byzantines* 14 (1988).

MacCoull forthcoming a
L. S. B. MacCoull. "More Coptic Papyri from the Beinecke Collection," in *Archiv für Papyrusforschung* 35 (1989).

MacCoull forthcoming b
L. S. B. MacCoull. "The Aphrodito Murder Mystery," forthcoming, in *Journal of Juristic Papyrology* (Warsaw).

MacCoull forthcoming c
L. S. B. MacCoull. "Coptic Law," in A. S. Atiya ed., *The Coptic Encyclopedia.* New York.

MacCoull and Worp 1989
L. S. B. MacCoull and K. A. Worp. "The Era of the Martyrs," in R. Pintaudi ed., *Miscellanea Papyrologica.* Florence, 1989.

MacLennan 1935
H. MacLennan. *Oxyrhynchus: An Economic and Social Study.* Princeton, 1935.

MacMillan Arensberg 1977
A. S. MacMillan Arensberg. "Dionysus: Late Antique Tapestry," in *BMFA* 75 (1977), pp. 4–25.

MacMullen 1986
R. MacMullen. "The Meaning of A.D. 312: The Difficulty of Converting the Empire," in *The 17th International Byzantine Congress: Major Papers.* Dumbarton Oaks / Georgetown University Washington, D.C., August 3–8, 1986. New York, 1986 (pp. 1–15).

Maguire 1987
H. Maguire. *Earth and Ocean: The Terrestrial World in Early Byzantine Art.* University Park, 1987.

Mango 1963
C. Mango. "Antique Statuary and the Byzantine Beholder," in *DOP* 17 (1963), pp. 53–75.

Mango 1972
C. Mango. *The Art of the Byzantine Empire* 312–1453. Englewood Cliffs, N.J., 1972.

Marshall 1911
F. H. Marshall. *Catalogue of the Jewellry, Greek, Etruscan, and Roman in the Department of Antiquities, British Museum.* London, 1911.

Martin 1984
A. Martin. "Les premiers siècles du Christianisme à Alexandrie," in *Rev Et* August 30 (1984), pp. 211–15.

Martin 1985
M. Martin. "Une lecture de l'Histoire des Patriarches d'Alexandrie," in *Proche-Orient Chrétien* 35 (1985), pp. 15–36.

Martin 1945
R. Martin. "Mummies," in *Chicago Natural History Museum, Popular Series: Anthropology* XXXVI (1945).

Martiniani-Reber 1986
M. Martiniani-Reber. *Lyons Musée historique des tissus. Soieries sassanides, coptes et byzantines Ve-XIe siècles*. Paris, 1986.

Maspero 1908
J. Maspero. "Bracelets-amulettes d'époque byzantine," in *ASAE* 9 (1908), pp. 246–58.

Mat'e and Ljapunova 1951
M. Mat'e and K. Ljapunova. *Khudozhestvennye tkani Koptskojo Egipta*. Moscow, 1951.

Mathews 1977
T. Mathews. *The Early Churches of Constantinople: Architecture and Liturgy*. University Park, 1977.

McCleary 1987
R. McCleary. *Portals to Eternity*. Kelsey Museum of Archaeology. University of Michigan. Ann Arbor, 1987.

McSorley 1957
J. McSorley. *An Outline History of the Church*. 10th edition. St. Louis, 1957.

Meindardus 1961
O. Meinardus. *Monks and Monasteries of the Egyptian Deserts*. Cairo, 1961.

Meinardus 1965
O. Meinardus. *Christian Egypt – Ancient and Modern*. Cairo, 1965.

Mélèze-Modrzejewski
J. Mélèze-Modrzejewski. "Le Statut des Hellènes dans l'Egypte Lagide," in *Revue des études grecques* 96 (1983), pp. 241–68

Metropolitan Museum of Art 1919
Metropolitan Museum of Art. *A Handbook of the Egyptian Rooms*. New York, 1919.

Metropolitan Museum of Art 1969
See Ostoia 1969.

Metropolitan Museum of Art 1979
Metropolitan Museum of Art. *Art of Spirituality. Late Antique and Early Christian Art. Third to Seventh Century* (ed. K. Weitzmann). New York, 1979.

Metzger 1981
C. Metzger. *Les Ampoules à Eulogie du Musée du Louvre*. Editions de la Réunions des Musées Nationaux. Paris, 1981.

Milburn 1988
R. Milburn. *Early Christian Art and Architecture*. Berkeley, 1988.

Millard 1987
Dom B. Millard OSB, "St. Christopher and the Lunar Disc of Anubis," in *JEA* 73 (1987), pp. 237–8.

Mitten and Doeringer 1967
D. Mitten and S. Doeringer. *Master Bronzes*. Fogg Art Museum. Cambridge, Mass., 1967.

Mond and Myers 1934
Sir R. Mond and O. H. Myers. *The Bucheum*. Egypt Exploration Society. London, 1934.

Mond and Myers 1940
Sir R. Mond and O. H. Myers. *Temples of Armant, A Preliminary Survey*. Egypt Exploration Society. London, 1940.

Monneret de Villard 1927
U. Monneret de Villard. *Il monastero di S. Simeone presso Aswan I*. Milan, 1927.

Moorhead 1981
J. Moorhead. "The Monophysite Response to the Arab Invasion," in *Byzantion* 51 (1981), pp. 579–91.

van Moorsel 1978
P. P. V. van Moorsel. "The Coptic Apse Composition and Its Living Creatures," in *Nubia, Recentes Recherches*. Cambridge, 1978, (pp. 325–33).

van Moorsel 1979
P. P. V. van Moorsel. *De Galaktotrophousa en de Monophysieten*, 1979.

Morenz 1960
S. Morenz. *Egyptian Religion*. Ithaca, 1960.

Morenz 1963
S. Morenz. "Fortwirken altägyptischen Elemente der christlicher Zeit," in Villa Hügel 1963 (pp. 54–59).

Morey 1942
C. R. Morey. *Early Christian Art. An Outline of the Evolution of Style and Iconography of Sculpture and Painting from Antiquity to the Eighth Century*. Princeton, 1942.

Morgan 1975
S. K. Morgan. *The Ancient Mediterranean*. Brockton, Mass., 1975.

Müller 1961
D. Müller. *Isis-Aretalogien*. Berlin, 1961.

Müller 1962
H. W. Müller. "Koptische Glasintarsien mit Figurlichen Darstellungen aus Antinoë – Mittelägypten," *Pantheon* 20 (1962), pp. 13–18.

Müller 1963
H. W. Müller. "Isis mit den Horuskinde," in *Münchner Jahrbuch der bildenden Kunst* 14 (1963), pp. 7–38.

Müller 1969
H. W. Müller. *Der Isis Kult im antiken Benevent und Katalog der Skulpturen aus den ägyptischen Heiligtumern im Museo del Sannio zu Benevent*. Berlin, 1969.

Müller-Wiener 1967
W. Müller-Wiener. "Abu Mena. 5 Vorläufiger Bericht," in *MDAIK* 22 (1967), pp. 216–7.

Murray 1935
M. A. Murray. "Coptic Painted Pottery," in *AEE* (1935), pp. 1–15.

Murray 1981
Sr. C. Murray. *Rebirth and Afterlife: a Study of the Transmutation of Some Pagan Imagery in Early Christian Funerary Art*. Oxford, 1981.

Musée du Louvre 1920
Musée du Louvre, Département des Antiquités Egyptiennes. *Catalogue des Etoffes coptes* (by P. du Bourguet). Paris, 1964.

Museum of Art, Rhode Island School of Design 1988
Museum of Art, Rhode Island School of Design. *A World of Costume and Textiles: A Handbook of the Collection* (ed. by S. A. Hay). Providence, 1988.

Museum of Fine Arts, Boston 1976
Museum of Fine Arts, Boston, Department of Classical Art. *Romans and Barbarians*. Boston, 1976.

Museum of Fine Arts, Boston 1982
Museum of Fine Arts, Boston. *Egypt's Golden Age*. (by Edward Brovarski). Boston, 1982.

Museum of Fine Arts, Boston 1988
Museum of Fine Arts, Boston. *Mummies and Magic* (ed. by P. Lacovara, S. D'Auria, and C. Roehrig). Boston, 1988.

Nauerth 1978
C. Nauerth. *Koptische Textilkunst im Spätantiken Ägypten. Die Sammlung Rautenstrauch im Städtlichen Museum Simeonstift Trier*. Trier, 1978.

Nauerth 1986
C. Nauerth. *Koptische Stoffe*. Frankfurt am Main. 1986.

Nauerth and Warns 1981
C. Nauerth and R. Warns. *Thekla*. Wiesbaden, 1981.

Naville 1913
E. Naville. *The XIth Dynasty Temple at Deir el Bahri, Part III*. London, 1913.

Needham 1979
P. Needham. *Twelve Centuries of Bookbindings, 400–1600*. New York and London, 1979.

Nersessian 1941
S. der Nersessian. "Pagan and Christian Art in Egypt: An Exhibition at the Brooklyn Museum," in *Art Bulletin* 23, 2 (June 1941), pp. 165–7.

The Newark Museum 1977
The Newark Museum. *Myth and Gospel* (by S. H. Auth). Newark, N.J., 1977.

Orlandi 1970
T. Orlandi. *Storia della Chiesa di Alessandria*. Milan, 1970.

Orlandi 1984
T. Orlandi. *Vite di Monaci Copti*. Rome, 1984.

Orlandi 1986
T. Orlandi, "Coptic Literature," in Pearson and Goehring 1986, pp. 51–81.

Orlandi 1988
T. Orlandi. *Paolo di Tamma, Opere*. Rome, 1988.

Osing 1976
J. Osing. *Der Spätägyptische Papyrus BM 10808*. Wiesbaden, 1976.

Ostoia 1969
V. K. Ostoia. *The Middle Ages: Treasures from the Cloisters and the Metropolitan Museum of Art*. Los Angeles, 1969.

Otto 1969
E. Otto. "Das 'Goldene Zeitalter' in einem ägyptischen Text," in *Religions en Egypte hellénistique et romaine*. Paris, 1969 (pp. 93–108).

Paris, Petit Palais, 1964
Paris, Petit Palais. *L'Art Copte*. Paris, 1964.

Parlasca 1963
K. Parlasca. "A Painted Egyptian Mummy Shroud of the Roman Period," in *Archaeology* 16, no. 4 (Winter, 1963), p. 266.

Parlasca 1966
K. Parlasca. *Mumienporträts und Verwandte Denkmaler*. Wiesbaden, 1966.

Parlasca 1978
K. Parlasca. "Der Übergang des spätrömischen zur frühkoptischen Kunst im Lichte des Grabreliefs von Oxyrhynchus," in *Enchoria* 8 (1978), pp. 115–20.

Parrish 1984
D. Parrish. *Season Mosiacs of Roman North Africa*. Rome, 1984.

Peacock and Williams 1986
D. P. S. Peacock and D. F. Williams. *Amphorae and the Roman Economy*. London, 1986.

Pearson 1976
B. A. Pearson. "The Pierpont Morgan Fragments of a Coptic Enoch Apocryphon," in G. Nickelsburg ed., *Studies on the Testament of Abraham*. Missoula, 1976 (pp. 227–83).

Pearson and Goehring 1986
B. A. Pearson and J. E. Goehring eds. *The Roots of Egyptian Christianity*. Philadelphia, 1986.

Perdrizet 1921
P. Perdrizet. *Les terres cuites grecques d'Egypte de la Collection Fouquet*. 2 vols. Nancy and Paris, 1921.

Peremans 1978
W. Peremans. "Les Revolutions égyptiennes sous les Lagides," in H. Maehler and V. M. Strocka eds., *Das ptolemaische Aegypten*. Mainz, 1978 (pp. 39–50).

Petersen 1954
T. Petersen, C. S. P. "The Paragraph Mark in Coptic Illuminated Ornament," in D. Miner ed., *Studies in Art and Literature for Belle Da Costa Greene*. Princeton, 1954 (pp. 295–330).

Petersen 1964
T. Petersen. *A Collection of Papyri*. Kraus Catalog 105. New York, 1964.

Peterson 1974
B. Peterson. "Der Traum von Paradiese. Gedanken zu einigen Grabreliefs aus Oxyrhynchos," in *From the Gustavianum Collections in Uppsala*. Stockholm, 1974.

Peterson 1959
E. Peterson. *Frühkirche, Judentum und Gnosis*. Freiburg, 1959.

Peterson 1933
E. E. Peterson. "The Temples of Pnepheros and Petesuchos," in A. E. Boak ed., *Karanis, the temples, coinhoards, botanical and zoological reports, Seasons 1924–31*. Ann Arbor, 1933 (pp. 17–55).

Petrie 1926
W. M. F. Petrie. *Weights and Measures*. London, 1926.

Petrie 1927
W. F. Petrie. *Objects of Daily Use*. British Museum School of Archaeology in Egypt. London, 1927.

Pfister 1932a
R. Pfister. "Les débuts du vêtement copte," in *Etudes d'orientalisme publiées par le Musée Guimet à la mémoire du Raymonde Linoissier* II. Paris, 1932 (pp. 433–59).

Pfister 1932b
R. Pfister. *Tissus coptes du Musée du Louvre*. Paris, 1932.

Pfister 1934–40
R. Pfister. *Textiles de Palmyre*. Paris, 1934–40.

Pfister 1936
R. Pfister. "Matériaux pour servir au classement des textiles égyptiens postérieurs à la conquête arabe," in *Revue des arts asiatiques* 10 (1936), pp. 1–16, 73–85.

Pharr 1952
C. Pharr. *The Theodosian Code and Novels, and the Sirmondia Constitution; A Translation with Commentary, Glossary and Bibliography*. New York, 1952.

Picard 1958
C. Picard. "La sphinge tricephale, dite 'panthée,' d'Amphipolis et la démonologie egypto-alexandrine," in *Monuments et memoires publies par l'Academie des Inscriptions et Belles-Lettres (Fondation Eugène-Piot)* 50 (1958), pp. 49–84.

Pritchard 1969.
J. B. Pritchard ed. *Ancient Near Eastern Texts*. 3rd edition. Princeton, 1969.

Quaegebeur 1983
J. Quaegebeur. "De l'Origine égyptienne du griffon Némésis," in *Mélanges Jacqueline Duchmin, Visages du Destin dans les Mythologies*, Paris, 1983 (pp. 41–54).

Quibell 1903
J. E. Quibell. "Kom Ishkau," in *ASAE* 3 (1903), pp. 85–8, pl. 2.

Quibell 1908
J. E. Quibell. *Excavations at Saqqara (1905–1906)*. Cairo, 1908.

Quibell 1909
J. E. Quibell. *Excavations at Saqqara (1907–1908)*. Cairo, 1909.

Quibell 1912
J. E. Quibell. *Excavations at Saqqara (1908–1909; 1909–10)*. Cairo, 1912.

Randall 1985
R. H. Randall, Jr. *Masterpieces of Ivory*. New York, 1985.

Redford 1976
D. B. Redford. "The Sun-Disc in Akhenaten's Program: Its Worship and Antecedents, I," in *JARCE* 13 (1976), pp. 47–61.

Redford 1986
D. B. Redford. *Pharaonic King-Lists, Annals and Day-Books*. Mississauga, 1986.

Reil 1913
T. Reil. *Beiträge zur Kenntnis des Gewerbes im hellenistischen Ägypten*. Borna-Leipzig, 1913.

Reisner and Wheeler 1967
G. A. Reisner and N. F. Wheeler. *Second Cataract Forts*. Museum of Fine Arts, Boston, 1967.

Remondon 1952
R. Remondon. "Egypte et la suprême résistance au christianisme (Ve-VIIe siècles)," in *BIFAO* 51 (1952), pp. 63–78.

Renner 1981
D. Renner. "Spätantike Figurliche Purpurwirkereien," in *Documenta Textilia: Festschrift für Sigrid Müller-Christencen* (ed. by M. Flury-Lemberg and K. Stollers). Munich, 1981 (pp. 82–94).

Renner 1982
D. Renner. *Die koptischen Textilien in den vatikanischen Museen.* Wiesbaden, 1982.

Ridgway 1972.
B. S. Ridgway. *Classical Sculpture.* Museum of Art, Rhode Island School of Design, Providence, R.I., 1972.

Riegl 1893
A. Riegl. "Koptische Kunst," in *Byzantinische Zeitschrift* 11 (1893), pp. 113 ff.

Rijksmuseum 1979
Rijksmuseum van Oudheden te Leiden. *Les Terres cuites grecques et romaines* (by P. Leyenaar-Plaisir). Leiden, 1979.

Roberts 1950
C. H. Roberts. *The Antinoopolis Papyri* I. London, 1950.

Roberts 1979
C. Roberts. *Manuscript, Society, and Belief in Early Christian Egypt.* London, 1979.

Roberts and Skeat 1983
C. Roberts and T. Skeat. *The Birth of the Codex.* London, 1983.

Robinson 1896
F. Robinson. *Coptic Apocryphal Gospels.* Cambridge, 1896.

Robinson 1967/68
J. Robinson. "The Coptic Gnostic Library Today," in *New Testament Studies* 14 (1967/68), pp. 356–401.

Robinson 1977
J. Robinson. "The Jung Codex: The Rise and Fall of a Monopoly," in *Religious Studies Review* 3 (1977), pp. 17–30.

Robinson 1984
J. Robinson. *The Facsimile Edition of the Nag Hammadi Codices: Introduction.* Leiden, 1984.

Robinson 1988
J. Robinson ed. *The Nag Hammadi Library in English.* 2nd edition. Leiden and San Francisco, 1988.

Robinson and Koester 1971
J. Robinson and H. Koester. *Trajectories Through Early Christianity.* Philadelphia, 1971.

Robinson et al. 1977
J. Robinson et al. *The Facsimile Edition of the Nag Hammadi Codices: Codex I.* Leiden, 1977.

Rodziewicz 1984
M. Rodziewicz. *Les habitations romaines tardives d'Alexandrie.* Warsaw, 1984.

Roeder 1956
Roeder. *Aegyptische Bronzefiguren.* Staatliche Museum zu Berlin. Berlin, 1956.

Root 1982
M. C. Root. *Wondrous Glass. Reflections on the World of Rome.* Kelsey Museum of Archaeology. University of Michigan. Ann Arbor, 1982.

Roscher 1894–97
W. Roscher. *Ausführliches Lexikon der griechischen und romanischen Mythologie.* Vols. 1–7. Hildesheim and New York, 1894–97.

Ross 1941
M. C. Ross. "Paganism and Christianity in Egypt," in *BSAC* VII (1941), pp. 47–50.

Ross 1947
M. C. Ross ed. *Early Christian and Byzantine Art at the Walters Art Gallery.* Exhibition held at the Baltimore Museum of Art. Baltimore, 1947.

Ross 1959
M. C. Ross. "A Coptic Marriage Lampstand in Bronze," in *Nelson Gallery and Atkins Museum Bulletin* (1959), pp. 1–4.

Ross 1962–65
M. C. Ross. *Catalogue of the Byzantine and Early Medieval Antiquities in the Dumbarton Oaks Collection.* New York, 1962–65.

Rouillard 1928
G. Rouillard. *L'administration civile de l'Egypte byzantine.* 2nd edition. Paris, 1928.

Rousseau 1985
P. Rousseau. *Pachomius: The Making of a Community in Fourth-Century Egypt.* Berkeley, 1985.

Rudolph 1983
K. Rudolph. *Gnosis: The Nature and History of Gnosticism.* Edinburgh and San Francisco, 1983.

Russell 1982
J. Russell. "The Evil Eye in Early Byzantine Society," in *XVI internationaler Byzantinistenkongress, Akten II/ 3* in *JÖB* 32/3 (1982), pp. 539–48.

Rutschowscaya 1979
M.-H. Rutschowscaya. "Boîtes à poids d'époque copte," in *Revue du Louvre* (1979/1), pp. 1–6.

Rutschowscaya 1986
M.-H. Rutschowscaya. *Catalogue des bois de l'Egypte copte.* Musée du Louvre. Paris, 1986.

von Saldern 1980
A. von Saldern. *Ancient and Byzantine Glass from Sardis.* Cambridge, Mass., 1980.

Saqqara 1908–12
See Quibell 1908–12.

Sauneron and Jacquet 1972
S. Sauneron and J. Jacquet. *Les ermitages chrétiens du desert d'Esna II.* Cairo, 1972.

Säve-Söderbergh 1961
T. Säve-Söderbergh. *Pharaohs and Mortals.* Indianapolis, 1961.

Säve-Söderbergh 1967
T. Säve-Söderbergh. "Gnostic and Canonical Gospel Traditions," in U. Bianchi ed. *Le Origini dello Gnosticismo.* Leiden, 1967 (pp. 552–62).

Säve-Söderbergh 1975
T. Säve-Söderbergh. "Holy Scriptures or Apologetic Documentations? The 'Sitz im Leben' or the Nag Hammadi Library," in J. E. Ménard ed. *Les Textes de Nag Hammadi. Colloque du Centre d'Histoire des Religions (Strasbourg, 23–25 octobre 1974).* Leiden, 1975 (pp. 3–14).

Säve-Söderbergh 1981
T. Säve-Söderbergh. "The Pagan Elements in Early Christianity and Gnosticism," in *Colloque international sur les textes de Nag Hammadi.* Quebec and Louvain, 1981.

Scanlon 1972
G. T. Scanlon. "Excavations at Kasr el-Wizz," in *JEA* 58 (1972), pp. 7–42.

Scharff 1956
P. Scharff. *A Select Library of Nicene and Post-Nicene Fathers of the Christian Church.* 2nd series. Grand Rapids, 1956.

Scheller 1963
R. W. Scheller. *A Survey of Medieval Model Books.* Haarlem, 1963.

Schenkel 1977
W. Schenkel. *Kultmythos und Martyrerlegende. Zur Kontinuität des ägyptischen Denkens.* Wiesbaden, 1977.

Schenkel 1986
W. Schenkel. "Schatten," in *LÄ* 5 (1984), cols. 535–6.

Schmidt 1919
V. Schmidt. *Sarkofager, Mumiekister, og Mumiehylestre i det Gamle Aegypten: Typologisk Atlas.* Copenhagen, 1919.

Schneider 1936
C. Schneider. "Studien zum Ursprung liturgischer Einzelheiten östlicher Liturgien," in *Kyrios* 1 (1936), pp. 57–73.